T0320153

THE SOCIAL VALUE OF NEW TECHNOLOGY

The Social Value of New Technology

Edited by

Albert N. Link

Virginia Batte Phillips Distinguished Professor, University of North Carolina at Greensboro, USA

and

John T. Scott

Professor of Economics, Dartmouth College, USA

EE Edward Elgar
PUBLISHING

Cheltenham, UK • Northampton, MA, USA

Published by
Edward Elgar Publishing Limited
The Lypiatts
15 Lansdown Road
Cheltenham
Glos GL50 2JA
UK

Edward Elgar Publishing, Inc.
William Pratt House
9 Dewey Court
Northampton
Massachusetts 01060
USA

A catalogue record for this book
is available from the British Library

Library of Congress Control Number: 2018967387

This book is available electronically in the **Elgar**online
Business subject collection
DOI 10.4337/9781788116336

ISBN 978 1 78811 632 9 (cased)
ISBN 978 1 78811 633 6 (eBook)
Printed and bound in Great Britain by TJ International Ltd, Padstow

Contents

PART III   OTHER EVALUATION METHODS

Acknowledgements

The editors and publishers wish to thank the authors and the following publishers who have kindly given permission for the use of copyright material.

Elsevier Ltd for articles: Albert N. Link and John T. Scott (2001), 'Public/Private Partnerships: Stimulating Competition in a Dynamic Market', *International Journal of Industrial Organization*, **19** (5), April, 763–94; David B. Audretsch, Albert N. Link and John T. Scott (2002), 'Public/Private Technology Partnerships: Evaluating SBIR-supported Research', *Research Policy*, **31** (1), January, 145–58.

National Academy of Sciences, courtesy of the National Academies Press for excerpts: John T. Scott (2000), 'An Assessment of the Small Business Innovation Research Program in New England: Fast Track Compared with Non-Fast Track Projects', in National Research Council (eds), *The Small Business Innovation Research Program (SBIR): An Assessment of the Department of Defense Fast Track Initiative*, Washington, DC, USA, 104–40; Albert N. Link (2000), 'An Assessment of the Small Business Innovation Research Fast Track Program in Southeastern States', in National Research Council (eds), *The Small Business Innovation Research Program (SBIR): An Assessment of the Department of Defense Fast Track Initiative*, Washington, DC, USA, 194–210.

Organisation for Economic Co-operation and Development (OECD) for article: John T. Scott (1998), 'Financing and Leveraging Public/Private Partnerships: The Hurdle-Lowering Auction', *STI Review*, **23**, 67–84.

Oxford University Press via the Copyright Clearance Center's RightsLink service for articles: Stuart D. Allen, Stephen K. Layson and Albert N. Link (2012), 'Public Gains from Entrepreneurial Research: Inferences about the Economic Value of Public Support of the Small Business Innovation Research Program', *Research Evaluation*, **21** (2), June, 105–12; Albert N. Link and John T. Scott (2012), 'On the Social Value of Quality: An Economic Evaluation of the Baldrige Performance Excellence Program', *Science and Public Policy*, **39** (5), October, 680–89.

SpringerNature via the Copyright Clearance Center's RightsLink service for articles: Albert N. Link and John T. Scott (2005), 'Evaluating Public Sector R&D Programs: The Advanced Technology Program's Investment in Wavelength References for Optical Fiber Communications', *Journal of Technology Transfer*, **30** (1/2), December, 241–51; John T. Scott (2009), 'Cost-Benefit Analysis for Global Public–Private Partnerships: An Evaluation of the Desirability of Intergovernmental Organizations Entering into Public–Private Partnerships', *Journal of Technology Transfer*, **34** (6), December, 525–59.

Taylor & Francis via the Copyright Clearance Center's RightsLink service for articles: Albert N. Link and John T. Scott (2006), 'An Economic Evaluation of the Baldrige National Quality Program', *Economics of Innovation and New Technology*, **15** (1), January, 83–100; David P. Leech and John T. Scott (2008), 'Intelligent Machine Technology and Productivity Growth', *Economics of Innovation and New Technology*, **17** (7&8), October/November, 677–87; Alan C. O'Connor, Albert N. Link, Brandon M. Downs and Laura M. Hillier (2015), 'The Impact of Public Investment in Medical Imaging Technology: An Interagency Collaboration in Evaluation', *Economics of Innovation and New Technology*, **24** (5), 510–31.

Introduction

Albert N. Link and John T. Scott

We have assembled in this book a collection of our prior research on program evaluation. This is a topic that has been on our 'front burner' for a number of decades. We became interested in program evaluation through requests from the National Institute of Standards and Technology (NIST) within the U.S. Department of Commerce to help the then Program Office develop a systematic approach to approximating the social value of new technology developed in, or with the assistance of, the NIST laboratories. Much of the new technology of interest to the Program Office was research and development (R&D) based, and our prior academic research had long been centered around R&D activities. A portion of the collection herein is focused on NIST programs, but over the years our application of evaluation methods and tools has found other application venues.

The papers that follow are divided into three groups. The first group of papers relies on what we call the counterfactual evaluation method, and the second group relies on what we call the spillover evaluation method. The proverbial third group contains papers that use other evaluation methods.

To frame the emphasis of these chapters as examples of program evaluation, it is important to distinguish between program assessment and program evaluation, regardless of whether or not the program is R&D or technology based. Although many use the terms *assessment* and *evaluation* interchangeably, we think that a distinction is warranted. Policy assessment is based primarily on the criterion of *effectiveness*: Has the program met its stated goals and objectives; have its designated outputs been achieved? Program evaluation is based on the criterion of *efficiency*: How do the social benefits associated with the program compare to the social costs? Critical to the program evaluation methods discussed in this book is who conducts the R&D under question: Is the publicly-funded R&D publicly performed or is it privately performed? The chapters that follow illustrate through example the appropriate methods.

As we explain in Chapter 1, 'The Theory and Practice of Public-Sector R&D Economic Impact Analysis' (Link and Scott, 2013), the counterfactual method asks a general question about publicly funded investments: What would the private sector have had to invest to obtain the same level of social benefits achieved through the public's investments? In other words: Are the public investments a more efficient way of generating the technology than private sector investments would have been? In comparison, the spillover method asks a general question about whether the public sector should be underwriting activities that occur in private-sector firms: What is the social rate of return from the program (including spillovers) compared to the private rate of return?

Chapters 2 and 3, 'An Economic Evaluation of the Baldrige National Quality Program' (Link and Scott, 2006) and 'On the Social Value of Quality: An Economic Evaluation of the Baldrige Performance Excellence Program' (Link and Scott, 2012), focus on the Baldrige National Quality Program, a national program administered at NIST. The evaluations in these two papers differ in time but not in method. Each evaluation of the program was done using a different set of information, but the conclusions from each evaluation were the same; the program is socially valuable.

Chapter 4, 'The Impact of Public Investment in Medical Imaging Technology: An Interagency Collaboration in Evaluation' (O'Connor et al., 2015), applies the counterfactual evaluation method to Canada's investments in medical imaging technology at national universities, and the evaluation reaches favorable conclusions about the social value relative to social cost.

Chapters 5 through 8 are applications of the spillover evaluation method. Chapter 5, 'Public/ Private Partnerships: Stimulating Competition in a Dynamic Market' (Link and Scott, 2001), illustrates a detailed application of this method to a NIST program, the Technologies for the Integration of Manufacturing Applications (TIMA) Program.

Chapter 6, 'Financing and Leveraging Public/Private Partnerships: The Hurdle-Lowering Auction' (Scott, 1998), proposes a theoretical mechanism – the hurdle-lowering auction – for leveraging the public funds invested in public/private partnerships to promote technology development.

Chapters 7 and 8, 'An Assessment of the Small Business Innovation Research Program in New England: Fast Track Compared with Non-Fast Track Projects' (Scott, 2000) and 'An Assessment of the Small Business Innovation Research Fast Track Program in Southeastern States' (Link, 2000), are empirical applications of the spillover method to a U.S. Department of Defense program. The method used in these two applications is similar, although the data in each come from companies in different regions of the United States.

The collection of papers in Chapter 9 through 13 are either based on a traditional method of program evaluation or on hybrids of the various methods. The conceptual arguments in Chapter 9, 'Cost-Benefit Analysis for Global Public–Private Partnerships: An Evaluation of the Desirability of Intergovernmental Organizations Entering into Public–Private Partnerships' (Scott, 2009), are focused on evaluations of global public–private partnerships that combine international intergovernmental organizations with national governments, businesses, and the non-profit organizations of civil society in order to allocate scarce resources to projects that, from an *international* perspective, are socially desirable. The paper considers the need for modifications to traditional cost-benefit analysis when evaluating the projects initiated by global partnerships, explaining why market-centered valuations are still needed despite the role of alternative valuations in such partnerships.

Chapter 10, 'Evaluating Public Sector R&D Programs: The Advanced Technology Program's Investment in Wavelength References for Optical Fiber Communications' (Link and Scott, 2004), is focused on a NIST-based program providing standard reference materials for measuring the wavelength of light, measurements needed to enable optical fiber communications. The paper applies, using interview or survey data, the Griliches/Mansfield methods for measuring the social rates of return to public sector innovative investments.

Chapter 11, 'Intelligent Machine Technology and Productivity Growth' (Leech and Scott, 2008), departs from the conventional benefit–cost metrics for program evaluation and provides information to guide future program investments by developing industrial experts' expectations about the path of the technology and its benefits. It defines the productivity gains to society from the adoption of intelligent machine technologies, and it presents industry's expectations for the productivity growth and the rate of return to R&D investments in those technologies.

Chapters 12 and 13, 'Public Gains from Entrepreneurial Research: Inferences about the Economic Value of Public Support of the Small Business Innovation Research Program' (Allen et al., 2012) and 'Public/Private Technology Partnerships: Evaluating SBIR-supported Research' (Audretsch et al., 2002), also focus on yet another publicly funded program, the U.S. Small Business Innovation Research (SBIR) program; and in both chapters, a variety of traditional evaluation methods and metrics are used to quantify the social value of new technology funded through that program.

Program evaluation is not, in our opinion, a passing fancy. In the United States, its origins date to the Presidency of Woodrow Wilson nearly a century ago, and we suspect that other nations that exercise public accountability have a similar history. In a global environment in which there are competing social needs for the public's funds, program evaluation is becoming more and more an, if not the, appropriate strategic policy approach for decision making. We hope that our collection of papers paints a broad picture of evaluation methods and practices, and that the picture not only serves to lead the way to effective implementations but also to inspire younger scholars entering the field.

PART I

COUNTERFACTUAL EVALUATION METHOD

2. The theory and practice of public-sector R&D economic impact analysis

Albert N. Link and John T. Scott

INTRODUCTION

This chapter summarizes the theory and practice of public-sector R&D economic analysis with specific reference to the National Institute of Standards and Technology's (NIST's) efforts to document the impact that their in-house R&D has had on society. Motivating this research is the general expectation and challenge for public institutions to be accountable for their use of public resources.[1] Economic impact analysis is one way that public institutions can quantify the social contribution of their activity. Impact analysis can also provide important lessons to management about the effectiveness of previous resource allocation decisions, and it can provide guidelines for future strategic planning.

To place R&D impact analysis in a broader perspective, we begin with a brief discussion of R&D evaluations. An evaluation of public-sector R&D programs is based on the criterion of efficiency.[2] The central question asked in an R&D evaluation is: How efficient are all attributes of a public-sector R&D program including the program's management, its strategic planning, and its investment strategy?[3]

One part of an R&D program evaluation is an economic impact analysis. The central question asked in an economic impact analysis is: How do the social benefits associated with the publicly supported R&D program compare to society's costs to undertake the program?[4]

Public interest in program evaluation is visible to the policy community as well as to the general public. For example, on 7 October, 2009, Peter Orszag, then Director of OMB, sent a memorandum to the heads of executive departments and agencies related to increased emphasis on program evaluations. Therein he wrote:

> Rigorous, independent program evaluations can be a key resource in determining whether government programs are achieving their intended outcomes. . ... Evaluations can help policymakers and agency managers strengthen the design and operation of programs. Ultimately, evaluations can help the [Obama] Administration determine how to spend taxpayer dollars effectively and efficiently (Orszag, 2009b).

16   *The theory and practice of program evaluation*

Following this memorandum, on 1 June 2010 the Science and Technology for America's Reinvestment: Measuring the Effect of Research on Innovation, Competitiveness and Science (STAR METRICS) initiative was announced. This is a multi-agency effort led by the National Institutes of Health (NIH), the National Science Foundation (NSF), and the White House Office of Science and Technology Policy (OSTP) to help the federal government document the value of its investments in R&D.

Our focus in this chapter is on impact analyses of NIST activities, retrospective analyses in particular. Although some of the NIST impact analyses reviewed below are partially prospective in nature (meaning that the time series of estimated expected benefits and costs extends into the future because the useful commercial lifetime of the technology studied extends beyond the date of the analysis), the analyses are still retrospective in the sense that they examine NIST programs from a historical investment perspective. However, we do discuss briefly prospective analyses in the concluding section of this chapter.

The remainder of this chapter is outlined as follows. We motivate the scope of our research in the second section with an overview of the theoretical and conceptual foundations for an economic impact analysis. Although academic in nature, there is both a management and strategic planning value to understanding the economic foundations upon which program evaluations and economic impact analyses are based. We stress these economic foundations for at least two reasons. First, individuals from a number of different disciplines are involved in the conduct of program evaluations and economic impact assessments. As such, discipline-specific terminologies for similar concepts are pervasive. And second, even within a given discipline, terminologies are misused because the evaluation questions are frequently misstated.

In the third section, we discuss 17 laboratory-based economic impact analyses, 16 of which were sponsored by the Program Office, and one that was sponsored by the Advanced Technology Program (ATP) at NIST.

In the fourth section, other widely used approaches for conducting an economic impact analysis are presented and illustrated with examples. The purpose of the discussion is to provide a general overview of other complementary approaches that management at NIST or other institutions engaged in public R&D might consider during the strategic planning phase that precedes the formulation and implementation of an economic impact analysis methodology.

In the final section, we offer guidelines about the conduct of future economic impact analyses, targeted toward NIST or other similar public-sector R&D agencies, especially guidelines related to real-time data collection by the research divisions to support any upcoming analysis.

ECONOMICS FOUNDATION FOR AN IMPACT ANALYSIS[5]

> In spite of efforts in the United States over the past decade to implement standardized methodologies for assessing the economic impact of government research programs, no generally accepted approach yet exists. (Tassey, 2003, p. 1).

Often overlooked, as agencies attempt to meet Government Performance and Results Act (GPRA) reporting requirements in a cost-efficient manner, is that there is an analytical and theoretical foundation or established methodology for conducting an impact analysis. This foundation, which has long been germane to the economics literature, is gaining prominence in the policy evaluation arena.[6]

Griliches (1958) pioneered the application of fundamental economic insight to the development of estimates of private and social rates of return to public investments in R&D.[7] Streams of investment outlays through time—the costs—generate streams of economic surplus through time—the benefits. Once identified and measured, these streams of costs and benefits are used to calculate rates of return, benefit-to-cost ratios, and other related metrics.[8]

In the simplest Griliches model, public-sector innovations are conceptualized as reducing the cost of producing a good sold in a competitive market at constant long-run unit cost, as shown in Figure 2.1. For any period, there is a demand curve for the good and, in the simplest model, a horizontal supply curve. Innovation lowers the unit cost of production, hence lowering the horizontal supply curve, increasing supply, and thereby, at the new lower equilibrium price, resulting in greater consumer surplus (the difference between the price consumers would have been willing to pay and the actual price they paid, summed over all purchases).[9]

The Griliches model for characterizing the benefits from a public-sector innovation has long been the traditional economics methodology for analyzing public-sector R&D programs. The Griliches model for calculating economic social rates of return adds the public and the private investments through time to determine social investment costs, and then the stream of new economic surplus generated from those investments is the benefit. Thus, the evaluation question that can be answered from such an analysis is: What is the social rate of return to the innovation, and how does it compare to the private rate of return?

This might not be the most appropriate question to ask from a public accountability perspective. Tassey (1997) developed the concept of using private and social hurdle rates to identify appropriate targets for government intervention. The fact that the social rate of return is greater than the

18   *The theory and practice of program evaluation*

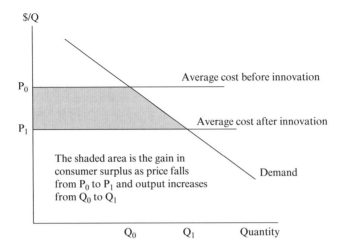

Source: Link and Scott (2011).

Figure 2.1   Gain in economic surplus from process innovation in a competitive market in the case of long-run constant unit costs

private rate of return could validate the role of government in innovation if the private sector would not have undertaken the research; but the question above ignores, for example, consideration of the cost effectiveness of the public sector undertaking the research as opposed to the private sector, and thus an alternative methodology might be more appropriate. Two alternative methodologies are discussed below, the counterfactual methodology and the spillover methodology, although the counterfactual methodology is the focus of the remainder of this chapter.

Counterfactual Methodology

The Griliches methodology assumes as the counterfactual situation the status quo technology (and hence the status quo demands and costs) that existed without the public R&D investments and the new technology (and hence new demands and costs) that resulted. However, with reference to what Link and Scott (1998, 2011), building on Tassey (1997), term a "counterfactual analysis", under a counterfactual economic impact analysis methodology, a different counterfactual scenario should be considered when publicly funded, publicly performed investments are evaluated, because typically the private sector would in some way have tried to replace the public investments and the technologies they produced. Link and Scott (1998) set out for the first time the distinctions between such a "counterfactual analysis" and the traditional analysis of economic surplus in the economics literature.[10] As explained there, in the extreme case that the public R&D output could be replaced with private R&D output of equal quality, holding constant the very stream of economic surplus that the Griliches model seeks to measure, and making no attempt to measure that stream, one should ask the counterfactual question: What would the private sector have had to invest to achieve those benefits in the absence of the public sector's investments?

In the less extreme case, where barriers to technology and market failures (discussed below) prevent the private sector from replacing the public R&D output with private R&D output of equal quality, the counterfactual question is: What would the private sector have invested in the attempt to replace the output of the public sector's investments and what would be the value lost because of the shortfall in the quality of the private sector's replacement R&D output?

The answer to the counterfactual question gives the benefits of the public's investments—namely, the costs avoided by the private sector.[11] With those benefits—obtained in practice through extensive interviews with administrators, federal research scientists, and those in the private sector who would have to duplicate the research in the absence of public performance—counterfactual rates of return and benefit-to-cost ratios can be calculated to answer the fundamental evaluation question: Are the public investments a more efficient way of generating the technology than private sector investments would have been?

The answer to this question is more in line with the public accountability issues implicit in GPRA, and certainly is more in line with the thinking of public sector stakeholders—or so we believe—who may doubt the appropriateness of government's having a role in the innovation process in the first place.

Spillover Methodolgy

There are important projects where economic performance can be improved with public funding of privately performed research. Another useful methodology that has been used to evaluate such privately performed R&D that is subsidized by public funds is what Tassey (1997), and later Link and Scott (2011), termed the "spillover analysis". It is not the approach used in the impact analyses discussed in the next section because they are all evaluating publicly performed R&D rather than R&D that is privately performed but publicly financed. The idea that public subsidy of privately performed R&D is justified by the positive externality associated with the spillover of knowledge generated by R&D investment is an old one, but the development of an implementable, interview-based, multiple-equation method for identifying social and private rates of return for publicly-subsidized and privately performed R&D—with an application to projects subsidized with ATP awards—is the unique contribution of Link and Scott (2001).

Under what Link and Scott (2011), building on Tassey (1997), refer to as the "spillover economic impact analysis methodology", the question asked is one that facilitates an economic understanding of whether the public sector should be underwriting the private-sector firms' research, namely: What is the social rate of return from the program (including spillovers) compared to the private rate of return? Or: What proportion of the total profit stream generated by the private firm's R&D and innovation does the private firm expect to capture; and hence, what proportion is not appropriated but is instead captured by other firms that imitate the innovation or use knowledge generated by the R&D to produce competing products for the social good?

The part of the stream of expected profits captured by the innovative firm along with its costs determine its private return, while the entire stream is the lower bound on the social rate of return (that would be compared to the social hurdle rate—the opportunity costs of the public's investment funds). In essence, this methodology weighs the private return, estimated through extensive interviews with firms receiving public support regarding their expectations of future patterns of events and future abilities to appropriate the value of R&D-based knowledge, against private investments. The social rate of return weighs the social returns against the social investments. The application of the spillover methodology to the evaluation of publicly funded, privately performed research is appropriate because the output of the research is only partially appropriable by the private firm, with the rest spilling over to society. The extent of the spillover of such knowledge with public good characteristics and its effect on private-sector rate-of-return estimates relative to a "hurdle rate" determines whether or not the public sector should fund the research.

Impact Analysis in Practice

While there is a rich economics-based theoretical foundation for impact analyses, there are pragmatic issues at play when applying the appropriate methodology. As the review of NIST impact analyses in the next section demonstrates, and as Tassey (2003, p. 15) perceptively noted, in practice the benefits estimated in an economic impact analysis of a specific R&D program or project are "frequently determined by data availability". Because of data limitations, the economic impact analyses for NIST's laboratories, and also for the Advanced Technology Program (ATP) at NIST, have often been able to estimate only a very small subset of the benefits identified when applying the counterfactual methodology appropriate for analyzing publicly financed and publicly performed R&D and collecting data relevant to quantifying the economic impacts of its investments in infrastructure technology (that is, infratechnology) research.

In the next section, we discuss 17 NIST retrospective economic impact analyses, making the point about data limitations in the context of discussing the proper scope of economic impact analyses and the actual examples of the subsets of estimated benefits from NIST's R&D to generate infrastructure technology.

NIST R&D ECONOMIC IMPACT ANALYSES

Overview of NIST Economic Impact Analyses

Much of NIST's research focuses on infrastructure technology, or infratechnology. According to Tassey (2007, p. 112): "Infratechnologies leverage the development and efficient use of technology at all three major stages of economic activity: R&D, manufacturing, and commercialization." Measurement and test methods are examples of infratechnologies. They are required for the efficient conduct of R&D, control of production, and many market transactions. Infratechnologies are also the basis for technical and functional interfaces among the products that constitute a system or tiers in a supply chain. Finally, product acceptance testing protocols and standards assure consumers that technology-based products perform as specified.[12]

This focus of NIST's research has both an institutional basis as well as an economics basis. The concept of government's involvement in standards traces to the Articles of Confederation signed on 9 July, 1778—"Congress assembled, shall also have the sole and exclusive right and power of . . . fixing the standard of weights and measures throughout the United States"—and this responsibility was reiterated in Article 1 of the Constitution of the United States. More to the point, the Omnibus Trade and Competitiveness Act of 1988 stated:

> The National Institute of Standards and Technology [shall] enhance the competitiveness of American industry while maintaining its traditional function as lead national laboratory for providing the measurement, calibrations, and quality assurance techniques which underpin United States commerce, technological progress, improved product reliability and manufacturing processes, and public safety. . . .

22 *The theory and practice of program evaluation*

From an economic perspective, infratechnologies have both public- and private-good characteristics; thus, they are often referred to as quasi-public goods and are jointly supplied by the public and private sectors. Infratechnologies have economic value only if they are uniformly and widely used. As such, the private sector will underinvest in infratechnologies because of its inability to appropriate fully the benefits from such investments. Thus, a theoretical basis for NIST's role in the provision of infratechnologies is based on the economic concept of market failure.

Market failure refers to the fact that the market—including both R&D-investing producers of a technology and the users of the technology—underinvests, from society's perspective, in a particular technology or technology application. Such underinvestment occurs because conditions or barriers exist that prevent organizations from undertaking or fully appropriating the benefits created by their investments.[13]

Table 2.1 lists 17 NIST-sponsored R&D laboratory and program impact analyses that are based on a counterfactual methodology, described above, for quantifying benefit information.[14] Also listed in the table is the stage or stages of economic activity benefiting from the infrastructure technology research studied in each analysis: R&D, production and commercialization. Finally, the table shows for each analysis the benefit-to-cost ratio (described below) estimated for the program studied.

There are typically benefits for R&D because NIST is doing the infrastructure technology R&D and because R&D is more difficult without good measurement. There are benefits for production because there is better process control. Also, there are benefits for commercialization because products are of higher quality (yielding more value to consumers or more efficient operation for producers using intermediate goods benefiting from the infratechnologies) and of known, consistent quality (reducing the transactions costs associated with commercialization). Table 2.1 provides a summary view of the stages focused on in the analyses, and distinguishes quantitative evaluations from those that are qualitative only.

As previously stated, each of the economic impact analyses in Table 2.1 is grounded in the counterfactual methodology of what would have happened in the absence of NIST. Then, in the first instance, the benefits from NIST's program under consideration are the costs avoided (that is, the avoided costs of activities to replace NIST's program) by industry. The counterfactual methodology is typically one in which firms incur costs in their attempts to replace the NIST infrastructure technology that is no longer available in the counterfactual situation. The benefits from NIST's infratechnology are the costs avoided by industry—costs that

Table 2.1   NIST R&D program economic impact analyses and measured economic impacts

Economic impact analysis	Stage of economic activity	Benefit-to-cost ratio*
"Economic Assessment of the NIST Thermocouple Calibration Program", Planning Report 97-1	R&D, production, and commercialization; commercialization for users of thermocouples evaluated qualitatively only	3-to-1
"Economic Evaluation of Radiopharmaceutical Research at NIST", Planning Report 97-2	R&D, production, and commercialization; some benefits for each stage of activity not quantified or quantified partially	97-to-1
"Economic Assessment of the NIST Alternative Refrigerants Research Program", Planning Report 98-1	R&D, production, and commercialization; commercialization benefits, including the value of better quality products, largely unquantified	4-to-1
"Economic Assessment of the NIST Ceramic Phase Diagram Program", Planning Report 98-3	R&D primarily, but also production (detecting and diagnosing abnormalities in production), and commercialization (because delays in the introduction of new materials were avoided); commercialization benefits of faster development of new products not quantified, and benefits for some segments of the ceramics industry not quantified	10-to-1
"Benefit Analysis of IGBT Power Device Simulation Modeling", Planning Report 99-3	R&D, production, and commercialization; production benefits for applications manufacturers and commercialization benefits of product quality for end users evaluated qualitatively only	23-to-1
"Economic Impact of Standard Reference Materials for Sulfur in Fossil Fuels", Planning Report 00-1	R&D, production, and commercialization; R&D benefits evaluated qualitatively only	113-to-1
"Economic Impact Assessment: NIST-EEEL Laser and Fiberoptic Power and Energy Calibration Services", Planning Report 00-3	R&D, production, and commercialization; some benefits at all stages of activity not measured, especially commercialization benefits related to product quality	11.3-to-1

24   *The theory and practice of program evaluation*

Table 2.1   (continued)

Economic impact analysis	Stage of economic activity	Benefit-to-cost ratio*
"The Economic Impacts of NIST's Cholesterol Standards Program", Planning Report 00-4	R&D, production, and commercialization; R&D benefits were not measured because it was assumed that industry would not have attempted to develop the accurate measurement technology provided by NIST, and the other benefits were not quantified completely because of insufficient data	4.5-to-1
"The Economic Impacts of NIST's Data Encryption Standard (DES) Program", Planning Report 01-2	R&D, production, and commercialization; R&D benefits not estimated because survey attempts failed, and other benefits were not quantified completely because of insufficient data	145-to-1
"Economic Evaluation of the Baldrige National Quality Program", Planning Report 01-3	R&D, production, and commercialization; commercialization benefits because of a shortfall in performance quality not estimated because it was assumed that the R&D and production costs avoided—i.e. that would have been incurred absent the program—would have successfully achieved the same quality performance as achieved using the Baldrige Criteria	207-to-1
"The Economic Impact of Role-Based Access Control", Planning Report 02-1	R&D, production, and commercialization; some benefits (because of sensitive proprietary information and because market penetration incomplete) at the commercialization stage not quantified	109-to-1
"The Economic Impact of the Gas-Mixture NIST-Traceable Reference Materials Program", Planning Report 02-4	Production, commercialization; benefits for some parts of the supply chain not quantified	21-to-1
"Economic Impact Assessment of the International Standard for the Exchange of Product	R&D, production, commercialization; benefits quantified are because NIST's participation reduced the	8-to-1

(continued overleaf)

Table 2.1   (continued)

Economic impact analysis	Stage of economic activity	Benefit-to-cost ratio*
Model Data (STEP) in Transportation Equipment Industries", Planning Report 02-5	development time but not quantified are benefits because NIST's participation resulted in higher quality of the infratechnology	
"Evaluation of ATP's Intramural Research Awards Program", NIST GCR 04-866	R&D, production, commercialization; some benefits from higher quality products not quantified	
Wavelength References for Optical Fiber Communications: SRM 2517a		267-to-1
Injectable Composite Bone Grafts		5400-to-1
Internet Commerce for Manufacturing		33-to-1
Polymer Composite Dielectrics for Integrated Thin-Film Capacitors		7-to-1
"Economic Analysis of NIST's Investments in Superfilling Research", Planning Report 08-1	R&D, production, commercialization; only the benefits of reduced R&D costs were quantified	6-to-1
"Economic Analysis of NIST's Low-k Materials Characterization Research", Planning Report 08-2	R&D, production, commercialization; only the R&D benefits were quantified	9-to-1
"Retrospective Economic Impact Assessment of the NIST Combinatorial Methods Center", Planning Report 09-1	R&D; commercialization benefits (resulting from the more efficient product R&D enabled by the infratechnology) for the users of the higher quality products not quantified	9-to-1

Notes:
Planning Reports are available at http://www.nist.gov/director/planning/impact_assessment.cfm. NIST GCR 04-866 is available at the preceding location under "Advanced Technology Program" and at http://www.atp.nist.gov/eao/eao_pubs.htm.
* Several other outcome metrics are in each Planning Report.

26   *The theory and practice of program evaluation*

would be incurred had industry tried to replace NIST's services in the counterfactual situation without NIST's program, provided in cooperative, public–private partnership between industry and NIST. Those costs would include not only the costs of activities to replace NIST's services, but also the lost economic value if the quality of industry's counterfactual alternative to the absence of NIST's services fell short of the quality of the NIST services being replaced. Such shortfalls in value are expected because the infratechnologies are quasi-public goods—they are provided through the public–private partnership of NIST and industry—and the ideal case typically entails a combined investment by NIST and industry. For that reason, the social costs of the NIST programs evaluated with economic impact analyses include not only NIST's costs, but the costs incurred by industry in its support of the NIST infratechnology programs.

It is this mixed case, where the private sector to some extent attempts to replace NIST's technology but does so incompletely, that is typically observed in the 17 economic impact analyses listed in Table 2.1. However, before reviewing the actual economic impact analyses, it will be important to set out clearly the two extreme and hypothetical, yet conceptually very important, special cases—the use of the status quo technology and the complete replacement case.

Status Quo Technology

In those cases where industry, because of severe barriers to technology development, would not have even attempted to replace NIST's program but instead would have simply worked with the technology available, the analysis is essentially the same as the traditional evaluation of social rate of return to public R&D investments in Griliches (1958). The counterfactual in the traditional method is the status quo without the innovation for which social rate of return is being evaluated. Thus, for Griliches' classic paper, the counterfactual is the old technology and associated unit cost of production before the innovation lowered unit cost.

Complete Replacement of Infrastructure Technology

In the case where industry does undertake to replace NIST's program, incurring the costs to replace it and doing so completely, the benefits of NIST's program are simply the costs avoided because industry did not have to incur the costs of establishing and operating the program in the private sector; there is no shortfall in the value generated with the replacement technology. Then, a benefit-to-cost ratio (discussed below) greater than

1.0 implies that the NIST program provided the infrastructure technology more efficiently than the private sector could have done. The costs to replace NIST's program are avoided by industry, and these avoided costs are the benefits from NIST's program. With a benefit-to-cost ratio greater than 1.0, those costs and hence the benefits exceed the total of NIST's and industry's costs for the NIST infrastructure technology program. Thus, in the extreme case of complete replacement of NIST's program by industry and the achievement of the same stream of economic surplus therefrom, the evaluation metrics compare the investment costs industry avoided (the benefits of NIST's program in the complete replacement scenario) with society's (NIST's and industry's) actual investment costs.

A Summarizing Restatement

At the extreme of the case of zero replacement by industry of NIST's infratechnology investments, the shortfall in value in the counterfactual situation absent NIST's program is complete, and the evaluation metrics compare the stream of economic surplus—the benefits from having NIST's program rather than the status quo ante technology—with the investment costs of NIST's program. The latter case where the shortfall in value is assumed to be complete may be the appropriate counterfactual scenario when barriers to technology development and use are especially severe and the discussions with industry support the belief that market failure would have prevented the private sector from investing in socially valuable infrastructure technology that NIST could provide in cooperation with industry.

However, barriers to technology may not preclude private-sector provision of the infratechnology, and in that case the counterfactual will have as benefits of NIST's program the replacement costs avoided by industry. When those replacement costs exceed the costs of NIST's program, then the benefit-to-cost ratio will exceed 1.0, net present value will be positive, and the social rate of return will exceed the opportunity costs of the public's funds (that is, society's hurdle rate).[15]

One could argue that in Griliches' classic article, the counterfactual used for evaluating the public's investment in developing hybrid corn was not the right one for providing an analysis of economic impact. In particular, if large manufacturers of farm supplies including seeds would, in the absence of the government R&D program, have undertaken their own development programs, the relevant counterfactual would not be the technology of the status quo ante, but instead the situation where the stream of economic surplus generated by hybrid corn was captured by private investment. Then, for the evaluation of the public R&D, the benefits to weigh against the government's investment costs would have been not the stream of economic surplus from hybrid corn but instead the costs avoided by the private sector because it did not have to do the investment. The government's program would be judged a success if it performed the research at a lower cost than the private sector's cost in the counterfactual situation.

Mixed Case Counterfactual Analysis

A review of the analyses in Table 2.1 shows the typical case is the mixed case where in the counterfactual situation the private sector to some extent attempts to replace the technology of NIST's program but does so incompletely. The prevalence of the mixed case is not surprising given that the NIST programs are providing quasi-public goods in the context of public–private partnership to develop and apply infratechnologies. Although the economic impact analyses in these tables span 22 years, and although they were conducted by different academics and contractors with varying backgrounds and skill sets, some generalities about the scope of the economic impact analyses and the availability of data can be gleaned.

Reviewing the projects in Table 2.1 suggests a generic set of data and associated evaluation approaches when NIST is conducting an impact analysis, or when doing economic evaluations more generally. For those managing NIST laboratory projects, the taxonomies of data and approaches, revealed by a review of the 17 analyses listed in Table 2.1, are described here. From the descriptions here, managers can identify data available for their projects that could be routinely collected on an ongoing basis and then periodically used for impact analysis.

Data about Economic Impacts

The first observation about data to measure economic impacts is that those impacts will be observed in the supply chains with benefits attributable to the infratechnologies provided by NIST. The scope of an impact analysis, in terms of the data about impacts that it should set out to observe, will depend on the structure of the supply chain. That point can be explained with two extreme, hypothetical examples.

First, consider a case where the infratechnology is embodied in an upstream manufacturer's product and then used in the supply chain's downstream markets. Suppose that the upstream firm is a perfectly price-discriminating monopolist (that is, it can collect all of the area under its demand curve) selling to a perfectly competitive downstream market that buys the monopolist's product and embodies it in the product it produces and then sells to the next stage of the supply chain. Assume moreover that all markets further downstream in the supply stream are also perfectly competitive. In this special case, collecting data about the infratechnology's effect on the first beneficiary in the supply chain will be sufficient to establish the benefits. In particular, one would gather data related to the outward shift in its demand curve because of the higher quality, and/or the downward shift in its average costs allowed by the NIST program's infratechnology, or about the private sector replacement costs to replicate NIST's technology and then, if there is a shortfall in quality, gather the data about the lost outward shift in demand and/or downward shift in costs.

Second, at the other extreme, imagine a case where the NIST program's developed infratechnology is used in a supply chain that is perfectly competitive at all stages of the supply chain. In that case, the social value of NIST's infratechnology can be captured by gathering data from the retail market for the product produced in the supply chain. In particular, one would gather data about the outward shift in the retail market's demand curve and/or about the downward shift in average costs or about the private sector's replacement costs to replicate the NIST program's infratechnology, and then, if there is a shortfall in quality, gather the data about the lost outward shift in demand and/or downward shift in costs.

Typically, the market structures of the supply chains benefiting from NIST's programs will not be either of these extreme cases, and consequently benefits occur and theoretically must be estimated through data collection and analysis at all levels of the supply chain.

However, the analyses in Table 2.1 reveal a limited ability of the evaluation teams to collect data of the theoretically desired scope.[16] More often than not, the analyses use only a small part of the supply chain from which to gather benefit data, even when it is clear that the scope of the benefits extended throughout many parts of the supply chain. The analyses then acknowledge this limitation and observe that the evaluation metrics are conservative in the sense that they will systematically underestimate the true benefits of NIST's infratechnology investments.

To improve the ability to document benefits throughout the supply chain, it is recommended that, to the extent practicable, NIST project managers maintain key contacts with the users of their projects' outputs at all stages of the supply chain and let those contacts know the types of data that will be needed to estimate benefits. However, experience has shown that tiers in a supply chain beyond those with which NIST has had direct contact (and therefore where the beneficiaries recognize that NIST has made significant contributions) do not have an incentive to cooperate and, in fact, do not.[17]

It is recommended that NIST project managers establish direct contact with those further down the supply chain who benefit from the NIST infratechnologies, explain those downstream benefits that are expected, and then request feedback about the extent to which those benefits are actually realized. In other words, with an educational outreach effort by NIST to those in tiers of a supply chain where traditionally there have not been direct contacts with NIST, the incentives to cooperate will be cultivated and NIST programs will be better attuned to industry's needs. Ideally, benefit data would be routinely gathered in real time on an ongoing basis. The availability of such data would allow periodic evaluations documenting impacts, thus facilitating NIST's ability to make possible adjustments that would better serve industry's needs and also allowing NIST to provide quality information about performance to support the mandate of the GPRA.

Numbers of respondents and statistical confidence intervals

Although several of the analyses in Table 2.1 provide upper and lower bounds for their estimated benefits, none of the analyses provides formal statistical confidence intervals for the estimates. In many cases a reason for this is that the numbers of respondents are two few to develop any formal statistics. The numbers of respondents providing information for the NIST economic impact analyses listed in Table 2.1 typically are far below what would normally be used in statistical analysis.[18] However, if project managers follow the recommendations for maintaining in real time key contacts throughout the supply chains benefiting from NIST projects and communicating regularly about the types of data that will be needed for evaluations, there will be many more respondents and the very real problem of small numbers of expert opinions about key benefits can, in some cases, be mitigated dramatically. With larger numbers of respondents providing estimates of benefits of particular types, it will at times be practical to produce formal statistical confidence intervals for the estimated benefits.[19]

Types of impact data

The analyses in Table 2.1 rely on many types of impact data that NIST project managers could request in real time from the key contacts throughout the supply chains benefiting from their projects' outputs. It is useful to discuss these examples in groups for a generic supply chain benefiting from NIST's infrastructure technology investments.

The analyses in Table 2.1 illustrate a range of different supply chains, but for illustrative purposes the generic supply chain will have the first level of beneficiaries being firms upstream that manufacture an input used downstream in the supply chain. The input produced by the first tier of beneficiaries could be an instrument that must be calibrated using the standards and calibration services developed at NIST, or it could be a reference material of field quality that is traceable to NIST standards. An example of a first tier of beneficiaries would be the suppliers of power meters and 249 nm excimer lasers used for photolithography allowing economic fabrication of miniaturized integrated circuits (see Planning Report 00-3). Another example would be the manufacturers of cholesterol measurement systems that are calibrated using NIST's cholesterol standard reference materials (SRMs) (see Planning Report 00-4).

The second tier of beneficiaries could be downstream manufacturers or service providers that must use the inputs purchased from the upstream firms to efficiently produce a product that will be sold to manufacturers or service providers further downstream in the supply chain. The second tier of firms, for example, might use an instrument that measures the wavelength of light to manufacture components that will be used in fiber optics communications systems.

For example, NIST standards and calibration services allow accurate calibration of instruments used in the manufacturing of specialized optical sources and detectors used in high performance communications systems. The NIST standards allow the manufacturers to characterize the frequency response of high-speed detectors that are essential to enabling many downstream areas of the telecommunications industry, including high-speed internet access. Or, the second tier of firms might use a reference material traceable to NIST standards to measure the sulfur content of a fuel that will be used in the production of energy. The goods produced by the second tier of firms benefiting from NIST's infrastructure technology are then used by firms further downstream; in the examples, those firms would be the providers of fiber-optic communications systems or the producers of energy.

Those firms in the third tier of the supply chain benefit from having inputs—the fiber-optic components or the fuel—with specifications traceable to NIST standards. Then, for the generic supply chain, the fourth tier will be the end users who also are beneficiaries of NIST's infratechnology. In the examples here, the end users would be the customers who use the services of a fiber optics communication system or those who use the energy produced with fuel with content meeting specifications traceable to NIST standards.

Table 2.2 provides examples of the types of data used in the analyses in Table 2.1 to estimate benefits of NIST's infratechnology investments for the various levels of the typical supply chain described in the preceding paragraph. Excepting the special cases discussed earlier in the text, benefits

32   *The theory and practice of program evaluation*

Table 2.2   Examples of impact data for a generic supply chain

Stage of the supply chain	Examples of impact data
First tier: Firms producing inputs—for example, materials with characteristics determined by characteristics data traceable to NIST	Avoided cost of using foreign national laboratories, rather than NIST, for traceability to standards Avoided cost of using commercial consultants, rather than NIST, for technical support services Avoided cost for users of reference materials with higher operations and production expenses because of their lowered confidence in their reference materials (e.g. manufacturers of field quality calibration gas that would have greater measurement uncertainty without NIST-traceable reference materials (NTRM), or manufacturers of instruments to monitor emissions) Avoided cost of additional measurement equipment Avoided cost of calibrating and maintaining in-house measurement systems Avoided cost of verifying the accuracy of measurements for customers Avoided cost of measurement disputes, without traceability to NIST, with customers Avoided cost of lost value because of delay in product reaching market Avoided R&D costs—labor and equipment Avoided cost of inefficient production processes Avoided costs of maintaining quality control and assurance systems Avoided cost that would be incurred to prevent interoperability problems (throughout the supply chain) before they occur and that would be incurred to address interoperability problems after they occur (e.g. for users of STEP, the international standard designed to address interoperability problems encountered in the exchange of digital product information)
Second tier: Firms producing inputs—for example, components, production equipment or other inputs with specifications	Avoided cost of using foreign national laboratories, rather than NIST, for traceability to standards Avoided cost of using commercial consultants, rather than NIST, for technical support services Avoided cost for users of reference materials with higher operations and production expenses because of their lowered confidence in their reference materials, instruments, and system components (e.g. manufacturers of systems for monitoring and controlling emissions) Avoided cost of additional measurement equipment

(continued overleaf)

Table 2.2   (continued)

Stage of the supply chain	Examples of impact data
traceable to NIST standards	Avoided cost of calibrating and maintaining in-house measurement systems
	Avoided cost of verifying the accuracy of measurements for customers
	Avoided cost of measurement disputes, without traceability to NIST, with suppliers or customers
	Avoided costs of implementation (risks and adoption costs) and interoperability across systems (e.g. software developers using infratechnologies supporting role-based access control (RBAC))
	Avoided cost of lost value because of delay in product reaching market
	Avoided R&D costs—labor and equipment
	Avoided cost of inefficient production processes
	Avoided costs of maintaining quality control and assurance systems
	Avoided cost that would be incurred to prevent interoperability problems (throughout the supply chain) before they occur and that would be incurred to address interoperability problems after they occur (e.g. for users of STEP, the international standard designed to address interoperability problems encountered in the exchange of digital product information)
Third tier: End user firms—for example, firms (such as OEMs) producing systems or outputs (autos, TVs, computers) with specifications traceable to NIST standards	Avoided cost of measurement disputes, without traceability to NIST, with suppliers or customers
	Avoided cost for end users that would have higher operations, maintenance and production expenses because of their lowered confidence in the accuracy of measurement technology (e.g. manufacturers using systems for monitoring and controlling their emissions)
	Avoided cost of additional measurement equipment
	Avoided cost of calibrating and maintaining in-house measurement systems
	Avoided cost of verifying the accuracy of measurements for customers
	Avoided cost of lost value because of delay in product reaching market
	Avoided R&D costs—labor and equipment
	Avoided cost of inefficient production processes
	Avoided cost of regulatory compliance for traceability to absolute standards (e.g. emissions control)

34   *The theory and practice of program evaluation*

Table 2.2   (continued)

Stage of the supply chain	Examples of impact data
	Avoided costs of maintaining quality control and assurance systems (e.g. clinical laboratories performing cholesterol tests)
	Avoided costs of implementation (risks and adoption costs) and interoperability across systems (e.g. end users of infratechnologies supporting RBAC)
	Avoided cost that would be incurred to prevent interoperability problems (throughout the supply chain) before they occur and that would be incurred to address interoperability problems after they occur (e.g. for users of STEP, the international standard designed to address interoperability problems encountered in the exchange of digital product information)
	Avoided loss in quality (product features, performance, reliability) of products as reflected in customers' decreased willingness to pay for the products [Note that care must be taken to avoid double-counting of this decreased willingness to pay; ideally the deterioration in quality at all levels of the supply chain and associated loss in customers' willingness to pay can be captured at the penultimate tier of the supply chain, with the cumulative effects of deterioration in quality throughout the supply chain reflected in the demand curve for the products of the end user firms by the decreased willingness to pay for their final product sold to the final consumers. At times the loss in value from quality deterioration may be captured in the downward shift of the demand curve for an upstream stage of the supply chain, but it must not then be also measured in the downstream markets.]
Fourth tier: Customers of end user firms—for example, consumers using the final goods and services provided by the third tier firms	Avoided cost of measurement disputes, without traceability to NIST, with suppliers
	Avoided costs of maintenance and repair (e.g. the users of refrigeration equipment with improperly functioning alternative refrigerants)
	Avoided costs of damage from, or costs of repeating, final consumption that had poor results because of inaccurate measurement (e.g. the patients at the end of the supply chain in the radiopharmaceuticals analysis; or, e.g. regarding costs of damage from poor measurement, the environmental damage without standard reference materials (SRMs) for the sulfur content of fossil fuels)

occur and are ideally measured at all levels of the supply chain. One should note that the examples given for each tier in the generic supply chain are all taken from the actual benefits documented in the analyses summarized in Table 2.1; however, in many cases a particular type of benefit that has been measured for a particular tier of the supply chain could also occur at other parts of the supply chain.

One can observe that the examples given in Table 2.2 include many different types of benefits from NIST's programs. These are benefits that could be quantified and collected in real time and used by NIST for more effective management. The types of benefits include avoiding costs that would be incurred by the firm in the counterfactual scenario without NIST's investments: investment, operating and maintenance costs to develop, use and maintain infrastructure technology and provide infratechnology services such as standard reference materials (SRMs) and calibrations services and traceability to national standards. Benefits to the firm also include avoiding increased time to market in the absence of NIST's programs, avoiding the loss of valuable knowledge that would not have been developed without NIST's infratechnologies increasing the performance of R&D investments (such knowledge is reflected in part in knowledge metrics such as patents and publications). Benefits include avoiding a loss in quality of products and services—that is, avoiding a loss in the firm's performance in the absence of NIST's investments. Benefits also include avoiding costly increases in time to meeting third party regulations or simply more difficulty in detecting whether or not the regulations are being met and that difficulty requires costly countermeasures to ensure that in fact the regulations are met.

Outcome Metrics

The outcome metrics traditionally used in the NIST retrospective economic impact analyses in Table 2.1 are the internal rate of return (*IRR*), the benefit-to-cost ratio (*B/C*), and net present value (*NPV*).[20]

Internal rate of return
The internal rate of return (*IRR*)—a real rate of return in the context of constant-dollar cash flows—is the value of the discount rate, i, that equates the net present value (*NPV*) of the stream of net benefits associated with a research project to zero. The time series runs from the beginning of the research project, $t = 0$, through a terminal point, $t = n$.
Mathematically:

$$NPV = [(B_0 - C_0)/(1 + i)^0] + \ldots + [(B_n - C_n)/(1 + i)^n] = 0 \quad (2.1)$$

where $(B_t - C_t)$ represents the net benefits associated with the project in year t, and n represents the number of time periods—years in the case studies below—being considered in the evaluation.

For unique solutions for i, from equation (2.1), the *IRR* can be compared to a value, r, that represents the opportunity cost of funds invested by the technology-based public institution. Thus, if the opportunity cost of funds is less than the internal rate of return, the project was worthwhile from an *ex post* social perspective.[21]

Benefit-to-cost ratio

The ratio B/C is the ratio of the present value of all measured benefits to the present value of all measured costs. Both benefits and costs are referenced to the initial time period, $t = 0$, when the project began as:

$$B/C = [\Sigma_{t = 0 \text{ to } t = n} B_t/(1 + r)^t]/[\Sigma_{t = 0 \text{ to } t = n} C_t/(1 + r)^t] \qquad (2.2)$$

A benefit-to-cost ratio of 1 is said to indicate a project that breaks even. Any project with $B/C > 1$ is a relatively successful project as defined in terms of benefits exceeding costs.

Fundamental to implementing the ratio of benefits-to-costs is a value for the discount rate, r. While the discount rate representing the opportunity cost for public funds could differ across a portfolio of public investments, the calculated metrics in the analyses in Table 2.1 follow the guidelines set forth by the OMB (1992) in Circular A-94: "Constant-dollar benefit–cost analyses of proposed investments and regulations should report net present value and other outcomes determined using the Office of Management and Budget (OMB) recommended real discount rate of 7 percent." The analyses listed in Table 2.1 are evaluating investment decisions—the allocation of capital across alternative investment options, and so the OMB-mandated 7 percent real discount rate has been used.[22]

Net present value

OMB circular A-94 states (OMB, 1992, p. 3):

> The standard criterion for deciding whether a government program can be justified on economic principles is net present value—the discounted monetized value of expected net benefits (i.e., benefits minus costs). Net present value is computed by assigning monetary values to benefits and costs, discounting future benefits and costs using an appropriate discount rate, and subtracting the sum total of discounted costs from the sum total of discounted benefits.

The information developed to determine the benefit-to-cost ratio can be used to determine *NPV* as:

$$NPV_{\text{initial year}} = B - C \qquad (2.3)$$

where, as in the calculation of *B/C*, *B* refers to the present value of all measured benefits and *C* refers to the present value of all measured costs, and where present value refers to the initial year or time period in which the project began, $t = 0$ in terms of the *B/C* formula in equation (2.2). Note that *NPV* allows, in principle, one means of ranking several projects *ex post*, providing investment sizes are similar.

It could be argued that for the purpose of public consumption of the finding from an economic impact analysis, *NPV* should be calculated as the difference between the present value of benefits and the present value of costs where both present values are referenced not to an initial period but rather to the time period that corresponds to when the analysis is conducted, $t = n$. The reason for this alternative approach (that is, alternative point of time reference to that implied by equation (2.3)) is that the use of *NPV* in a retrospective economic impact analysis is different from its conventional use as described in corporate finance textbooks. In the latter case, objectives include comparing alternative investments subject to a corporate constraint on funds available for investments, or deciding which investments will add to the value of the corporation's stock. All estimates are in current dollars, as the "present" is the time of decision. In the case of a retrospective analysis, and all of the analyses in Table 2.1 are retrospective in scope, the analysis takes place some considerable amount of time after the project was initiated (the "present" time in the corporate finance use of this metric). Because the results of retrospective analyses are read by policy makers and other stakeholders some time—in most cases, many years—after the project was initiated, these stakeholders will compare results in a "current-dollar" context. Hence, the reference of *NPV* to the time of the analysis can allow stakeholders to compare the results with current investment options. In other words, the following formula for *NPV* should be considered:

$$NPV_{\text{year of the analysis}} = [\Sigma_{t=0 \text{ to } t=n} B_t \times (1+r)^{n-t}] - [\Sigma_{t=0 \text{ to } t=n}$$

$$C_t \times (1+r)^{n-t}] = (NPV_{\text{initial year}}) \times (1+r)^n \qquad (2.4)$$

After the experience with the investment, a positive $NPV_{\text{initial year}}$ shows that at the outset of the investment, the value of the stream of benefits exceeded the value of the stream of costs by the amount $NPV_{\text{initial year}}$. The intuitive story for $NPV_{\text{year of the analysis}}$ is that at the time the investment is put in place, its stream of benefits could, theoretically, be sold for the stream's present value, and then a portion of the proceeds equal to the present value of the costs could be invested to release the stream of costs needed for the project, leaving the $NPV_{\text{initial year}}$ as an excess of value above and beyond costs. That value could at that time have been invested, and then the resulting value from the project by the time of the analysis would have been $NPV_{\text{year of the analysis}}$.

OTHER TECHNIQUES RELEVANT TO AN ECONOMIC IMPACT ANALYSIS

The economics-based methodologies discussed above provide analyses that are theoretically sound and more commonly used with reference to R&D- and technology-based programs, especially for analyses of R&D programs funded by US agencies. However, other retrospective techniques, some of which are also economics-based or can be used to evaluate an economics-based measure of performance, have been used to assess or to support economic impact analyses of public-sector R&D programs. Following Polt and Rojo (2002), these other techniques include econometric models, productivity models, benchmarking analysis, innovation surveys, expert panels and peer review, and network analysis.[23] Each of these other techniques is discussed below. In the concluding section of this chapter we suggest that, when possible, these techniques be considered as tools to complement the economics-based methodologies discussed earlier.

Econometric Models

> An ideal analytical approach [for a retrospective evaluation] is the construction of a time series of economic activity of affected industries that includes a period before government intervention. At some point in the time series, a government funded project . . . occurs and the subsequent portion of the time series reflects the technical and economic impacts of the intervention. (Tassey, 2003, p. 15).

Econometric models (more specifically models that are estimated using econometric methods) quantify the level of a predefined performance variable before and after the public-sector R&D program being considered had an effect.[24] The time series data that are used in these models relate to policy-relevant economic units such as a sector, an industry, a firm, an organization or institution, or an individual. Generally, the data, when available, pertain to individual firms' performances before and after the public-sector R&D program.

Define a performance variable for the ith firm as P_i. Consider two series of data. The first is a time series of data on the observed performance of k firms, $i = 1$ to $i = k$, before and after the effect from the public-sector R&D program. After the public-sector R&D program is operating, each of the k firms will be affected, but not necessarily in the same degree. If performance data are available from time periods $t = 0$ to $t = n$, and if the public-sector R&D program became effective at time period $t = t^*$, then the relevant comparison is between the performance of the k firms before the R&D program, $P_{i, \text{ for } t = 0 \text{ to } t = t^* - 1}$, and their performance after the R&D program, $P_{i, \text{ for } t = t^* \text{ to } t = n}$.

The second series of data could be on the performance of affected and non-affected firms (that is, matched pairs of firms) after the public-sector program was initiated at t^*. If performance data are only available from time $t = t^*$ to $t = n$ for k affected firms, $P_{i, i = 1 \text{ to } i = k}$, and for m non-affected firms, $P_{j, j = 1 \text{ to } j = m}$, then, for each matched pair of firms, the relevant comparison is over time between P_i and its matched P_j.[25] The counterfactual situation, that is the situation without the public-sector R&D program, is the performance of the m non-affected firms.

In the case of the first series of data that quantifies pre- and post-R&D program performance, pooled cross-sectional and time series data could be used to estimate a model that takes the general form:

$$P_{i, t} = a_0 + a_1 RD_{t^*} + \text{control variables} + \varepsilon \tag{2.5}$$

where $P_{i, t}$ represents the relevant performance variable of the ith firm at time t; RD represents the public-sector R&D program being evaluated that was initiated or became effective at time t^*—RD takes on a value of 0 for the time period before t^* and a value of 1 at t^* and afterwards;[26] and ε is a normally distributed random error term.

Estimated regression parameters from equation (2.5) allow one to interpret the economic impact of the public-sector R&D program. For example, the estimated coefficient on RD in equation (2.5) quantifies the impact of the R&D program on the average performance of the sample of k firms. If the estimated value of a_1 is positive and statistically significant, then the public-sector R&D program had a measurable positive impact on firm performance, all other factors held constant. If the public program is hypothesized to change the extent to which various control variables affect performance, then interaction terms would be added to the specification with each interaction multiplying RD with a control variable for which impact would be affected. For example, the public R&D program might have not only an "intercept effect" but also have a "slope effect" for a variable such as the firm's own R&D investment, which could be more effective given the public R&D investments.

In the case of the matched pairs of firms in which the counterfactual situation is approximated by the performance of firms not affected by the target R&D program, cross-sectional time series data could be used to estimate a model that takes the general form:

$$P_t = b_0 + b_1 E + \text{control variables} + \varepsilon \qquad (2.6)$$

The variable E divides the sample of firms into those affected by the R&D program and those matched pairs that are not affected: E takes on a value of 0 for the m non-affected matched firms and a value of 1 for the k affected matched firms. If the estimated value of b_1 is positive and statistically significant, then the R&D program had a measurable positive impact on firm performance relative to the performance of "similar" firms not affected by the program, other things held constant.[27]

There are a number of important data issues related to the use of the econometric models discussed above, and one of those issues relates to how the performance variable, P, is measured. If P is measured in terms of the stated goals of the public-sector R&D program, then the use of econometric models might be an appropriate tool for an economic assessment. If, however, there are spillovers and they are the focus of the public R&D program, then measuring firm performance, P, rather than a broader measure of performance will not work for an evaluation of the public R&D.

To illustrate, one notable economic assessment analysis by Busom (2000) is based on a model that is, in concept, equivalent to that in equation (2.6) above. She examined a sample of 154 Spanish firms that conducted R&D in 1988. About 45 percent of the firms received public support of their R&D through an agency of the Spanish Ministry, and a stated goal of this public-support program was to leverage private R&D. Other factors held constant, Busom found that participation in the public program did increase private R&D effort.[28]

Productivity Models

Productivity models are a special case of a performance model (that is, P in the previous section) that has been estimated using econometric tools. The special case is highlighted here because many of the innovation-based policy responses to the productivity slowdown in the early 1970s and then again in the late 1970s were based on what economists frequently call production function analysis. A production function is a mathematical representation of the relationship between a firm's (or other unit of analysis) output and the inputs that generate that output. For example, it is generally assumed that a firm's flow of labor (L), its stock of physical plant and equipment or capital (K), and its stock of technical knowledge (T) are relevant inputs in the production of a firm's output (Q) as:

$$Q = F(L, K, T) \tag{2.7}$$

Under a set of stylistic assumptions, such as the functional form for F($\bullet$) and the relationship between T and the firm's investments in R&D, an econometric model can be derived from which one can estimate the rate of return to the firm's investments in R&D. An estimate of the rate of return to investments in R&D could be useful for an economic impact analysis if the model is estimated before and after an R&D program.[29] Generally, however, such productivity models have not been used for this purpose but rather for justification of future public-sector R&D programs to support firm-level investments in R&D.

Benchmarking Analysis

Benchmarking analysis involves the comparison of the performance of firms affected by a public-sector R&D program relative to a theoretical objective or goal, to the best practice of all of the firms being studied, or to some other exemplary standard. For example, if the performance of k firms affected by the public-sector R&D program is denoted as $P_{i, i = 1 \text{ to } i = k}$, and if the theoretical objective or goal of the program is for firm performance to reach the level P^*,[30] then the relevant comparison is the performance of each of the k firms to the benchmark P^*, that is the relevant comparison is between P^* and $P_{i, i = 1 \text{ to } i = k}$.

Because benchmarking analysis is designed not only for impact analysis, but also for improved program management, k firm-specific indices can be calculated as $(P^* - P_i)$ and then each index can be compared to a set of firm characteristics. In other words, one could quantify the characteristics of firms that are related to their performance being "closer" (that is, $(P^* - P_i) > 0$ but relatively small in value) or "farther away" (that is, $(P^* - P_i) > 0$ but relatively large in value) from the theoretical objective or goal of the program.

As an example, the interaction between public sector R&D (mostly within universities) and firm performance has been called by Polt et al. (2001) a dimension of "industry–science relations (ISR)". In the 1990s

42   *The theory and practice of program evaluation*

throughout Europe two paradoxical trends were being observed: high performance in science and deteriorating industrial competitiveness. In response to this widely observed "European paradox", the European Commission, DG Enterprise, and the Austrian Federal Ministry of Economy and Labor commissioned a benchmark analysis of ISR in eight EU countries (Austria, Belgium, Finland, Germany, Ireland, Italy, Sweden and the UK) and the United States and Japan. Examining multiple indicators on ISR, such as university–industry research collaboration, faculty consulting with industry, patent applications, and new business start-ups related to public research, Polt et al. (2001) analyzed factors that determined the highest level of university performance in each dimension of ISR. In other words, the performance of ISR across universities within each country was benchmarked against the most efficiently performing country in each dimension (for example, the most efficient countries in terms of new business start-ups related to public research are those that support campus-based infrastructures to provide management and financial support for start-ups).

Innovation Surveys

Innovation surveys, although referred to by Polt and Rojo (2002) and others (for example, Licht and Sirilli, 2002) as an evaluation methodology, are in our opinion a data collection tool that can be used for both an economic assessment and an economic impact analysis. Large publicly administered innovation surveys are an effective means to collect data related to various aspects of the innovation process from a national perspective.[31] The surveyed units are generally firms or enterprises, but aggregation to an industry or national level is not uncommon.

European countries have sponsored broader and more detailed innovation surveys than has the United States. Noteworthy are the Community Innovation Surveys (CIS) throughout the European Union. The surveys began in 1992 and have continued more or less on a biannual basis. A hallmark of the CIS efforts is their breadth of coverage of multiple dimensions of the innovation process (for example sources of information that firms use to enhance their innovation strategy) and their documentation of a variety of government innovation policy schemes (Licht and Sirilli, 2002). The National Science Foundation's Survey of Industrial Research and Development pales in comparison to the CIS efforts in terms of its ability to collect information to quantify multiple R&D spending dimensions of the innovation process.

Information collected through the CIS efforts lends itself to the estimation of econometric models like those in equations (2.5), (2.6) and (2.7) above. Information collected through NSF's R&D survey could be used in econometric models like those in equations (2.5), (2.6) and (2.7), subject to accessibility to firm responses, but only when other external information is imposed on the model (for example, time series R&D data from the NSF survey can be used in a model like that in equation (2.5) to test for changes in R&D spending pre- and post-policy periods).

Expert Panels and Peer Reviews

Following the United Nations' definition (2005, p. 17):

> Peer review can be described as the systematic examination and assessment of the performance of an entity by counterpart entities, with the ultimate goal of helping the reviewed entity improve its policy making, adopt best practices, and comply with established standards and principles.

The peer review process is widely used to assess the quality of scientific endeavors ranging from manuscripts submitted for publication in a scholarly journal to the social impact of a public sector program's research programs (for example, US Department of Energy, 1982, 1991; Office of Naval Research, 1989). To generalize, experts are asked to review public sector research projects on a number of dimensions. In the case of the US Department of Energy (1982) evaluation of basic energy sciences projects, several evaluation factors were considered, ranging from the scientific merit of the research to the expected impact of the research on the energy mission of the agency.

Ormala (1994), for example, notes that evaluation panels are used widely throughout Europe for public sector policy and program evaluation, especially those related to public sector R&D evaluation. One especially noteworthy effort was, according to Ormala, the Commission of the European Communities evaluation of the first European Community R&D Framework Program.[32]

The National Academy of Sciences (1999, p. 38) recommended that federal agencies, in compliance with GPRA, should rely on expert review to assess the quality of basic research that they fund: "Federal agencies should use expert review to assess the quality of research they support, the relevance of that research to their mission, and the leadership of the research."

The Academy (1999, p. 39) was also of the opinion: "The most effective way to evaluate research programs is by expert review. The most commonly used form of expert review of quality is peer review. This operates on the premise that the people best qualified to judge the quality of research are experts in the field of research."

CONCLUSIONS

Although prospective analyses are beyond the scope of this chapter, thinking about them adds useful perspective to the discussion of retrospective analyses. There are examples of economic impact analyses in Table 2.1 where the time series of expected benefits and costs are extended into the future because the NIST infrastructure technology being evaluated had a commercial lifetime extending beyond the date of the analysis. Nonetheless, those analyses are retrospective because they evaluate NIST programs that started in the past; the programs are expected to generate benefits into the future; prospective analyses would entail evaluations of potential public investment in new projects.

In thinking about altogether new technology programs and projects, according to Martin (1995, pp. 139–40):

> It is widely agreed that new technologies . . . will have a revolutionary impact on the economy and society over the coming years. . . . [Government is thus under pressure to answer the question:] how can one identify the most promising research areas and the emerging technologies on which to concentrate resources and, hence, derive the fullest socio-economic benefits? . . . Foresight represents one response to these pressures. [Foresight] is the process involved in systematically attempting to look into the longer-term future of science, technology, the economy and society with the aim of identifying the areas of strategic research and the emerging generic technologies likely to yield the greatest economic and social benefits.

Technology assessment/economic impact, in contrast, is a process to project the economic impacts associated with the allocation of resources toward new science and technology.

Foresight differs from technology assessment/evaluation in at least one important dimension. Foresight is a management tool, not an assessment or evaluation tool, method, or methodology.[33] In contrast, technology assessment/evaluation is a policy tool used to approximate the economic impacts associated with science and technology resource allocations.[34]

In the United States, technology assessment as a policy tool gained visibility through the Congressional Office of Technology Assessment (active from 1974–95).[35] Technology assessment/evaluation is a tool that could effectively be used for prospective economic impact analyses, but prospective analyses have not been conducted to any great extent, and are conspicuously absent from the NIST analyses summarized in Table 2.1.[36]

Because the policy tool of technology assessment/evaluation examines resource allocations to science and technology, a key question for such evaluations of economic impact, whether retrospective or prospective, is: Why should government rather than the private sector fund and perform the activity being evaluated? The analyses reviewed in Table 2.1 answer this fundamental question in a variety of ways depending on the context of each particular analysis, but the short answer is "market failure". Each of the analyses in Table 2.1, based on discussions with industry experts, found significant sources of market failure underlying the need for the publicly financed and publicly performed infratechnology investment being evaluated.

Whether economic impact analyses are retrospective or prospective, identification of the market failure that provides the reason for public investment plays an integral role in the analyses themselves because understanding the market failure helps to formulate the crucial counterfactual scenario that must be clearly stated if benefits from the public investment are to be identified. Are barriers to technology so severe that the private sector would not even attempt to replicate the public investment (extant investment for a retrospective analysis and proposed investment in a prospective analysis)? In that case, the counterfactual scenario is the status quo ante technology absent the public investment, and a "traditional" economic impact analysis in the sense of Griliches (1958) is appropriate.

Or, would the private sector, absent the public investment and despite barriers to technology, undertake investment to provide a substitute for the infratechnology generated with the public investment? In that case, what Link and Scott (2011) call "counterfactual analysis" is the appropriate approach for an economic impact analysis, with the benefits of the public's investment being the costs avoided by the private sector—the investment costs the private sector would have incurred to replicate the public infratechnology and any shortfall in the value of the counterfactual privately developed infratechnology from the value of the technology developed publicly (often by means of the cooperative efforts of NIST and industry in public–private partnership).

As explained earlier, the "counterfactual analysis" is equivalent to the "traditional" approach when that approach is appropriate for the evaluation of publicly financed and performed R&D, that is, when barriers imply the private sector would not attempt to provide the infratechnology. Thus, the "counterfactual analysis" actually covers both approaches. As the discussions in the second and third sections explain and as the economic impact analyses in Table 2.1 illustrate, in practice both approaches are useful—both the traditional approach, with its counterfactual of the status quo ante technology, and the approach for which the counterfactual scenario entails private investment to provide the infratechnology that the public program provides.

46   *The theory and practice of program evaluation*

The timing of an economic impact analysis is important—sufficient time must have passed for the effects of the infratechnology to be observed. For example, the analysis of the Thermocouple Calibration Program, Planning Report 97-1, was premature. The analysis was supposed to estimate the benefits of a new international standard for calibration data. But, the international body did not understand that industry was committed and happy with the existing standard; that is, industry did not yet need to shift to the new standard. Similarly, in the analysis of role-based access control, Planning Report 02-1, the analysis was premature because there had not yet been sufficient market penetration of the infratechnology being evaluated.

The timing of an economic impact analysis is also important because the time during which the greatest effects of the infratechnology were realized must not be so far in the past that gathering good information about the benefits is not possible. An analysis can be done too late; in contrast to the thermocouple analysis, that of NIST's Cholesterol Standards Program, Planning Report 00-4, was done too late because as a practical matter it is not typically possible to gather the quantitative information about benefits in a period about which the institutional memory of respondents—even if appropriate respondents can be found—has faded.

Benefit data for most economic impact analyses came from detailed interviews or surveys, but possibilities for using published data (in conjunction with or in place of gathering new survey data) should be considered and used when appropriate information is available, as in the analysis of NIST's Data Encryption Standard (DES) Program, Planning Report 01-2.

When benefit data are gathered by survey, the study team should be given access to the addresses and other contact information for the entities surveyed. For example, in the analysis of the Baldrige National Quality Program, Planning Report 01-3, the American Society for Quality (ASQ) sent the survey to its members, but the study team did not have access to the email list of the recipients of the survey. The predictable result was the low response rate because although the ASQ could follow up with a mass email to its members, the opportunity for the study team to implore each member to participate was absent.

Before an infratechnology investment is undertaken, NIST should be sure that a significant underinvestment gap exists. The relatively small reduction in R&D costs found in the analysis of NIST's investments in superfilling research, Planning Report 08-1, suggests as a methodological lesson that when deciding to undertake an investment project, project managers should be sure that there is a significant underinvestment gap.

NIST project managers can maintain key contacts with the users of their projects' outputs at all stages of the supply chain and communicate with those contacts about the types of data that will be needed to estimate benefits. Ideally such data would be routinely gathered in real time on an ongoing basis. The availability of such data would allow periodic evaluations documenting impacts, thus facilitating NIST's ability to make possible adjustments that would better serve industry's needs and also allowing NIST to provide quality information about performance to support the mandate of the GPRA.

When NIST initiates a new program and also in real time as program directors and project managers gather information useful for evaluating their projects, they can also work with their industry contacts to develop understanding of the nature of the market failure to which the public provision of infratechnology investment is responding. Developing that understanding will inform the direction of the infratechnology investment in a way that increases its beneficial economic impact.

A project manager's key contacts in industry throughout the relevant supply chain can also provide access to greater numbers of industrial respondents to surveys about the economic impact of the project. Key contacts could be asked on an ongoing basis about other industrial users of the infrastructure technology, and project managers could maintain lists of industrial users in real time and on an ongoing basis. With larger numbers of respondents to provide estimates of benefits of particular types when surveys of industry are administered, it will be possible to produce formal statistical confidence intervals for the estimated benefits.

The other techniques, discussed in the fourth section, relevant for an economic impact analysis can be used to complement the approach of the economic impact analyses that has been discussed in the third section.

Should NIST standardize the supply chain used in the economic impact analyses? In our opinion, the answer is no. Instead, the place to begin is with the abstract, general understanding of how the economic impact of NIST's infrastructure technologies occurs throughout the idealized supply chain based on the four-tier model identified in this chapter. Then, with that idealized model in mind, the project leaders deciding on infratechnology investments or the study team planning an economic impact analysis can develop the actual supply chain where benefits are realized.

Should NIST replace the current approach that is often driven by the availability of data for assessment of benefits with a more standardized application of the cost/benefit methodology? As a practical matter, the answer in our opinion is no, but future economic impact analyses should continue to identify qualitatively, as the past analyses have done, all of the benefits and costs, ensuring that the metrics presented are conservative and explaining why that is so. The current approach can only be characterized as data driven in the sense that all data that can be reliably collected and reasonably quantified is included in the calculations of metrics, but the analyses are not data driven in that they try to identify qualitatively all of the benefits and costs. Thus, the quantitative metrics are data driven (as of course must be the case), but the overall evaluation is not. The result is that estimated cost–benefit ratios can differ for reasons other than differential impacts between research programs, and for that reason it is crucial that each analysis continue to identify all effects qualitatively and state clearly what is missing from the estimated evaluation metrics and emphasize that readers should not simply compare benefit-to-cost ratios or other metrics across the analyses. Instead, the conservative metrics, along with a good understanding of what is missing from the metrics, must be in mind when comparing the economic impacts of the analyses. While some analyses are able to quantify impact for a single tier of the supply chain, others quantify benefits for three tiers. Some analyses are able to extrapolate benefits to draw conclusions regarding impacts at the industry level while others are able only to characterize the direct impacts on survey respondents. Some analyses are able to quantify future benefits while others must restrict the analysis to quantification of past benefits even if the NIST technical outputs remain state-of-the-art. The end point for benefits to be realized in the future must of course be determined by a conservative estimate of the future impact horizon, and the likely proportion of future benefits that is conservative may be very different across analyses given the information available.

Summarizing, by following the recommendations about gathering benefit and cost data for the economic impact of an infratechnology project on all affected parts of the supply chain, NIST will have, to the extent practicable, the type of data that it needs to evaluate the project. As a review of the previous economic impact analyses shows, the type of data will often differ by project and by the tier of the supply chain affected. In our experience, benefits extending into the future are even more difficult for industry's beneficiaries to estimate, but if the recommendation for ongoing, real-time gathering of benefit and cost data are followed, a better fix on the benefits and costs and the expected commercial lifetime will be available than has been available for the extant analyses. The expected commercial lifetimes vary across the different infrastructure technologies because the pace of technological change varies widely across different industries and even within industries across different types of infratechnology applications. Real-time and ongoing data collection will also make possible more accurate extrapolations of benefits from the respondents to the industry-wide level. The previous economic impact analyses have differed in the extent to which they extrapolate, simply because it is not always possible to develop a good understanding of how representative an individual respondent is of the entire industry. The real-time and ongoing maintenance of industry contacts and data collection will, because such benefits are often more difficult to quantify, also enable more analyses that measure the economic impact of basic measurement research (as contrasted with the evaluation of the calibration services that take such science as given) such as in the evaluation of the investment in developing the basic science of wavelength references for optical fiber communications in the analysis of ATP's Intramural Research Awards Program (in NIST GCR 04-866). As the analysis shows, the industrial benefits from developing basic measurement science can be immensely important for innovation and the productive evolution of technology.

NOTES

1. The concept of fiscal accountability in the United States is rooted in the fundamental principles of representation of the people, by the people. Following Link and Scott (1998, 2011), issues of fiscal accountability can be traced at least to as far back as President Woodrow Wilson's reforms, and in particular to the Budget and Accounting Act of 1921. This Act of 10 June, 1921 not only required the President to transmit to Congress a detailed budget on the first day of each regular session, but also it established the General Accounting Office (GAO) to settle and adjust all accounts of the government. More recently, the Government Performance and Results Act (GPRA) of 1993 stated that: "Congressional policymaking, spending decisions and program oversight are seriously handicapped by insufficient attention to program performance and results." GPRA mandated that the head of each government agency submit to the Director of the Office of Management and Budget (OMB): "a strategic plan for program activities.... [The plan] shall contain . . . a description of the program evaluations used in establishing or revising general goals and objectives, with a schedule for future program evaluations." GPRA was at the time of its passage: "the most significant advance in bringing accountability to government programs.... Unfortunately, the implementation of this law has fallen short of its authors' hopes. Agency plans are plagued by performance measures that are meaningless, vague, too numerous, and often compiled by people who have no direct connection with budget decisions" (President's 2004 Budget, pp. 48–9). In response, President George W. Bush's 2004 budget presented a new assessment, not evaluation, tool: the Program Assessment Rating Tool (PART). There have also been policy discussions to replace PART with a new performance improvement and analysis framework called Putting Performance First (Orszag, 2009a).

2. Many point in the United States to President George H.W. Bush's 1990 US Technology Policy as our nation's first formal domestic technology policy statement, although, as Kahin and Hill (2010) point out, US innovation policies trace as far back as President George Washington's 1790 address to Congress. However, US Technology Policy, like its predecessors, has failed to articulate a foundation for government's role in supporting innovation and technology. Rather, it has implicitly assumed that government has a role, and then sets forth the general statement (Executive Office of the President 1990, p. 2): "The goal of US technology policy is to make the best use of technology in achieving the national goals of improved quality of life for all Americans, continued economic growth, and national security." President William Clinton took a major step

50   *The theory and practice of program evaluation*

forward from this 1990 policy statement in his 1994 "Economic report of the President" by articulating first principles about why government should be involved in the technological process (Council of Economic Advisers, 1994, p. 191): "The goal of technology policy is not to substitute the government's judgment for that of private industry in deciding which potential 'winners' to back. Rather, the point is to correct market failure". Relatedly, Martin and Scott (2000, p. 438) observed: "Limited appropriability, financial market failure, external benefits to the production of knowledge, and other factors suggest that strict reliance on a market system will result in underinvestment in innovation, relative to the socially desirable level. This creates a *prima facie* case in favor of public intervention to promote innovative activity." For a detailed discussion about the economic justification for government's role in the innovation process see Link and Scott (2005, 2011).

3. NIST defines an evaluation in this broad manner. What NIST refers to as an economic impact analysis is to many, including Link and Scott (1998, 2011) and the references therein, an economic impact evaluation. However, the NIST terminology is maintained throughout this chapter.

4. It is important to distinguish between assessment and impact analysis, although the terms are frequently used interchangeably. A distinction is offered herein, as discussed below, to define the boundaries of this chapter, although (for example in the titles of the economic impact analyses reviewed in Table 2.1) the distinction is not made uniformly throughout this chapter. Policy assessment is based primarily on the criterion of effectiveness, not efficiency, and the question asked is: Has the R&D program met its stated goals and objectives, and have its designated outputs been achieved?

    Also, regarding effectiveness versus efficiency, some areas of government, notably regulation, have the explicit requirement to demonstrate efficiency.

5. This section draws directly from Link and Scott (2011), which is based in part on Link and Scott (1998). Both sources refer to the following discussion under the rubric of an economic evaluation as noted in note 3 above.

6. It is important to emphasize the difference between the terms *methodology* and *method*. The terms are often used interchangeably, although it is incorrect to do so. A *methodology* is the theoretical foundation or practices within a discipline that determine or guide how to engage in an inquiry; a *method* is a tool or technique used to implement the inquiry.

7. The Mansfield et al. (1977) seminal article applied the Griliches methodology to private sector innovations, and it expanded the methodology to accommodate imperfect competition in certain circumstances.

8. These metrics are discussed in the third section.

9. Additionally, for market settings more complicated than the simplest model, the Griliches model accounts for producer surplus, measured as the difference between the price the producers receive per unit and the actual marginal cost, summed over the output sold, minus any fixed costs. Social benefits are then the streams of new consumer and producer surpluses—economic value above and beyond the opportunity costs of the resources used to create value, while private benefits for a firm that invests in innovation are the portions of the streams of producer surplus appropriated by the investor. Not all of the appropriated producer surplus is necessarily new because the surplus gained by one producer might be cannibalized from the pre-innovation surplus of another producer or from pre-innovation consumer surplus. Social and private costs will, in general, also be divergent.

10. See specifically pages 12–16 in Link and Scott (1998).

11. Observe that this does not assume that the private sector would make the same level of investment, and it does not assume that the resulting R&D output would be of equal quality. The costs avoided are the costs that the private sector would have spent on developing replacement technology and the loss in value because the replacement technology was not of equal quality to the technology developed with the public R&D. Observe that if the barriers to technology and market failure are sufficiently severe that

the private sector would not have attempted to replace the public R&D investment at all, then the counterfactual is the status quo ante technology and there are no private sector replacement costs and only the lost value from the shortfall in quality of the technology used with the public investment—exactly the counterfactual of the traditional analysis.

12. This description of infratechnologies draws on Tassey (2007). He notes (pp. 112–13): "if you cannot measure, you cannot do R&D; if you cannot test, you cannot control the production process for yield and quality; if you cannot pass a variety of complex data from machine to machine and from company to company, you cannot control cost or schedule; and if you cannot provide a customer with standardized test data for a product, you cannot assure that buyer that performance specifications have been met."

13. The causes for an underinvestment in R&D or in technology are discussed in detail in Tassey (2007) and Link and Scott (2011). Link and Scott (2011) discuss eight factors or barriers to technology that lead to technological market failure: (1) High technical risk means the outcomes of the firm's R&D might not be technically sufficient to meet its needs. This might cause market failure, given that when the firm is successful, the private returns fall short of the social returns. An underinvestment in R&D will result. (2) High technical risk can be related to high commercial or market risk, when the requisite R&D is highly capital intensive. Such investments could require too much capital for a firm to fund the outlay; thus, the firm will not make the investment, even though it would be better off if it had been able to finance the investment, and so would society. (3) Many R&D projects are characterized by a lengthy time interval until a commercial product reaches the market. The time expected to complete the R&D, and the time until commercialization of the R&D results, are long; thus, the realization of a cash flow is distant and in conjunction with differing private and social discount rates can result in market failure. (4) It is not uncommon for the scope of potential markets to be broader than the scope of the individual firm's market strategies, so the firm will not perceive economic benefits from all potential market applications of the technology. (5) The evolving nature of markets requires investment in combinations of technologies that, if they existed, would reside in different industries that are not integrated. Because such conditions often transcend the R&D strategy of individual firms, such investments are not likely to be pursued. (6) The nature of the technology may make difficult the assignment of intellectual property rights. (7) Industry structure can raise the cost of market entry for applications of the technology. (8) Situations can exist where the complexity of a technology makes agreement with respect to product performance costly between buyers and sellers. Infrastructure technology investments by NIST can allow many such barriers to be overcome—reducing costs of entry or costs of agreement about performance so that the benefits outweigh NIST's costs. Stated alternatively in the language of the "counterfactual method" described in the second section, the social cost for the investments in infratechnologies are lower with NIST and industry working together in public–private partnership than with the private sector attempting to accomplish the same ends without NIST.

14. These analyses were sponsored by the Program Office at NIST except for one that was sponsored by ATP. For additional impact assessments sponsored by ATP, see http://www.atp.nist.gov/eao/eao_pubs.htm.

15. This argument is developed in greater detail in Link and Scott (2011).

16. This statement is not intended as a criticism of the evaluators' abilities or due diligence. Rather, it underscores the difficulty in collecting retrospective data subject to resource constraints.

17. Even when it is possible to interview the beneficiaries in a downstream tier of the supply chain, they are often unable to quantify the benefits they receive from NIST's program. For example, in the analysis (Planning Report 97-1) of NIST's Thermocouple Calibration Program, benefits for domestic users were not quantified because they are more indirect and difficult to quantify than the benefits for the wire suppliers (providing materials for thermocouple assemblies) and thermocouple suppliers.

52   *The theory and practice of program evaluation*

18.   Even when all of the beneficiaries are interviewed, the numbers are often quite small. For example, in the analysis of the radiopharmaceutical research program at NIST (Planning Report 97-2), there are only seven respondents even though those seven respondents were 100 percent of the US manufacturers participating in the program.

19.   One detailed example of the use of formal statistical confidence intervals in a journal article based on a NIST-sponsored analysis is Leech and Scott (2008).

20.   Tassey (2003) refers to these metrics as corporate finance measures; they have traditionally been discussed in corporate finance textbooks' development of a firm's capital budgeting decision.

21.   For the archetypal illustrative case to explain the concept of internal rate of return, the net cash flows of benefits minus the costs begin as negative and then become positive, with just a single reversal in the sign for the series of flows. There is then at most a single real solution for the internal rate of return. Of course, for actual investment projects there can be multiple reversals in the signs for the net cash flows, and then using the internal rate of return concept for a cost–benefit analysis requires some additional work with the time series of benefits and costs. For an actual example with an explanation of how to treat the issue, see Link and Scott (1998, p. 46).

22.   Commenting on the 7 percent real discount rate, OMB (2003, p. 33) observed: "The 7 percent [real] rate is an estimate of the average before-tax rate of return to private capital in the US economy. It is a broad measure that reflects the returns to real estate and small business capital as well as corporate capital. It approximates the opportunity cost of capital, and it is the appropriate discount rate whenever the main effect of a regulation is to displace or alter the use of capital in the private sector. OMB revised *Circular A-94* in 1992 after extensive internal review and public comment." Further, OMB (2003, p. 33) observed: "The pre-tax rates of return better measure society's gains from investment. Since the rates of return on capital are higher in some sectors of the economy than others, the government needs to be sensitive to possible impacts of regulatory policy on capital allocation." However, OMB (2003, p. 33) also observed: "The effects of regulation do not always fall exclusively or primarily on the allocation of capital. When regulation primarily and directly affects private consumption (e.g., through higher consumer prices for goods and services), a lower discount rate is appropriate." Hence, if one were evaluating a policy where, instead of alternative uses of investment capital in public R&D investment decisions, the issue evaluated were a regulatory policy (for example, for health care) that would directly and primarily affect the stream of real income to consumers (for example, alternative health plans with streams of different magnitudes and different timings), then the OMB has directed (OMB, 2003, pp. 33–4) that "for regulatory analysis" (p. 34), rather than an evaluation of an investment, the real discount rate of 3 percent should be used and compared to the results using the 7 percent real discount rate. OMB explains that for consumers' decisions, 3 percent better approximates their real rate of time preference.

  OMB (2003, p. 33) explicitly stated that the 7 percent real required rate of return that is based on the average rate of return to private capital investment is "a default position"; yet, the market failure story recognizes that for investments (not just "regulatory policy") the social rate of return and the private rate of return can (and are expected to) diverge, with the social required rate of return being less than the private hurdle rate. As it turns out, in practice, a 7 percent social hurdle rate for public investments is not inconsistent with that logic because the 7 percent is based on the average. However, for the R&D investment projects we have evaluated in case studies, the firms report higher private hurdle rates. OMB appears to be taking the least controversial approach by using for the social hurdle rate for investments an average return for private capital investments and by advising consideration of the variance in private returns in different activities. Clearly, as we have noted, there is no reason society should be constrained in its assessments of value by prices determined in markets where there are market failures and the prices give the wrong signals. Hence, the private rate of return on investment should not be expected to equal the social opportunity cost of investment funds; the private rates of return may be based on prices that do not reflect social value. We know that with positive externalities such as non-appropriated spillovers that benefit those who did not invest, social rates of return can be high when private rates of return are low. Moreover, the private rate of return can be high even when the social rate of return is low or even negative. For example, in the context of R&D investment, the results of a privately profitable R&D investment may simply cannibalize previously existing economic surplus, causing the investment to have a negative social rate of return for a period of time. OMB's approach is a solution in the absence of a practical way to determine what the theoretical social hurdle rate should be in any given situation.

23. These techniques are widely cited by the European Commission (Polt and Rojo, 2002) as methodologies. In our opinion they are a potpourri of methodologies, methods and data collection tools rather than all being methodologies, and they vary greatly in their relation to the theory of value and opportunity costs that underlies economics-based methodologies. All of these techniques are discussed because of their general visibility.

24. As Jaffe (2002) explains, identifying the effect of the public program is difficult.

25. There are many issues related to how one defines a matched firm (for example, size, level of own R&D, industry), but that discussion is beyond the scope of this chapter.

26. The specification in equation (2.5) is simplified for purposes of an introductory explanation because it assumes the R&D program's impact occurred at time t^* and that impact remained constant through subsequent time periods. More sophisticated variations of equation (2.5) are possible.

27. Again, if the program is hypothesized to affect the impacts of control variables (that is, if it will have "slope effects" as well as "intercept effects"), then interaction terms that multiply E with each affected control variable would be entered in the specification.

28. This finding could be interpreted as showing that public R&D complements private R&D rather than substitutes for it (that is, crowds it out). See David et al. (2000) and the references therein.

29. Hall et al. (2010) provide an excellent review of the academic literature on such productivity models.

30. P^* could be the performance level of the most efficient firm in the sample, the average performance of all firms in the sample, or some other performance index related to best practices.

31. Such publicly administered surveys also have economic value in the sense that they are within the public domain (controlled for confidentiality issues), and thus, analyses based on the collected data can be replicated.

32. The Framework Program was initially designed to assist small- and medium-sized enterprises, technology-based enterprises in particular, compete in globalized markets.

33. The importance of foresight as a strategic management tool is not independent of government's role in the innovation process, which is based on the economic concept of market failure. Market failure refers to the market—including both the R&D-investing producers of a technology and the users of the technology—underinvesting, from society's standpoint, in a particular technology or technology application. Such underinvestment occurs because conditions exist that prevent organizations from fully realizing or appropriating the benefits created by their investments. To elaborate on the concept of market failure, consider a marketable technology to be produced through an R&D process where conditions prevent the R&D-investing firm from fully appropriating the benefits from technological advancement. Other firms in the market, or in related markets, will realize some of the benefits (economic profits—revenues in excess of the opportunity costs of the resources used by these other firms) from the innovation, and of course consumers will typically place a higher value on a product than the price paid for it. The R&D-investing firm will then calculate, because of such conditions, that the marginal benefits it can receive from a unit investment in such R&D will be less than could be earned in the absence of the conditions reducing the appropriated benefits of R&D below their potential, namely the full social benefits. Thus, the R&D-investing

54   *The theory and practice of program evaluation*

firm might underinvest in R&D, relative to what it would have chosen as its investment in the absence of the conditions.

There are a number of factors that can explain why a firm will perceive that its expected private rate of return will fall below its hurdle rate, even when the social rate of return exceeds the social hurdle rate. See Link and Scott (2011) for a more detailed explanation, and see note 13 for enumeration and brief discussion of eight factors that constitute barriers to innovation and technolology. The eight factors lead to a private underinvestment in R&D.

34. The importance of technology assessment/evaluation as a policy tool is not independent of identifying which of the barriers to innovation and technology brought about the market failure and then understanding the extent to which allocated resources will overcome those barriers.
35. Schot and Rip (1997) offer examples of technology assessment used in the Netherlands.
36. An exception is Leech and Scott (2008) which provides an economics-based prospective analysis to look ahead to the expected impact of intelligent machine technology and to explain that new public infratechnology investments would increase that future impact.

REFERENCES

Busom, Isabel (2000), 'An empirical evaluation of the effects of R&D subsidies', *Economics of Innovation and New Technology*, **9**, 111–48.

Council of Economic Advisers (annual), 'Economic report of the President', Washington, DC: US Government Printing Office.

David, Paul A., Bronwyn H. Hall and Andrew A. Toole (2000), 'Is public R&D a complement for private R&D?', *Research Policy*, **29**, 497–529.

Executive Office of the President (1990), 'US technology policy', Washington, DC: Office of Science and Technology Policy.

Griliches, Zvi (1958), 'Research costs and social returns: hybrid corn and related innovations', *Journal of Political Economy*, **66**, 419–31.

Hall, Bronwyn H., Jacques Mairesse and Pierre Mohnen (2010), 'Measuring the returns to R&D', in Bronwyn H. Hall and Nathan Rosenberg (eds), *The Economics of Innovation*, Amsterdam: Elsevier, pp. 1033–82.

Jaffe, Adam B. (2002), 'Building programme evaluations into the design of public research-support programs', *Oxford Review of Economic Policy*, **18**, 22–34.

Kahin, Brian and Christopher T. Hill (2010), 'United States: the need for continuity', *ISSUES in Science and Technology*, **26**, 51–60.

Leech, David P. and John T. Scott (2008), 'Intelligent machine technology and productivity growth', *Economics of Innovation and New Technology*, **17**, 677–87.

Licht, Georg and Giorgio Sirilli (2002), 'Innovation surveys', in Gustavo Fahrenkrog, Wolfgang Polt, Jaime Rojo, Alexander Tübke and Klaus Zinöcker (eds), *RTD Evaluation Toolbox*, Seville: European Commission, pp 71–81.

Link, Albert N. and John T. Scott (1998), *Public Accountability: Evaluating Technology-based Institutions*, Norwell, MA: Kluwer Academic Publishers.

Link, Albert N. and John T. Scott (2001), 'Public/private partnerships: stimulating competition in a dynamic market', *International Journal of Industrial Organization*, **19**, 763–94.

Link, Albert N. and John T. Scott (2005), *Evaluating Public Research Institutions: The US Advanced Technology Program's Intramural Research Initiative*, London: Routledge.

Link, Albert N. and John T. Scott (2011), *Public Goods, Public Gains: Calculating the Social Benefits of Public R&D*, New York: Oxford University Press.

Mansfield, Edwin, John Rapoport, Anthony Romeo, Samuel Wagner and George Beardsley (1977), 'Social and private rates of return from industrial innovations', *Quarterly Journal of Economics*, **91**, 221–40.

Martin, Ben R. (1995), 'Foresight in science and technology', *Technology Analysis and Strategic Management*, **7**, 140–68.

Martin, Stephen and John T. Scott (2000), 'The nature of innovation market failure and the design of public support for private innovation', *Research Policy*, **29**, 437–47.

National Academy of Sciences (1999), *Evaluating Federal Research Programs: Research and the Government Performance and Results Act*, Washington, DC: National Academy of Sciences.

Office of Management and Budget (OMB) (1992), 'Circular No. A–94: Guidelines and discount rates for benefit–cost analysis of federal programs', Washington, DC: Government Printing Office.

Office of Management and Budget (OMB) (2003), 'Circular No. A–4: Regulatory analysis', Washington, DC: Government Printing Office.

Office of Naval Research (1989), 'Significant accomplishments: Office of Naval Research sponsored programs', Washington, DC: Office of Naval Research.

Ormala, Erkki (1994), 'Impact assessment: European experience of qualitative methods and practices', *Evaluation Review*, **18**, 41–51.

Orszag, Peter R. (2009a), 'Testimony of Peter Orszag before the Subcommittee on Financial Services, Committee on Appropriations, on May 20, 2009', Washington, DC: House of Representatives, US Congress.

Orszag, Peter R. (2009b), 'Memorandum for the Heads of Executive Departments and Agencies', Office of Management and Budget, Executive Office of the President, 7 October.

Polt, Wolfgang and Jaime Rojo (2002), 'Evaluation methodologies', In Gustavo Fahrenkrog, Wolfgang Polt, Jaime Rojo, Alexander Tübke and Klaus Zinöcker (eds), *RTD Evaluation Toolbox*, Seville: European Commission, pp. 65–70.

Polt, Wolfgang, Christian Rammer, Helmut Gassler, Andreas Schibany and Doris Schartinger (2001), 'Benchmarking industry–science relations: the role of framework conditions', *Science and Public Policy*, **4**, 247–58.

President's 2004 Budget (2003), available at: <http://www.gpoaccess.gov/usbudget/fy04/pdf/budget/performance.pdf>.

Schot, Johan and Arie Rip (1997), 'The past and the future of constructive technology assessment', *Technological Forecasting and Social Change*, **54**, 251–68.

Tassey, Gregory (1997), *The Economics of R&D Policy*, Westport, CT: Quorum Books.

Tassey, Gregory (2003), 'Methods for Assessing the Economic Impacts of Government R&D', NIST Planning Report 03-1, Gaithersburg, MD.

Tassey, Gregory (2007), *The Technology Imperative*, Cheltenham, UK and Northampton, MA, USA: Edward Elgar Publishing.

US Department of Energy (1982), 'An assessment of the basic energy sciences program', Washington, DC: Office of Energy Research.

US Department of Energy (1991), 'Procedures for peer review assessments', Washington, DC: Office of Energy Research.

United Nations Development Programme (2005), 'Peer assessment of evaluation in multilateral organisations', Koege, Denmark: Ministry of Foreign Affairs of Denmark.

[2]

Econ. Innov. New Techn., 2006, Vol. 15(1), January, pp. 83–100

AN ECONOMIC EVALUATION OF THE BALDRIGE NATIONAL QUALITY PROGRAM

ALBERT N. LINK[a,*] and JOHN T. SCOTT[b,†]

[a]*Department of Economics, University of North Carolina at Greensboro, Greensboro, NC 27402, USA;* [b]*Department of Economics, Dartmouth College, Hanover, NH 03755, USA*

(Received 4 February 2004; Revised 27 June 2004; In final form 3 November 2004)

All federal programs are accountable for their use of public funds. This paper presents conservative estimates of the net social benefits associated with the Baldrige National Quality Award Program, established within the National Institute of Standards and Technology in 1987. On the basis of survey data from members of the American Society for Quality, we estimate cost savings benefits to members, extrapolate those benefits to the economy as a whole, and compare the benefits to the social costs associated with the Program. Our estimation method implies that the ratio of economy-wide benefits to social costs probably exceeds 207:1, supporting the hypothesis that the public investments in quality-standards infrastructure are worthwhile.

Keywords: Evaluation methods; Public program evaluation; Social benefits and costs

1 INTRODUCTION

In response to the productivity decline in the non-farm US economy in the mid-1970s and early-1980s, a number of economic policy initiatives were introduced in the early- and mid-1980s in an effort to reverse the downward productivity trend by stimulating innovative activities within firms. One such initiative was the Malcolm Baldrige National Quality Improvement Act of 1987 (PL 100-107) that declared:[1]

> [T]he leadership of the United States in product and process quality has been challenged strongly (and some-times successfully) by foreign competition, and our Nation's productivity growth has improved less than our competitors over the last two decades; . . . a national quality award program . . . in the United States would help improve quality and productivity by –
>   (A) helping to stimulate American companies to improve quality and productivity for the pride of recognition while obtaining a competitive edge through increased profits,

---

* Corresponding author. E-mail: al_link@uncg.edu
† Tel.: +1 603-646-2941; E-mail: john.t.scott@dartmouth.edu
[1] As Townsend and Gebhardt (1996) explained, the origins of the Baldrige Award grew from 'alarm over the Japanese challenge to the American economy' (p. 6), and they concluded (p. 13):

> [T]he Baldrige will retain its position of importance, a position earned by being perhaps the major factor in positioning American business for the 21st century. The Baldrige didn't just shift the paradigm for American business – it defined a whole new way to go about doing things. As a result, business communities throughout the world once again can look to America to learn how to get things done.

ISSN 1043-8599 print; ISSN 1476-8364 online © 2006 Taylor & Francis
DOI: 10.1080/1043859042000332204

(B) recognizing the achievements of those companies which improve the quality of their goods and services and providing an example to others,
(C) establishing guidelines and criteria that can be used by businesses, industrial, governmental, and other organizations in evaluating their own quality improvement efforts, and
(D) providing specific guidance for other American organizations that wish to learn how to manage for high quality by making available detailed information on how winning organizations were able to change their cultures and achieve eminence.
[And] there is hereby established the Malcolm Baldrige National Quality Award.

Physically and administratively located at the National Institute of Standards and Technology, the Program has been supported by federal and private funding since its establishment. On the federal side, support for the Program has increased from $200,000 in 1988 to $5,344,000 in 2000.

Albeit a small program by fiscal standards, the Baldrige National Quality Program may be one of the better-known competitiveness programs sponsored by the government. Certainly, the Malcolm Baldrige National Quality Award is one of the most widely publicized of all public sector sponsored performance awards.

Regardless of the size or visibility of the Program, it is like any federal program accountable for its use of public funds. The Government Performance and Results Act (GPRA) of 1993 – to improve the confidence of the American people in the performance capability of the federal government and to improve federal program effectiveness – requires each federal program to develop a process of identifying and quantifying the economic benefits of the program's outcomes.

The purpose of this paper is to present estimates of the net social benefits associated with the Baldrige National Quality Program. In Section 2, various institutional aspects of the Program are overviewed including a discussion of the Award criteria, trend in applications, and anecdotal information related to the social benefits associated with the Program. In Section 3, systematic approaches to program evaluation are discussed, and our counterfactual approach is contrasted with traditional approaches. In Section 4, results from the application of the counterfactual evaluation method are presented. Fundamental to our application of the counterfactual evaluation method is our use of very detailed survey response data that, as a practical matter, will always come from a relatively small sample. Given the smallness of our sample of members of the American Society for Quality (ASQ), we use a statistical procedure that controls for selection into the small sample and uses the standard errors of our estimates to ensure that we arrive at a conservative estimate of the Program's social benefit-to-cost ratio. That conservatively estimated benefit-to-cost ratio is 207:1. Finally, in Section 5, we offer concluding observations.

2   AN OVERVIEW OF THE BALDRIGE NATIONAL QUALITY PROGRAM

Although the Program's federally funded budget has increased since the Program's inception, as shown in Figure 1, the number of applicants to the Program for the Award has not, as shown in Figure 2. There has been speculation that the decline in the number of applicants since 1991 reflects the increasing opportunity costs for organizations to conform to the Baldrige Criteria for Performance Excellence (Tab. I). The increase in applicants for 1999 and 2000 is because the Program's scope was broadened to include awards for educational organizations and health care providers.

The companies that received the Malcolm Baldrige National Quality Award through 2000 are listed in Table II. At that time, 43 Awards had been announced.

EVALUATION OF BALDRIGE NATIONAL QUALITY PROGRAM   85

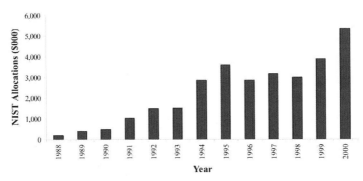

FIGURE 1   NIST Allocations to the Baldrige National Quality Program (thousands of dollars: $000), 1988–2000.

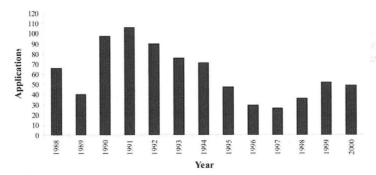

FIGURE 2   Applications to the Baldrige National Quality Program, 1988–2000.

One important motivation for selecting the Baldrige National Quality Program for an evaluation study was the rich empirical literature related to investments in quality that strongly suggested that there were measurable spillover benefits associated with the Baldrige Criteria, and thus with the Award. For example, George and Weimerskirch (1994, pp. 5–6) champion

TABLE I   Overview of the Baldrige Criteria for Performance Excellence.

The Baldrige Criteria for Performance Excellence provide organizations with an integrated, results-oriented framework for implementing and assessing processes for managing all operations. The Baldrige Criteria are also the basis for making the Baldrige Award and providing feedback to applicants. The Baldrige Criteria consist of seven categories:

1. *Leadership*: The company's leadership system, values, expectations, and public responsibilities.
2. *Strategic planning*: The effectiveness of strategic and business planning and deployment of plans, with a strong focus on customer and operational performance requirements.
3. *Customer and market focus*: How the company determines customer and market requirements and expectations, enhances relationships with customers, and determines their satisfaction.
4. *Information and analysis*: The effectiveness of information collection and analysis to support customer-driven performance excellence and marketplace success.
5. *Human resource development and management*: The success of efforts to realize the full potential of the work force to create a high-performance organization.
6 *Process management*: The effectiveness of systems and processes for assuring the quality of products and services.
7. *Business results*: Performance results, trends, and comparison to competitors in key business areas – customer satisfaction, financial and marketplace, human resources, suppliers and partners, and operations.

Source: NIST (1997b).

TABLE II   Malcolm Baldrige National Quality Award winners, 1988–2000.

Year	Recipients
1988	Motorola Inc., Westinghouse Electric Corporation – Commercial Nuclear Fuel Division, Globe Metallurgical Inc.
1989	Milliken & Company, Xerox Corporation – Business Products and Systems
1990	Cadillac Motor Car Company, IBM Rochester, Federal Express Corporation, Wallace Co., Inc.
1991	Solectron Corporation, Zytec Corporation, Marlow Industries, Inc.
1992	AT&T Network Systems Group – Transmission Systems Business Unit, Texas Instruments Incorporated – Defense Systems and Electronics Group, AT&T Universal Card Services, The Ritz-Carlton Hotel – Company, Granite Rock Company
1993	Eastman Chemical Company, Ames Rubber Corporation
1994	AT&T Customer Communications Services, GTE Directories Corporation, Wainwright Industries, Inc.
1995	Armstrong World Industries Inc. – Building Products Operation, Corning Incorporated – Telecommunications Products Division
1996	ADAC Laboratories, Dana Commercial Credit Corporation, Custom Research, Inc., Trident Precision Manufacturing, Inc.
1997	3M Dental Products Division, Solectron Corporation, Merrill Lynch Credit Corporation, Xerox Business Services
1998	Boeing Airlift and Tanker Programs, Solar Turbines, Incorporated, Texas Nameplate Company, Inc.
1999	STMicroelectronics, Inc.-Region Americas, BI, The Ritz-Carlton Hotel Co., LLC, Sunny Fresh Foods
2000	Dana Corp.-Spicer Driveshaft Division, KARLEE Company, Inc., Operations Management International, Inc., Los Alamos National Bank

Source: Available online at: http://www.quality.nist.gov.

the Baldrige Criteria as the leading model of total quality management with the following observations:

> No other model has gained such widespread global acceptance. As evidence, consider these facts.
>
> - Since the Baldrige Program was introduced in 1988, the National Institute of Standards and Technology has distributed more than a million copies of the criteria. It estimates that people have made at least that many copies for their own use.
> - More than half the states in the country now have state quality award programs based on the Baldrige criteria.
> - Several countries, including Argentina, Australia, Brazil, Canada, and India, are developing or have implemented quality award programs based on the Baldrige criteria.
> - The criteria for the European Quality Award, first presented in 1992, are patterned after the Baldrige criteria.
> - Companies, such as Honeywell, Intel, IBM, Carrier, Kodak, and AT&T, have adopted the Baldrige criteria as their internal assessment tool and criteria for their corporate quality awards. Many other large companies are asking suppliers to assess their organizations by the Baldrige criteria.

From the mid-1980s to the mid-1990s, the service sector of the US economy grew faster than the non-service sector by an order of magnitude (Scott, 1999). The rapidly evolving service sector is using the Baldrige Criteria to ensure comprehensive management of quality; Blodgett (1999, p. 74) thus observes:

> Service organizations are adopting the criteria in two main ways: They are conducting self-assessments against this robust organizational management model to help identify their strengths and opportunities for improvement, and they are applying for the increasing number of Baldrige-based quality awards in place at the state and local level.

In addition to these general observations about aspects of the social benefits associated with the Program, the Criteria have been adopted by states as a foundation or benchmark for their own quality award programs, thus signifying one dimension of spillover benefits (Tab. III).

Table IV provides a concise perspective of the extant empirical economic and management literature related to measurable firm performance effects associated with all aspects of the

TABLE III   Application of Baldrige Criteria to State and Local Quality Award Programs.

Year	Number of states with award programs tied to Baldrige Criteria	Number of service and manufacturing organizations that applied for state and local quality awards
1991	8	111
1992	12	144
1993	19	357
1994	29	428
1995	37	574
1996	42	804
1997	43	974
1998	44	830

Source: Blodgett (1999) and NIST (1998).

TABLE IV   Empirical literature related to measurable firm performance effects associated with the Baldrige National Quality Program.

Aspects of performance	Authors
Award winners have stronger financial performance and greater increases in their market value	Wisner and Eakins (1994) Helton (1995) Lawler *et al.* (1995) Huselid and Becker (1996) Easton and Jarrell (1998) NIST (1996, 1997a, 2000) Hendricks and Singhal (2001)
Application of Baldrige Criteria improved employee relations, lowered costs, improved customer satisfaction	GAO (1991)
Application of Baldrige Criteria improved competitiveness	Council on Competitiveness (1995) Banker *et al.* (1998)
Application of Baldrige Criteria increased worker productivity	Ichniowski *et al.* (1995) Black and Lynch (1996a,b)

Program. Although it is beyond the scope of this evaluation paper to discuss the literature in detail, the table does show that scholars have identified several aspects of the social benefits associated with the Program, the Award, and the underlying Criteria. Therefore, our *a priori* expectations are that the net social benefits associated with the Program are substantial.

3   SYSTEMATIC APPROACHES TO PROGRAM EVALUATION

With any publicly funded program, in principle, the government has an economically justifiable role in supporting investment because of market failures stemming from the public-good nature of the investments associated with the private sector's inability to appropriate returns to the investments or to accept their risks.[2] When the public-good nature of investments provides a justifiable role for government in a publicly funded program, systematic program evaluation will demonstrate that the program's social benefits exceed its social costs.

3.1   Traditional Economic Evaluation Methods

Griliches (1958) and Mansfield *et al.* (1977) pioneered the application of fundamental economic insight to the development of measurements of private and social rates of return to

---

[2] The origin of this view can be traced at least to Bush (1945); Link and Scott (2001) place it in a specific policy context.

innovative investments. Streams of investment costs generate streams of economic benefits over time. Once identified and measured, these streams of costs and benefits are used to calculate such performance metrics as social rates of return and benefit-to-cost ratios.

For example, for a process innovation adopted in a competitive market, using the traditional framework, the publicly funded innovation being evaluated is thought to lower the cost of producing a product to be sold in a competitive market. As the innovation lowers the unit cost of production, consumers will actually pay less for the product than they paid before the innovation and less than they would have been willing to pay – a gain in consumer surplus. The social benefits from the innovation include the total savings that all consumers receive as a result of producers adopting the cost-reducing innovation. Thus, the evaluation question that can be answered from this traditional approach is 'given the investment costs and the social benefits, what is the social rate of return to the innovation?'

Asking the question in the foregoing way is not the most appropriate approach from a public accountability perspective. Certainly, the approach allows the evaluation to show the benefits of a socially useful innovation, as intended. However, for publicly funded and publicly performed research, the procedure ignores consideration of the cost effectiveness of the public sector undertaking the research as opposed to the private sector. In other words, the procedure ignores the efficiency with which social benefits are being achieved. Is the public performance less costly than performing the research in the private sector? For publicly funded and privately performed research, the procedure does not by itself distinguish the private rates of return with and without public funding from the social rate of return. As a result, the benefits from the public funding are not identified.

In our opinion, the following 'counterfactual' evaluation method is more appropriate for publicly funded and publicly performed infrastructure research and development (R&D) (as well as related operations and maintenance investments in the infrastructure more generally) than the traditional economic approaches.[3]

3.2   The Counterfactual Evaluation Method

When publicly funded and publicly performed investments are being evaluated, holding constant the economic benefits that the Griliches–Mansfield model measures, and making no attempt to measure that stream, the relevant counterfactual question to ask is 'what would the private sector have had to invest to achieve those same benefits in the absence of the public sector's investments?'

The answer to this question yields the benefits of the public investments, namely, the private sector's costs avoided through the public's investments plus the benefits from the public sector's investments that industry would be unable or unwilling to duplicate.[4] With those benefits – obtained in practice through extensive interviews with administrators, federal research scientists, and those in the private sector who would have to duplicate the investments in the absence of public performance – counterfactual rates of return and benefit-to-cost ratios can be

---

[3] For discussion and illustrations of the method, as well as an alternative method for use with publicly funded but privately performed R&D investments, see Link and Scott (1998, 2000, 2001).

[4] In the extreme case where industry would not have made the investments at all, there are no private-sector costs avoided. However, because the private-sector performance shortfall is complete, the entire, traditional Griliches–Mansfield-like (whether their cost-reducing innovations or surplus-creating innovations more generally) stream of returns to the R&D investments is valued as benefits. In that special case, the Link–Scott approach is identical to the Griliches–Mansfield approach except that it has the advantage of having pointed out that government could do the work more efficiently – in this special case because industry would not do it at all; see Link and Scott (1998) for more details about the counterfactual evaluation method. Consistent with what our respondents have told us, and further to be conservative in our estimate of the benefits of the Baldrige Program, we assume throughout this paper that the private sector could – for the additional costs identified in our survey – have replicated the results of the Program.

calculated. These metrics answer the fundamental evaluation question: are the public investments a more efficient way of generating the technology than the private sector investments would have been?

The answer to this fundamental question aligns with the public accountability issues implicit in GPRA, and certainly addresses a key question of public-sector stakeholders who may doubt the appropriateness of government having a role in the innovation process in the first place. Further, in the context of investments with a public-good nature, the hypothesized answer to the fundamental evaluation question is yes; the counterfactual method tests that hypothesis.

3.3 Evaluation Method Applicable to the Baldrige National Quality Program

In a broad sense, the Baldrige National Quality Program is a measurement-and-standards infrastructure R&D investment program, with the associated investments in operations and maintenance. Publicly funded and publicly performed infrastructure R&D and related operations and maintenance investments occur within the Program in the sense that therein the Baldrige Criteria were originally developed and therein, through the Baldrige Award process, appropriate applications of the criteria for performance excellence are evaluated. In this broad sense, the Baldrige National Quality Program is similar to a NIST laboratory that performs infrastructure technology R&D investments and sets performance standards (i.e. the Baldrige Criteria) and then continually calibrates bench standards used in private-sector laboratories to achieve a predetermined level of performance (i.e. the Baldrige Award process).

Thus, we apply the counterfactual evaluation method to the evaluation of the Baldrige National Quality Program. Benefits to the economy from the Program are systematically quantified in terms of the cost savings organizations realized by having the Baldrige Criteria to follow as opposed to organizations, on their own, developing and testing comparable criteria.

Benefit data were collected through surveys to selected members of the ASQ and then extrapolated to the aggregate economy as discussed in the following section. Cost data were provided by the Baldrige National Quality Program Office at NIST. The relevant evaluation metric is a benefit-to-cost ratio, with all benefits and all costs referenced to year 2000.

4 APPLICATION OF THE COUNTERFACTUAL EVALUATION METHOD TO THE BALDRIGE NATIONAL QUALITY PROGRAM

4.1 American Society for Quality[5]

The ASQ agreed to a request from the management of the Baldrige National Quality Program Office on our behalf to have a mail survey distributed to its 875 US private-sector companies and public-sector organizations (hereafter 'members').[6]

ASQs stated mission is to advance individual and organizational performance excellence on a worldwide basis by providing members opportunities for learning, quality improvement, and knowledge exchange. As stated at its web site, the Society's objectives for 2000 are as follows:

- to be our members' best resource for achieving professional and organizational excellence;
- to be a worldwide provider of information and learning opportunities related to quality;

---

[5] Available online at: http://www.asq.org.

[6] In addition to these US organizational members, there are over 200 international organizational members plus over 120,000 individual members.

TABLE V   Baldrige National Quality Program operating costs.

(1) Fiscal year	(2) NIST allocations ($)	(3) Foundation allocations ($)	(4) Company reimbursed examiner expenses ($)	(5) Examiner time (h)	(6) Total operating costs ($2000)
1988	200,000	*600,000*	*190,000*	*37,995*	3,689,349
1989	408,000	*600,000*	*190,000*	*37,995*	3,910,205
1990	488,000	*600,000*	*190,000*	37,995	3,951,030
1991	1,018,000	*600,000*	*190,000*	46,510	5,059,093
1992	1,482,000	*600,000*	*190,000*	49,763	5,750,259
1993	1,525,000	*600,000*	*190,000*	46,223	5,516,050
1994	2,860,000	728,973	190,453	45,944	7,072,918
1995	3,611,000	694,669	188,137	51,259	8,092,820
1996	2,865,000	652,017	160,230	44,143	6,683,663
1997	3,174,000	778,600	171,803	44,090	7,073,404
1998	3,010,000	808,713	157,879	43,662	6,840,293
1999	3,877,000	1,159,337	186,052	51,735	8,553,566
2000	5,334,000	1,187,543	160,363	51,349	9,891,218

Notes: Column (2): NIST allocation data were provided by the Award office. For inclusion in column (6), these data were inflated to $2000 using the chain-type price index for gross domestic product from Table B-7, 'Chain type-price indexes for gross domestic product, 1959–2000' Council of Economic Advisers (2001, p. 284). *Column (3):* Foundation allocation data were provided by the Award office for 1994–2000. The upper-bound on pre-1994 data was estimated (italics), with advice from the Award office. For inclusion in column (6), these data were inflated to $2000 using the chain-type price index for GDP in Council of Economic Advisers (2001, p. 284). *Column (4):* Foundation reimbursements of 70% were paid in 1999 and 2000 for examiners in the education and health care areas; all other examiners were reimbursed at 60% of their expenses. From these data, provided by the Award office, company reimbursed expenses were calculated for 1994–2000. The upper-bound on pre-1994 company costs was estimated (italics), with advice from the Award office. For inclusion in column (6), these data were inflated to $2000 using the chain-type price index for GDP in Council of Economic Advisers (2001). *Column (5):* Examiner time was provided by the Award office. The upper-bound on pre-1990 examiner time was estimated (italics), with advice from the Award office. Based on the management background of the numerous examiners involved in the program, the Award office estimates that the current fully burdened value of a man-year of examiner time is $125,000 ($2000 based on 2000 h per year). The estimated value of examiner time is included in column (6) without additional adjustment.

- to be the leader in operational excellence and delivering customer value;
- to be the recognized leader worldwide for advancing individual and organizational performance excellence.

The Society was formed on 16 February 1946.

4.2   Social Costs of Operating the Baldrige National Quality Program

The public source of funds for the Baldrige National Quality Program is an annual allocation from the NIST budget. Column (2) of Table V shows the Program's annual allocations from NIST by fiscal year beginning with its first year of operation, 1988.

The Malcolm Baldrige National Quality Improvement Act of 1987 states that:

> The Secretary [of Commerce] is authorized to seek and accept gifts from public and private sources to carry out the program.

In addition to the public funding through NIST, there are private sources of funds. The Program was initially endowed by private industry with $10 million. A Foundation was established to manage these funds and to allocate the interest earned to the Program for award ceremonies, publication costs, and partial training and travel costs for examiners whose companies would not pay for such expenses. In column (3) of Table V are the Program's annual allocations from the Foundation. In column (4) are annual estimates of company expenditures for examiner travel that were not reimbursed by the Foundation through the Program.[7]

---

[7] The Foundation reimburses between 60% and 70% of examiner travel costs, and the remainder is paid by the examiner's company or organization.

Industry also supports the Program through volunteer examiners during the application and evaluation process. In column (5) of Table V are the total man-hours of examiner time devoted to training, application review, and site visits.

Column (6) of Table V reports the estimated Program costs in year-2000 dollars (year-2000 dollars will be denoted as '$2000' from this point on), by year. The present value of these costs, brought forward at the real social rate of return of 7% to account for the social opportunity costs of these funds following the guidelines of OMB (1992), is $118,617,000.

Thus, $119 million (rounded in $2000) is used to represent the present value of the total social costs (to date) associated with the Baldrige National Quality Program.

4.3   Social Benefits Associated with the Baldrige National Quality Program

A five-step approach is used to estimate the net social benefits associated with the Baldrige National Quality Program. Each step is discussed subsequently in detail, but here is a brief overview.

Benefit data were collected by survey from a sample of the membership of ASQ. These benefit data were extrapolated first to the ASQ membership as a whole and then to the economy as a whole.

The present value of the conservative estimate of the net private benefits received by the ASQ members as a result of the Baldrige National Quality Program is $2.17 billion (rounded in $2000).

If the entire economy benefits to the same extent as the ASQ members, the present value of the conservative estimate of the net social benefits associated with the Baldrige National Quality Program is $24.65 billion (rounded in $2000).

The net private benefits to ASQ members and net social benefits were estimated as follows.

Step 1: Estimating the Probability of Survey Response from ASQ Members.   As noted earlier, the ASQ agreed to a request from the management of the Baldrige National Quality Program Office at NIST on our behalf to distribute a survey administered by the Program Office to its 875 US members. Sixty-five organizations returned completed or partially completed survey instruments.[8]

Step 1 quantifies the probability that an ASQ member who received a survey would respond to the survey. Obviously, the average probability of response is 65 returned surveys out of 875 sent surveys, or a 7.43 response rate. However, for the statistical analysis, an estimated probability of response for each of the 875 members is needed as a control variable used in Step 2.[9]

The probability of a member responding to the survey is estimated using an industry effects model represented as

$$\text{Prob(response)} = F(\text{2-digit SIC industry variables}) \qquad (1)$$

where the dependent variable used to estimate Eq. (1) equals 1 if the member returned a completed or partially completed survey and 0 otherwise, and where the 2-digit Standard Industrial Classification (SIC) industry variable categories are as described in the note to Table VI.[10] Equation (1) then posits that the probability of a member responding can be

---

[8] ASQ sent an electronic reminder to each survey recipient ∼3 weeks after the initial mailing. No member-specific information is reported herein to ensure confidentiality.

[9] As explained in the discussion of Step 2, we include a variable for response in the belief that it will capture substantive effects of the complete model of the probability of self-assessment.

[10] ASQ provided the 2-digit industry for ∼75% of its members. Public domain information was used to determine the remaining classifications, including the *Thomas Register* and other Internet search mechanisms. The simple

TABLE VI   Probit results for probability of response to the survey ($n = 859$).

Variable	Estimated coefficient
dnonmin	0.743
	(1.46)
dchempet	−0.008
	(−0.03)
dmcneqin	−0.076
	(−0.37)
dtrcomut	0.020
	(0.06)
dwholret	0.035
	(0.11)
dfire	−0.047
	(−0.12)
dserv	−0.586**
	(−2.02)
dbusser	0.350
	(1.49)
dhealth	0.795**
	(2.07)
dpubadm	−0.215
	(−0.75)
Intercept	−1.418*
	(−8.73)
Log likelihood	−220.297
Psuedo-R^2	0.043
χ^2 (10)	19.94**

Note: The 16 observations in the miscellaneous category (members who could not be assigned to a 2-digit SIC industry or who were assigned to miscellaneous manufacturing) were dropped because the miscellaneous category predicted non-response perfectly. dnonmin = 1 for the agriculture, forestry, fisheries, minerals, and construction industries, and 0 otherwise; includes SICs < 20. dchempet = 1 for chemicals, petroleum, and rubber, and miscellaneous plastics, and 0 otherwise; includes SICs 28, 29, and 30. dmcneqin = 1 for machinery and equipment, both non-electric and electric and electronic, and instruments, and 0 otherwise; includes SICs 35, 36, 37, and 38. dmats = 1 for the remaining manufacturing SICs, and 0 otherwise; includes SICs 20 through 27 and SICs 31 through 34; observations with dmats = 1 are in the intercept. dtrcomut = 1 for transportation, communications, and utilities, and 0 otherwise; includes all 2-digit SICs greater than 39 and less than 50. dwholret = 1 for wholesaling and retailing, and 0 otherwise; includes all 2-digit SICs greater than 49 and less than 60. dfire = 1 for finance, insurance, and real estate, and 0 otherwise; includes all 2-digit SICs greater than 59 and less than 70. dserv = 1 for other services other than business services and health services, and 0 otherwise; includes all 2-digit SICs greater than 69 and less than 90 except for SIC 73 and 80. dbusser = 1 for business services, and 0 otherwise; includes SIC 73. dhealth = 1 for health services, and 0 otherwise; includes SIC 80. dpubadm = 1 for public administration, and 0 otherwise; includes 2-digit SICs greater than 89 and less than 100. Asymptotic *t*-statistics in parentheses.
*Significant at 0.01 level, **significant at 0.05 level, and ***significant at 0.10 level.

predicted on the basis of the industry in which that member produces. The probit results from Eq. (1) are in Table VI.

For each of the 875 surveyed members, Eq. (1) produces a predicted value for the probit index, z, for the probability of response.[11,12]

industry effects model is significant; more elaborate models that add other available characteristics of the members have no greater explanatory power – the additional variables are not statistically significant.

[11] There are 16 cases that were assigned to a miscellaneous category because either a member could not be matched uniquely to a 2-digit SIC industry or was assigned to miscellaneous manufacturing. None of those 16 members responded. Consequently, the categorical variable for the group predicted non-response perfectly, and the 16 observations were dropped from the sample used to estimate the model and assigned a probability of response of 0.

[12] On the basis of Eq. (1), the hazard rate is also computed as $h(z) = F'(z)/[1 − F(z)]$, where $F(z)$ is the probability of response given the probit index z (hence, it is the cumulative density function for the standard normal variable

Step 2: Estimating the Probability of Self-assessment for Responding Members.   Step 2 quantifies the probability that an ASQ member who received a survey conducted a quality-based self-assessment. A probability of self-assessment is needed in the estimation of net benefits. First, a probability of self-assessment model is estimated, and secondly, a prediction of the probability of self-assessment for each ASQ member is calculated in Step 3.

The probability of a member having conducted a self-assessment in the past, given that the member returned a completed or partially-completed survey, is estimated using a model written as

$$\text{Prob(self-assessment)} = F(\text{2-digit SIC industry variables, competitiveness}$$
$$\text{variables, control variables}) \qquad (2)$$

where the dependent variable used to estimate the model equals 1 if the member responded in the affirmative to at least one of the following survey statements, and 0 otherwise:

Has your organization performed a self-assessment using the Baldrige Criteria for Performance Excellence or related criteria (and by related criteria we mean criteria informed or derived by the Baldrige Criteria)? If yes, in what year(s)?

Has your organization applied for the Malcolm Baldrige National Quality Award? If yes, in what year(s)?

Has your organization applied for a state quality award? If yes, in what year(s)?

and where the competitiveness variables noted in Eq. (2) are defined in terms of a member's Likert responses (7 = strongly agree to; 1 = strongly disagree) with the following two survey statements:[13]

1. the possibility or threat of new competition is significant (comp);
2. our customers have a significant ability to bargain on the price of our primary products (barg);

and where the relevant control variables are based on estimates of the probability of response (probres) to the survey from Eq. (1). We introduce a control for the probability of response to the survey because our model of the probability of assessment is exploratory and unlikely to be complete with just the variables other than the probability of response. We do not believe the response variable is simply controlling for the effect of a correlation in random errors in the model of response and the complete model of the probability of self-assessment. Instead, we view the variable probres as capturing substantive effects of the complete model that otherwise would be left in the error term and that are related to the probability of responding to the survey. Thus, probres completes our substantive model, capturing systematic effects on the probability of self-assessment that vary with the characteristics of the ASQ members that are associated with their probability of response. Those ultimate characteristics may not be those in our response model, but associated with them and therefore with response.

---

at the value z) and $F'(z)$ is the density of the standard normal variable at z for each observation. The hazard rate is the conditional probability of response for a small increase in z. Conditional on no response for the observation, the probability of response for a small increment in z is $F'(z)dz/[1 - F(z)]$. A 'non-selection' hazard rate used in traditional two-step methods to control for selection is defined analogously.

[13] The mean value of comp ($n = 65$) = 5.6. The mean value of barg ($n = 65$) = 4.6. The inclusion of these competitiveness variables follows from the economic and management literatures related to quality shown in Table IV. Firms facing greater competitive pressures or buyers with greater bargaining strength are expected to be more likely to invest heavily in quality management; see for example Lau (1996) who develops information about his responding firms' competitive environments, including the possibility or threat of new competition.

TABLE VII   Probit results for probability of self-assessment ($n = 60$).

Variable	Estimated coefficient
dwholret	0.899
	(1.33)
dpubadm	1.932*
	(2.46)
comp	−0.189
	(−1.36)
barg	0.234***
	(1.80)
probres	4.248
	(1.25)
Intercept	−1.276
	(−1.40)
Log likelihood	−32.096
Psuedo-R^2	0.124
χ^2 (5)	9.11***

Note: There are 65 observations available to estimate the model in Eq. (2); however, the 2-digit industry variables, *dtrcomut* and *dfire*, are dropped along with the five observations where they equal 1 because they predict assessment perfectly. Thus, the results mentioned earlier are based on 60 observations. Asymptotic *t*-statistics in parentheses. *Significant at 0.01 level, **significant at 0.05 level, and ***significant at 0.10 level.

Twenty-three of 65 members had performed a self-assessment. The probit results from Eq. (2) are in Table VII.[14, 15]

Step 3: Predicting the Probability of Self-assessment for Members of ASQ.   The statistical output from this Step 3 is an estimate of the probability of conducting a self-assessment for each of the 875 members of ASQ using the results from Eq. (2) presented in Table VII.

With reference to Eq. (2), a probit index for each of the 875 members is estimated by multiplying the actual value of each independent variable for each member by the estimated probit coefficient reported in Table VII.[16, 17]

---

[14] When the hazard rate is included in Eq. (2) in place of the probability of response, the estimated probit model performed almost identically to the model reported in Table VII. Those results are available from the authors on request. Further, other available, potential explanatory variables were insignificant and did not add importantly to the model's explanatory power.

[15] The model in Eq. (2) is estimated with 65 observations, however the 2-digit industry variables, dtrcomut and dfire, are dropped along with the five observations where they equal 1 because they predict assessment perfectly. Thus, the results in Table VII are based on 60 observations.

[16] As noted with reference to the estimation of Eq. (2), data are available for 65 members on comp and barg. The mean value of these two variables ($n = 65$) is imputed to the other 810 (875 − 65) ASQ members for predicting the probability of self-assessment.

[17] The mean value of the probit index ($n = 810$) = −0.7041409, corresponding to a probability of assessment = 0.2602325. In the following calculations, a lower-bound probit index is used rather than the predicted value averaged here. Note from the foregoing footnote that there are 65 ASQ members that responded to the survey. Also there are by happenstance 65 of 875 members where dtrcomut and dfire equal 1, so there is no probit index for them from the estimation of Eq. (2) – recall from an earlier footnote that those two categories are perfect predictors of assessment – and hence $n = 810$. In the following calculations, rather than imposing a probability of self-assessment of 1.0 on each of the additional 65 members in the perfect prediction categories, the average lower-bound probability of self-assessment from Eq. (2) is imputed to them; thus, producing in these instances, a more conservative estimate. The average lower-bound probability, as contrasted with the average probability, is explained subsequently.

Step 4: Estimating the Net Social Value of the Baldrige National Quality Program to ASQ Members.   Of the 23 members of ASQ that performed a self-assessment, 14 responded to the following survey statement:

> In the absence of the Malcolm Baldrige National Quality Award – and therefore without the information and assistance that it provides about performance management/quality improvement assessments and therefore with the need to incur expenditures to develop and acquire such knowledge and assistance from other sources – what expenditures (fully burdened) would your organization have incurred to achieve the same level of expertise in performance management/quality improvement that you now have?
> $____ per year over the previous____ years.

As discussed earlier with reference to the counterfactual evaluation method, members' responses to this statement represent credible time-specific estimates of the benefits (i.e. the costs avoided reported in $2000) associated with the Baldrige National Quality Program. Thus, for each of the 14 responding members, a time series of real benefits received is formulated.

Regarding costs to compare to this time series of benefits, each of the 14 members responded to the following two questions:

> If your organization has been an award applicant, what was the total economic cost (fully burdened) to your organization to obtain, understand, collect relevant information, and comply with the Baldrige Criteria or state application requirements?
> $____ per year during the year(s)____.

and,

> If your organization did not apply for the Malcolm Baldrige National Quality Award or state award, but nonetheless performed a self-assessment using the Baldrige Criteria or related criteria, what was the total economic cost (fully burdened) to your organization to perform the self-assessment?
> $____ per year during the year(s)____.

Thus, for each of the 14 responding members, a time series of real ($2000) costs incurred to make the Baldrige Criteria operational is also developed.[18]

The net present value of each member's benefits is calculated using these survey data by first calculating the present value (referenced to the earlier of the first year of benefits or the first year of costs, hereafter the base year) of each member's benefits and each member's costs. The discount rate for this calculation is $r = (k - 0.03)/(1 + 0.03)$, where k is each member's reported hurdle rate and where the prevailing rate of price inflation over the reported time intervals is estimated at 3%.[19] Thus, net present value is the difference between the present value of benefits less the present value of costs, both referenced to the base year. Each member's net present value of benefits is then re-referenced to 2000 using a 7% growth rate to account for the social opportunity costs of these moneys (OMB, 1992).

The following model is estimated using the 14 calculated net present values:[20]

$$NPV_{2000} = F(\text{2-digit industry variables, size variables}) \qquad (3)$$

---

[18] Such costs are often referred to as pull costs; see Link and Scott (1998).
[19] Regarding the hurdle rate, each member was asked to respond to the following statement:

> What is your company's hurdle rate for investments (the minimum rate of return that your company must anticipate if it is to consider new investment worthwhile)?
> ____ percent.

The real rate of return will be $r = (k - a)/(1 + a)$, where a is the anticipated rate of inflation. If one invests X and receives Y, the nominal return for the period is k such that $X(1 + k) = Y$ and $k = (Y - X)/X$. Given an anticipated rate of inflation a, the real rate of return r is such that $X(1 + a)(1 + r) = Y$ as that yields the rate of return r in constant dollars: $X(1 + r) = Y/(1 + a)$. As $X(1 + a + r + ra) = X(1 + k)$, then $k = (a + r + ra)$ and $r = (k - a)/(1 + a)$. The mean value of $k = 0.1821$.
[20] The mean value of NPV_{2000} $(n = 14) = \$17.7$ million.

TABLE VIII   Least-squares results for
net present value of benefits ($n = 14$).

Variable	Estimated coefficient
size	−83844.49**
	(−2.48)
size^2	13.33**
	(2.27)
dtrcomut	4.90e+07***
	(2.10)
Intercept	9.45e+07**
	(2.71)
$F_{(3,10)}$	3.51***
R^2	0.513

Note: The explanatory member-size variable is
measured in millions of dollars, whereas the
dependent variable for value is measured in
dollars. *t*-statistics in parentheses. *Significant
at 0.01 level, **significant at 0.05 level, and
***significant at 0.10 level.

where member size was provided by ASQ for 874 of the 875 members. The least-squares results from Eq. (3) are in Table VIII.[21]

The estimated coefficients in Eq. (3) are used to forecast the net present value of benefits for each of the 874 members of ASQ for which member size was available.

The predicted values from Eq. (2) represent point estimates for the probability of each member of ASQ conducting a self-assessment. The predicted values from Eq. (3) represent point estimates of the net present value of benefits associated with the Baldrige Program conditional on a member conducting a self-assessment. The product of these two estimates gives a point estimate of the expected net present value from the Baldrige Program for a member of ASQ. Using the standard errors of our predictions from Eqs. (2) and (3), we shall control to the extent possible for the relatively small sample of members that provided the detailed information about their net benefits from the Program.

Thus, in an effort to present conservative estimates of the net present value of benefits associated with the Baldrige Program to members of ASQ, the following adjustments are made.

First, regarding the predicted values of the probability of a self-assessment from Eq. (2), a 0.4142 confidence interval is calculated for each member of ASQ, and the lower-bound on that interval is used as the relevant predicted value of the probability of self-assessment for that member. The lower-bound on a 0.4142 confidence interval implies that there is a 0.7071 probability that the true value of the probability of self-assessment is greater than the value being used.[22]

Secondly, regarding the predicted value, conditional on self-assessment, of the net present value of benefits associated with the Baldrige Program from Eq. (3), a 0.4142 confidence interval is calculated for each ASQ member using the standard errors for the linear combination of the estimated coefficients and for the error in equation. The lower-bound on that interval is then used as the conservative net present value conditional on self-assessment by the member.

---

[21] Other available, potential explanatory variables, including various hazard rates or associated probabilities and other sector effects, were insignificant and did not add importantly to the explanatory power of the model.

[22] Each tail in a 0.4142 confidence interval contains 0.2929 of the distribution, so there is 0.7071 probability (0.4142 + 0.2929) that the true value is greater than the value being used.

The product of the lower-bound of the probability of self-assessment from Eq. (2) and the lower-bound of the net present value of benefits from Eq. (3) yields for each member an estimate of net present value of benefits. That estimate may be lower or higher than the true value of the net present value of benefits. The true value has greater than a 50% probability ($0.7071 \times 0.7071 = 0.50$) of being larger than the value being used as the estimate, because the probability that both estimates multiplied are exceeded by their true value is 0.50. Of course, in some cases where the true value of one but not the other of the two estimates being multiplied falls short of the lower-bound, the true value of net present value benefits may still exceed the estimate used. Hence, the true value has more than a 50% probability of being greater than the one used.

The sum of the conservative, lower-bound derived value of net benefits for ASQ members is $2.17 billion.[23]

Thus, if it is assumed that there is no value associated with the Baldrige National Quality Program other than that received by the ASQ members, the conservative present value for net private benefits is $2.17 billion. When compared with the present value of the total social cost associated with the Program of $119 million, the ratio of ASQ benefits to social costs is 18.2:1.

Step 5: Estimating the Aggregate Net Social Value of the Baldrige National Quality Program. If the entire economy benefits from the Baldrige National Quality Program to the same extent as the ASQ members,[24] then total social benefits can be forecast using the following formula:

$$\text{Economy Value} = \frac{\text{Value for ASQ}}{\begin{array}{c}\text{Proportion taken by the ASQ members in the}\\ \text{50 represented industrial sectors}\end{array}} \qquad (4)$$

where the denominator is calculated to be 0.0880285.[25]

Thus, under this assumption, the conservative present value of social benefits is $24.65 billion.[26] When compared with the present value of the total social cost associated with the Program of $119 million, the ratio of economy-wide benefits to social costs is 207:1.[27]

4.4 Ratio of Net Social Benefits to Social Costs Associated with the Baldrige National Quality Program

As derived in the previous section, the conservative estimate of the present value of aggregate economy-wide net social benefits associated with the Program through 2000 is $24.65 billion (rounded in $2000). As also explained earlier, the present value of the social costs to operate the Program through 2000 is $119 million (rounded in $2000). From an evaluation perspective, these values yield a benefit-to-cost of 207:1.

---

[23] The mean value of the conservative estimate of value ($n = 874$) = $2,478,039.

[24] This extrapolation is similar in procedure to that used by Scherer (1982).

[25] The size data for industrial sectors were assembled using information in US Census (1997) and Council of Economic Advisers (2001). Size data for 1997 were inflated using the chain-type price index for gross domestic product from Table B-7, 'Chain-type price indexes for gross domestic product, 1959–2000' Council of Economic Advisers (2001, p. 284) to be comparable with the ASQ 1999 sales data. When 1997 sector size data were unavailable, 1992 data were used and then inflated to 1999.

[26] $2.17 billion/0.088025 = $24.65 billion.

[27] All but a few ASQ members could be separated into the manufacturing sector and the service sector. Recalculating, using only these two broad industrial categories and omitting industrial categories where there are very few members (SIC < 20 sectors with only eight ASQ members), yields a conservative estimate of the aggregate manufacturing sector's net benefits of $7.6 billion and a conservative estimate of the aggregate service sector's net benefits of $13.0 billion. Thus, when the sum of these estimates is compared with total social costs of $119 million, the resulting benefit to cost ratio is 173:1.

5   CONCLUDING REMARKS

This paper reports the findings from an economic evaluation of Baldrige National Quality Program. Extrapolating from the ASQ membership to the entire economy – under the assumption that the entire economy benefits from the Program to the same extent as ASQ members – implies a social benefit-to-cost ratio of 207:1. Yet the organizations outside of the ASQ may benefit even more than the ASQ membership. The ASQ members represent by member size 8.8% of the 50 industrial sectors with ASQ members. Through 2000, 11 of the 43 Baldrige Awards were received by ASQ members. Further, on the basis of requests for Baldrige application materials and criteria, as well as the many winners from outside the ASQ, many companies outside of the ASQ are using and benefiting – conceivably even more than ASQ members – from the Baldrige Criteria. Thus, extrapolating from the net social benefits of the Program for ASQ members to the economy as a whole may underestimate the true social benefits associated with the Program.[28] In that case, the social benefit-to-cost ratio derived in this paper would understate, even beyond the conservative estimation procedure used in this study, the true benefits of the Program.

Certainly, the estimated benefit-to-cost ratio of 207:1 supports the hypothesis that the public's investment in quality-standards infrastructure is worthwhile. The Baldrige National Quality Program at NIST provides another NIST standards-infrastructure investment, although in contrast to NIST's investments in infratechnologies focused on engineering, measurement, and science, the Baldrige Program is focused on management. These public investments in management standards appear to be worthwhile when evaluated using the benefit-to-cost ratio. However, although a benefit-to-cost ratio greater than 1.0 logically implies that the Program is worthwhile given the standard assumptions behind evaluation analysis, the assumptions are important.[29] As Scott (2000) explains, the benefit-to-cost ratio assumes that we really do know the opportunity costs of the resources invested by the public in a program. Although the social benefits greatly outweigh the costs as measured, there may be even higher yields on other potential uses of the public's funds. We have simply assumed, albeit following OMB (1992), that a yield of 7% covers the opportunity costs for the public's invested funds. Further, the value of resources has been measured by the preferences given the current distribution of income. Finally, the public may want to use its investments to promote goals, such as diversity, that are not measured by values of resources as determined by demands for goods and services and the costs of technologies available for providing them.

The economics and management literature cited in Table IV describes benefits from the Baldrige Program because it leverages private sector investments in quality management. Thus, the literature about the Program and the Award suggests that the large benefit-to-cost ratio for the Baldrige Program is realistic and not unexpected. Taken together, the literature about the Program and the benefit-to-cost ratio estimated in this paper support the hypothesis that NIST's National Quality Award Program is an efficient infrastructure investment in standards that are important for the effective operation of organizations.

Acknowledgements

We appreciate the comments and suggestions of Daniel Barton, Lee G. Branstetter, Charles C. Brown, Joseph E. Cooper, Susan Cozzens, Barry Diamondstone, Harry Hertz, Steven Martin,

---

[28] There is, on the other hand, a possible upward bias from extrapolation because the ASQ population has a proportionally greater number of Baldrige Award winners than does industry as a whole.

[29] Of course, a benefit-to-cost ratio greater than 1.0 does not by itself justify the use of public money to support this program. A discussion of elements of market failure, which the Baldrige Program seeks to overcome, is in Link and Scott (2005).

Troy J. Scott, Gregory Tassey, and two anonymous referees on aspects of earlier versions of this paper. Any remaining errors or omissions are our responsibility.

References

Banker, R.D., Khosla, I. and Sinha, K.K. (1998) Quality and Competition. *Mangement Science*, **44**(9), 1179–1192.

Black, S.E. and Lynch, L.M. (1996a) Human Capital Investments and Productivity. *American Economic Review*, 263–267.

Black, S.E. and Lynch, L.M. (1996b) How to Compete: The Impact of Workplace Practices and Information Technology on Productivity. Harvard University and US Department of Labor.

Blodgett, N. (1999) Service Organizations Increasingly Adopt Baldrige Model. *Quality Progress*, 74–76.

Bush, V. (1945) *Science – the Endless Frontier*. Washington, DC: US Government Printing Office.

Council on Competitiveness. (1995) *Building on Baldrige: American Quality for the 21st Century*. Washington, DC: Council on Competitiveness.

Council of Economic Advisers. (2001) *Economic Report of the President*, January 2001. Washington, DC: US Government Printing Office.

Easton, G.S. and Jarrell, S.L. (1998) The Effects of Total Quality Mangement on Corporate Performance: an Empirical Investigation. *The Journal of Business*, **71**(2), 253–307.

George, S. and Weimerskirch, A. (1994) *Total Quality Management: Strategies and Techniques Proven at Today's Most Successful Companies*. New York: John Wiley & Sons, Inc.

Griliches, Z. (1958) Research Costs and Social Returns: Hybrid Corn and Related Innovations. *Journal of Political Economy*, **66**, 419–431.

Helton, B.R. (1995) The Baldie Play. *Quality Progress*, **28**(2), 43–45.

Hendricks, K.B. and Singhal, V.R. (2001) The Long-Run Stock Price Performance of Firms with Effective TQM Programs. *Management Science*, **47**(3), 359–368.

Huselid, M.A. and Becker, B.E. (1996) High Performance Work Systems and Firm Performance: Cross-Sectional versus Panel Results. *Industrial Relations*, **35**(3), 400–423.

Ichniowski, C., Shaw, K. and Prennushi, G. (1995) The Effects of Human Resource Management Practices on Productivity. NBER Working Paper No. 5333.

Lau, R.S.M. (1996) A Survey of Competitiveness and Manufacturing Practices. *South Dakota Business Review*, **54** 1, 4–9.

Lawler, E.E., III, Mohrman, S.A. and Ledford, G.E. Jr. (1998) *Creating High Performance Organizations: Practices and Results of Employee Involvement and Total Quality Management in Fortune 1000 Companies*. San Francisco: Jossey-Bass.

Link, A.N. and Scott, J.T. (1998) *Public Accountability: Evaluating Technology-Based Institutions*. Norwell, Mass.: Kluwer Academic Publishers.

Link, A.N. and Scott, J.T. (2000) Estimates of the Social Returns to Small Business Innovation Research Projects. In Charles W. Wessner (Ed.) *The Small Business Innovation Research Program*. Washington, DC: National Academy Press, 275–290.

Link, A.N. and Scott, J.T. (2001) Public/Private Partnerships: Stimulating Competition in a Dynamic Market. *International Journal of Industrial Organization*, **19**, 763–794.

Link, A.N. and Scott, J.T. (2005) *Evaluating Public Research Institutions: The U.S. Advanced Technology Program's Intramural Research Initiative*. London: Routledge.

Mansfield, E., Rapoport, J., Romeo, A., Wagner, S. and Beardsley, G. (1977) Social and Private Rates of Return from Industrial Innovations. *Quarterly Journal of Economics*, **91**, 221–240.

NIST. (1996) Study Finds 'Quality Stocks' Yield Big Payoff. *Update*, February 5. Available online at http://www.quality.nist.gov/qualstok.htm.

NIST. (1997a) Results of Baldrige Winners' Common Stock Comparison, Third NIST Stock Investment Study. Available at http://www.quality.nist.gov/96stok.htm.

NIST. (1997b) Malcolm Baldrige National Quality Award: 1997 Criteria for Performance Excellence. Gaithersburg, Maryland: National Institute of Standards and Technology. Available online at http://www.quality.nist.gov/.

NIST. (1998) *Ten Years of Business Excellence for America*. Gaithersburg, MD: National Institute of Standards and Technology.

NIST. (2000) 'Baldrige Index' Outperforms S&P 500 by Almost 5 to 1. Commerce News, February 25. Available at http://www.nist.gov/public_affairs/releases/g00-26.htm.

Office of Management and Budget (OMB). (1992) Circular No. A-94: *Guidelines and Discount Rates for Benefit-Cost Analysis of Federal Programs*. Washington, DC: Office of Management and Budget.

Scherer, F.M. (1982) Interindustry Technology Flows in the United States. *Research Policy*, **11**, 227–245.

Scott, J.T. (1999) The Service Sector's Acquisition and Development of Information Technology: Infrastructure and Productivity. *Journal of Technology Transfer*, **24**, 37–54.

Scott, J.T. (2000) The Directions for Technological Change: Alternative Economic Majorities and Opportunity Costs. *Review of Industrial Organization* **17**, 1–16.

Townsend, P. and Gebhardt, J. (1996) The Importance of the Baldrige to the US Economy. *Journal for Quality and Participation*, 6–13.

US General Accounting Office (GAO). (1991) *Management Practices: U.S. Companies Improve Performance Through Quality Efforts*. Washington, DC: General Accounting Office, GAO/NSIAD-91-190.

US Census Bureau. (1997) *Economic Census, 1987 SIC Basis, Sales, Receipts or Shipments in 1997*. Available online at http://www.census.gov/epcd/ec97sic/E97SUS.HTM along with related material at http://www.census.gov/epcd/www/sic.html.

Wisner, J.D. and Eakins, S.G. (1994) A Performance Assessment of the U.S. Baldrige Quality Award Winners. *International Journal of Quality and Reliability Management*, 11(2), 8–25.

Science and Public Policy 39 (2012) pp. 680–689
Advance Access published on 19 July 2012

doi:10.1093/scipol/scs052

On the social value of quality: An economic evaluation of the Baldrige Performance Excellence Program

Albert N. Link[1],* and John T. Scott[2]

[1]*Department of Economics, University of North Carolina at Greensboro, Greensboro, NC 27402-6165, USA*
[2]*Department of Economics, Dartmouth College, Hanover, NH 03755-3514, USA*
Corresponding author. Email: anlink@uncg.edu.

This study estimates the net social value of the Baldrige Performance Excellence Program. It focuses specifically on a survey population of 273 applicants for the Malcolm Baldrige National Quality Award since 2006. Using a counterfactual evaluation method, social benefits have been quantified from the responses of 45 Award applicants to a web-based survey. We estimate the ratio of all measured social benefits to costs to be between 351:1 and 820:1. This finding certainly supports the belief that the Baldrige Program creates considerable value for the US economy.

Keywords: Baldrige Award; quality; performance excellence; program evaluation.

1. Introduction

Productivity in the non-farm US economy fell in the early-1970s and then fell again in the early to mid-1980s.[1] Associated with these declines was the loss of world market shares by firms in many critical industries. In response, a number of economic policy initiatives were introduced in the early-1980s in an effort to reverse the downward productivity trend by stimulating innovative activities within firms. These initiatives included: the Bayh–Dole Act of 1980 and the Stevenson–Wydler Innovation Act of 1980 to encourage technology transfer from universities and federal laboratories, respectively, to the private sector; the Economic Recovery and Tax Act of 1981 that contained provisions for a research and experimentation (R&E) tax credit; the Small Business Innovation Development Act of 1982 that established the Small Business Innovation Research (SBIR) Program; and the National Cooperative Research Act of 1984 that encouraged collaborative research activity among firms.

Further, Congress declared as part of the Malcolm Baldrige National Quality Improvement Act of 1987 (US Public Law (PL) 100-107) that:

> ...the leadership of the United States in product and process quality has been challenged strongly (and sometimes successfully) by foreign competition, and our Nation's productivity growth has improved less than our competitors over the last two decades;...a national quality award program...in the United States would help improve quality and productivity by:

(A) helping to stimulate American companies to improve quality and productivity for the pride of recognition while obtaining a competitive edge through increased profits,
(B) recognizing the achievements of those companies which improve the quality of their goods and services and providing an example to others,
(C) establishing guidelines and criteria that can be used by businesses, industrial, governmental, and other organizations in evaluating their own quality improvement efforts, and

(D) providing specific guidance for other American organizations that wish to learn how to manage for
high quality by making available detailed information on how winning organizations were able to
change their cultures and achieve eminence.

...[and] There is hereby established the Malcolm Baldrige
National Quality Award...

The goal of the Malcolm Baldrige National Quality
Improvement Act of 1987 was to enhance the competitiveness of US businesses. Applicants for the Award originally
represented three categories of US firms: manufacturing
firms, small businesses, and service sector firms.

The criteria for the Malcolm Baldrige National Quality
Award have evolved over time. In 1997, the name of the
Award Criteria was changed to the Criteria for Performance Excellence, and in 2010 the Program was renamed
the Baldrige Performance Excellence Program.[2] The
name of the award has remained the Malcolm
Baldrige National Quality Award. The scope of the
Program has also evolved. It was expanded to include
health care and education organizations in 1999 and
nonprofit/government organizations in 2006. Table 1
shows the number of applicants, by year and by sector,
for the Award.

The Program is a public–private partnership (Link 2006).
The public aspect of the Program involves its reliance on
governmental resources to support the Program Office
within the National Institute of Standards and Technology
(NIST). The private aspect of the partnership involves
monetary and in-kind resource support (e.g. examiner's
time to evaluate applications for the Award).

In 2001, we estimated the net social benefits associated
with the Baldrige National Quality Program using interview data from members of the American Society for
Quality (ASQ)[3] (Link and Scott 2001, 2006). We concluded from that study that the ratio of ASQ benefits
(i.e. benefits to the population of ASQ members) to the
total social costs associated with the Program was 18.2:1.
Projecting the benefits to the economy as a whole, the
benefit–cost ratio was estimated to be 207:1. Thus, at
one level, this paper represents a decennial re-evaluation
of the Program given that scope of the Program has
evolved. At another level, this paper represents an
exercise to determine the accountability of public resources
devoted to the Program.

On 7 October 2009, Peter Orszag, Director of the Office
of Management and Budget (OMB), sent a memorandum
to the heads of executive departments and agencies on the
subject of increased emphasis on program evaluations.
He wrote:

Rigorous, independent program evaluations can be a key
resource in determining whether government programs are
achieving their intended outcomes...Evaluations can help
policymakers and agency managers strengthen the design
and operation of programs. Ultimately, evaluations can

Table 1. Number of award applicants, by year and by sector

Year	Manufacturing	Service	Small business	Education	Health care	Nonprofit	Total
1988	45	9	12	n/a	n/a	n/a	66
1989	23	6	11	n/a	n/a	n/a	40
1990	45	18	34	n/a	n/a	n/a	97
1991	38	21	47	n/a	n/a	n/a	106
1992	31	15	44	n/a	n/a	n/a	90
1993	32	13	31	n/a	n/a	n/a	76
1994	23	18	30	n/a	n/a	n/a	71
1995	18	10	19	n/a	n/a	n/a	47
1996	13	6	10	n/a	n/a	n/a	29
1997	9	7	10	n/a	n/a	n/a	26
1998	15	5	16	n/a	n/a	n/a	36
1999	4	11	12	16	9	n/a	52
2000	14	5	11	11	8	n/a	49
2001	7	4	8	10	8	n/a	37
2002	8	3	11	10	17	n/a	49
2003	10	8	12	19	19	n/a	68
2004	8	5	8	17	22	n/a	60
2005	1	6	8	16	33	n/a	64
2006	3	4	8	16	45	10	86
2007	2	4	7	16	42	13	84
2008	3	5	7	11	43	16	85
2009	2	4	5	9	42	8	70
2010	3	2	7	10	54	7	83
Total	357	189	368	161	342	54	1,471

Source: <http://www.nist.gov/baldrige/about/faqs_recipients.cfm> accessed 27
June 2012.

help the [Obama] Administration determine how to
spend taxpayer dollars effectively and efficiently...(Orszag
2009)

The remainder of the paper is outlined as follows.
In Section 2, the methodology used in this evaluation is
overviewed and the counterfactual evaluation method
which is used is discussed in detail. The process used to
collect relevant benefit and cost data is described in Section
3. The data used in the economic evaluation are presented
in Section 4 along with calculated benefit–cost ratios.
Section 5 includes a discussion of the findings and a brief
concluding statement.

2. Evaluation methodology

Traditional economics-based evaluation methods are
frequently referenced to the research by Griliches (1958)
and Mansfield et al. (1977). They pioneered the application
of fundamental economic insights to the development of
estimates of the private and social rates of return to
investments in R&D. Streams of investment outlays
through time (the costs) generate economic surplus
through time (the benefits). Once identified and
measured, these streams of costs and benefits are used to
calculate rates of return, benefit–cost ratios, and other
related metrics.

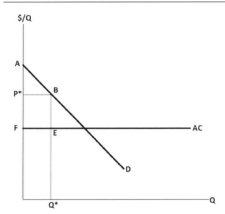

Figure 1. Consumer surplus and producer surplus.

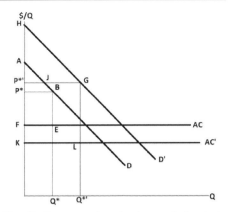

Figure 2. Consumer surplus and producer surplus from implementing Baldrige Criteria.

In a broad sense, the Baldrige Performance Excellence Program is a measurement-and-standards infrastructure R&D investment program. Publicly funded, publicly performed infrastructure R&D developed the Baldrige Criteria. Continuing investments have occurred within the Program throughout the Baldrige Award process to measure business performance and apply the Criteria.

The Griliches–Mansfield model for calculating economic social rates of return is generally viewed as the traditional evaluation method to use when considering the impact of a publicly funded technology. However, following Link and Scott (1998, 2011, 2012), it is not the most appropriate model to use from a public accountability perspective and therefore it is not employed in this study. Rather, the counterfactual evaluation method is implemented, and the evaluation question asked is: What would the private sector have had to invest to achieve the same level of benefits as provided through the publicly funded Baldrige Performance Excellence Program?[4]

When there are shortfalls in benefits, despite such investment with the aim of achieving the same level of benefits, the counterfactual evaluation method is expanded here to also include the gains in producer and consumer surplus associated with a firm or organization (hereafter 'firm' in the theoretical discussion in this section) implementing the Baldrige Criteria rather than incurring costs to establish performance excellence in the absence of the Baldrige Program.

Fig. 1 shows a firm, with average cost AC and facing demand D, that sells its differentiated product or service in amount Q* at price P* in a market with other sellers.[5] The area defined by the triangle ABP* represents the consumer surplus. Producer surplus is represented by the rectangle P*BEF.

Fig. 2 shows the same firm after it has implemented the Baldrige Criteria. The firm's demand has increased from D to D′ because of the firm's higher quality product, and its average cost has fallen from AC to AC′ because of more efficient operations. This firm's implementation of the Baldrige Criteria has created a net gain of HGJA in total surplus because of new consumer surplus and a net gain of JBEFKLG in total surplus because of new producer surplus.[6]

Fig. 2 depicts the annual effect resulting when the firm implements a performance excellence program using the Baldrige Criteria. Over time, other firms with competing differentiated products and efficient processes could erode the firm's profitability and hence the producer surplus. In a long-run equilibrium, producer surplus may even be eliminated by price competition among the sellers of the general type of differentiated product or service, although the benefits to consumers of higher quality products of that type will increase as prices fall and numerous competitors offer the higher quality products, resulting in more consumer surplus as the producer surplus is competed away.

Therefore, given the social costs—the public and private costs to operate the Baldrige Performance Excellence Program—the counterfactual evaluation method is used to estimate the three following public benefits of the Program:

(1) The counterfactual cost savings as measured by what the private sector would have had to invest in its attempt to achieve the same level of benefits as provided through the publicly funded Baldrige Performance Excellence Program.
(2) The annual shortfall from HGJA in Fig. 2, given the alternative performance excellence programs developed by firms in the absence of the Baldrige

Criteria (i.e., the annual gains in consumer surplus because the Baldrige Criteria were available rather than the counterfactual alternatives).

(3) The annual shortfall from JBEFKLG in Fig. 2, given the alternative performance excellence programs (i.e. the annual gains in producer surplus because the Baldrige Criteria were available rather than the counterfactual alternatives).

3. Data collection process

Two sets of data are needed to implement the counterfactual evaluation method. The first set of data relates to the costs to operate the Baldrige Performance Excellence Program. The second set relates to the three categories of benefits described above: the implementation costs (of performance excellence programs in the absence of the Baldrige Program) avoided by the private sector, the avoided shortfalls in the gains in consumer surplus, and the avoided shortfalls in the gains in producer surplus. The three categories of benefits—the avoided implementation costs and the avoided shortfalls in consumer and producer surplus gains—are costs avoided because of having the Baldrige Program rather than having to use the counterfactual alternatives to the Baldrige Criteria. Annual program costs for the period 1988–2010 were provided by the Baldrige Performance Excellence Program Office.

On the benefit side, the Program Office provided the email addresses of applicants to the Malcolm Baldrige National Quality Award for the period 2007–10, 2007 being the first application year after the scope of the Program was expanded. During the period 2007–10, there were 322 applications for the Malcolm Baldrige National Quality Award. These 322 applications were from 273 firms and organizations. The 49 additional applications were repeat applications from some of the 273 firms and organizations. The 273 firms and organizations that applied for the Award in the period 2007–10 were asked to complete a web-based survey instrument.[7] A total of 45 firms and organizations responded to the survey request—a response rate of 16.5%—and the results from an evaluation analysis based on those responses were used to calculate the benefits associated with the Program.[8]

Because the survey respondents are all Award applicants, an additional cost was considered in the evaluation analysis. Specifically, the following question was asked about the costs of applying for the Award (see Box 1):[9]

The counterfactual cost savings, as measured by what the private sector would have had to invest in an attempt to achieve the same level of benefits as provided through the publicly funded Baldrige Performance Excellence Program, were obtained from responses to the survey question given in Box 2:

The avoided shortfalls (of what would be obtained with the counterfactual effort to replace the Baldrige

---

Box 1

If your organization has been an Award applicant, what was the total monetary cost (fully burdened and in current dollars) to your organization to obtain, understand, collect relevant information, and comply with the Baldrige Award or state application requirements?

Approximately   between $_____   and $_____(in current dollars) per year over the year(s) ____ to ____.

Box 2

Please consider the following hypothetical or counterfactual situation. Assume the Baldrige Criteria and related processes had not been available, and as a result your organization could not have used the Baldrige Criteria or related criteria to perform an organizational performance self-assessment or submit an award application to receive feedback on organizational performance from a panel of trained Baldrige examiners. We would like to know how much your organization would have had to spend in the absence of the Baldrige Criteria or related criteria, and over what years, to achieve the same level of expertise in performance excellence that your organization now has.

Counterfactual Cost Savings
In the absence of the Baldrige Performance Excellence Program—and therefore without the information and assistance that it provides about performance excellence assessments and therefore with the need to incur expenditures to develop and acquire such knowledge and assistance from other sources—what expenditures (fully burdened and in current dollars) would your organization have incurred to achieve the same level of expertise in performance excellence that you now have?

Approximately   between $_____   and $_____(in current dollars) per year over the years ____ to ____.

Criteria from what was obtained with the Baldrige Criteria) in consumer surplus and producer surplus were measured from responses to the survey questions given in Box 3:[10]

4. Estimation of net social benefits

One method, and clearly the most conservative method, for calculating the net social benefit associated with the Baldrige Performance Excellence Program is to employ a cluster approach.[11] A cluster approach to evaluation compares the benefits for a sample of identified

---

Box 3

Above, you estimated, in the hypothetical or counterfactual situation without the Baldrige Criteria or related criteria for guidance, the additional costs that your organization would have incurred to achieve same level of expertise in performance excellence that your organization has now achieved using these criteria. However, even with such additional effort, if performance excellence were achieved in the absence of the Baldrige Criteria, customers may have undervalued the products and services of your organization and investors may have not recognized as fully the performance excellence achieved. Or, possibly, despite efforts to achieve the same level of performance excellence, there would have been a performance shortfall without the Baldrige Criteria to guide organizational self-assessment and improved performance. This question allows you to quantify any such shortfalls in quality performance that would have been experienced in the hypothetical situation where your organization had not had the Baldrige Criteria or related criteria and instead used the substitution of additional efforts to make up for the loss of the Criteria to organize the management of performance excellence.

Consumer Surplus

Because a key aspect of quality performance is ensuring customer satisfaction, it is expected that the value customers place on your organization's products or services increased because of performance improvement efforts. Because of the competition your organization faces, customers' willingness to pay for the products or services of your organization will typically exceed what they actually do pay. If the Baldrige Criteria or criteria based on them had not been available as a guide, and instead your organization had incurred the costs for improvement as reported above, as a percentage of your organization's total sales/revenues or the appropriate analogous measure, what would have been the approximate reduction annually in the excess amount (beyond what they actually paid) in your customers' collective willingness to pay for your organization's products or services because improvement took place in the absence of the Baldrige Criteria? Please mark the most appropriate answer:

0% 5%-10% 10%-20% 20%-30% 30%-40% 40%-50%
50%-60% 60%-70% 70%-80% 80%-90% 90%-100% other___%

Producer Surplus

If your organization had not had the Baldrige Criteria as a guide, and instead had incurred the costs for quality improvement as reported above, as a percentage of your organization's total sales/revenues or the appropriate analogous measure (for example, for a health care organization, revenues might include third party reimbursements, or for an organization in education the tuition fees and grants, or for a public school perhaps simply the annual budget, or for a charitable organization the donations and grants it receives, and so forth), what would have been the shortfall in annual earnings before interest and taxes (or the most appropriate analogous measure reflecting the difference between revenues and costs for your organization) for your organization because improvement took place in the absence of the Baldrige Criteria? Please mark the most appropriate answer:

0% 5%-10% 10%-20% 20%-30% 30%-40% 40%-50%
50%-60% 60%-70% 70%-80% 80%-90% 90%-100% other ___%

---

private-sector benefit recipients from the population of potential benefit recipients to the total operating costs of the publicly funded, publicly performed program. Stated differently, a cluster approach in effect assumes that the subset of affected parties for which benefit information is available is the entire population of affected parties. Thus, while we noted above that our survey response rate was on par with other studies of innovative and competitive behavior, our response rate is not relevant in the sense that we are comparing the benefit responses from 45 firms to the total Quality Award budget.

In addition to the pronounced conservative (i.e. downward biased) basis from using the cluster approach focused on only the applicants for the Baldrige National Quality Award, an even more conservative measure of social benefits associated with the Baldrige Performance Excellence Program would be to use for the cluster of applicants only the sum of implementation cost savings (category 1, see numbered list in Section 2) obtained

from the sample of 45 survey respondents. Thus, a decidedly lower bound estimate of benefits associated with the Baldrige Performance Excellence Program is the ratio of the present value of implementation cost savings for the 45 survey respondents to the present value of total Program operating costs. Below we present evaluation metrics using only implementation cost savings as well as metrics adding the consumer and producer surplus benefits.

Program costs, provided by the Program Office, are reported in Table 2 in 2010 US dollars ($2010). The present value of total Program operating costs is derived from Table 2. Each annual value of operating costs, in 2010 dollars ($2010), is referenced forward to 2010 by a 7% real rate (see column (3) of Table 3).[12] The application costs, as quantified from the survey of Award applicants, and the present value of those costs are also included in Table 3 (columns (4) and (5)).

Table 2. Baldrige Performance Excellence Program operating costs ($2010 thousands)[a]

(1) Fiscal year	(2) NIST allocations	(3) Foundation allocations[b]	(4) Firm reimbursed examiner expenses[b]	(5) Examiner time (hours)[b]	(6) Total operating costs[c]
1988	$249.67	*$749.01*	*$237.19*	*37,995*	$4,218.47
1989	$509.33	*$749.01*	*$237.19*	*37,995*	$4,478.13
1990	$609.19	*$749.01*	*$237.19*	37,995	$4,577.99
1991	$1,270.82	*$749.01*	*$237.19*	46,510	$5,908.04
1992	$1,850.05	*$749.01*	*$237.19*	49,763	$6,742.64
1993	$1,903.73	*$749.01*	*$237.19*	46,223	$6,518.43
1994	$3,570.27	$910.01	$237.75	45,944	$8,324.64
1995	$4,507.78	$867.19	$234.86	51,259	$9,633.66
1996	$3,576.51	$813.94	$200.02	44,143	$8,055.70
1997	$3,962.25	$971.96	$214.47	44,090	$8,609.75
1998	$3,757.52	$1,009.55	$197.09	43,662	$8,391.63
1999	$4,839.84	$1,447.25	$232.26	51,735	$10,580.55
2000	$6,658.68	$1,482.46	$200.19	51,349	$12,372.23
2001	$7,080.60	$1,807.14	$117.70	50,760	$12,990.10
2002	$6,786.43	$1,397.59	$94.54	48,720	$12,103.08
2003	$7,098.57	$1,134.57	$99.46	49,560	$12,223.05
2004	$6,691.37	$1,110.56	$104.34	52,800	$12,051.07
2005	$6,028.64	$841.24	$104.93	54,600	$11,260.91
2006	$7,863.71	$1,681.21	$253.48	63,840	$14,809.84
2007	$8,371.55	$1,133.21	$276.94	63,480	$14,764.89
2008	$8,636.94	$1,360.76	$318.63	66,600	$15,544.43
2009	$9,529.57	$993.49	$268.33	70,200	$16,302.10
2010	$9,907.60	$387.62	$291.52	68,880	$15,993.82

[a]Cost data were provided by the Program Office in current dollars. These values were converted to $2010 using the chain-type price index for gross domestic product. See <http://www.gpoaccess.gov/eop/tables11.html>, Table B-7, accessed 27 June 2012.
[b]Values in italics were estimated by the Program Office. In addition to public funding through NIST, there are private sources of funds. The Program was initially endowed by private industry with $10 million. The Foundation for Malcolm Baldrige National Quality Award was established to manage these funds and to allocate the interest earned to the Program for award ceremonies, publication costs, and partial training and travel costs for examiners.
[c]The value of examiner time is included. The value of a fully-burdened 2000-hour examiner year in $2010 is $157,000, as suggested by the Baldrige Program Office.

The present value of counterfactual cost savings, in $2010, is similarly calculated by referencing forward annual counterfactual cost savings to 2010 by a 7% rate (see Table 4).

Regarding the calculation of the shortfalls avoided in consumer surplus and producer surplus from responses to the respective questions above, it is assumed that both are social benefits of the Baldrige Program that should be accounted for, and it is assumed that both begin in the year that the firm applied for the Baldrige Award (see Table 5). However, as mentioned above, over time producer surplus is expected to decline because of market competition. Here, we conservatively assume that profits persist for 5 years, declining by 20% of the base year each year until in year 6 the producer surplus equals 0.[13]

Table 3. Present value of Baldrige Performance Excellence Program operating costs and application costs

(1) Fiscal year	(2) Total operating costs ($2010 K)	(3) Present value of total operating costs ($K)	(4) Total application costs ($K)[b]	(5) Present value of application costs ($K)
1988	$4,218.47	$18,689.52[a]	$1,050.00	$4,651.92
1989	$4,478.13	$18,541.96	$1,050.00	$4,347.59
1990	$4,577.99	$17,715.39	$1,050.00	$4,063.17
1991	$5,908.04	$21,366.61	$1,050.00	$3,797.35
1992	$6,742.64	$22,789.66	$1,050.00	$3,548.93
1993	$6,518.43	$20,590.50	$1,050.00	$3,316.76
1994	$8,324.64	$24,575.69	$1,050.00	$3,099.77
1995	$9,633.66	$26,579.56	$1,050.00	$2,896.98
1996	$8,055.70	$20,771.90	$1,050.00	$2,707.46
1997	$8,609.75	$20,748.16	$1,275.00	$3,072.55
1998	$8,391.63	$18,899.56	$2,412.50	$5,433.41
1999	$10,580.55	$22,270.48	$3,987.50	$8,393.10
2000	$12,372.23	$24,338.04	$3,987.50	$7,844.02
2001	$12,990.10	$23,881.76	$4,100.00	$7,537.68
2002	$12,103.08	$20,795.35	$4,116.00	$7,072.05
2003	$12,223.05	$19,627.55	$4,453.50	$7,151.35
2004	$12,051.07	$18,085.40	$4,408.50	$6,615.97
2005	$11,260.91	$15,794.01	$3,498.50	$4,906.83
2006	$14,809.84	$19,412.68	$4,881.00	$6,398.00
2007	$14,764.89	$18,087.62	$5,241.00	$6,420.45
2008	$15,544.43	$17,796.82	$5,608.50	$6,421.17
2009	$16,302.10	$17,443.24	$5,416.00	$5,795.12
2010	$15,993.82	$15,993.82	$4,633.00	$4,633.00
Total	$236,455.13	$464,795.28	$67,468.50	$120,124.63

[a]$4,218.47 × (1.07)^{22} = $18,689.52.
[b]One firm/organization in sample first applied for the Award in 1988; no other firm/organization applied until 1997. The survey question asks for application costs per year.

For the sample of 45 Award applicants, the ratio of all social benefits to social costs is calculated as the ratio of the sum of the present value (PV) of counterfactual implementation cost savings plus the PV of shortfalls avoided in consumer surplus plus the PV of shortfalls avoided in producer surplus to the sum of the PV of total operating costs plus the PV of application costs:

$$B/C_{n=45} = \frac{\left(\begin{array}{l}\text{PV counterfactual implementation cost}\\\text{savings} + \text{PV counterfactual avoided}\\\text{shortfalls in consumer surplus} + \text{PV}\\\text{counterfactual avoided shortfalls in}\\\text{producer surplus}\end{array}\right)}{\left(\begin{array}{l}\text{PV total operating costs}\\+ \text{PV application costs}\end{array}\right)}$$

(1)

Based on the survey data from only the cluster of respondents (n = 45), the ratio of social benefits to total social costs is 351:1.

To generalize to the survey population of the 273 Baldrige applicants, the benefits of the preceding

Table 4. Present value of counterfactual cost savings

(1) Fiscal year	(2) Counterfactual cost savings ($2010 K)	(3) Present value of counterfactual cost savings ($K)
1988	$5,500.00	$24,367.21[a]
1989	$5,500.00	$22,773.09
1990	$5,500.00	$21,283.26
1991	$13,000.00	$47,014.86
1992	$13,000.00	$43,939.12
1993	$13,000.00	$41,064.60
1994	$13,000.00	$38,378.13
1995	$14,000.00	$38,626.44
1996	$14,125.00	$36,421.79
1997	$14,917.50	$35,948.86
1998	$15,957.50	$35,939.35
1999	$16,032.50	$33,746.04
2000	$16,050.00	$31,572.78
2001	$20,775.50	$38,194.91
2002	$20,815.50	$35,764.90
2003	$20,748.00	$33,316.75
2004	$20,550.50	$30,840.76
2005	$18,350.50	$25,737.53
2006	$22,038.00	$28,887.32
2007	$23,088.00	$28,283.79
2008	$24,438.00	$27,979.07
2009	$23,988.00	$25,667.16
2010	$23,838.50	$23,838.50
Total	$378,213.00	$749,586.23

[a]$5,500.00 × (1.07)^{22} = $24,367.21.

Table 5. Present value of shortfalls avoided in consumer surplus and producer surplus

(1) Fiscal year	(2) Consumer Surplus ($2010 K)	(3) Present value of consumer surplus ($K)	(4) Producer Surplus ($2010 K)	(5) Present value of producer surplus ($K)
1988	$97,500.00	$431,964.17	$97,500.00	$431,964.17
1989	$97,500.00	$403,704.83	$78,000.00	$322,963.87
1990	$97,500.00	$377,294.24	$58,500.00	$226,376.54
1991	$97,500.00	$352,611.43	$17,289,000.00	$62,526,144.55
1992	$97,500.00	$329,543.40	$13,819,500.00	$46,708,974.08
1993	$97,500.00	$307,984.48	$10,350,000.00	$32,693,737.43
1994	$97,500.00	$287,835.97	$6,900,000.00	$20,369,929.87
1995	$97,500.00	$269,005.58	$3,450,000.00	$9,518,658.82
1996	$109,875.00	$283,316.44	$6,187.50	$15,954.68
1997	$145,475.00	$350,572.20	$31,750.00	$76,512.58
1998	$320,475.00	$721,771.10	$130,152.50	$293,128.37
1999	$320,475.00	$674,552.43	$102,555.00	$215,863.09
2000	$980,475.00	$1,928,742.73	$494,957.50	$973,656.32
2001	$1,141,725.00	$2,099,014.84	$565,610.00	$1,039,850.92
2002	$1,222,481.25	$2,100,450.39	$497,718.75	$855,173.48
2003	$1,222,481.25	$1,963,037.75	$340,485.00	$546,744.51
2004	$1,389,112.50	$2,084,683.29	$370,882.50	$556,594.62
2005	$1,407,487.50	$1,974,074.03	$201,322.50	$282,365.22
2006	$1,505,425.00	$1,973,305.08	$189,325.00	$248,166.45
2007	$1,537,587.50	$1,883,610.80	$144,915.00	$177,527.11
2008	$1,666,962.50	$1,908,505.37	$222,368.75	$254,589.98
2009	$1,666,962.50	$1,783,649.88	$144,572.50	$154,692.58
2010	$1,666,962.50	$1,666,962.50	$100,102.50	$100,102.50
Total	$17,083,962.50	$26,156,192.92	$55,585,405.00	$178,589,671.72

benefit–cost ratio and the application costs portion of the costs can be multiplied by the ratio of the total sales of the survey population of all 273 applicants to the total sales of the sample of 45 responding applicants (sales ratio = 3.563).[14] Thus, the ratio of social benefits to social costs for the population of all Baldrige Award applicants in the period 2007–10 is 820:1.[15]

Table 6 compares these benefit–cost ratios for the cluster of 45 respondents and the generalization to the survey population of 273 applicants, which are based on all categories of benefits, to ratios calculated using sub-categories of benefits. From an economic perspective, all of the benefit categories should be considered, but for purposes of comparison to related evaluation analyses, the other benefit–cost ratios are useful, especially those ratios which are calculated using only implementation cost savings.

As discussed above with reference to the expanded scope of the Program in 1999 and again in 2006 (see Table 1), we disaggregated the 45 responses by applicant sector. We found that 25 of the 45 applicants who responded, listed their primary sector of activity: 5 from education, 13 from health care, and 7 from manufacturing. In an exploratory manner, given the small sector samples, we calculated a benefit–cost ratio, by sector. For benefits, we considered

Table 6. Disaggregated analysis of components of ratio of social benefits to social costs

Categories of benefits	B/C$_{n=45}$	B/C$_{Baldrige}$ Award applicants
Counterfactual implementation cost savings	1.3:1	3.0:1[a]
Counterfactual implementation cost savings + avoided shortfalls in consumer surplus	46:1	107:1[b]
Counterfactual implementation cost savings + avoided shortfalls in consumer surplus + avoided shortfalls in producer surplus	351:1	820:1[c]

[a]($749,586.23 × 3.563)/($464,795.28 + ($120,124.63 × 3.563)).
[b](($749,586.23 + $26,156,192.92) × 3.563)/($464,795.28 + ($120,124.63 × 3.563)).
[c](($749,586.23 + $26,156,192.92 + $178,589,671.27) × 3.563)/($464,795.28 + ($120,124.63 × 3.563)).

the sum of the PV of implementation cost savings plus the PV of the avoided shortfalls in consumer and producer surplus; for costs, we considered the sum of the PV of total operating costs for the Award Program plus the PV of the application costs for the sample of sectorial respondents. Finally, we extrapolated these ratios to the survey population of all Award applicants, by sector. This analysis resulted in a benefit–cost ratio for the education sector of 119:1, for the health care sector of 456:1, and for the manufacturing sector of 357:1.[16]

We refrain from generalizing from these disaggregated calculations about the relative importance of the Baldrige application process to different sectors because of the limited number of responses, by sector. However, our findings do suggest that the net benefits to the Program as reported in Table 6 are not specific to any one sector but reflect benefits realized across all of the sectors.

5. Discussion and conclusions

As reported in Table 6, even the most conservative estimates for the benefit–cost ratios show substantial benefits from the Baldrige Program. All of the ratios in Table 6 compare benefits for selected subsets of beneficiaries and categories of benefits to all of the Program costs. Were one to completely ignore consumer and producer surplus shortfall benefits, the ratio of just the category of social benefits for avoided implementation costs to social costs (including all of the Program's operating costs) for the survey population of applicants since 2006 is 3.0:1. Adding to the social benefits only the shortfalls in consumer surplus, under what might be viewed as a heroic assumption that producer surplus is immediately competed away, yields a ratio of social benefits–social costs of 107:1.

The most inclusive benefit–cost ratios are those that are based on the broadest categorization of benefits. And for those, the ratio of the sample of 45 firms is 351:1, and for all applicants it is 820:1. The lower bound on this range compares all of the social costs of the Baldrige Program to only the social benefits for the surveyed applicants for the Baldrige Award.[17] The calculation also assumes that the producer surplus created by the use of the Baldrige Criteria to establish performance excellence is eroded quite rapidly by competition.[18,19] The upper end of this range is based on an extrapolation from the sample of 45 firms to all award applicants based on the ratio of sales of all applicants to sales of the sample. We are aware that some may not appreciate such an extrapolation, but for those who do appreciate it, the upper end of the ratio range is an important datum.

As observed in Section 2, the Baldrige Performance Excellence Program is, in a broad sense, a measurement-and-standards infrastructure R&D investment program, with the associated investments in operations and maintenance. Publicly funded and publicly performed infrastructure R&D, and related operations and maintenance investments, occur within the Program in the sense that the Baldrige Criteria were originally developed in that context and, through the Baldrige Award process, appropriate applications of the criteria for performance excellence are evaluated.

In this broad sense, the Baldrige Performance Excellence Program is similar to a NIST laboratory that performs infrastructure technology R&D investments and sets performance standards (i.e. the Baldrige Criteria) and then continually calibrates bench standards used in private-sector laboratories to achieve a predetermined level of performance (i.e. the Baldrige Award process). As an infrastructure R&D investment program, it is therefore reasonable to ask how the benefit–cost ratio of 820:1 compares with the ratios estimated in several evaluations of economic impact of infrastructure technology investments in the laboratories at NIST.

Link and Scott (2012) have reviewed the previous evaluations of economic impact at NIST, and discussed six evaluations that have found benefit–cost ratios of 100:1 or greater. In all six cases, as with the present study, the evaluations were able to quantify the benefits from avoiding shortfalls in consumer and producer surplus. Apart from measuring the benefit of avoiding the costs of developing an alternative to NIST's program, typically the studies were able to measure portions of the reductions in costs for R&D, or for production, or for sales efforts that were made possible by having the NIST infrastructure technology project rather than the counterfactual alternative. Those reductions in costs were not simply a measure of greater producer surplus, but instead a mixture of consumer and producer surplus because the lower costs are in part passed on as a benefit to consumers in the form of lower prices. The evaluations of economic impact with benefit–cost ratios of roughly 100:1 or greater included evaluations of NIST programs in: radiopharmaceutical research, standard reference materials for sulfur in fossil fuels, data encryption standards, role-based access control, wavelength references for optical fiber communications, and injectable composite bone grafts. All of these studies relate to public investments in infrastructure, as do the investments by the Baldrige Program.

To conclude, the benefit–cost ratio of 820:1 reported in Table 6 was developed from the responses to the survey of individual firms and organizations, all of which have shown great interest in management for performance excellence given that they all have applied for the Malcolm Baldrige National Quality Award, and those individual responses are all sensible, believable, and entirely credible. Examining those observations and thinking about the expected benefits for an organization intent on pursuing performance excellence with the implementation of the Baldrige Criteria, the benefit–cost ratio of between 351:1 and 820:1—using only the benefits for the group of surveyed applicants for the National Quality Award since 2006 but using all of the social costs of the Baldrige Program—is not surprising. If the social costs were compared to the benefits for the economy as a whole, the benefit–cost ratio would be considerably higher. The estimated range of benefit–cost ratios certainly supports the belief that the Baldrige Program creates great value for the US economy.

The Baldrige Performance Excellence Program is a public–private partnership that—with the imprimatur of national leadership and a prominent national award presented by the President—creates great value that could not be replicated by private sector actions alone. That said, the current economic conditions in the USA have necessitated Congressional budget cuts. On 18 November 2011, the Consolidated and Further Continuing Appropriations Act of 2012 (PL112-55) was signed into law. The Act eliminated public support for the Baldrige Program for the 2012 fiscal year, although the Program will continue to operate at a reduced level in the 2012 fiscal year through funding support from the Foundation for the Malcolm Baldrige National Quality Award.

Notes

1. See Link and Siegel (2007) for a detailed discussion of the productivity slowdown.
2. As stated: After 23 years as the 'Baldrige National Quality Program,' the nation's public–private partnership dedicated to performance excellence has decided to highlight that mission with a new name— the Baldrige Performance Excellence Program. 'Performance excellence' describes a focus on overall organizational quality, and for years, followers of the Baldrige Criteria for Performance Excellence have indicated that this term best reflects what makes Baldrige work. <http://www.nist.gov/baldrige/baldrige_100510.cfm> accessed 27 June 2012.
3. For the earlier study, ASQ graciously agreed to send the survey instrument for the study to their institutional members, who cover a wide range of types of organizations. ASQ is a global community of experts and the leading authority on quality in all fields, organizations, and industries. As a professional association, ASQ advances the professional development, credentials, knowledge and information services, membership community, and advocacy on behalf of its more than 85,000 members worldwide. ASQ members are driven by a sense of responsibility to enrich their lives, to improve their workplaces and communities, and to make the world a better place by applying quality tools, techniques, and systems. Long-known as the American Society for Quality and established in 1946, ASQ has assisted NIST in the administration of the Malcolm Baldrige National Quality Program Award since 1991. <http://asq.org/about-asq/who-we-are/index.html> accessed 27 June 2012.
4. Many evaluation studies at NIST have been done using the counterfactual method. Link and Scott

(2012) have reviewed these. See also Link and Vonortas (forthcoming) for additional examples of the application of the counterfactual approach.
5. The market might have so many other sellers that there is no strategic interaction among them, and in that case such markets with differentiated products are called 'monopolistically competitive' in the economics literature. If there are fewer competitors and strategic interaction, the economics literature typically describes the equilibrium price and output for the firm as an outcome in a Nash noncooperative equilibrium for price-setting oligopolists selling differentiated products. In either case, the depiction in Fig. 1 is appropriate.
6. The new consumer surplus is net of previously existing consumer surplus AJP*'. The new producer surplus is net of P*'JBP* which was previously existing consumer surplus and net of P*BEF which was the producer surplus existing before the performance excellence program. The movement from P* to P*' reflects the movement to the new profit-maximizing equilibrium after the implementation of the Baldrige Criteria.
7. To assure the confidentiality of the respondents, our survey instrument was administered on the web by RTI International.
8. This response rate is on par with other studies that are related to innovation and competitive behavior. For example, the response rate for the congressionally mandated study of NASA SBIR award recipient firms by the National Research Council (2009) was 23%.
9. The mean value reported on this survey question, and on those that follow, was used in the evaluation analysis.
10. Recall that, for the counterfactual evaluation method, the consumer surplus benefits and producer surplus benefits of the Baldrige Program are not the areas HGJA and JBEFKLG identified in Fig. 2 (those would be the benefits in the traditional Griliches–Mansfield approach) but instead the shortfalls from those areas if the counterfactual replacement of the Baldrige Program is used rather than the Program itself.
11. Ruegg and Jordan (2011) advocated a cluster approach for the evaluation of the retrospective benefit-cost studies of technologies developed from the Department of Energy (DOE) Office of Energy Efficiency and Renewable Energy (EERE). Ruegg and Jordan argue that one can compare the benefits for a cluster of technologies funded by EERE to the entire EERE budget in an effort to obtain a lower bound on a measure of net social benefits.
12. The use of a 7% real rate corresponds to the guidelines set forth by the Office of Management and Budget (1992) in Circular A-94:

Constant-dollar benefit-cost analyses of proposed investments and regulations should report net present value and other outcomes determined using a real discount rate of 7 percent.

Rather than discounting all operating costs to 1988, the first year of data on costs, and similarly discounting all benefits to 1988, we chose to bring all values forward for ease of interpretation.

13. For those firms for which producer surplus began in year 2007 or later, the straight line depreciation is truncated in year 2010.

14. This extrapolation, based on the distribution of firm size, from the sample to the population assumes that the sample of respondents is representative of the population of surveyed applicants. Of course, there will be differences in respondents apart from the differences in their sizes. For that reason, the 351:1 ratio is much more conservative than the 820:1 ratio.

15. $B/C_{\text{Baldrige Award Applicants}} = (B_{n=45} \times 3.563)/$ (total program operating costs + (application costs$_{n=45} \times 3.563$)) = 820 : 1.

16. More details on this exploratory analysis are available from the authors.

17. As Link and Scott (2001) showed, many firms that never apply for the Award, utilize the Baldrige Criteria.

18. Theory and evidence (Mueller 1977, 1986) in the economics literature about industrial organization show that the profitability of firms that establish competitive advantages persists over time. Indeed, graduate business schools teach executives ways to pursue *sustainable* competitive advantage (Porter 1985).

19. An earlier evaluation by Link and Scott (2001, 2006) of the Baldrige Program, based on ASQ members rather than Award applicants, yielded a 18.2:1 ratio. In that study, the narrowest category of benefit net of any application costs for 875 ASQ members was compared to all of the Program costs. Here, the same narrowest category of benefit, but not net of the applicant's application costs for 45 firms, is compared to all of the Program costs plus the application costs for the firms. Thus, for a rough comparison of the estimated benefits relative to the costs in the two studies, controlling for the different sample sizes and different treatment of application costs (i.e. 875 ASQ members compared to 273 Award applicants), we have the estimate of 18.2:1 in the first study and the extrapolated estimate of 15.5:1 for the second study. Projecting to economy-wide benefits from these similar findings for the two populations for the sampled beneficiaries would yield similar findings for the economy-wide benefit–cost ratio. Given that in contrast to the earlier study which surveyed mostly

industrial corporations, the present study reflects the composition of applicants for the Award and includes firms and organizations from the education, health care, and nonprofit sectors, the findings of the two studies are remarkably consistent.

References

Griliches, Z. (1958) 'Research costs and social returns: Hybrid corn and related innovations', *Journal of Political Economy*, 66: 419–31.

Link, A. N. (2006) *Public/Private Partnerships: Innovation Strategies and Policy Alternatives*. New York: Springer.

Link, A. N. and Scott, J. T. (1998) *Public Accountability: Evaluating Technology-Based Institutions*. Norwell, MA: Kluwer.

——. (2001) 'Economic evaluation of the Baldrige National Quality Program', NIST Planning Report 01-03. Gaithersburg, MD: National Institute of Standards and Technology.

——. (2006) 'An economic evaluation of the Baldrige National Quality Program', *Economics of Innovation and New Technology*, 15: 83–100.

——. (2011) *Public Goods, Public Gains: Calculating the Social Benefits of Public R&D*. New York: OUP.

——. (2012) 'The theory and practice of public sector R&D economic impact analysis', NIST Planning Report 11-1. Gaithersburg, MD: National Institute of Standards and Technology.

Link, A. N. and Siegel, D. S. (2007) *Innovation, Entrepreneurship, and Technological Change*. Oxford, UK: OUP.

Link, A. N. and Vonortas, N. S. (forthcoming) *Handbook on Program Evaluation*. Cheltenham, UK: Edward Elgar.

Mansfield, E., Rapoport, J., Romeo, A., Wagner, S. and Beardsley, G. (1977) 'Social and private rates of return from industrial innovations', *Quarterly Journal of Economics*, 91: 221–40.

National Research Council. (2009) *An Assessment of the Small Business Innovation Research Program at the National Aeronautics and Space Administration*. Washington, DC: National Academics Press.

Mueller, D. C. (1977) 'The persistence of profits above the norm', *Economica*, 44: 369–80.

——. (1986) *Profits in the Long Run*. Cambridge, UK: Cambridge University Press.

Office of Management and Budget. (1992) *OMB Circular A-94: Guidelines and Discount Rates for Benefit-Cost Analysis of Federal Programs*. Washington, DC: Government Printing Office.

Orszag, P. R. (2009) 'Memorandum for the Heads of Executive Departments and Agencies', Office of Management and Budget, Executive Office of the President, 7 October 2009. Washington, DC: Office of Management and Budget.

Porter, M. E. (1985) *Competitive Advantage: Creating and Sustaining Superior Performance*. New York: Free Press.

Ruegg, R. and Jordan, G. (2011) 'Guide for conducting benefit-cost evaluation of realized impacts of public R&D programs,' Draft report prepared for the US Department of Energy, Office of Energy Efficiency and Renewable Energy. Washington, DC: US Department of Energy.

[4]

Economics of Innovation and New Technology, 2015
Vol. 24, No. 5, 510–531, http://dx.doi.org/10.1080/10438599.2014.988518

The impact of public investment in medical imaging technology: an interagency collaboration in evaluation

Alan C. O'Connor[a], Albert N. Link[b*], Brandon M. Downs[c] and Laura M. Hillier[c†]

[a]*RTI International, 3040 Cornwallis Road, Research Triangle Park, 27709, NC, USA;* [b]*Department of Economics, Bryan School of Business and Economics, University of North Carolina at Greensboro, 1000 Spring Garden Street, 27402 Greensboro, NC, USA;* [c]*Evaluation and Outcome Assessment, Canada Foundation for Innovation, 450-230 rue Queen St., Ottawa, Ontario, Canada K1P 5E4*

(*Received 15 August 2014; final version received 7 November 2014*)

The Canada Foundation for Innovation (CFI) and the Canadian Institutes of Health Research (CIHR) allied to analyze the impact of their investments in medical imaging research. The CFI funds capital and operating programs for research infrastructure, and CIHR's mandate concentrates its funding on research activity. It happens that CIHR-funded research consumes CFI-funded infrastructure as an input in the innovation process. Apart from a few partnered programs, by design there is no coordination between CFI and CIHR funding decisions. Together, these agencies invested $916 million over a 14-year-period. In this paper, we evaluate the economic and health benefits from advancements in one funded area, namely computed tomography perfusion (CTP). CTP is an imaging technique that uses computed tomography to measure blood flow in organs and tissues. It is mostly used to assess acute ischemic stroke. The net social benefits attributable to these investments are substantially positive: the benefit-to-cost ratio is estimated to be between 6.66-to-1 and 9.99-to-1. We review how public investments from multiple funders comingle in the innovation process to deliver social value and improved health outcomes.

Keywords: cost-benefit analysis; innovation; technology; medical imaging research; innovation; CT perfusion; stroke; Canada

1. Introduction

This paper presents an economic analysis of investments made by two independent but complementary Canadian funding agencies that entered into an alliance to jointly evaluate the impact of their research investments. The Canada Foundation for Innovation (CFI) and the Canadian Institutes of Health Research (CIHR) are significant federal investors in Canada's university-based health research enterprise. Both are charged with individually funding scientific excellence, with the CFI's mandate focused on research infrastructure and CIHR's focused on research activity. It happens that CIHR-funded research consumes CFI-funded infrastructure as an input in the innovation process, though by design there

---

*Corresponding author. Email: anlink@uncg.edu
†Formerly of Canadian Institutes of Health Research.

This article was originally published online with errors. This version has been amended. Please see Corrigendum (10.1080/10438599.2015.1013781).

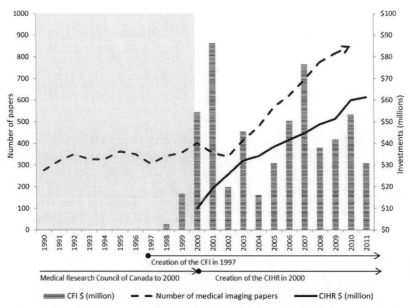

Figure 1.   Growth in Canadian Scientific Publishing in Medical Imaging, 1990–2011.
Source: Larivière and Lemelin (2012), CFI, and CIHR.

is no coordination between CFI and CIHR funding decisions. What is more, CFI funds up to 40% of an individual infrastructure project, and its awarding of funding leverages financial support from provincial authorities, universities, or other partners. As such, it is often the case that a technology or research finding stems from facilities and research programs receiving support from a spectrum of funders.

In Canada, as elsewhere, there is an imperative to evaluate public investments in science and technology (S&T). One of the policy commitments contained in the Government of Canada's Science and Technology Strategy was to increase government's accountability to Canadians by improving its ability to measure and report on the impact of S&T expenditures (Industry Canada 2009). Health and related life sciences and technologies is one of four priority areas that the Government of Canada, through the National Science & Technology Strategy, has committed to strengthening over time (Industry Canada 2009).[1]

As a subset of the health and life sciences focus, investments in medical imaging and related health research by CFI and CHIR align with this larger national strategy. CFI and CIHR play the important role of supporting university scientists conducting basic and applied research in the field of medical imaging. Without this support there would not be concepts to commercialize and thus enhance competitiveness and improve the quality of clinical care for patients.

Research conducted by Larivière and Lemelin (2012) provides a lens into the growth in scientific output pre- and post-CFI and CIHR creation in 1997 and 2000, respectively. The study revealed an inflection point in publishing, a first-order measure of scientific output, in the years following these agencies' creation (see Figure 1). Additionally, these publications were found to have above-average impact factors. Given this research excellence, the question of interest for CFI and CIHR became: To what extent have these investments translated into socioeconomic benefits for all Canadians?

This was the question that motivated CFI and CIHR to undertake an interagency collaboration in evaluation that explored in depth the net economic and health benefits that resulted from their investments. This paper reviews and presents the findings from one important piece of that evaluation: a case study of publicly-supported imaging R&D involving the comingling of complimentary public expenditures by these two agencies. The case study is that of computed tomography perfusion (CTP), an imaging study that uses computed tomography (CT) to measure blood flow in organs and tissues and is most commonly used in assessing moderate to severe acute ischemic stroke.

The remainder of the paper is outlined as follows. In Section 2, we review CFI's, CIHR's, and partners' investments in medical imaging technology. In Section 3, we explain CTP and its emergence as an imaging study, review CFI and CIHR support for its development, and discuss its advantages. The categories of social benefits attributable to CTP are discussed and quantified in Section 4. In Section 5, we present evaluation metrics associated with CFI's and CIHR's investments in CTP. The paper ends with brief concluding remarks in Section 6.

2. CFI, CIHR, and partner investments in medical imaging

CIHR is Canada's federal agency charged with funding health research, and it is the largest public-sector investor in Canada's health research enterprise. CIHR awards research grants based on their scientific merit through annual funding competitions. It does not fund research infrastructure (e.g. facilities, laboratories, instrumentation, equipment), but rather it funds labor, materials, and the like for research projects that make productive use of infrastructure.

A substantial amount of federal funding for research infrastructure is channeled through the CFI, which awards through competitions infrastructure projects and operating support based on funding applications' scientific merit. Funding from CFI is sometimes likened to a 40 cent dollar because the CFI provides up to 40% of the infrastructure cost, with an average of 40% coming from the provincial authorities and 20% from another partners (e.g. universities, foundations, private companies). Because of this project financing design, when analyzing CFI investments, one analyzes others' contributions as well.

This study makes no claim about the relative effectiveness of one funder's dollar over another's. The focus is on contribution, not on attribution. In other words, all parties – CFI, provinces, universities, and other partners – share attribution equally.

The cost basis for this study was composed of infrastructure and operating funds awarded for medical imaging infrastructure under CFI projects plus CIHR grants from FY1998/1999 (CFI) and FY2000/2001 (CIHR) through the close of FY2011/2012. Neither CFI nor CIHR had an identifier solely for medical imaging-related projects. Therefore, to develop the cost basis, project lists were assembled by each organization using common search terms, and then the costs for projects appearing on the list were summed.[2]

CFI project costs for all medical imaging-related projects totaled $491.81 million between FY1998/1999 and FY2011/2012, consisting of $195.25 million in CFI cash disbursements (40%) and $296.56 million in province and partner disbursements (60%) (e.g. university, foundation, corporate partner) (see Table 1).

Total CIHR funding for medical imaging-related health research grants and awards across Canada amounted to $423.78 million between FY2000/2001 and FY2011/2012.[3]

Table 1. CFI project and CIHR funding for medical imaging research, FY1998/1999–2011/2012 ($million).

	CFI project			CIHR	
Fiscal year	(1) CFI share	(2) Provincial and partner share	(3) Total CFI project funding	(4) CIHR research funding	(5) Combined CFI and CIHR funding
1998/1999	0.78	1.22	2.00		2.00
1999/2000	6.31	6.10	12.41		12.41
2000/2001	16.95	25.08	42.03	7.77	49.80
2001/2002	27.33	40.13	67.46	15.02	82.48
2002/2003	5.35	10.48	15.83	20.18	36.01
2003/2004	16.56	20.73	37.29	26.12	63.41
2004/2005	6.16	7.55	13.71	28.68	42.39
2005/2006	10.26	16.74	27.00	33.45	60.45
2006/2007	18.35	26.83	45.18	37.14	82.32
2007/2008	28.51	41.78	70.29	41.15	111.44
2008/2009	14.86	21.49	36.35	46.74	83.09
2009/2010	16.38	23.13	39.51	48.25	87.76
2010/2011	16.05	35.67	51.72	57.97	109.69
2011/2012	11.40	19.63	31.03	61.31	92.34
Total	195.25	296.56	491.81	423.78	915.59

Source: CFI and CIHR.

Table 2.   Combined CFI project and CIHR funding (millions $2011).

	Canada			
Fiscal year	(1) Calendar year	(2) CFI	(3) CIHR	(4) Total
1998/1999	1998	2.75	–	2.75
1999/2000	1999	16.76	–	16.76
2000/2001	2000	54.48	10.07	64.55
2001/2002	2001	86.50	19.26	105.76
2002/2003	2002	20.07	25.59	45.66
2003/2004	2003	45.77	32.06	77.83
2004/2005	2004	16.31	34.11	50.42
2005/2006	2005	31.10	38.53	69.63
2006/2007	2006	50.69	41.68	92.37
2007/2008	2007	76.43	44.75	121.18
2008/2009	2008	37.96	48.82	86.78
2009/2010	2009	42.06	51.36	93.42
2010/2011	2010	53.50	59.95	113.45
2011/2012	2011	31.02	61.31	92.33
Total		565.40	467.49	1032.89

Notes: Because fiscal years (April–March) and calendar years (January– December) do not align, to simplify calculations the main calendar year into which the fiscal year falls (from April to December) was chosen as the index for the entire fiscal year. For example, costs in FY1998/1999 were inflated to 2011 using the corresponding index value for 1998. In addition, to simplify presentation of costs (calculated by fiscal year) and benefits (calculated by calendar year), costs were assigned to each fiscal year's primary calendar year. All of FY1998/1999s costs were placed in 1998, for example.

Table 2 combines the disbursements in Table 1 and converts each monetary datum to 2011 dollars ($2011) using the Canadian Gross Domestic Product index as reported by Statistics Canada. In real terms, the combined CFI and CIHR funding of medical imaging-related infrastructure and research projects amounted to $1032.93 million.

A.C. O'Connor et al.

To analyze in-depth how multiple public funding streams combine to support imaging research and improve health outcomes, the case of CTP was selected, from among all imaging research projects receiving public support, as the most appropriate case study.[4] See Sinclair (1998) for a review of other funded imaging research.

3. CTP and the Role of CFI and CIHR in its emergence as an imaging study

3.1. Use of CTP to assess stroke

There are three broad categories of strokes: ischemic (related to blood clots), hemorrhagic (bleeding), and transient ischemic attack (TIA). In this evaluation study, the condition of interest is acute ischemic stroke, for which CTP is most commonly used.[5] Put simply, a stroke occurs when blood flow in the brain is interrupted, usually from a clot, which causes brain cells to rapidly die off because of an inadequate supply of oxygen and nutrients. Depending on which part of the brain is affected and the severity of the stroke, the patient may recover, suffer paralysis or other impairments, or even die.

After a physical exam, the first imaging study used to assess the effects of a stroke in an acute setting (e.g. hospital emergency room) is an unenhanced CT to rule out brain hemorrhage (Canadian Stroke Network 2011). CTP can be used immediately following the unenhanced CT to provide the treating physician with additional information about the area of dead brain cells (infarct), the surrounding area of brain cells at risk but potentially salvageable (penumbra), and quantitative measures of blood flow in the area. It can more conclusively assess a patient's condition, including whether the patient may be a candidate for thrombolysis (Hopyan et al. 2010). Thrombolysis is the use of pharmaceuticals (namely, tissue plasminogen activator, tPA) delivered intravenously to break up the blood clot that is the source of the stroke. tPA is commonly used in instances of acute ischemic stroke but prescribing it is not without risk because it acts by thinning the blood and therefore presets risk for hemorrhage.

The most commonly used perfusion measures are (1) cerebral blood flow (CBF), (2) cerebral blood volume (CBV), and (3) mean transit time (MTT). CBF, CBV, and MTT are quantified using software embedded with algorithms that analyze images captured at regular intervals by the CT scanner. While undergoing the CT scan, the patient receives a contrast agent intravenously, and the raw radiographic data are transmitted from the scanner to the software, which then calculates measures. CTP adds between 5 and 10 minutes to the imaging time (Wintermark et al. 2002a; Miller et al. 2008).

3.2. CFI and CIHR support for CTP development

The first commercially available software for CTP was released in 2000 by GE Healthcare, one of the four major manufacturers of CT scanner systems. The algorithms and protocols in this software package for quantifying CBF, CBV, and MTT were developed by Dr Ting-Yim Lee. Lee has multiple affiliations and positions in London, Ontario: the Lawson Health Research Institute of the London Health Sciences Centre and St Joseph's Health Care, the Robarts Research Institute, and Western University.

CTP algorithm and software development has been a career focus for Dr Lee. He spent 8 years as a hospital physicist before pursuing a career in research. As a consequence of that experience, Dr Lee told us during interviews that he had a distinct interest in tools that had direct clinical application. The underlying motivation for investigating CT's application in perfusion imaging was to convert imaging data from qualitative information into objective

Table 3.   CFI and CIHR CTP project costs (millions $2011).

Fiscal year	(1) CFI	(2) CIHR	(3) Total
2000/2001	2.50	0.77	3.27
2001/2002	0.57	0.16	0.73
2002/2003	0.50	0.15	0.65
2003/2004	–	0.16	0.16
2004/2005	–	0.11	0.11
2005/2006	–	0.02	0.02
2006/2007	–	0.17	0.17
2007/2008	–	0.10	0.10
2008/2009	3.37	0.15	3.52
2009/2010	–	0.24	0.24
2010/2011	–	0.10	0.10
2011/2012	–	0.14	0.14
Total	6.94	2.27	9.21

indicators using readily available scanners and that did not require specially trained personnel to interpret. Funding from CIHR and the CFI was fundamental to Lee's research program and provided the needed infrastructure and operating grants that supported the development of algorithms that GE Healthcare commercialized as 'CT Perfusion' in 2000 (Version 1), 2002 (Version 2), 2003 (Version 3), and 2008 (Version 4). As of this writing, GE Healthcare holds an exclusive license to the algorithms and software implementation of the CTP method developed by Lee.

Two CFI projects provided the necessary CT instrumentation. The first (CFI Project 317) was for magnetic resonance imaging (MRI), electroencephalography (EEG), and CT instrumentation valued at $8,720,301 (cash only, nominal terms), of which CFI contributed $2,864,000 and the province and university contributed $5,853,601. The project supported multiple imaging research initiatives; the CT component was distinct in the budget and accounted for $2,763,910. The funds allowed Dr Lee to upgrade CT scanning capabilities at St Joseph's Hospital and to increase access to the scanning facilities for software development and research. The second (CFI Project 11358) was a large-scale capital facilities development and instrumentation investment program valued at $23,193,652. As before, the CT component was distinct in the budget and accounted for $3,095,280 to support the acquisition of a CT scanner with a 4-cm wide detector. After adjustment to real terms using real GDP (chained), the CT-specific CFI project cost for CTP research only amounts to $6,931,994 (2011$).

Lee's research into CTP was seeded in 1995 with a small grant from the Medical Research Council (MRC), CIHR's predecessor agency, and began in earnest following the award of CFI projects and CIHR grants.[6] MRC and CIHR operating support covered the core application area of acute stroke and development for emerging clinical applications for myocardial infarction (heart attack) and oncology (cancerous tumors). CIHR has funded CTP R&D continuously since 2000 through six awards.[7] Collectively, these operating grants represent $2,259,446 (2011 dollars) in research support through the close of FY2011/2012.[8] These grants funded algorithm development, testing, and evaluation, including validation using CT scanning infrastructure.

Table 3 reports these CTP investments, by year. Total public investments for the development of the enabling algorithms and protocols for CTP software was $9.21 million of which 75% was for CFI-funded projects and 25% was for CIHR research.

3.3. Emergence of CTP as an imaging study

CTP progressed rapidly from discussion and validation in the literature in the late 1990s and the 2000s to a tool that is now being used in hospitals around the world to assess the condition of patients, particularly those experiencing moderate to severe acute ischemic stroke.

The concept of using imaging scans to study CBF was first proposed by Axel (1980), but the concept was impractical at the time given technical limitations of then-available imaging systems (Axel 1980). In subsequent decades, sophisticated CT scanning systems and the associated computing infrastructure needed to process images eliminated those limitations, and neuroradiologists began studying the appropriateness and diagnostic accuracy of CTP. Perfusion measurements can also be done by MR, which will provide greater detail than a CT as well as provide supplemental information about the patient's condition. However, MR systems are not as ubiquitous as CT systems and MR studies would take 20 to 40 minutes longer to conduct. In an acute stroke situation, the ubiquity, speed, and ease of scheduling of CT erode MR's advantages (Parsons 2008).

Wintermark et al. (2002a) validated the accuracy of CTP in quantifying CBF, predicting the final infarct size, and evaluating the clinical prognosis for acute stroke patients in an emergency department setting. Their research was subsequently followed by other studies that compared CTP with MR and concluded that CT correlated closely with MR in quantification of perfusion (Wintermark et al. 2002b; Eastwood et al. 2003). The software used in these studies was CTP, which had received U.S. Food and Drug Administration approval in 2000.

In the years following CTP's clinical validation, papers reviewing CTP's clinical advantages, role in supporting acute stroke care, and recommended protocols entered the scientific literature. In addition to 11 trials associated with stroke treatment, trials are underway for other conditions.[9]

Hoeffner et al. (2004) published a review of CTP as a technique and noted its clinical potential not only for stroke but also for vasospasm and tumors. Shetty and Lev (2005) noted that CTP's speed, simplicity, and accuracy would have implications for stroke patients worldwide. Other clinicians offered reviews, recommendations, and assessments of its clinical utility (Srinivasan et al. 2006; de Lucas et al. 2008; Parsons 2008; Lui et al. 2010), including from the nursing perspective (Summers and Malloy 2011). In a study supported by CIHR, Hopyan et al. (2010) documented that a stroke protocol that includes CTP increases diagnostic performance.[10]

3.4. Advantages of CTP in Canadian clinical settings

It is estimated that there are more than 50,000 hospitalizations per year for stroke in Canada and approximately 300,000 people are living with the effects of a stroke. A report prepared for Public Health Agency of Canada (PHAC) quantified the national cost of stroke for 2000 alone to be $3.6 billion (PHAC 2009).[11]

CTP offers several advantages in Canadian emergency department settings for acute stroke. Current indications for thrombolysis are that tPA should be administered within 4.5 hours of stroke onset and ideally within 3 hours (Canadian Stroke Network 2011).

Interviews with leading neuroradiologists in Canada and the USA, as well as a review of the extant literature, emphasize the advantages of CTP:

- quantification of CBF, CBV, and MTT to inform acute stroke care;
- use of CT scanning technology that is readily and increasingly available in Canadian trauma settings (CIHI 2012);

- lack of availability of MR scans in trauma settings, which would be the alternative to acquiring indicators in the absence of CT;
- rapidity with which CTP scans can be conducted, particularly because of lengthy travel times from location of stroke onset to trauma unit; and
- low cost and ease of use.

3.5.   *Impact of CTP on health outcomes*

A cost-effectiveness analysis of using CTP for acute stroke diagnosis and patient selection for thrombolysis relative to unenhanced CT and MR was published in 2012 by Earnshaw et al. That study used a decision-analytic model in which clinical trial, costs, efficacy, and utility information were collected and analyzed from the published literature on stroke and CTP. The model concluded that inclusive of direct and indirect costs CTP saved costs and enhanced quality of life. Patients selected for thrombolysis were determined to have 0.12 additional quality-adjusted life years (QALYs), on average, because of enhanced diagnosis and course of treatment decisions.[12]

4.   Estimating the social benefits attributable to CTP

Estimation of the social benefits attributable to CTP requires accurate specification of the counterfactual introduction to the healthcare market of CTP algorithms in the absence of CFI's infrastructure and CIHR's research support.[13] Mainly, how much longer would the development and commercialization of CTP algorithms have taken, and to what extent would the quality and utility of the state-of-the-art CTP technology be different, had the investments by CFI and CIHR not been made?

To answer these questions, the perspectives and opinions of scientists and physicians knowledgeable about the development and use of CTP technology were elicited through in-depth interviews, conducted by telephone and a number of site visits, and augmented with e-mail exchanges. Over the course of the collection of benefit data, 66 individuals provided information that complemented literature reviews and other data collection methods. Thirteen experts provided information that specified the final counterfactual CTP.[14]

The consensus among participating neuroradiologists and stroke neurologists was that the CTP research and the licensing of the algorithms and protocols to GE Healthcare accelerated the clinical use of CTP between 5 and 7 years.[15] These experts also estimated that without the public funds from CFI and CIHR, not only would the introduction of CTP software have been delayed, but the software that would have emerged would likely have been inferior in the accuracy and precision of measurement of CBF, CBV, and MTT.[16]

Following GE Healthcare's release of CTP, other manufacturers moved to emulate the work, with varying degrees of success. When challenged to support the claim of not only induced innovation (see O'Connor and Rowe 2008) but also of inferior quality in the absence of Lee's research, interviewees noted that first-released CTP was using principles, such as deconvolution, that others were not using. Yet, within a span of 3 years most competing software products had adopted those principles. Conversely, these same individuals noted that, by the late 2000s, most software products had matured and it became routine to see an advance first appearing in one package being emulated in another. It was noted that CTP can also be used for perfusion studies in the heart, the liver, and tumors, but other software products generally are not. Further, CTP is the benchmark software being used for clinical trials studying the efficacy of using CTP for stroke and cancer.

A.C. O'Connor et al.

Table 4.   Estimated number of strokes in Canada for 2004–2009.

	Ischemic	Hemorrhagic	TIA	Total
2004–2009	137,557	28,746	43,669	209,972
5-year average	27,511.4	5749.2	8733.8	41,994.4

Source: Krueger et al. (2012).
Note: Excludes strokes in persons under the age of 20.

Despite anecdotal evidence and scientific literature suggesting widespread usage, the prevalence of CTP is not well documented. The panel of neuroradiologists participating in this case study estimated prevalence in Canada at 40–60% in 2011, with a high of 70% and a low reported as unknown penetration for moderate to severe acute ischemic strokes.

The estimation of specific benefits requires the following elements:

- number of moderate to severe acute ischemic strokes per year,
- probability of visiting an emergency department with CTP capabilities,
- current prevalence and the rate of growth in CTP from its introduction in 2000,
- QALYs associated with using CTP,
- monetary value imputed for each QALY,
- costs of conducting CTP studies, and
- public investments in CTP research.

Analyzing such measure will provide an estimate of the dollar-denominated net social value of CTP.

4.1.   *Estimated annual number of moderate to severe accute ischemic strokes*

Neuroradiologists and stroke neurologists participating in this study indicated that CTP was generally only used for moderate to severe acute ischemic strokes. Patients with TIA, hemorrhagic, or mild ischemic stroke are either contraindicated or not expected to receive a CTP study.

To estimate the relevant number of strokes, we analyzed data from a recent study that quantified the national number of strokes by stroke type. Unfortunately, that study's results did not distinguish stroke severity. Therefore, a study performed in the USA on stroke severity was used to assign stroke severity to the Canadian data. We then converted the subsequent results to the Canadian Neurological Scale (CNS) for stroke severity and calculated the number of moderate to severe acute ischemic strokes. The remainder of this section describes the relevant calculations.

The number of acute ischemic strokes per year is approximated by the 5-year annual average calculated by Krueger et al. (2012). They analyzed administrative data from 2004 to 2009 from the Canadian Institute of Health Information (CIHI) Discharge Abstract Database to determine the number of hospital episodes with strokes. Rather than recalculate the number of strokes per year, Krueger et al.'s estimate is assumed to be a representative of all years.[17]

Table 4 shows the 5-year total and annual average breakdown of strokes by stroke type. Of the 41,994 average number of strokes per year in Canada, 27,551 were ischemic strokes. This would be a conservative estimate for 2000 through 2004, in particular, because an assessment prepared by PHAC (2009) reports that the incidence of all strokes was likely higher in this period.[18]

Table 5.   Severity of acute ischemic stroke using the NIHSS stroke scale.

(1) NIHSS scale[a]	(2) Percentage of strokes	(3) Number of cases[b]
1	2.82%	776
2	2.26%	621
3	6.67%	1835
4	6.93%	1906
5	7.44%	2047
6	10.52%	2894
7	5.64%	1553
8	5.13%	1412
9	2.82%	776
10	8.98%	2470
11	2.82%	776
12	4.10%	1129
13	2.82%	776
14	2.82%	776
15	3.85%	1059
16	1.54%	423
17	1.54%	423
18	5.13%	1412
19	2.31%	635
20	2.31%	635
21	2.05%	565
22	1.54%	423
23	2.82%	776
24	2.31%	635
25	0.77%	212
26	0.77%	212
27	0.77%	212
28	0.00%	–
29	0.00%	–
30	0.51%	141

[a]Johnston et al. (2000).
[b]Krueger et al. (2012).

To estimate the proportion of strokes that could be considered moderate to severe, we relied on Johnston et al. (2000) who measured the severity of strokes using the US NIH Stroke Scale (NIHSS) for Medicare Fee-For-Service patients. Because a similar distribution was not available for Canada, Canadian strokes were assumed to be distributed similarly. Table 5 maps the Canadian stroke estimates onto the NIHSS distribution. The NIHSS scale goes from 1 to 30, ranging from least severe to most severe.

The CNS uses a different numbering system than the NIHSS. The CNS ranges from 0 to 11 with 0 being most severe and 11 being least severe. Nilanont et al. (2010) created a simple conversion formula to calculate CNS scores when given NIHSS scores:

$CNS = (NIHSS - 21)/(-2)$. Using NIHSS scores to create CNS scores has been verified in other works. Muir et al. (1996) verified the high correlation between NIHSS and CNS scores. Mapping the distribution in Table 5 and renumbering negative values to become 0 results provide a distribution of strokes on a 12-point CNS scale (see Table 6).

Siposnik (2010) created a binning of stroke severity with mild ($CNS \geq 8$), moderate (CNS of $5 < 8$), and Severe (CNS of $0 < 5$). Applying this distribution of CNS severity to Table 6, there were 8539 severe strokes and 7339 moderate strokes. Thus, we estimate that the annual average of moderate to severe acute ischemic strokes in Canada to be 15,878.

Table 6. Severity of acute ischemic stroke, CNS stroke scale.

(1) CNS scale[a,b]	(2) Number of cases[c]
11.0	776
10.5	621
10.0	1835
9.5	1906
9.0	2047
8.5	2894
8.0	1553
7.5	1412
7.0	776
6.5	2470
6.0	776
5.5	1129
5.0	776
4.5	776
4.0	1059
3.5	423
3.0	423
2.5	1412
2.0	635
1.5	635
1.0	565
0.5	423
0	2188

[a]Johnston et al. (2000).
[b]Nilanont et al. (2010).
[c]Krueger et al. (2012).

4.2. Estimated prevalence of CTP

The Canadian Stroke Network (2011) estimated that 70% of stroke hospitalizations occur at facilities with thrombolysis capabilities.[19] This probability was used as the probability that a person would arrive at a hospital with CTP capabilities. Applying the exact percentage to the estimated number of acute strokes (15,878) yields 11,116 in-scope stroke hospitalizations. Thus, the maximum number of CTP hospitalizations for which CTP could be performed is 11,116.

Interviewees estimated that the prevalence of CTP studies in Canada in 2011 was in the range of 40% to 60% of moderate to severe acute ischemic strokes. It is estimated that in 2011 between 4446 and 6670 CTP studies were performed in Canada. This range was estimated by applying the lower and upper bounds of the prevalence range to the relevant number of stokes per year[20] (see Table 7).

4.3. Estimated QALYs gained

Earnshaw et al. (2012) estimated the health outcomes benefits to be 0.12 QALYs. In economic studies, human health benefits are quantified in terms of QALYs, or the additional quantity of life an intervention offers a patient, recognizing the fact that the person has suffered an adverse health event or has an illness. Assuming that this benefit has been constant over time, multiplying the estimated number of CTP studies by this benefit value yields a time series of the QALYs gained for stroke patients benefiting from CTP (see Table 8).

Table 7. Estimated prevalence of CTP for acute stroke diagnosis, 2000–2011.

Calendar year	(1) Estimated cumulative penetration, as a proportion of ultimate 2011 penetration[a]	(2) Lower-bound estimated penetration (40%)[b]	(3) Upper-bound estimated penetration (60%)[c]	(4) Estimated annual moderate-severe acute ischemic strokes[d]	(5) Estimated number of CTP studies, lower bound[e]	(6) Estimated number of CTP studies, upper bound[f]
2000	0.017	0.68%	1.02%	11,116	75.59	113.38
2001	0.068	2.72%	4.08%	11,116	302.36	453.53
2002	0.128	5.12%	7.68%	11,116	569.14	853.71
2003	0.198	7.92%	11.88%	11,116	880.39	1320.58
2004	0.276	11.04%	16.56%	11,116	1227.21	1840.81
2005	0.369	14.76%	22.14%	11,116	1640.72	2461.08
2006	0.461	18.44%	27.66%	11,116	2049.79	3074.69
2007	0.552	22.08%	33.12%	11,116	2454.41	3681.62
2008	0.649	25.96%	38.94%	11,116	2885.71	4328.57
2009	0.738	29.52%	44.28%	11,116	3281.44	4922.16
2010	0.877	35.08%	52.62%	11,116	3899.49	5849.24
2011	1.000	40.00%	60.00%	11,116	4446.40	6669.60

[a]These data are based on the diffusion of the licenses over time. These secondary data were supplied by Western University, but the primary data remain confidential to Western.
[b]Column (2) is column (1) × 100 × 0.40.
[c]Column (3) is column (1) × 100 × 0.60.
[d]See the text for a discussion of these data.
[e]Column (5) is column (2) × column (4).
[f]Column (6) is column (3) × column (4).

Table 8.   Estimated gain in QALYs from CTP, 2000–2011.

Calendar year	(1) Estimated number of CTP studies, lower bound[a]	(2) Estimated number of CTP studies, upper bound[a]	(3) QALYs gained per stroke case receiving CTP study[b]	(4) Estimated QALYs gained, lower bound[c]	(5) Estimated QALYs gained, upper bound[d]
2000	75.59	113.38	0.12	9.07	13.61
2001	302.36	453.53	0.12	36.28	54.42
2002	569.14	853.71	0.12	68.30	102.45
2003	880.39	1320.58	0.12	105.65	158.47
2004	1227.21	1840.81	0.12	147.26	220.90
2005	1640.72	2461.08	0.12	196.89	295.33
2006	2049.79	3074.69	0.12	245.97	368.96
2007	2454.41	3681.62	0.12	294.53	441.79
2008	2885.71	4328.57	0.12	346.29	519.43
2009	3281.44	4922.16	0.12	393.77	590.66
2010	3899.49	5849.24	0.12	467.94	701.91
2011	4446.40	6669.60	0.12	533.57	800.35
Total	23,712.65	35,568.98		2845.52	4268.28

[a]Columns (1) and (2) are from Table 7.
[b]See the text for a discussion of these data.
[c]Column (4) is column (1) × column (3).
[d]Column (5) is column (2) × column (3).

4.4.   Value of QALYs gained

As in Krueger et al. (2012), the value of 1 QALY is the average annual Canadian wage regardless of the patient's age or work status. Therefore, three data series from Statistics Canada were acquired to monetize the QALYs:

- the average hourly wage for persons 15 or over (Statistics Canada 2012b),
- the average number of working hours per week (Statistics Canada 2012c), and
- the GDP index, which is used to adjust for the time value of money (Statistics Canada 2012a).

As shown in Table 9, the average annual wage in 2011 was $43,515. The data for 2000 through 2010 were adjusted backwards using the Canadian GDP index. Table 10 presents the value of QALYs gained for 2000 through 2011 in 2011 dollars ($2011).

4.5.   Estimated costs of CTP studies

The average incremental cost of a CTP study in 2011 was estimated to be $88.06 (Earnshaw et al. 2012), of which 80% was the cost of the contrast agent. As previously noted, the time for conducting the imaging study was estimated to be between 5 and 10 minutes, and the time for processing and interpreting the results is estimated to take no more than 5 to 6 minutes.

Even in real terms, it is unlikely that the costs for conducting a CTP study remained constant over time. Therefore, prior years' costs for CTP were estimated by deflating costs using the healthcare services component of the Consumer Price Index (Statistics Canada 2012d) – see column (3) in Table 11. Table 11 presents the costs of applying CTP in a stroke setting.

Table 9.   Valuation of one QALY, 2000–2011.

Calendar year	(1) Average hourly wage rate[a]	(2) Average number of hours worked per week[b]	(3) Number of weeks per year	(4) Annual wage rate	(5) Annual wage rate ($2011)
2000	16.66	37.9	52	32,833.53	42,569.44
2001	17.21	37.3	52	33,380.52	42,797.26
2002	17.66	37.1	52	34,069.67	43,200.34
2003	18.05	36.5	52	34,258.90	42,052.55
2004	18.50	36.9	52	35,497.80	42,224.40
2005	19.09	37.2	52	36,927.70	42,528.90
2006	19.72	36.9	52	37,838.74	42,459.75
2007	20.40	37.2	52	39,461.76	42,913.82
2008	21.31	36.8	52	40,778.82	42,592.70
2009	22.04	36.0	52	41,258.88	43,926.33
2010	22.53	36.2	52	42,410.47	43,863.36
2011	22.99	36.4	52	43,515.47	43,515.47

[a]Statistics Canada (2012b). Labour force survey estimates (LFS), wages of employees by type of work, National Occupational Classification for Statistics (NOC-S), sex and age group, unadjusted for seasonality, annual (current dollars unless otherwise noted), (CANSIM Table 282–0069).
[b]Statistics Canada (2012c). LFS, by total and average usual and actual hours worked, main or all jobs, type of work, sex and age group, annual (CANSIM Table 282–0028).
[c]Column (4) is column (1) × column (2) × column (3).

Table 10.   Valuation of QALYs gained, 2000–2011.

Calendar year	(1) Estimated number of QALYs gained, lower bound[a]	(2) Estimated number of QALYs gained, upper bound[a]	(3) Annual wage rate ($2011)[b]	(4) Value of QALYs gained, lower bound (million $2011)[c]	(5) Value of QALYs gained, upper bound (million $2011)[d]
2000	9.07	13.61	42,569.44	0.39	0.58
2001	36.28	54.42	42,797.26	1.55	2.33
2002	68.30	102.45	43,200.34	2.95	4.43
2003	105.65	158.47	42,052.55	4.44	6.66
2004	147.26	220.90	42,224.40	6.22	9.33
2005	196.89	295.33	42,528.90	8.37	12.56
2006	245.97	368.96	42,459.75	10.44	15.67
2007	294.53	441.79	42,913.82	12.64	18.96
2008	346.29	519.43	42,592.70	14.75	22.12
2009	393.77	590.66	43,926.33	17.30	25.95
2010	467.94	701.91	43,863.36	20.53	30.79
2011	533.57	800.35	43,515.47	23.22	34.83
Total	2845.52	4268.28		122.80	184.20

[a]Columns (1) and (2) are from Table 8.
[b]Column (3) is from Table 9.
[c]Column (4) is column (1) × column (3).
[d]Column (5) is column (2) × column (3).

4.6.   Estimated benefits of applying CTP in an acute stroke setting

The net economic benefits for health plans and patients is therefore the monetized value of QALYs gained less the costs of conducting CTP (see Table 12). We estimate that the value of QALYs gained to be between $122.80 million and $184.20 million. Less costs of conducting CTP, net economic benefits over the period of 2000–2011, before assessing attribution to Lee and public support, would be between $120.78 million and $181.17

Table 11.   Costs of performing CTP studies in an acute stroke setting, 2000–2011.

Calendar year	(1) Estimated number of CTP studies, lower bound[a]	(2) Estimated number of CTP studies, upper bound[a]	(3) Estimated cost per study (2011$)	(4) Estimated cost of CTP studies, lower bound (million $2011)[b]	(5) Estimated cost of CTP studies, upper bound (million $2011)[c]
2000	75.59	113.38	77.22	0.01	0.01
2001	302.36	453.53	78.81	0.02	0.04
2002	569.14	853.71	80.68	0.05	0.07
2003	880.39	1320.58	80.68	0.07	0.11
2004	1227.21	1840.81	81.06	0.10	0.15
2005	1640.72	2461.08	82.07	0.13	0.20
2006	2049.79	3074.69	82.97	0.17	0.26
2007	2454.41	3681.62	83.17	0.20	0.31
2008	2885.71	4328.57	82.54	0.24	0.36
2009	3281.44	4922.16	87.19	0.29	0.43
2010	3899.49	5849.24	88.51	0.35	0.52
2011	4446.40	6669.60	88.06	0.39	0.59
Total	23,712.65	35,568.98		2.02	3.02

[a]Columns (1) and (2) are from Table 8.
[b]Column (4) is column (1) × column (3).
[c]Column (5) is column (2) × column (3).

Table 12.   Estimated benefits of CTP for acute stroke, 2000–2011 (millions $2011).

Calendar year	(1) Value of QALYs gained, lower bound[a]	(2) Value of QALYs gained, upper bound[a]	(3) Estimated cost of CTP studies, lower bound[b]	(4) Estimated cost of CTP studies, upper bound[b]	(5) Incremental economic benefit of CTP studies, lower bound[c]	(6) Incremental economic benefit of CTP studies, upper bound[d]
2000	0.39	0.58	0.01	0.01	0.38	0.57
2001	1.55	2.33	0.02	0.04	1.53	2.29
2002	2.95	4.43	0.05	0.07	2.90	4.36
2003	4.44	6.66	0.07	0.11	4.37	6.56
2004	6.22	9.33	0.10	0.15	6.12	9.18
2005	8.37	12.56	0.13	0.20	8.24	12.36
2006	10.44	15.67	0.17	0.26	10.27	15.41
2007	12.64	18.96	0.20	0.31	12.44	18.65
2008	14.75	22.12	0.24	0.36	14.51	21.77
2009	17.30	25.95	0.29	0.43	17.01	25.52
2010	20.53	30.79	0.35	0.52	20.18	30.27
2011	23.22	34.83	0.39	0.59	22.83	34.24
Total	122.80	184.20	2.02	3.02	120.78	181.17

[a]Columns (1) and (2) are from Table 10.
[b]Columns (3) and (4) are from Table 11.
[c]Column (5) is column (1) − column (3).
[d]Column (6) is column (2) − column (4).

million. This range reflects the value to patients of additional quantity of life, after adjusting for the quality of that life.

These net economic benefits would be attributable to CFI and CIHR if in the absence of their support Lee's research would not have been supported by any other organization and no other entity in Canada or elsewhere developed commercially viable CTP algorithms before 2012. However, such a scenario is unlikely given that research about CTP was published (Wintermark et al. 2002a) and given the highly competitive CT scanner

Table 13.   Economic benefits of CTP attributable to CIHR, CFI, and partners, 2000–2011 (millions $2011).

Calendar year	(1) Economic benefit of CTP studies, lower bound[a]	(2) Economic benefit of CTP studies, upper bound[a]	(3) Economic benefits under a 5-year delay, lower bound	(4) Economic benefits under a 5-year delay, upper bound	(5) Attributable economic benefits, lower bound[b]	(6) Attributable economic benefits, upper bound[c]
2000	0.38	0.57	–	–	0.38	0.57
2001	1.53	2.29	–	–	1.53	2.29
2002	2.90	4.36	–	–	2.90	4.36
2003	4.37	6.56	–	–	4.37	6.56
2004	6.12	9.18	–	–	6.12	9.18
2005	8.24	12.36	0.38	0.57	7.86	11.79
2006	10.27	15.41	1.53	2.29	8.74	13.12
2007	12.44	18.65	2.90	4.36	9.53	14.30
2008	14.51	21.77	4.37	6.56	10.14	15.21
2009	17.01	25.52	6.12	9.18	10.89	16.34
2010	20.18	30.27	8.24	12.36	11.94	17.91
2011	22.83	34.24	10.27	15.41	12.55	18.83
Total	120.78	181.17	33.82	50.73	86.96	130.45

[a]Columns (1) and (2) are from Table 12.
[b]Column (5) is column (1) – column (3).
[c]Column (6) is column (2) – column (4).

market. Thus, to account for attribution, the evaluation analysis turns to the question of how and when would the benefits in Table 12 have accrued in the absence of CFI and CIHR support.

4.7.   Net economic benefits attributable to CFI, CIHR, and partners

Under the counterfactual scenario without CFI and CIHR, the consensus among neuro-radiologists who participated on expert panels for background information was that the acceleration effect attributable to CFI and CIHR funding would have been at least 5 years. That is, CFI and CIHR funding accelerated the commercial availability of CTP software by not less than 5 years. To quantify this attribution effect, actual benefits accrued less the corresponding value under a 5-year delay would represent the net economic benefits attributable to CFI and CIHR funding.

We thus estimate in Table 13 that the economic benefits attributable are between $87.0 million and $130.49 million. Delaying benefits 5 years and taking the difference between the actual benefits and counterfactual benefits equate to the benefit attributable to public support.

The attributable economic benefit estimates in columns (5) and (6) of Table 13 are conservative estimates because experts reported that the quality of algorithms that would otherwise have been introduced would have been lower. This would mean that the slope of the CTP penetration curve (see column (1) of Table 7) would have been lower in the counterfactual scenario and thus the counterfactual benefits stream lower. However, our panel of experts was unable to measure such changes in quality, and the analysis, therefore, had to assume that the penetration curve under the counterfactual scenario was of the same slope as was estimated for 2000–2011.

Table 14.   Net economic benefits attributable to CIHR, CFI, and partners, 2000–2011 (millions $2011).

Calendar year	(1) Attributable economic benefits, lower bound[a]	(2) Attributable economic benefits, upper bound[a]	(3) CT public development[b]	(4) Net attributable economic benefits, lower bound[c]	(5) Net attributable economic benefits, upper bound[d]
2000	0.38	0.57	3.27	− 2.89	− 2.70
2001	1.53	2.29	0.73	0.80	1.56
2002	2.90	4.36	0.65	2.25	3.71
2003	4.37	6.56	0.16	4.21	6.40
2004	6.12	9.18	0.11	6.01	9.07
2005	7.86	11.79	0.02	7.84	11.77
2006	8.74	13.12	0.17	8.57	12.95
2007	9.53	14.30	0.10	9.43	14.20
2008	10.14	15.21	3.52	6.62	11.69
2009	10.89	16.34	0.24	10.65	16.10
2010	11.94	17.91	0.10	11.84	17.81
2011	12.55	18.83	0.14	12.41	18.69
Total	86.96	130.45	9.21	77.75	121.24

[a]Columns (1) and (2) from Table 13.
[b]Column (3) from Table 3.
[c]Column (4) is column (1) – column (3).
[d]Column (5) is column (2) – column (3).

5.   Evaluation metrics associated with CFI's and CIHR's investments in CTP

Public investments of $9.21 million for Lee's CT research (see column (3) of Table 3) are subtracted from the benefits stream to yield net benefits in Table 14. Thus, the net economic benefits attributable to public support of CTP are estimated to be between $77.75 million and $121.24 million over the years 2000 through 2011.

We calculated two measures of economic returns to the CT-related costs: net present value (NPV) and a benefit-to-cost ratio (BCR). Table 15 presents the PV of costs when a narrow cost basis of only CT-related project costs is included in the cost basis. Cash flows

Table 15.   Present value of CFI, CIHR, and partner costs, 2000–2011 (millions $2011).

Calendar year	(1) Period number	(2) CT costs[a]	(3) Present value of costs (base year = 2000)
2000	0	3.27	3.27
2001	1	0.73	0.68
2002	2	0.65	0.56
2003	3	0.16	0.13
2004	4	0.11	0.08
2005	5	0.02	0.01
2006	6	0.17	0.11
2007	7	0.1	0.06
2008	8	3.52	1.90
2009	9	0.24	0.12
2010	10	0.1	0.05
2011	11	0.14	0.06
Total		9.21	7.02

[a]Column (2) is from Table 14.

Table 16.   Present value of economic benefits attributable to CFI, CIHR, and partners, 2000–2011 (millions $2011).

Calendar year	(1) Period number	(2) Attributable economic benefits, lower bound[a]	(3) Attributable economic benefits, upper bound[a]	(4) Present value of attributable economic benefits lower bound (base year = 2000)	(5) Present value of attributable economic benefits, lower bound (base year = 2000)
2000	1	0.38	0.57	0.35	0.53
2001	2	1.53	2.29	1.31	1.97
2002	3	2.90	4.36	2.31	3.46
2003	4	4.37	6.56	3.21	4.82
2004	5	6.12	9.18	4.16	6.25
2005	6	7.86	11.79	4.95	7.43
2006	7	8.74	13.12	5.10	7.65
2007	8	9.53	14.30	5.15	7.72
2008	9	10.14	15.21	5.07	7.61
2009	10	10.89	16.34	5.05	7.57
2010	11	11.94	17.91	5.12	7.68
2011	12	12.55	18.83	4.98	7.48
Total		86.96	130.45	46.77	70.16

[a]Columns (2) and (3) are from Table 14.

Table 17.   Evaluation metrics (CT costs only).

Metric	Estimate
NPV of net benefits (base year = 2000)	$39.75 million to $63.14 million
Benefit-to-cost ratio	6.66-to-1 to 9.99-to-1

are discounted using the real social discount rate recommended by the Treasury Board Secretariat (TBS) of Canada based on Canada's economic opportunity cost of capital (TBS 2007), which is 8% per annum (Jenkins and Kuo 2007). The PV of costs is $7.02 million.

The NPV is the present value (base year = 2000) of benefits less the PV of costs. Because costs are assumed to be incurred at the beginning of a period and benefits at the end, benefits are discounted one additional period than costs. Table 16 presents the PV of net attributable benefits. Subtracting the PV of costs from the PV of benefits yields an NPV between $39.75 million[21] and $63.14 million[22] (see Table 17).

The BCR is the ratio of the PV of benefits to the PV of costs, using the same 8% social discount rate. Thus, under a narrow cost definition, the BCR of CTP is between 6.66-to-1[23] and 9.99-to-1.[24]

6.   Concluding remarks

The high BCRs estimated in this case study reflect the inherent value of sophisticated, yet simple to use, diagnostic tools that can inform clinical care. The estimates provided in this case study reflect the benefits to Canadians of CTP for stroke alone; however, Dr Lee and others are developing protocols and testing, with CIHR support, CTP for the heart, the liver, and tumor imaging. CTP is used around the world, but we limited our lens to Canada in order to compare costs and benefits of publicly-funded R&D.

The case of CT perfusion is an excellent example of the profound effect public support and acceleration of R&D in the public interest can have on health outcomes. The right tools were placed in the hands of researchers who knew what to do with them, and the support was there over the long term for researchers to put those tools to good use. This study documented the connection between research infrastructure support and research program support in the innovation process, and how different funders supporting different facets of the innovation process each have an enabling role to play. The ultimate beneficiaries are stroke sufferers whose doctors are better equipped to rapidly diagnose their condition and more confidently recommend a course of treatment.

Disclosure statement

No potential conflict of interest was reported by the authors.

Notes

1. The other three are environmental science and technologies, natural resources and energy, and information and communication technologies.
2. French and English keyword search terms that were relevant included those related to modalities (e.g. CT, positron emission tomography (PET), MRI) and/or advanced image processing, development of biomarkers, comparative image analysis, quantitative analyses of imaging data for screening and early disease detection, directing of image-guided treatment, disease diagnosis and staging, and use of imaging to evaluate the effectiveness of treatment. Searches were performed using Perl compatible regular expression-compliant regular expressions with case and accent insensitivity. Fields searched included those for keywords, project abstract, and project title. Searches of CFI's databases were performed by CFI's Information Systems group, and the resulting project list was reviewed by the Evaluation and Outcome Assessment group. Searches of CIHR's databases were performed by the Corporate Measurement and Data Unit, and the resulting project list was reviewed by the CIHR Institute of Cancer Research. CFI and CIHR exchanged project lists for review. The Assistant Director of the Institute of Cancer Research performed the final quality review of a combined CFI and CIHR project list.
3. Funding data prior to 2000 from CIHR's predecessor agency, the MRC, were not available.
4. Case selection criteria included: receipt of CFI and CIHR funding, multiple awards, year(s) of award(s), commercialization status, and documented impact on health outcomes. See also O'Connor and Link (2013).
5. CTP can also be used to measure blood flow in other conditions of the brain such as tumors or vascular malformations and in other organs such as the heart or the liver (Hoeffner et al. 2004).
6. In fact, Dr Lee submitted multiple applications to the MRC to have CTP research funded before finally being granted funding in 1995.
7. CIHR 61010, Multi-slice CT and MR CBF Perfusion Mapping in Thrombolytic Treatment of Stroke; CIHR 64574, CT Cardiac Perfusion Imaging; CIHR 98017, Development of New PET/CT Techniques for Imaging Tumour Hypoxia; CIHR 146177, Perfusion and Lipid Imaging with a Liver Specific CT Contrast Agent to Detect Progression of Cirrhosis to Hepatocellular Carcinoma; CIHR 167357, Developing CT Functional and Molecular Imaging Techniques for the Diagnosis of Disease and Monitoring of Treatment Effects in Stroke, Cancer, and Heart Diseases; and CIHR 226667, Quantitative CT Myocardial Perfusion Imaging.
8. Future commitments for these grants total $584,705 for a total funding amount of $1,945,933.
9. These include Perfusion CT Imaging to Evaluation Treatment Response in Ovarian Cancer Patients Participating in GOG-0262 (sponsored by the US National Cancer Institute/American College of Radiology Imaging Network); Multi-institution Study of DCE CT Imaging Biomarkers of Tumor Microvasculature in Metastatic Renal Cell Carcinoma Treated with Sunitinib – Reproducibility and Response Prediction (sponsored by Ontario Institute of Cancer, High Impact Clinical Trial Program); and CIHR Medical Imaging Trial Network of Canada (MITNEC) project to measure perfusion in the heart of CAD patients and compare the measurement with clinical gold standards

10.   CTP software is currently available from GE Healthcare, Siemens, Philips, and Toshiba, all of which market CT scanning systems globally.

11.   That estimate is composed of direct healthcare costs and the indirect costs of lost productivity and premature mortality.

12.   The range of QALY in Earnshaw et al. (2012) is 0.12 to 0.13. The 0.12 QALY benefit estimate is used below as a measure of the social value of CTP to a person suffering from moderate to severe acute ischemic stroke.

13.   For a discussion of the counterfactual evaluation methodology, see Link and Scott (1998, 2011a, 2011b).

14.   Data collection was conducted under assurances of confidentiality for private-sector participants or assurances that names would not be associated with specific remarks for university researchers. This step was taken to enable interviewees to speak candidly about their research activities or the impact of those activities. Representative titles included Chief of Neuroradiology; CT Product Line Director; Medical Director, CT and MR Imaging; and Professor of Radiology.

15.   Other experts who were interviewed simply stated 'many' years or stated that there was an acceleration effect but they were uncertain how great that effect was.

16.   Interviewees noted that Lee has an uncommon background beyond his research career as both an imaging physicist and a mathematician. This background coupled with what was characterized as an intense interest in developing simple tools using readily available technology were offered in explanation of the novelty of Lee's accomplishments.

17.   Kruger et al. (2012) applied two exclusion criteria. First, hospital transfers were excluded to prevent one stroke episode from being counted more than once in the analysis. Second, the researchers excluded stroke episodes for those younger than 20 years old. Also, The CIHI database did not include data for Quebec. To estimate Quebec, the researchers used their CIHI data, broken down by age category, and then applied this to population figures for Quebec (Krueger et al. 2012).

18.   The age-standardized rate of hospitalization for stroke per 100,000 population has declined since 1980. PHAC notes that the decrease may reflect few hospital admissions because of changes in patterns of care, better preventative care and health management, and healthier habits. However, an aging population and increased rates of diabetes and obesity may cause the rate to increase again (PHAC 2009).

19.   70.01% to be exact.

20.   See the notes in Table 9.

21.   (46.77–7.02).

22.   (70.16–7.02).

23.   (46.77/7.02).

24.   (70.16/7.02).

References

Axel, L. 1980. "Cerebral Blood Flow Determination by Rapid-Sequence Computed Tomography: Theoretical Analysis." *Radiology* 137 (3): 679–686.

Canadian Stoke Network. 2011. *The Quality of Stroke Care in Canada*. Ottawa: Canadian Stroke Network.

CIHI (Canadian Institute for Health Information). 2012. *National Survey of Selected Medical Imaging Equipment, 2003–2011*. Ottawa: CIHI.

Earnshaw, S. R., C. McDade, A.-M. Chapman, D. Jackson, and L. Schwamm. 2012. "Economic Impact of Using Additional Diagnostic Tests to Better Select Patients with Stroke for Intravenous Thrombolysis in the United Kingdom." *Clinical Therapeutics* 34 (7): 1544–1558.

Eastwood, J. D., M. H. Lev, M. Wintermark, C. Fitzek, D. P. Barboriak, D. M. Long, T.-Y. Lee, et al. 2003. "Correlation of Early Dynamic CT Perfusion Imaging with Whole-Brain MR Diffusion and Perfusion Imaging in Acute Hemispheric Stroke." *American Journal of Neuroradiology*, 24 (9): 1869–1875.

Hoeffner, E. G., I. Case, R. Jain, S. K. Gujar, G. V. Shah, J. P. Deveikis, R. C. Carlos, B. G. Thompson, M. R. Harrigan, and S. K. Mukherji. 2004. "Cerebral Perfusion CT: Technique and Clinical Applications." *Radiology* 231 (3): 632–644.

Hopyan, J., A. Ciarallo, D. Dowlatshahi, P. Howard, V. John, R. Yeung, L. Zhang, et al. 2010. "Certainty of Stroke Diagnosis: Increment Benefit with CT Perfusion over Noncontrast CT and CT Angiography." *Radiology* 255 (1): 142–153.

Industry Canada. 2009. *Mobilizing Science and Technology to Canada's Advantage: Progress Report 2009*. Ottawa: Industry Canada. http://www.ic.gc.ca/eic/site/icgc.nsf/eng/h_04709.html

Jenkins, G., and C.-Y. Kuo. 2007. "The Economic Opportunity Cost of Capital for Canada – An Empirical Update." Queen's Economics Department Working Paper Number 1133. Kingston, ON: Queen's University.

Johnston, K. C., A. F. Connors, D. P. Wagner, W. A. Knaus, X.-Q. Wang, and E. C. Haley. 2000. "A Predictive Risk Model for Outcomes of Ischemic Stroke." *Stroke* 31 (2): 448–455.

Krueger, H., P. Lindsay, R. Cote, M. K. Kapral, J. Kaczorowski, and M. D. Hill. 2012. "Cost Avoidance Associated with Optimal Stroke Care in Canada." *Stroke* 43 (8): 2198–2206.

Larivière, V., and P. Lemelin. 2012. "Scientific and Technological Impact of CFI Researchers' Papers and Patents in the Area of Medical Imaging, 1990–2010." Report submitted to the Canada Foundation for Innovation by Observatoire des sciences et des technologies, February 29.

Link, A. N., and J. T. Scott. 1998. *Public Accountability: Evaluating Technology-Based Institutions*. Norwell, MA: Kluwer Academic Publishers.

Link, A. N., and J. T. Scott. 2011a. *Public Goods, Public Gains: Calculating the Social Benefits of Public R&D*. New York: Oxford University Press.

Link, A. N., and J. T. Scott. 2011b. "The Theory and Practice of Public Sector R&D Economic Impact Analysis." NIST Planning Report 11–01, Gaithersburg, MD: National Institute of Standards and Technology.

de Lucas, E. M., E. Sanchez, A. Gutierrez, A. Consales Mandly, E. Ruiz, A. Fernandez Florez, J. Izquierdo, et al. 2008. "CT Protocol for Acute Stroke: Tips and Tricks for General Radiologists." *RadioGraphics* 28 (6): 1673–1687.

Lui, Y. W., E. R. Tang, A. M. Allmendinger, and V. Spektor. 2010. "Evaluation of CT Perfusion in the Setting of Cerebral Ischemia: Patterns and Pitfalls." *American Journal of NeuroRadiology* 31 (8): 1552–1563.

Miller, J. C., M. H. Lev, L. H. Schwamm, J. H. Thrall, and S. I. Lee. 2008. "Functional CT and MR Imaging for Evaluation of Acute Stroke." *Journal of the American College of Radiology* 5 (1): 67–70.

Muir, K. W., C. J. Weir, G. D. Murray, C. Povey, and K. R. Lees. 1996. "Comparison of Neurological Scales and Scoring Systems for Acute Stroke Prognosis." *Stroke* 27 (10): 1817–1820.

Nilanont, Y., C. Komoltri, G. Saposnik, R. Cote, S. Di Legge, Y. Jin, N. Prayoonwiwat, N. Poungvarin, and V. Hachinski. 2010. "The Canadian Neurological Scale and the NIHSS: Development and Validation of a Simple Conversion Model." *Cerebrovascular Disease* 30 (2): 120–126.

O'Connor, A. C., and A. N. Link. 2013. "Pilot Socioeconomic Impact Analysis of CFI and CIHR Funding: Medical Imaging R&D." RTI Report 0213907. Prepared for the Canada Foundation for Innovation and the Canadian Institutes of Health Research.

O'Connor, A. C., and B. R. Rowe. 2008. "Public-Private Partnership to Develop Technology Infrastructure: A Case Study of the Economic Returns of DNA Diagnostics." *Economics of Innovation and New Technology* 17 (7): 651–663.

Parsons, M. W. 2008. "Perfusion CT: Is It Really Useful?" *International Journal of Stroke* 3 (1): 41–50.

PHAC (Public Health Agency of Canada). 2009. *Tracking Heart Disease and Stroke in Canada*. Ottawa: Public Health Agency of Canada.

Shetty, S. K., and M. H. Lev. 2005. "CT Perfusion in Acute Stroke." *Neuroimaging Clinics of North America* 15 (3): 481–501.

Sinclair, A. 1998. "Medical Imaging Discussion Paper." Report to Health Industries Branch, Industry Canada, Ontario, Canada. Report No.: 98-X11-C06-1534-1.

Siposnik, G. 2010. "Canadian Neurological Scale – Iscore." http://www.sorcan.ca/iscore/cns.html

Srinivasan, A., M. Goyalm, F. Al Azri, and C. Lum. 2006. "State-of-the-Art Imaging of Acute Stroke." *RadioGraphics* 26 (Suppl. 1): S75–S95.

Statistics Canada. 2012a. "CANSIM (database)." Table 380–0056 – Gross domestic product (GDP) indexes, annual (2002 = 100).

Statistics Canada. 2012b. "Labour Force Survey Estimates (LFS), Wages of Employees by Type of Work, National Occupational Classification for Statistics (NOC-S), Sex and Age Group,

Unadjusted for Seasonality, Annual (current dollars unless otherwise noted)." CANSIM Table 282–0069.

Statistics Canada. 2012c. "Labour Force Survey Estimates (LFS), by Total and Average Usual and Actual Hours Worked, Main or All Jobs, Type of Work, Sex and Age Group, Annual". CANSIM Table 282–0028.

Statistics Canada. 2012d. "Table 326–0021 – Consumer Price Index (CPI), 2009 basket, annual (2002 = 100 unless otherwise noted)." CANSIM (database).

Summers, D., and R. Malloy. 2011. "CT and MR Imaging in the Acute Ischemic Stroke Patient: A Nursing Perspective." *Journal of Radiology Nursing* 30 (3): 104–115.

TBS (Treasury Board Secretariat of Canada). 2007. "Canadian Benefit-Cost Analysis Guide (Regulatory Proposals)." Catalogue No. BT58–5/2007.

Wintermark, M., M. Reichart, J.-P. Thiran, P. Maeder, M. Chalaron, P. Schnyder, J. Bogousslavsky, and R. Meuli. 2002a. "Prognostic Accuracy of Cerebral Blood Flow Measurement by perfusion Computed Tomography, at the Time of Emergency Room Admission, in Acute Stroke Patients." *Annals of Neurology* 51 (4): 417–432.

Wintermark, M., M. Reichart, O. Cuisenaire, P. Maeder, J.-P. Thiran, P. Schnyder, J. Bogousslavsky, and R. Meuli. 2002b. "Comparison of Admission Perfusion Computed Tomography and Qualitative Diffusion- and Perfusion-Weighted Magnetic Resonance Imaging in Acute Stroke Patients." *Stroke* 33 (8): 2025–2031.

PART II

SPILLOVER EVALUATION METHOD

ELSEVIER

International Journal of Industrial Organization
19 (2001) 763–794

International Journal of
Industrial
Organization

www.elsevier.com/locate/econbase

Public/private partnerships: stimulating competition in a dynamic market

Albert N. Link[a,*], John T. Scott[b]

[a]*Department of Economics, University of North Carolina at Greensboro, Greensboro, NC 27412,
USA*
[b]*Department of Economics, Dartmouth College, Hanover, NH 03755, USA*

Abstract

This paper sets forth a public/private partnership competition policy that mitigates the appropriability problems associated with innovation that occur in a dynamic market when competitive pressures are present. We illustrate the applicability of our policy proposal using the results from an analysis of research projects jointly funded by the Advanced Technology Program (ATP) and the private partners. Our analysis illustrates that in the absence of ATP funding these projects would not have been undertaken by private-sector firms, and that the social rate of return from the projects is substantial. We also posit a mechanism whereby ATP, or any public agency, can partner with industry to ensure that its public funds are being efficiently allocated. . 2001 Elsevier Science B.V. All rights reserved.

Keywords: Public/private partnership; Advanced Technology Program; R&D; Technology policy

JEL classification: O31; D62

1. Introduction

An effective competition policy in a dynamic market encourages innovative behavior, given the knowledge that innovation encourages technological advance and technological advance stimulates economic growth and the competitiveness of firms. However, technology-based competition erodes appropriability and in-

---

*Corresponding author. Tel.: +1-336-334-5146; fax: +1-336-334-4089.
E-mail addresses: al_link@uncg.edu (A.N. Link), john.t.scott@dartmouth.edu (J.T. Scott).

764   A.N. Link, J.T. Scott / Int. J. Ind. Organ. 19 (2001) 763–794

creases risk. Both of these factors can work against the social goals of an effective competition policy because large firms in concentrated markets may be the outcome of a market's adjustments to a regime of rapid innovation. For example, if numerous firms compete through investments in research and development (R&D), each may anticipate many competing innovations in a post-innovation market or each may anticipate a low probability that it will itself innovate. In either case, anticipated appropriable profits from the R&D investments may be too small, and the risk that the post-innovation market profits for the firm would fall below its required rate of return may be too large, to allow socially optimal innovative investments in such competitive markets. Schumpeter (1950) reasoned that the large firms that dominate industrial markets —markets with resources concentrated in the control of a few leading firms —would be able to use the profits from their market power in pre-innovation markets to provide internal finance and insurance funds to cover the risks of innovative investments.

The tradeoff between multiple independent firms competing and the benefits of coordination to reduce risk and appropriability problems is not new to the arena of competition policy, and there are at least two policy responses. One policy approach to deal with the tradeoff was the passage of the National Cooperative Research Act (NCRA) of 1984 (PL-98-462). This Act culminated a five-year effort to ease the antitrust treatment of collaborative research by creating a registration process, later expanded by the National Cooperative Research and Production Act (NCRPA) of 1993 (PL-103-42), under which research joint ventures (RJVs) can disclose the names of their members and their research intentions to the U.S. Department of Justice. RJVs gain two significant benefits from such voluntary filing: if subjected to antitrust action, they are evaluated under a rule of reason that considers a venture's effects on social welfare; and if found to fail a rule-of-reason analysis, they are subject to actual rather than treble damages.[1] However, in certain circumstances cooperative R&D may result in the loss of socially desirable competitive pressures (Scott, 1993). Competitive pressures may be desirable because they would provide socially useful parallel paths for research or desirable diversity, but if such pressures are incompatible with sufficient appropriability of returns, then a second policy might prove useful to allow desirable innovative investment at the same time that competitive pressure exists.

A second policy approach to deal with the tradeoff is the one posited and evaluated in this paper. This policy mechanism involves partial public funding of privately-performed research. The objective of such 'public/private partnership competition policy' is to mitigate the appropriability and risk problems that would inevitably occur in a dynamic market when substantial competitive pressures are present. Such a policy would not only complement the existing RJV-related

---

[1] Filing with the Department of Justice is distinct from the decision of whether to form an RJV or not. For a review of analyses of the formation decision see Hagedoorn et al. (2000).

A.N. Link, J.T. Scott / Int. J. Ind. Organ. 19 (2001) 763–794   765

policies, but it would also specifically benefit small and medium-sized enterprises (SMEs). A large body of literature suggests that SMEs face significant finance constraints.[2] In particular, SMEs are most likely to face imperfect financial markets where transaction costs preclude access to impacted information. Thus, given the market structures now encouraged by antitrust and competition policy, SMEs may require public funding to achieve socially desirable research.

There is a tradeoff between SMEs, that bring many independent sources of innovative ideas, and large, dominant firms with market power. Large firms with market power may be able to realize advantages of firm size, and their market power may stimulate R&D investment as well. In fact, Schumpeter (1950, p. 87) emphasized that market power might be necessary to provide internal funds for R&D investments:

> *We must ... recognize the ... fact that restrictive practices [monopoly restriction of output to raise price] ... acquire a new significance in the perennial gale of creative destruction, a significance which they would not have in a stationary state or in a state of slow and balanced growth. In either of these cases restrictive strategy would produce no result other than an increase in profits at the expense of buyers except that, in the case of balanced advance, it might still prove to be the easiest and most effective way of collecting the means by which to finance additional investment. But in the process of creative destruction, restrictive practices may do much to steady the ship and to alleviate temporary difficulties.*

There are typically different ways of creating innovative solutions to problems. Given the assumption that numerous firms, perhaps to avoid rent-destroying competition in post-innovation markets, independently pursue different solutions (Scott, 1991; Cohen and Klepper, 1992), society would like competition and independent sources of initiative to survive in the market. Under such conditions, however, it may be difficult to finance R&D. In fact, because of difficulties appropriating sufficient returns, it may be difficult to even justify investing in R&D. The policy we set forth overcomes the appropriability hurdle; it allows for more competitive market structures and independent sources of innovative initiative (with associated appropriability problems as numerous competitors can benefit from the innovative investments of any particular firm), while still generating sufficient R&D investments.

In Section 2, we discuss market failure and the concomitant problem of underinvestment in R&D. In Section 3, we describe the illustrative case analysis for this paper, namely a set of privately-performed projects that received partial

---

[2] See Lerner (1996); Hall (1992); Hao and Jaffe (1993); Himmelberg and Petersen (1994) and Hubbard (1998).

766   *A.N. Link, J.T. Scott / Int. J. Ind. Organ. 19 (2001) 763–794*

public funding from the Advanced Technology Program (ATP) at the National Institute of Standards and Technology (NIST). In Section 4, we set forth a conceptual model for estimating the expected private rate of return and the expected social rate of return associated with these research projects, and we implement our model using these ATP project data. Our analysis in this section quantifies the size of the gap between the social and private rate of return. Section 5 concludes the paper with a recapitulation of our quantitative estimates, and then draws on the implications of those estimates to generalize about how policy makers might proceed to formulate a public/private partnership competition policy to effectively stimulate innovative behavior in the private sector. We observe that one implication of the gap between the social and private rate of return (private rate of return with and without public support) is that 'financial engineering' could be used to leverage the public funds that stimulate innovative investment.[3] We posit that if a bidding mechanism were implemented, following Scott (1998), there would be net social cost savings.

2. Market failure and underinvestments in R&D

The purpose of this section is threefold: to provide an overview of the economic concept of market failure, to provide interview information to demonstrate that the projects analyzed in Section 3 would not have been undertaken in the absence of public ATP support, and to describe the elements of market failure that would have brought about such an underinvestment in R&D.

2.1. Underinvestments in R&D

Many point to President Bush's 1990 *U.S. Technology Policy* as the Nation's first formal domestic technology policy statement. Albeit an important initial policy effort, it however failed to articulate a foundation for government's role in technology. Rather, it implicitly assumed that government had a role, and then set forth the general statement (1990, p. 2):

> *The goal of U.S. technology policy is to make the best use of technology in achieving the national goals of improved quality of life for all Americans, continued economic growth, and national security.*

President Clinton took a major step forward from the 1990 policy statement in

---

[3] According to Scott (1998), financial engineering, a primarily European term, refers to the optimal amount and design of public funding of privately performed investments in technology and innovation carried out by public/private partnerships.

A.N. Link, J.T. Scott / Int. J. Ind. Organ. 19 (2001) 763–794   767

his *Economic Report of the President* (1994) by articulating first principles about why government should be involved in the technological process (1994, p. 191):

> *The goal of technology policy is not to substitute the government's judgment for that of private industry in deciding which potential 'winners' to back. Rather, the point is to correct market failure* ...[4]

Subsequent Executive Office policy statements have echoed this theme; *Science in the National Interest* (1994) and *Science and Technology: Shaping the Twenty-First Century* (1998) are the most recent such examples.

Market failure, as we address it in this paper and of the type which could specifically be termed "technological or innovation market failure," refers to a condition under which the market, including both the R&D-investing producers of a technology and the users of the technology, underinvests from society's standpoint in a particular technology. Such underinvestment occurs because conditions exist that prevent organizations from fully realizing or appropriating the benefits created by their investments. In our explanation of market failure and the reasons for market failure, we essentially reiterate and apply the seminal work of Arrow (1962) in which he identified three sources of market failure related to knowledge-based innovative activity —uncertainty, non-exclusivity, and public goods.

To explain, consider a marketable technology to be produced through an R&D process where conditions prevent full appropriation of benefits. Other firms will realize some of the profits from the innovation, and of course consumers will typically place a higher value on a product than the price paid for it. A firm will then calculate, because of such conditions, that the marginal benefits it can receive from a unit investment in such R&D will be less than could be earned in the absence of the conditions reducing the appropriated benefits of R&D below their potential, namely the full social benefits. Then, the firm may underinvest in R&D relative to what it would have chosen as its investment in the absence of the conditions. Stated alternatively, the firm may determine that its private rate of return is less than its private hurdle rate and therefore will not undertake socially valuable R&D.

2.2. Barriers to technology

Risk and difficulties appropriating returns create barriers to technology, and as a result, there may be an underinvestment in or underutilization of a technology. The premise that markets may fail to undertake socially optimal amounts of R&D has

---

[4] The conceptual importance of identifying market failure for policy is also emphasized, although without any operational guidance, in Office of Management and Budget (1996).

768   A.N. Link, J.T. Scott / Int. J. Ind. Organ. 19 (2001) 763–794

long been accepted by economists and is now being invoked by policy makers, as the quoted passage from President Clinton above makes clear.[5] Much of the technological market failure literature focuses on underinvestments in the creation or production of technology through R&D. However, the arguments set forth below are generalizable to the purchase and utilization of the technology that results from R&D.

As a starting point to discuss barriers to technology, the concept of risk must be defined. In its most general form, risk measures the probability that actual outcomes will deviate from the expected outcome. So defined, risk can be characterized in terms of the variance of the distribution of possible outcomes centered around the expected outcome.

Our definition of risk, for the purpose of this paper and for the purpose of proffering a public/private partnership competition policy, follows from the following general statement. We use a definition of risk that is focused on the operational concern with the downside outcomes for an investment. The shortfall of the private expected outcomes from society's expected returns reflects appropriability problems. As Arrow (1962) explained, investments in knowledge entail uncertainty of two types —technical and market. The technical and market results from technology may be very poor, or perhaps considerably better than the expected outcome. Thus, a firm is justifiably concerned about the risk that its R&D investment will fail, technically or for any other reason. Or, if technically successful, the R&D investment output may not pass the market test for profitability. Further, the firm's private expected return typically falls short of the expected social return as previously discussed. We elaborate on this concept of downside risk in Section 4 below.

There are several related technological and market factors that will cause private firms to appropriate less return and to face greater risk than society does. These factors underlie what Arrow (1962) identifies as the non-exclusivity and public good characteristics of investments in the creation of knowledge. The private firms' incomplete appropriation of social returns in the context of technical and market risk can make risk in its operational sense unacceptably large for the private firm considering an investment. Operationally, Tassey (1997), for example, defines risk as the probability that a project's rate of return falls below a required, private rate of return or private hurdle rate (as opposed to simply deviating from an expected return). As we illustrate below (both in concept and in terms of the specific ATP-funded projects), for many socially desirable investments, the private firm faces an unacceptably large probability of a rate of return that falls short of its private hurdle rate. Yet, from society's perspective, the probability of a rate of

---

[5] There is an excellent theoretical and empirical literature that concludes that the private sector will underinvest in R&D because of market failures. A survey of that literature is beyond the scope of this report, but one recent review is in Martin and Scott (1998, 2000).

return that is less than the social hurdle rate is sufficiently small that the project is still worthwhile.

There are a number of factors that can explain why a firm will perceive that its expected private rate of return will fall below its hurdle rate. Individuals will differ not only about a listing of such factors because they are not generally mutually exclusive, but also they will differ about the relative importance of one factor compared to another in whatever taxonomy is agreed upon.

First, high technical risk (that is, outcomes may not be technically sufficient to meet needs) may cause market failure given that when the firm is successful, the private returns fall short of the social returns. The risk of the activity being undertaken is greater than the firm can accept, although if successful there would be very large benefits to society as a whole. Society would like the investment to be made, but from the perspective of the firm, the present value of expected returns is less than the investment cost and is thus less than the amount yielding its acceptable return on investment.

Second, high risk can relate to high commercial or market risk (although technically sufficient, the market may not accept the innovation —reasons can include factors listed subsequently such as imitation or competing substitutes or interoperability issues) as well as to technical risk when the requisite R&D is highly capital intensive. The project may require too much capital for any one firm to feel comfortable with the outlay. The minimum cost of conducting research is thus viewed as excessive relative to the firm's overall R&D budget, which considers the costs of outside financing and the risks of bankruptcy. In this case, the firm will not make the investment, although society would be better off if it had, because the project does not appear to be profitable from the firm's private perspective.

Third, many R&D projects are characterized by a lengthy time interval until a commercial product reaches the market. The time expected to complete the R&D and the time until commercialization of the R&D results are long, and the realization of a cash flow from the R&D investment is in the distant future. If a private firm faces greater risk than society does, and as a result requires a greater rate of return and hence applies a higher discount rate than society does, it will value future returns less than does society. Because the private discount rate exceeds the social discount rate, there may be underinvestment, and the underinvestment increases as the time to market increases because the difference in the rate is compounded and has a bigger effect on returns further into the future.

Fourth, it is not uncommon for the scope of potential markets to be broader than the scope of the individual firm's market strategies so the firm will not perceive or project economic benefits from all potential market applications of the technology. As such, the firm will consider in its investment decisions only those returns that it can appropriate within the boundaries of its market strategies. While the firm may recognize that there are spillover benefits to other markets, and while it could possibly appropriate them, such benefits are ignored or discounted heavily relative

770   A.N. Link, J.T. Scott / Int. J. Ind. Organ. 19 (2001) 763–794

to the discount weight that would apply to society. A similar situation arises when the requirements for conducting R&D demand multidisciplinary research teams; unique research facilities not generally available with individual companies; or 'fusing' technologies from heretofore separate, non-interacting parties. The possibility for opportunistic behavior in such thin markets may make it impossible, at reasonable cost, for a single firm to share capital assets even if there were not R&D information sharing difficulties to compound the problem. If society, perhaps through a technology-based public institution, could act as an honest broker to coordinate a cooperative multifirm effort, then the social costs of the multidisciplinary research might be less than the market costs.[6]

Fifth, the evolving nature of markets requires investments in combinations of technologies that, if they existed, would reside in different industries that are not integrated. Because such conditions often transcend the R&D strategy of firms, such investments are not likely to be pursued. That is not only because of the lack of recognition of possible benefit areas or the perceived inability to appropriate whatever results, but also because coordinating multiple players in a timely and efficient manner is cumbersome and costly. Again, as with the multidisciplinary research teams, society may be able to use a technology-based public institution to act as an honest broker and reduce costs below those that the market would face.

Sixth, a situation can exist when the nature of the technology is such that it is difficult to assign intellectual property rights. Knowledge and ideas developed by a firm that invests in technology may spill over to other firms during the R&D phase or after the new technology is introduced into the market. If the information creates value for the firms that benefit from the spillovers, then other things being equal, the innovating firms may underinvest in the technology. Relatedly, when competition in the development of new technology is very intense, each firm, knowing that the probability of being the successful innovator is low, may not anticipate sufficient returns to cover costs. Further, even if the firm innovates, intense competition in application can result because of competing substitute goods, whether patented or not. Especially when the cost of imitation is low, an individual firm will anticipate such competition and may therefore not anticipate returns sufficient to cover the R&D investment costs. Of course, difficulties appropriating returns need not always inhibit R&D investment (Baldwin and Scott, 1987). First-mover advantages associated with customer acceptance and demand as well as increasing returns as markets are penetrated and production expanded can imply that an innovator wins most of the rewards even if it does not 'take all.'

Seventh, industry structure may raise the cost of market entry for applications of

---

[6] See Leyden and Link (1999) on the role of a federal laboratory as an honest broker.

A.N. Link, J.T. Scott / Int. J. Ind. Organ. 19 (2001) 763–794   771

the technology. The broader market environment in which a new technology will be sold can significantly reduce incentives to invest in its development and commercialization because of what some scholars have called technological lock-in and path dependency.[7] Many technology-based products are part of larger systems of products. Under such industry structures, if a firm is contemplating investing in the development of a new product but perceives a risk that the product, even if technically successful, will not interface with other products in the system, the additional cost of attaining compatibility or interoperability may reduce the expected rate of return to the point that the project is not undertaken. Similarly, multiple sub-markets may evolve, each with its own interface require- ments, thereby preventing economies of scale or network externalities from being realized. Again, society, perhaps through a technology-based public institution, may be able to help the market's participants coordinate successful compatibility and interoperability.

Eighth, situations exist where the complexity of a technology makes agreement with respect to product performance between buyer and seller costly. Sharing of the information needed for the exchange and development of technology can render the needed transactions between independent firms in the market prohibi- tively costly if the incentives for opportunistic behavior are to be reduced to a reasonable level with what Teece (1980) calls obligational contracts. Teece emphasizes that the successful transfer of technology from one firm to another often requires careful teamwork with purposeful interactions between the seller and the buyer of the technology. In such circumstances, both the seller of the technology and the buyer of the technology are exposed to hazards of opportun- ism. Sellers, for example, may fear that buyers will capture the know-how too cheaply or use it in unexpected ways. Buyers may worry that the sellers will fail to provide the necessary support to make the technology work in the new environ- ment; or they may worry that after learning about the buyer's operations in sufficient detail to transfer the technology successfully, the seller would back away from the transfer and instead enter the buyer's industry as a technologically sophisticated competitor. Once again, if society can use a technology-based public institution to act as an honest broker, the social costs of sharing technology may be less than market costs.

These eight factors that create, individually or in combination, barriers to technology and thus lead to a private underinvestment in R&D are listed in Table 1. While we have discussed these factors individually above, and have listed them

---

[7] See David (1987) for detailed development of the ideas of path dependency in the context of business strategies and public policy toward innovation and diffusion of new technologies.

Table 1
Factors creating barriers to technology in the TIMA projects

1. High technical risk associated with the underlying R&D	2
2. High capital costs to undertake the underlying R&D	6
3. Long time to complete the R&D and commercialize the resulting technology	1
4. Underlying R&D spills over to multiple markets and is not appropriable	7
5. Market success of the technology depends on technologies in different industries	2
6. Property rights cannot be assigned to the underlying R&D	5
7. Resulting technology must be compatible and interoperable with other technologies	7
8. High risk of opportunistic behavior when sharing information about the technology	0

in the table as if they are discrete phenomena, they are interrelated and overlapping, although in principle any one factor could be sufficient to cause a private firm to underinvest in R&D (see Tassey, 1997).

3. Overcoming market failure through public/private partnerships

3.1. The Advanced Technology Program

The Advanced Technology Program (ATP) was established within the National Institute of Standards and Technology (NIST) through the Omnibus Trade and Competitiveness Act of 1988, and modified by the American Technology Preeminence Act of 1991. The goals of the ATP, as stated in its enabling legislation, are to assist U.S. businesses in creating and applying the generic technology and results necessary to "[c]ommercialize significant new scientific discoveries and technologies rapidly, and refine manufacturing technologies."[8] More specifically:[9]

> The goal of the ATP is to benefit the U.S. economy by cost-sharing research with industry to foster new, innovative technologies. The ATP invests in risky, challenging technologies that have the potential for a big pay-off for the nation's economy. These technologies create opportunities for new, world-class products, services and industrial processes, benefiting not just the ATP participants, but other companies and industries and ultimately consumers and taxpayers as well. By reducing the early-stage R&D risks for individual

---

[8] The term 'generic technology' does not have a generally accepted definition. It is not a National Science Foundation reporting category of R&D spending (Link, 1996). Tassey (1992, pp. 98–99) offers the following definition: "generic technology research is a major step in the sequential evolution of a typical industrial technology. It is the organization of scientific principles into a *functional technical concept*."

[9] http://www.atp.nist.gov/atp/imp_fact.htm.

A.N. Link, J.T. Scott / Int. J. Ind. Organ. 19 (2001) 763–794   773

companies, the ATP enables industry to pursue promising technologies which otherwise would be ignored or developed too slowly to compete in rapidly changing world markets.

ATP received its first appropriation from Congress in FY 1990, and held its first general competition in that same year. Since 1994, ATP has sponsored a number of focused program competitions in addition to its general competitions. According to ATP:[10]

> [*Focused programs are*] *multi-year efforts aimed at specific, well-defined technology and business goals. These programs, which involve the parallel development of a suite of interlocking R&D projects, tackle major technology problems with high payoff potential which cannot be solved by an occasional project coming through the general competition.*

One such focused program is the Technologies for the Integration of Manufacturing Applications (TIMA) Program. There was a TIMA competition in 1995 from which four research projects were selected to receive ATP support, and in 1997 there was a second TIMA competition from which six research projects were funded.

3.2. The TIMA focused research program

The overall goal of the TIMA focused program is to develop and demonstrate the technologies needed to create affordable, integrable manufacturing systems. Many manufacturing companies need to respond more rapidly to changing markets and evolving opportunities if they are to remain competitive in global markets. Although this need is widely recognized, manufacturers find it difficult to implement the technologies needed for them to become more agile producers. Even highly automated plants and factories struggle to adapt successfully and efficiently and reconfigure production processes to accommodate design changes and new product lines. Customized systems integration efforts are often needed to achieve such changes, but they are not undertaken primarily because of idiosyncrasies in manufacturing software and incompatibilities among software applications.

Typically, factory-floor information systems focus on the operation of production equipment and the control of processes. The systems communicate neither directly nor regularly with administrative information systems, or with design and engineering systems. As a result, upstream information systems are unaware of

---

[10] http://www.atp.nist.gov/atp/focusprg.htm.

774   *A.N. Link, J.T. Scott / Int. J. Ind. Organ. 19 (2001) 763–794*

important manufacturing details. Middle-level information systems, known as manufacturing execution systems (MES), bridge this critical information gap.

MES solutions, complex and burdensome as they may be, can be solved by contracting with a large systems provider or integrator. However, once a manufacturer has incurred such a substantial investment it is likely to become dependent on that single vendor and thereby become unaware of, or if aware likely ignore, other vendors that may have more economical or innovative solutions. Because the initial solution involves a re-engineering of the manufacturer's business processes to be compatible with the vendor's requirements, even large manufacturers that can afford the up-front investment cost will by-pass the use of MES technology.

TIMA technologies are expected to benefit a range of companies: companies that employ MES by providing them with a wider range of powerful, integrable applications that will dramatically improve the manufacturer's ability to reconfigure, scale, and adapt their processes; small- and medium-sized manufacturers by making MES more affordable and by providing a direct path toward greater automation through incremental addition of compatible applications; and vendors of MES products by expanding the market, lowering barriers to entry, stimulating innovation, and technical specialization. Consumers may benefit from the adoption of these technologies in at least two ways, a higher quality product and a lower priced product to the extent that greater automation increases competition.

ATP identified a contact person for each of the ten ATP-funded TIMA projects.[11] We interviewed seven individuals corresponding to eight of the ten funded projects.[12] Each of these individuals was asked: *In the absence of ATP funding, would this research have been undertaken?* Three of the eight projects are single participant projects and five are joint ventures. All five of the research joint-venture respondents answered that no, in the absence of ATP funding, the joint venture would not have been formed and that in the absence of the joint venture their companies would not have undertaken the research. For the three

---

[11] Detailed project descriptions are available from the authors upon request. The ten projects, along with the sponsoring companies, are: Model-Driven Application & Integration Components for MES, sponsored by Vitria Technology, Inc.; An Agent-Based Framework for Integrated Intelligent Planning–Execution, sponsored by IBM Manufacturing Solutions Unit; Advanced Process Control Framework Initiative, sponsored by Honeywell Technology Center; Solutions for MES-Adaptable Replicable Technology (SMART), sponsored by National Industrial Information Infrastructure Protocols Consortium; Virtual Reality Telecollaborative Integrated Manufacturing Environment (VRTIME), sponsored by Searle; Process Integration Using Model-Driven Engines, sponsored by Vitria Technology, Inc.; Agent-Enhanced Manufacturing System Initiative, sponsored by Advanced Micro Devices; EECOMS: Extended Enterprise Coalition for Integrated Collaborative Manufacturing Systems, sponsored by IBM Corporation, CIIMPLEX; Distributed Factory System Framework; sponsored by Consilium, Inc.; ANTS Scheduling and Execution System, sponsored by Denab Robotics, Inc.

[12] One respondent was the contact person for two projects. Vitria Technology, Inc. chose not to participate in this study without explanation. Vitria Technology is involved in two research projects.

A.N. Link, J.T. Scott / Int. J. Ind. Organ. 19 (2001) 763–794   775

single participant projects, one respondent reported that the research would not have been undertaken without ATP funding. One reported that maybe the research would have been undertaken but it would have been at a reduced level. One reported that maybe the research would have been undertaken but it would have been at a slower pace.

Respondents were asked to describe their understanding of the characteristics of technical risk (the project being technically successful) and market risk (the project being commercially successful) associated with the research project, and how that risk affected the fact that their company could not have undertaken the research at all or at the same level, scope, and speed in the absence of ATP funding. Of course, risks inherent in the project are viewed in the context of the respondent's firm, and we cannot be certain to what degree the perceived risk reflects risk inherent in the project and to what degree it reflects the capabilities of the firm. Table 1 is used as a summary device for generalizing from the responses given during the interviews and tallying the responses indicating the various barriers. Again, these barriers to technology are listed as if they are discrete phenomenon, when in reality they are interrelated. More than eight responses are recorded in Table 1; there were numerous occasions where we inferred from the respondent's discussion that there was more than one barrier to technology, that is, more than one reason for their underinvestment in R&D.

The tally in Table 1 captures our interpretation of the discussions with the project leaders of the TIMA projects. As such, the tally may underestimate the magnitude of the importance of some of the barriers to technology that can lead to market failure. Given this caveat, at least two interesting patterns emerge from Table 1. One, the TIMA research projects are characterized by both technical and market risk. Technical risk is explicitly cited only twice, although it may be evident in the cases where there are concerns about the large capital cost needed to undertake the research and in the cases of concern about interoperability with other technologies. Market risk is primarily evident in the need for the resulting technology (generic technology to be applied to software development) to interface with users' information technology. The respondents discussed with us each aspect of risk, and they emphasized the interfacing issues and interoperability issues. We concluded those issues were the major sources of risk contributing to market failure.

4. Toward a public/private partnership competition policy

4.1. The conceptual model

Jaffe (1998, p. 18) argues that for ATP to be effective in achieving its statutory objectives, it "must try to determine which projects proposed to it will generate large spillovers ... "[13] His arguments that lead to this conclusion assume that ATP should only select those projects that would not be funded by the private sector in the absence of ATP funding, or if funded would be funded at a considerably lower level so that only partial results would have been realized and these results would have taken longer to occur. Jaffe points to a number of ATP-sponsored studies and an independent study by the General Accounting Office. These studies conclude that ATP grantees are of the opinion that their research would not have taken place in the absence of ATP funding or would have been funded at a considerably lower level and hence would have taken place only partially and would have taken considerably longer to complete. However, Jaffe's argument also sets general parameters for a broader public/private partnership competition policy, as we discuss in the concluding section of this paper.

Fig. 1 illustrates Jaffe's conclusion.[14] The social rate of return is measured on the vertical axis along with society's hurdle rate on investments in R&D; the private rate of return is measured on the horizontal axis along with the private hurdle rate on R&D. A 45-degree line (dashed) is imposed on the figure under the assumption that the social rate of return from an R&D investment will at least equal the private rate of return from that same investment. Two separate research

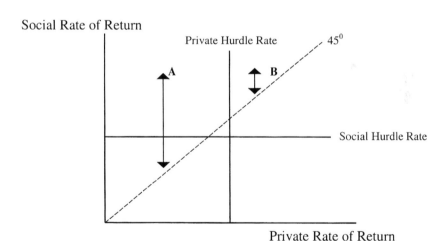

Fig. 1. Spillover gap between social and private rates of return to R&D.

---

[13] Jaffe does not quantify what a 'large' spillover is. Neither he nor we can define such a concept in the absence of a benchmark. Rather, we present below an estimate of the size of the spillover gap that characterizes the TIMA projects.

[14] See Link (1998, 1999) for a more detailed discussion of public/private partnerships and related public policy relative to this diagram.

projects are labeled Project A and Project B. Each, for our purposes, is shown with the same expected social rate of return.

For project A, the private rate of return is less than the private hurdle rate because of barriers to technology. As such, the private firm will not choose to invest in project A, although the social benefits from undertaking the project would be great. The vertical distance marked by project A is, in the Jaffe sense, the spillover gap; it results from the additional value society would receive above what the private firm would receive if project A were undertaken. Project A is precisely the type of project in which the public should invest, namely one in which the private sector would not invest because of market failure and one from which society would greatly benefit. In contrast, project B yields the same social rate of return as project A, but most of that return is capturable by the innovator, and the private rate of return is greater than the private hurdle rate. Hence, project B is one in which the private sector has an incentive to invest on its own or, alternatively stated, there is no economic justification for public funds being allocated to support project B.

Referring back to the interview information suggesting that the research projects would not have been undertaken or would have been undertaken at a reduced level or pace, we conclude that the TIMA research projects have similar characteristics to those of Project A in Fig. 1 in that each of the respondents views the expected private rate of return absent ATP funds to be less than his company's private hurdle rate. Hence, these TIMA projects are valid candidates for ATP support in the Jaffe sense, and in the broad sense these are the types of projects that a public/private partnership competition policy could affect.

Fig. 1 is the conceptual basis for understanding the result that public funding has on projects subject to market failure, as discussed above. And, Fig. 1 is useful for motivating the formulation of the competition policy that we set forth in Section V below. However, for completeness, it is also important as groundwork to illustrate what happens to the entire distribution of the rate of return as ATP (or any public agency) adds funds to a project like Project A in Fig. 1. This illustration emphasizes the concept of risk that underlies the above discussion of market failure.

ATP support of a private research project, whether it be a project with a single participant or a joint venture, reduces the risk that characterizes the project. In terms of Fig. 1, ATP's support shifts project A to the right so that the firm's private rate of return is then greater than its private hurdle rate.

In Fig. 2, we alternatively illustrate that reduction in risk in terms of a rightward shift in the distribution of the rate of return for the private firms. We illustrate the rate of return in Fig. 2 in order to illustrate our previous conceptualization of operational risk. The rightward shift of the distribution, and the concept of reducing the probability of returns lower than acceptable to the private investors, applies equally well to the absolute level of net return (absolute return minus private investment) expected from the project.

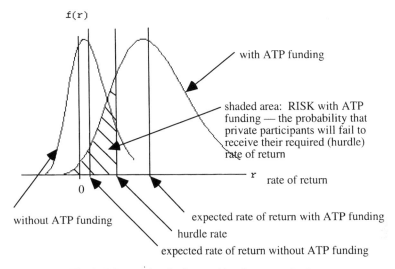

Fig. 2. Private risk reduction resulting from ATP funding.

For each distribution in Fig. 2 —without ATP funding (left distribution) and with ATP funding (right distribution) —the expected rate of return is shown. [15] As drawn, with ATP funding the expected private rate of return and the variance in the private rate of return from the research project will increase. One can generalize that this will always be the case.[16]

Consider the left distribution —the distribution of the rate of return for the private firm without ATP funding. As drawn, the private hurdle rate is to the right of the expected rate of return without ATP funding, meaning that the private firm will not undertake this research because the firm will not receive its required rate of return. The risk of the project equals the area under this without-ATP distribution that is to the left of the private hurdle rate. For those used to thinking of the variance of the distribution as the measure of risk, the downside risk —

---

[15] Note that the expected rate of return does not necessarily correspond to the greatest frequency or probability density because the distribution of rates of return need not be symmetric.

[16] The expected private rate of return with ATP support is: $r=[\text{return}-(\text{total project cost}-\text{ATP funding})]/[\text{total project cost}-\text{ATP funding}]$. Let $Z=(\text{total project cost}-\text{ATP funding})$. Then, $r=(\text{return}-Z)/Z=[(\text{return}/Z)-1]$. The variance of r is: $[(1/Z)^2\text{Var(return)}]$, and it is a general proposition that as ATP funding increases (and hence Z decreases) the variance in the private rate of return increases (since $(1/Z)$ gets larger). It is also a general proposition that the expected private rate of return $=E[(\text{return})/Z]-1]$ must increase for the same reason. Further, neither the expected social rate of return nor the variance in the social rate of return change at all. The social cost is the same and the social return is the same.

A.N. Link, J.T. Scott / Int. J. Ind. Organ. 19 (2001) 763–794   779

which is the probability of a rate of return less than the hurdle rate —may seem unusual. Variance measures the possibility that outcomes can differ from the expected outcome, while the downside risk measures the probability of an outcome departing to the downside of the hurdle rate. Note that the technical risk and the market risk for the project are reflected in the variance of the distribution —the technical goals may exceed or fall short of expectations and market acceptance of the project's technical outcomes may do the same. The downside risk refers to the outcomes that fall short of the hurdle rate.

Consider the right distribution —the distribution of the rate of return for the private firm with ATP funding. With ATP funding, the private firm will expect a return greater than its hurdle rate —the expected private rate of return with ATP funding is drawn to the right of the private hurdle rate.[17] While ATP funding will not increase the probability that the research will be successful, assuming hypothetically that it were undertaken absent ATP funding, it will reduce private risk by increasing the expected private rate of return because the expected rate of return will be based on a smaller private outlay.[18] Hence, ATP funding leverages the private firm's investment as illustrated by a greater expected return and a greater variance in the distribution as explained above.

The shaded area in Fig. 2 is what we call the downside risk of the project — that is, it is the probability that the project will yield a rate of return less than the private hurdle rate even with ATP funding. Hence, the amount of downside risk with ATP funding is visually less than the downside risk associated with the research project in the without-ATP funding case.

Although we will conclude that ATP funding reduces risk, as defined operationally in terms of reducing the probability of a rate of return below the private hurdle rate, we emphasize that our analysis below is in no way wed to any particular measure of risk or any particular model of capital asset pricing with associated systematic and non-systematic risk. Instead, our treatment encompasses any and all such models because the relevant risk, however it is perceived by private firms, is captured in the private hurdle rate, and the distributions of returns are otherwise represented by their expected values. In describing the effect of ATP funding on the distribution of private rates of return, we are describing an underlying reality that would be reflected in the private hurdle rate —as determined by some model —and in the expected value of the returns. Thus, Fig. 3 re-specifies Fig. 1 and shows specifically the implications of ATP funding reducing downside risk.

---

[17] ATP funding need not affect the firm's private hurdle rate; that rate is set by corporate policy in most cases. Conceivably, because the operational measure of risk falls, the hurdle rate might fall as well in the presence of ATP funding, and the simulative effect of ATP funding would hold a fortiori.

[18] To capture the idea of limited liability for investors, we bound that return below by zero. Thus, the rate of return can be quite negative when the return falls below the amount invested, but because the return is bounded below at zero, the rate of return is bounded below by (-100%).

Social Rate of Return

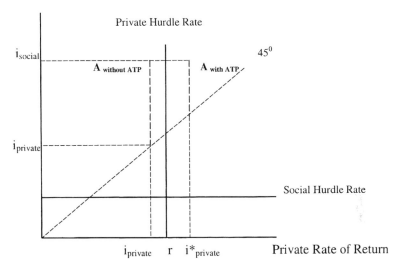

Fig. 3. Spillover gap between social and private rates of return to ATP-funded TIMA research.

4.2. Quantifying the conceptual model

Based on our extensive interviews with contact individuals in the TIMA projects, we collected quantitative information on the variables noted in the first two columns of Table 2.

We relied on these project-specific data to calculate the critical values shown above in Fig. 3. In particular, we calculate the expected social rate of return associated with the TIMA projects, i_{social}; the private rate of return without ATP funding, $i_{private}$; and the private rate of return with ATP funding, $i^*_{private}$. Given our understanding developed in the interviews along with the derived estimates for these critical values we conclude:

- The private rate of return to TIMA projects is less than the private hurdle rate, hence these projects would not have been pursued without ATP support, as initially inferred from interviews.
- There are spillover benefits to society associated with these TIMA projects as evidenced by the size of the spillover gap, $(i_{social} - i_{private})$.

For our calculation of the expected social rate of return from TIMA research projects, we calculate a lower bound for the expected social rate of return in two different ways. One, we calculate the expected social rate of return for each of the eight TIMA projects studied, and then we average across the rates; and two, we first average the eight project-specific data for each relevant variable, and then

A.N. Link, J.T. Scott / Int. J. Ind. Organ. 19 (2001) 763–794   781

Table 2
Descriptive statistics on values used in the estimation of the social rate of return ($n=8$)

Variable	Definition	Mean	Standard deviation
d	Duration of the ATP project	2.51 years	0.578
C	Total cost of the ATP project	$12,749,125	1.16e+07
A	ATP funding	$6,421,875	5.48e+06
r	Private hurdle rate	0.25	0.063
z	Duration of the extra period of development	1.03 years	0.619
F	Additional cost for the extra period of development	$1,644,784	1.35e+06
T	Life of the commercialized technology	7.69 years	3.96
m	Proportion of producer surplus appropriated by the participants in their particular application of the generic technology	0.675	0.152
k	Proportion of total applications of the generic technology developed by the project addressed by the participants' applications	0.216	0.118
v	Proportion of producer surplus appropriated	0.135	0.071
L	Lower bound for expected annual private return to investing firm	$5,250,439	5.59e+06
U	Upper bound for expected annual private return to the investing firm	$9,885,615	1.05e+07

second estimate one expected social rate of return based on average data for each variable. We will use the latter calculation in our exposition, but the results of both methods are presented. Neither of these methods precisely characterizes the expected social rate of return to the TIMA research program, but each approximates what might be called an expected social rate of return for an average TIMA research project.

The calculation of the expected social rates of return using each of our two methods relies on information collected during the telephone interviews and information published by ATP about each project. Interview respondents were assured that their individual responses would remain confidential; hence only the average values of interview data and derived metrics are reported herein. The mean values and standard deviations for all of these variables are in the last two columns of Table 2.

Data related to project duration, d, total project cost, C, and the level of ATP funding, A, are reported in ATP's Project Brief for each project provided to us by ATP. Data on the next six variables — r, z, F, T, m, and k —were obtained through the interview process.

Respondents were asked the following question about their private hurdle rate, r: *For projects like this one, what is your company's hurdle rate or minimum expected rate of return over the life of the project?*

Regarding the duration of the extra period of development, z, and the additional research cost for the extra period of development, F, respondents were asked:

Approximately, how soon after the project's completion will the technology be commercialized? And, *Approximately, what is the level of the additional investment expenditures expected to be made by your company during this period?*

Once commercialized, the life of the technology, *T*, was determined from responses to the question: *Approximately, what is the projected life of the technology being developed?*

The variable *v* represents the proportion of producer surplus appropriated by the project team; larger (smaller) values of *v* are interpreted to mean that less (more) spillover of technical knowledge is anticipated and thus appropriability problems are less (more) critical. From an analytical perspective, this is a critical value for our analysis. We calculated *v* as the product of two information data collected from the interviews. It equals the product of the proportion (*m*) of total profits anticipated from the development and commercialization of the specific software being developed, and the proportion (*k*) of all possible applications of the generic technology addressed by the specific software being researched in the ATP project.[19] Thus *v*, the product of these two interview elements, is the total proportion of the value of the technology appropriable by the researching firms. Loosely speaking, and focusing on the mean values in Table 2, the funded firms expect to appropriate about 70 percent (*m*) of the market value of the software they are developing in the 20 percent (*k*) (by value) of the applications areas they are focusing on. Roughly, the funded firms expect to capture about 14 percent of the profit potential of the generic technology being developed, and 86 percent of the profit potential associated with the generic technology being developed will spill over to imitators.

The variables *L* and *U* are discussed just below.

Given the published data in the Project Briefs and interview data on each of the variables noted in Table 2, the first step in the calculation of the expected social rate of return is to calculate the variable *L*, the lower bound for the annual expected private return from a TIMA research project. *L* is a derived variable. It was derived for each of the eight projects using project-specific data as reported in Table 2. It was also calculated separately using the averaged values of each relevant variable, as discussed in our exposition below of the 'average' TIMA project.

Eq. (1) consists of three general terms. Each term represents the present value for a particular flow that is realized over a particular time period. The first term in the equation represents the present value of the negative cash flows that result to the firm from the cost of conducting the project, $C - A$, from its start to its expected completion, $t = 0$ to *d*. The second term is the present value of the future negative cash flows from the additional cost, *F*, of taking the generic technology

---

[19] Seven of the eight participants offered an estimate of *m* and *k*. For the eighth project we imputed a value of *m* and *k* equal to the average of the reporting seven. Thus, eight observations are used for the calculation of each mean in Table 2.

A.N. Link, J.T. Scott / Int. J. Ind. Organ. 19 (2001) 763–794   783

from the ATP project, at $t = d$, and commercializing it, at $t = d + z$. Finally, the third term is the present value of the expected net cash flows from the project, L, after it has been commercialized, at $t = d + z$, over its estimated life, to $t = d + z + T$. Note that the discount rate in Eq. (1) is the firm's hurdle rate, r. Therefore, the value for L that solves Eq. (1) is the value for which the private firm just earns its hurdle rate of return on the portion of the total investment that it must finance. The firm would not invest in the ATP project unless it expected at least L for the average annual private return so that its hurdle rate would exactly be met. Thus, L is a lower bound estimate.

$$-\int_0^d \left(\frac{C-A}{d}\right) e^{-rt}\, dt - \int_d^{d+z} \left(\frac{F}{z}\right) e^{-rt} dt + \int_{d+z}^{d+z+T} L\, e^{-rt}\, dt = 0$$

$$\Rightarrow\ -\left(\frac{C-A}{d}\right)\left(\frac{-1}{r}\right) e^{-rt}\, \big|_0^d -\left(\frac{F}{z}\right)\left(\frac{-1}{r}\right) e^{-rt}\, \big|_d^{d+z} +(L)\left(\frac{-1}{r}\right) e^{-rt}\, \big|_{d+z}^{d+z+T} = 0$$

$$\Rightarrow\ \left(\frac{C-A}{dr}\right)\left(e^{-rd} - 1\right) +\left(\frac{F}{zr}\right)\left(e^{-r(d+z)} - e^{-rd}\right) -\left(\frac{L}{r}\right)\left(e^{-r(d+z+T)} - e^{-r(d+z)}\right) = 0$$

$$(1)$$

Given specific values for the variables d, C, A, r, z, F, and T, Eq. (1) is solved for the unknown variable, L. To illustrate using the mean values for these seven variables from Table 2, Eq. (1) solves for L equal to $3,883,680. Again, this derived value of L is the lower bound for the estimate of the expected annual private return using the mean values of the relevant variables in Table 2. Since we will illustrate the solution of the three equations that follow also using the mean values of the relevant variables in Table 2, we will refer for ease of exposition to the solutions as those for the 'average' TIMA project.

The second step in the calculation of the estimated social rate of return is to calculate the variable U, the upper bound for the expected annual private return for each TIMA project. U was derived for each of the eight projects, by solving Eq. (2) using values for the variables in Table 2. Note that the first term in Eq. (2) is the total negative cash flow from the cost of conducting the research project, C. Thus, U is an upper bound for the annual private return because a return greater than U would imply that the firm would earn a rate of return in excess of its hurdle rate in the absence of ATP funding, and therefore ATP funding would not be required for the project. Note that all reference to ATP is purposively absent in Eq. (2) because we are calculating the expected annual private return that would result in the private firm just meeting its hurdle rate in the absence of ATP involvement.

$$-\int_0^d \left(\frac{C}{d}\right) e^{-rt}\, dt - \int_d^{d+z} \left(\frac{F}{z}\right) e^{-rt}\, dt + \int_{d+z}^{d+z+T} U\, e^{-rt}\, dt = 0$$

$$\Rightarrow\ -\left(\frac{C}{d}\right)\left(\frac{-1}{r}\right) e^{-rt}\, \Big|_0^d -\left(\frac{F}{z}\right)\left(\frac{-1}{r}\right) e^{-rt}\, \Big|_d^{d+z} +(U)\left(\frac{-1}{r}\right) e^{-rt}\, \Big|_{d+z}^{d+z+T} = 0$$

$$\Rightarrow\ \left(\frac{C}{d}\right)\left(e^{-rd} - 1\right) +\left(\frac{F}{zr}\right)\left(e^{-r(d+z)} - e^{-rd}\right) -\left(\frac{U}{r}\right)\left(e^{-r(d+z+T)} - e^{-r(d+z)}\right) = 0. \quad (2)$$

To illustrate the solution of Eq. (2), values for the variables d, C, r, z, F, and T are given. Thus, Eq. (2) solves for U. To illustrate using the mean values for these given variables in Table 2, the derived value of U is \$7,267,910. This value represents the upper bound of the annual private return for the 'average' TIMA project.

Using the mean values (other than L and U) in Table 2, an estimate of the average expected annual private return to the firm is calculated as $[(L + U)/2]$, the mean of the upper and lower bounds on the average expected annual private return for the 'average' TIMA project.[20] The average expected annual private return to the participating firm or firms equals v times the average expected annual return that will be captured by all producers using the technology (producer surplus). Knowing the average expected annual private return is $[(L + U)/2)]$ and knowing the portion of producer surplus that is appropriable, v, then total producer surplus equals $[(L + U)/2v]$ and hence this value is a lower bound for the average expected annual social return. It is a lower bound because consumer surplus has not been measured.

The expected private rate of return without ATP funding is the solution to i in Eq. (3), given solution values for L and U from Eqs. (1) and (2). The solution value of i in Eq. (3), represents the rate of return that just equates the present value of the expected annual private return to the firm to the present value of research and post-research commercialization costs to the firm in the absence of ATP funding.

$$-\int_0^d \left(\frac{C}{d}\right) e^{-it}\, dt - \int_d^{d+z} \left(\frac{F}{z}\right) e^{-it}\, dt + \int_{d+z}^{d+z+T} \left(\frac{L+U}{2}\right) e^{-it}\, dt = 0$$

$$\Rightarrow \left(\frac{C}{di}\right)(e^{-id} - 1) + \left(\frac{F}{zi}\right)(e^{-i(d+z)} - e^{-id}) - \left(\frac{L+U}{2i}\right)(e^{-i(d+z+T)} - e^{-i(d+z)}) = 0$$

$$(3)$$

The expected private rate of return without ATP funding, i, was estimated for each of the eight TIMA projects by solving Eq. (3) given the values for d, C, z, F, T, L, and U. To illustrate the solution of Eq. (3) using the mean values of the relevant variables in Table 2 along with the values derived from Eqs. (1) and (2)

---

[20] We want an estimate of the average expected annual return, and the simple average of the lower and upper bounds is the natural measure. Alternatively, one could use both L and U and obtain an upper and lower bound on each solution to Eqs. (3), (4) and (5) below. One could then think of their average as a better estimate. However, our procedure is more direct and more simply exposited, and because we have presented the values for L and U, readers interested in re-estimating Eqs. (3), (4) and (5) can do so. As we show below, our results are in general quite insensitive to the choice of computing disaggregated metrics and then aggregating across individual results, versus aggregating variables and computing a single aggregated metric.

A.N. Link, J.T. Scott / Int. J. Ind. Organ. 19 (2001) 763–794   785

of L and U for the 'average' project, the expected private rate of return for the 'average' TIMA project is 0.20 or 20 percent.

Finally, the lower bound on the social rate of return is found by solving Eq. (4) for i, given values for the other variables. Note that Eq. (4) is identical to Eq. (3) with the exception that the average expected annual private return, $[(L + U)/2]$, is replaced with the lower bound for the average expected annual social return, $[(L + U)/2v]$.

$$-\int_0^d \left(\frac{C}{d}\right) e^{-it} \, dt - \int_d^{d+z} \left(\frac{F}{z}\right) e^{-it} \, dt + \int_{d+z}^{d+z+T} \left(\frac{L+U}{2v}\right) e^{-it} \, dt = 0$$

$$\Rightarrow \left(\frac{C}{di}\right)(e^{-id} - 1) + \left(\frac{F}{zi}\right)(e^{-i(d+z)} - e^{-id}) - \left(\frac{L+U}{2iv}\right)(e^{-i(d+z+T)} - e^{-i(d+z)}) = 0$$

$$(4)$$

As with each of Eqs. (1) through (3), Eq. (4) was estimated for each of the eight TIMA projects. Again, to illustrate the solution of Eq. (4) using the average values of d, C, z, F, T, and v from Table 2 with the derived values of L and U for the 'average' project, the expected social rate of return for the 'average' TIMA project is derived to be at least 0.63 or 63 percent.

To summarize, we have extracted an expected social rate of return from our model. We first designed a set of questions that allowed us to gather the additional information, to supplement the information in the Project Briefs, needed to derive an estimate of the private benefit stream anticipated by the participants. Second, we gathered information revealing the benefits created by the project that would be captured by producers that are not participants in the project. We then had an estimate of the total producers' benefits from the project to compare with the project's costs. Thus, we use the private participant's expected benefits and the project's costs to compute the private expected rate of return. We use the total expected benefits, to all producers whether they are participants or not, to compare to the total costs for the project to compute the lower bound on the social rate of return. It is a lower bound, because we have not measured the consumer surplus created by the project for the ultimate consumers of the final goods that are made using the project's technology.

We can summarize the findings from our analysis for the 'average' TIMA research project, based on the mean values in Table 2 (excepting those for L and U) and the derived values from Eqs. (1) through (4). There are two important points to be made. First, the average expected private rate of return in the absence of ATP funding is 20 percent, clearly less than the average private hurdle rate of 25 percent since the estimate of the upper bound for the average cash flows would just allow the hurdle rate to be reached. Thus, in the absence of ATP funding the TIMA firms would not have undertaken this research, and in fact they expressed this fact explicitly as noted earlier. Second, the expected social rate of return associated with ATP's funding of the TIMA projects is at least 63 percent, and hence the projects are expected to be socially valuable.

As discussed above, we estimated Eqs. (1) through (4) for each of the eight projects. Doing so, we derived eight values for L and eight values for U (the averages for these values are shown in Table 2 and are somewhat higher than the single values derived for the 'average' project and reported in the text), and eight lower bound estimates of the expected social rate of return —one set of rates for each TIMA project. For each of the eight projects, just as for the 'average' project, the private rate of return without ATP funding of course falls short of the private hurdle rate, yet because of the spillovers the projects are all socially valuable. The average of the eight expected private rates of return absent ATP funding is 19 percent (0.19 with a standard deviation of 0.06); the average expected social rate of return is 72 percent (0.72 with a standard deviation of 0.22). These derived rates of return are observably close to our 'average' project's private and social rates of return of 20 percent and 63 percent respectively. Thus, we are comfortable using these figures to characterize the 'average' TIMA project.

Our broad-brush approach to estimating the various rates of return does not try to build in more detail for the model than the data can support. For example, instead of trying to develop the details of an unknown diffusion pattern for the generic technology, we estimated the average expected annual return over the lifetime of the technology. Our methodology gives a reasonable fix on the average expected annual private returns to the ATP project participants because we can solve for what they must be expecting as lower and upper bounds, and then we average the two expectations. What we do not know with certainty is the multiplier to apply to the participants' average annual expected returns to estimate returns to all producers. Our multiplier is based on the interview responses that estimate the variables m and k, and hence v. We do not have a good estimate of the lag from $d + z$, when the ATP project's technology is commercialized, until the technology is imitated not only by producers copying the particular application of the generic technology but also by producers developing new applications of the generic technology. Thus, because there will be some lag before imitation and because there will be some development costs for producers using the generic technology, the net average expected annual earnings to all producers using the generic technology will be somewhat less than $[(L + U)/2v]$ unless diffusion is instantaneous and costless. For the particular information technology that we are studying, the diffusion may well be relatively quick and additional development costs may well be minimal; however, the possibility that it is not the case can be modeled by lowering our multiplier $(1/v)$ to reflect the fact that if diffusion is not rapid, then the ATP participants' average annual returns are actually a larger proportion of the average social returns than the proportion v. To estimate the sensitivity of our results to the speed of the diffusion of the technology, we varied v in the following experiment. If v is increased by 10 percent, the estimated social rate of return for the 'average' TIMA project falls from 63 percent to 61 percent; if v is increased

A.N. Link, J.T. Scott / Int. J. Ind. Organ. 19 (2001) 763–794   787

by 50 percent, the estimated social rate of return falls to 54 percent; and if v is increased by 100 percent, the estimated social rate of return falls to 47 percent. Thus, our conclusion that ATP's TIMA projects are socially valuable is robust with respect to the parameter v when it is increased to capture slower diffusion rates (and any development costs to be netted out) for the applications of the generic technology.[21]

It is important to re-emphasize that the profit potential of the generic technology being developed that is appropriated by the TIMA firms represents producer surplus. Our analysis does not, as we have previously stated, attempt to capture consumer surplus, and of course consumer surplus would not be appropriated by the researching firms. Thus, when we refer to a lower bound estimate of the expected social rate of return we are explicitly acknowledging that there are social benefits to the consumer surplus generated from the TIMA research-based software, but we are just not capturing them. Thus, our social rate of return estimate for the 'average' TIMA project is clearly a lower-bound estimate.

Finally, we explicitly note that our model in Eqs. (1) through (4) is a continuous time model, as is appropriate. However, if the model is approximated as a discrete time model, we calculated that the estimated social rate of return for the 'average' TIMA project is again 63 percent, given the rounding of times to the nearest whole year and given appropriate placement (a particular choice of beginning or end of years that results in replicating the solution found with the continuous model) of the discrete cash flows. As would be expected, however, in the discrete model, the estimation is not insensitive to the placement of the cash flows, and for that reason we present and solve the more accurate continuous time model.

5. Formulating a public/private partnership competition policy for a dynamic market

The case-based analyses presented in this paper can be summarized as follows. The TIMA projects under study would not have been undertaken in the absence of ATP's public funding. Because of technical and market risk and because of appropriability issues —key elements of market failure —firms perceive that their expected rate of return had they pursued this research in the absence of ATP's support would have been less than their required rate of return. ATP funding of these projects reduces risk to the private firm. And, as a result of ATP funding, these projects are being researched and the expected social rate of return from them is estimated to be at least 63 percent.

Of course, one cannot conclude that a social rate of return of at least 63 percent is 'good' or 'bad,' or 'better' or 'worse' than expected. Those are non-axiomatic

---

[21] We thank Jeanne Powell of the ATP for raising this interesting issue.

conclusions. However, one can compare our estimate of the lower bound of the social rate of return to the opportunity cost of public funds. Following the guidelines set forth by the Office of Management and Budget (1992) to use a real discount of 7 percent for constant-dollar benefit-to-cost analyses of proposed investments and regulations, then clearly a nominal social rate of return of 63 percent is above that rate and thus is socially worthwhile.[22]

Consider Fig. 4. Project A characterizes the 'average' TIMA project. Shown is our estimated private rate of return absent ATP funding of 20 percent, and our estimated lower bound on the social rate of return of 63 percent. Hence the spillover gap associated with the average TIMA project is at least 43 percent.

In comparison to these estimates, we calculated the private rate of return with ATP funding to be 33 percent. This rate comes from the solution to Eq. (5) for i, given the mean values of d, C, A, z, F, and T from Table 2 and the derived values of L and U from Eqs. (1) and (2).

$$-\int_0^d \left(\frac{C-A}{d}\right) e^{-it} \, dt - \int_d^{d+z} \left(\frac{F}{z}\right) e^{-it} \, dt + \int_{d+z}^{d+z+T} \left(\frac{L+U}{2}\right) e^{-it} \, dt = 0$$

$$\Rightarrow \left(\frac{C-A}{di}\right)(e^{-id} - 1) + \left(\frac{F}{zi}\right)(e^{-i(d+z)} - e^{-id}) - \left(\frac{L+U}{2i}\right)(e^{-i(d+z+T)} - e^{-i(d+z)})$$

$$= 0 \tag{5}$$

Social Rate of Return

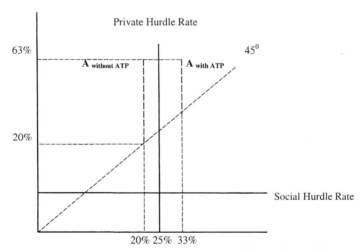

Fig. 4. Spillover gap between social and private rates of return to ATP-funded TIMA research.

[22] Link and Scott (1998) discuss the use of this guideline for NIST economic impact assessments.

A.N. Link, J.T. Scott / Int. J. Ind. Organ. 19 (2001) 763–794   789

The estimated rate of return with ATP funding of 33 percent is perhaps reasonably close to the private hurdle rate of 25 percent.[23,24] Had ATP funding been greater (less), the estimated rate of return with ATP funding would have been greater (less). However, there is no way for ATP to have calculated the optimal level of funding for these TIMA projects unless, as part of the focused program proposal, all relevant data, including hurdle rates, could have been assessed.[25] In the absence of such information, which in practice would be difficult to obtain because of, if nothing else, self-serving reporting by proposers, the funding scheme that ATP has implemented appears to be close to optimal.[26]

In principle, a bidding mechanism could be used by ATP to ensure that the

---

[23] Our estimation procedure has not forced the closeness of these rates. Although greater ATP funding (an increase in A) has no effect on our estimate of U, it does of course require that our estimate of L and hence of $[(L + U)/2]$ be lower. However, the initial private investment ($C - A$) falls as ATP funding increases, and that effect dominates causing our estimate of the private rate of return to increase as ATP funding increases. For example, if ATP funding for the average TIMA project were increased by 50 percent, our estimate of the private rate of return with ATP funding would have risen from 33 percent to 42 percent.

[24] The expected private rate of return with ATP funding was calculated for each of the eight projects. The mean of these eight rates is 0.35 or 35 percent, with a standard deviation of 0.094.

[25] The reader will note that it is mathematically possible to solve Eq. (5) for the level of ATP funding, A^*, that would equate the estimated private rate of return with ATP funding to the hurdle rate of 25 percent. Such an exercise may lack policy relevance in the sense that the calculation has the benefit of hindsight and information collected after ATP funding was allocated and furthermore we do not know the true weights for our estimated upper and lower bounds. We assume the equal weights of 0.5 for each, but although our basic conclusions about the relation between the social and private rates of return are not sensitive to that assumption, the calculation of A^* is dependent on whether the actual expected annual returns are closer to the upper or the lower bound. We believe it is safer for the ATP funding to be on the 'high side' in any case. In a separate study (Hall et al., 1998), we have found that greater ATP funding dramatically reduced the probability of termination of ATP information technology projects. The theoretical reason is clear; having more ATP funds shifts the distribution of the project to the right and lowers the probability that the private participants in the project, who are constantly monitoring the progress of the project, would want to terminate the project because the probability of an unacceptably low rate of return was too high.

[26] The above findings should be interpreted in light of three particular limitations of this paper. First, the conclusions presented here are based in part on interview data collected from a key participant in each TIMA project. As such, there is obviously some uncertainty built into the expressed estimates, although they are the best point estimates available. Perhaps more important, this interview information may be time dependent, meaning that it was collected at this particular early point in the progress of the research project. As such, the estimates presented herein are not definitive estimates to be expected at the completion of each project, but rather characterizations of the expected social benefits at this point in time. Second, we have referred to our lower bound estimate of 63 percent —although this caveat refers to any of the calculated social rates of return —as a metric to characterize the 'average' TIMA project. And third, our analyses have not specified any diffusion paths. We refrained from going beyond the limits of our data and did not attempt to model much less quantify when in time rivals will imitate the participants' applications of the generic technology, or when in time others will commercialize other aspects of the generic technology. Still, with these limitations in mind, it appears at this point in the progress of the TIMA projects that they are socially worthwhile.

private participants in TIMA research projects earn just a normal rate of return. Such a bidding mechanism is what Scott (1998) refers to as a hurdle-lowering auction.

Motivated by the case analysis of the ATP-funded TIMA projects, a broad public/private partnership competition policy should address three broad questions:

1. How can the public get the best private partner for each partnership?
2. How can society determine the optimal level of public funding for the partnership, not too much yet enough to overcome the underinvestment resulting from market failure?
3. How can society avoid the potential for opportunistic behavior to which both the government and the private sector's partners are exposed?

Below we list several premises that we argue should motivate the formulation of a public/private competition policy, along with the implementation implications of those premises.

Premise 1: The private sector knows more than the government about the investment characteristics of the technology projects —or at least has the resources to make the best estimate of the streams of returns and the risk.

Implication 1: A competition policy should include a mechanism for setting up a public/private partnership that provides the incentive for private parties to determine who is best suited to be the private partner in a public/private partnership.

Premise 2: The government desires to overcome the project's underinvestment resulting from market failure and to do so at the least cost to the public.

Implication 2: A competition policy should include a mechanism that gives the selected private partner for the public/private partnership an incentive to undertake the desired level of investment while providing a proportion of the project's funding that is consistent with a normal expected private rate of return given the appropriability and risk characteristics of the project.

Premise 3: All parties related to the public/private partnership want to overcome the potential for opportunistic behavior by the other party.

Implication 3: Policy should include a mechanism that provides both the public- and the private-sector partners an incentive to participate in the project in a way that maximizes the total value of the project's expected outcome rather than the value to the individual partner that could of course use opportunistic behavior to benefit at the expense of the overall project's results.

General characteristics of the mechanism design: What are the general characteristics of the optimal mechanism design for public/private partnerships that will achieve the desired incentives for the private sector to choose the best private partner, for the private partner(s) to carry out the desired amount of investment at the least cost to the public, and for avoiding opportunistic behavior by either the public or the private partner?

A.N. Link, J.T. Scott / Int. J. Ind. Organ. 19 (2001) 763–794   791

Consideration of the questions suggests that the optimal mechanism design for what we advocate and call a public/private competition policy would have the private parties use a contingent valuation method to bid for the right to be the private partner. In particular, the bidding could be a hybrid bidding mechanism that combines an up-front bid, a periodic payment bid, and finally a royalty bid: private firms would bid for the right to be the private partner in the public/private partnership project that the government would fund.[27] Alternatively, instead of bids being accepted directly from the companies that will be performing the R&D, private venture capital companies that would manage the public investments might bid for the rights to manage the projects.

As a simple example of how a bidding process would deliver the public funding to a public/private partnership such as any of the TIMA projects discussed in this paper, consider the following. Suppose that from society's perspective, an R&D investment project would cost $100 now and generate the expectation of $130 in one year and nothing thereafter. Suppose further that the threshold rate of return justifying public funding —society's hurdle rate —is 10 percent. Thus, the R&D project yields a social rate of return of 30 percent, which exceeds society's hurdle rate of 10 percent, and of course the net present value of $[(130/(1.1)) - 100]$ is greater than zero. Suppose that from a private perspective the project costs $100 and, because of incomplete appropriation of returns, yields the expectation of just $105 in one year. Suppose further that given the private risk the private hurdle rate is 15 percent. Thus, the private sector would not undertake the project which has an internal rate of return of 5 percent, which is less than the hurdle rate of 15 percent; and, of course, net present value is then negative.

In the context of the foregoing example, which conceptually describes each of the TIMA projects, the bidding process would work as follows. The government announces that it will 'buy' the R&D project, paying the $100 investment cost.[28] The government then opens the bidding for the right to be the private partner in the public/private partnership. Private firms will bid the amount $X such that $X(1.15)=$105, implying that $X=$91.30. The cost to the public of the project would then be $8.70. With great uncertainty about the future returns, the use of royalty bidding rather than the up-front bidding can yield more to the government. Also, private firms with better capabilities for doing the project would be expected to bid higher than those firms that are less well suited to the project.

Suppose the ATP, or the government in general, wanted to use a public/private partnership to develop a project. It would announce that it would provide an

[27] There is a large literature describing bidding mechanisms in great detail. McAfee and McMillan (1987) provide an excellent review, and they set out the general hybrid mechanism with the up-front bid as well as the royalty bid. Hansen (1985) and Samuelson (1986) provide analyses of the royalty bidding and bidding for the up-front fee and the royalty rate simultaneously.

[28] Martin and Scott (2000) provide detailed discussion of the circumstances in which market failure and underinvestment would be expected to occur; the discussion is needed to inform the identification of projects that would be funded.

up-front payment of $F to support the R&D investment project to be conducted by the winning bidder in an auction to determine the private partner(s) for the public/private partnership (and when there are several partners as in an RJV we are viewing the RJV as the partner). Further, the government pledges to provide a periodic flow of funds $C throughout the project's life to support the flow costs of the R&D project. The fixed cost $F, and the flow cost $C, correspond to the typical abstraction of the structure of costs for R&D investment projects.[29] Bidders vie for the right to be the private partner in the project by submitting a three-part bid —first a bid for how much the private firm will pay the government up-front, and second a bid on the periodic flow payment during the life of the R&D project, and third a bid on the royalty rate that it would pay the government on the innovation produced by the public/private partnership and licensed (perhaps exclusively) to the private partner.

As McAfee and McMillan (1987) make clear, in the context of the appropriate combinations of assumptions about the characteristics of the asset being auctioned and the participants in the auction and their beliefs about the value of the asset, there are nontrivial choices to be made about the exact nature of the auction. Apart from the usual choices for auctions in general, there would be choices specific to the new institutional use of auctions to determine the private partner for the public/private partnership. For example, institutional arrangements must be designed to ensure that the government's payments of $F and $C go solely for the purchase of R&D investments; the private partner's profits from the R&D investment project will come after the innovation is introduced. However, for this paper, full details of the ideal auction in different circumstances will not be developed. Instead, the paper presents the basic idea and observes that the three-part bidding mechanism proposed has the potential for leveraging public funding optimally. Should the Advanced Technology Program have undertaken such a hurdle-lowering auction ex ante, in terms of Fig. 4, the expected rate of return to the TIMA projects with ATP funding (actually estimated to be 33 percent in our model) would not have exceeded the project participant's private hurdle rate (25 percent). Hence, society would have been better off in terms of a more optimal allocation of R&D resources.

Finally, two things must be emphasized. First, the high social rates of return estimated and reported for the TIMA projects are very conservative, lower-bound estimates because they do not include consumer surplus in the benefit stream. The profits that will be generated by the technology are obviously a small proper subset of the social benefits that the technology will generate, but the estimation method measures only the return in the form of profits to the innovator and to other producers of the technology. Second, one might be skeptical about the TIMA respondents' earnest belief that the projects would not have been undertaken, or at

---

[29] See Lee and Wilde (1980).

A.N. Link, J.T. Scott / Int. J. Ind. Organ. 19 (2001) 763–794   793

least would not have been undertaken to the same extent or at the same speed, without ATP funding. If the research would have occurred without public funding, the estimated upper bound and hence the average of the upper and lower bounds for expected private returns would be too low, and the actual lower bounds for the social rates of return would be even higher than we have estimated. Further, the gap between the social and private rates of return would remain, although that would not in itself justify the public funding of the projects.

Acknowledgements

We would like to thank David B. Audretsch, William L. Baldwin, and an anonymous referee for helpful comments and suggestions.

References

Arrow, K.J., 1962. Economic welfare and the allocation of resources for invention. In: Universities — National Bureau Committee for Economic Research, The Rate and Direction of Inventive Activity. Princeton University Press, Princeton, pp. 609–625.

Baldwin, W.L., Scott, J.T., 1987. Market Structure and Technological Change. Harwood Academic Publishers, London.

Cohen, W.M., Klepper, S., 1992. The tradeoff between firm size and diversity in the pursuit of technological progress. Small Business Economics 4, 1–14.

David, P.A., 1987. Some new standards for the economics of standardization in the information age. In: Dasgupta, P., Stoneman, P. (Eds.), Economic Policy and Technological Performance. Cambridge University Press, Cambridge, England, pp. 206–239.

Economic Report of the President, 1994. Government Printing Office, Washington, DC.

Executive Office of the President, 1990. U.S. technology policy. Office of Science and Technology Policy, Washington, DC.

Hagedoorn, J., Link, A.N., Vonortas, N., 2000. Research partnerships. Research Policy 29, 567–586.

Hall, B.H., 1992. Investment and research and development: Does the source of financing matter? University of California at Berkeley Working Paper No. 92–194.

Hall, B.H., Link, A.N., Scott, J.T., 1998. Universities as partners in ATP-funded research projects. Preliminary final report submitted to the Advanced Technology Program.

Hansen, R.G., 1985. Auctions with contingent payments. American Economic Review 74, 862–865.

Hao, K.Y., Jaffe, A.B., 1993. Effect of liquidity on firms' R&D spending. Economics of Innovation and New Technology 2, 275–282.

Himmelberg, C.P., Petersen, B.C., 1994. R&D and internal finance: A panel study of small firms in high-tech industries. Review of Economics and Statistics 76, 38–51.

Hubbard, R.G., 1998. Capital-market imperfections and investment. Journal of Economic Literature 36, 193–225.

Jaffe, A.B., 1998. The importance of 'spillovers' in the policy mission of the Advanced Technology Program. Journal of Technology Transfer 23, 11–19.

Lee, T., Wilde, L.L., 1980. Market structure and innovation: a reformulation. Quarterly Journal of Economics 94, 429–436.

Lerner, J., 1996. The government as venture capitalist: The long-run impact of the SBIR program. NBER Working Paper 5753.

Leyden, D.P., Link, A.N., 1999. Federal laboratories as research partners. International Journal of Industrial Organization 17, 572–592.

Link, A.N., 1996. On the classification of R&D. Research Policy 25, 379–401.

Link, A.N., 1998. Public/private partnerships as a tool to support industrial R&D: Experiences in the United States. Final report prepared for the working group on technology and innovation policy, division of science and technology at OECD.

Link, A.N., 1999. Public/private partnerships in the United States. Industry and Innovation 6, 191–216.

Link, A.N., Scott, J.T., 1998. Public Accountability: Evaluating Technology-based Institutions. Kluwer Academic Publishers, Norwell, Massachusetts.

McAfee, R.P., McMillan, J., 1987. Auctions and bidding. Journal of Economic Literature 25, 699–738.

Martin, S., Scott, J.T., 1998. Financing and leveraging public/private partnerships. Final report prepared for the working group on technology and innovation policy, division of science and technology at OECD.

Martin, S., Scott, J.T., 2000. The nature of innovation market failure and the design of public support for private innovation. Research Policy 29, 437–447.

Office of Management and Budget, 1992. Circular No. A-94: Guidelines and discount rates for benefit-cost analysis of federal programs. Washington, DC.

Office of Management and Budget, 1996. Economic analysis of federal regulations under Executive Order 12866. Washington, DC.

Office of Science and Technology Policy, 1994. Science in the national interest. Executive Office of the President, Washington, DC.

Office of Science and Technology Policy, 1998. Science and technology: Shaping the twenty-first century. Executive Office of the President, Washington, DC.

Samuelson, W.F., 1986. Bidding for contracts. Management Science 32, 1533–1550.

Schumpeter, J.A., 1950. Capitalism, Socialism and Democracy. Harper & Row, New York.

Scott, J.T., 1991. Research diversity induced by rivalry. In: Acs, Z.J., Audretsch, D. (Eds.), Innovation and Technological Change. Harvester-Wheatsheaf, London, pp. 132–151.

Scott, J.T., 1993. Purposive Diversification and Economic Performance.. Cambridge University Press, Cambridge, England.

Scott, J.T., 1998. Financing and leveraging public/private partnerships: The hurdle-lowering auction. STI Review 23, 67–84.

Tassey, G., 1992. Technology Infrastructure and Competitive Position. Kluwer Academic Publishers, Norwell, Massachusetts.

Tassey, G., 1997. The Economics of R&D Policy. Quorum Books, Westport, Connecticut.

Teece, D.J., 1980. Economies of scope and the scope of the enterprise. Journal of Economic Behavior and Organization, September 1, 223–247.

[6]

FINANCING AND LEVERAGING PUBLIC/PRIVATE PARTNERSHIPS: THE HURDLE-LOWERING AUCTION

TABLE OF CONTENTS

This article was written by John T. Scott of the Department of Economics at Dartmouth College, Hanover, New Hampshire, United States. The author would like to thank Jean Guinet, Robert G. Hansen, Meir G. Kohn, Albert Link, Stephen Martin, F.M. Scherer, Gregory Tassey and the participants at the OECD Workshop for advice on the issues addressed in this article.

I. INTRODUCTION

The purpose of this article is to propose a mechanism – the *hurdle-lowering auction* – for leveraging the public funds invested in public/private partnerships to promote technology. The article addresses *financial engineering* – the optimal amount and design of public funding of privately performed investments in technology and innovation carried out by *public/private partnerships*. Public/private partnerships are joint research ventures combining public and private resources to invest in the research and development of technology and innovations.[1] Thus, financial engineering concerns the design of mechanisms for public funding of public/private partnerships that generate the maximum *leverage* of the public funds on the private investment and performance. By maximum leverage of public funding, is meant maximum effectiveness of the funds in ensuring the use of the least amount of public funds to get the desired results and ensuring the necessary incentives to get those results given the appropriate amount of public funding.

Obviously "desired results" can mean different things in different circumstances, but in the context of this study good results mean correcting the underinvestment that would result in the absence of the public funding. The social objective of the public funding is to correct market failure which results in underinvestment in technology and innovation. Martin and Scott (1998) develop a taxonomy of innovation modes and associated market failures and appropriate policy responses, and in that context suggest circumstances where the mechanism discussed in this article might usefully be developed and reduced to practice. The aim of this brief article is simply to sketch the idea of the proposed mechanism.

Changes in the nature of technological competition compel the development of a new approach to leverage public investments in public/private partnerships. The review of the literature in Martin and Scott (1998) points to the following observations:

- There is an important role for public support of R&D, and there is support for two very different views of the appropriate use of public funding of R&D.
- One is a very cautious view that technology policy should foster ongoing institutional arrangements, either at or in connection with universities, that will encourage innovation and dissemination of new knowledge over the long run. Broadly, such arrangements would be focused on the basic and generic end of the spectrum of research and not on the applied research that is closer to the commercialisation of innovations.

– The other view is an aggressive view that a revolution in the nature of technological change combined with a revolution in the extent of global competition and transformations of financial markets dealing with technology and innovation investments have reinforced one another to create a new technology and policy regime in which public funding of public/private partnerships is more important, and more feasible than ever before, to correct market failures that extend beyond the basic and generic end of the research spectrum and into the development and commercialisation of innovations.

The revolution in technological change is centred on information technology, which is fraught with appropriability difficulties and risks that cause market failure and underinvestment.[2] Broadly speaking, the technological networking issues to be addressed with R&D investments must be solved in a global economy that is increasingly "networked" with regard to complex and interdependent information technology, and in this new technological and competitive environment, public/private partnerships are more important than ever. At the same time, new developments in venture capital markets make old-style public funding of technology investments obsolete; in the current high-technology environment, the selection of investment projects will need interactive involvement with evolving technologies that will be difficult for governments to provide, and the investments themselves will need a type of "hands-on" monitoring that will be difficult for governments to provide directly.

In this new policy regime, lessons from the past about not using public funds for development work that is close to the commercialisation stage may be challenged for three reasons. First, past difficulties may have reflected circumstances where the legitimacy of public funding was not as compelling as it is in the new policy regime. Second, new developments in venture capital markets and new understanding of those markets place new demands on public funding of ventures dealing with the new regime of technological change. Third, past difficulties may have resulted because insufficient attention was paid to the design of the mechanisms for public funding.

– Attention must be paid, in the implementation of public funding for R&D, to the appropriate design of mechanisms to stimulate desirable investment responses from the private partners in public/private partnerships.
– Given the new reasons to believe that public funding to overcome market failure and underinvestment in R&D is needed more than ever before, and given that the past difficulties for public/private partnerships may be attributable to inadequate design of the public funding mechanisms, the hurdle-lowering auction is proposed as a mechanism for delivering public funding to public/private partnerships more effectively.

The new technological and competitive environment makes public/private partnerships compelling; poor performance for some earlier public/private partnerships suggests the need for new approaches to public funding of the partnerships, and the case for new approaches is especially compelling now that venture capital markets are developing rapidly to deal with investments in emerging technologies. If one accepts the argument that public funding should extend beyond basic and generic research, government needs to do something better than simply pick the technology area where commercial results are to be supported and then throw money at the chosen projects. That leads to the next question:

- How can government *ensure* that such support exert a maximum leverage on private investment?

The leverage question has been focused to get beyond the prescription of "do the socially optimal amount of funding to correct the underinvestment that resulted from the market failure". Technology policy must do more than offer the theoretically correct, but operationally empty, prescription that says to provide enough public funds to bring investment up to the point where social marginal benefit and marginal cost of investment coincide. How does the government optimise such public funding? What is the form and the optimal amount of public support, and how can the government ensure that such support exerts maximum leverage on private investment? The extent of market failure and underinvestment varies by type of innovative investment done by the project and by type of industrial setting. The mechanisms for the delivery of public funding for public/private partnerships must be flexible enough to work well in different technological and economic environments.

Further, because venture capital markets require a hands-on, ongoing relationship between investors and entrepreneurs that is expected to be difficult and costly for public agencies to conduct successfully, the mechanisms should rely on private markets and to the extent possible not supplant private market decision making. To provide more reliance on private decision making to answer key questions about the incidence of public funding and about the form of the funding and its optimal amount, this article proposes a flexible bidding process to determine the extent of public funding at the various stages of the investment projects. Certainly it is beyond the scope of this initial paper to develop complete details of the bidding process, but it is sketched in sufficient detail to justify and explain the approach and introduce its essential ideas; Martin and Scott (1998) place the idea in the context of the literature and propose further development of the idea for future research.[3]

II. PUBLIC/PRIVATE PARTNERSHIPS
TO CORRECT MARKET FAILURE

Market failure in general refers to situations where the divergence of private and public benefits or costs cause market solutions to differ from socially optimal ones. This article focuses on market failures that result in underinvestment in technology and innovation. Although there are market failures that can cause too much R&D investment (Baldwin and Scott, 1987), those are obviously not the market failures addressed with public funding to counter a shortfall of private R&D investment.

Two broad and interrelated sources of the market failures cause underinvestment in technology and innovation: appropriability difficulties – private firms typically do not appropriate all of the social returns from their innovative investments; and risk and uncertainty – private firms typically are concerned about the downside risk of their innovative investment because of bankruptcy costs and the firm-specific human capital of the managers and employees of the firms.

These two sources of market failure and underinvestment are related because appropriability difficulties make unacceptable downside outcomes for an investment project more likely. Thus, if appropriability differences imply that two projects with the same variance in return have different expected returns, the one with lower appropriation of returns and hence lower expected outcome creates a greater risk for the firm because the probability of an outcome below a minimal acceptable level is greater. The appropriability difficulties and the uncertainty stem from spillovers of knowledge, from "the paradox of information", from unappropriated consumer surplus with even monopoly pricing, from the competition that drives price towards marginal costs in a post-innovation market, and from technological risks and market risks facing firms doing R&D.

Public funding through public/private partnerships for R&D investment corrects underinvestment by increasing the rate of return on the private firm's R&D investment, thereby giving the private firm the incentive to carry out the investment project. The public funding directly eliminates the problems of appropriability difficulties and risk by changing the probability distribution over the outcomes for the private firm's investment in the project. The public funding would typically shift the distribution of rate of return on the private firm's own investment in the project to the right, increasing the company's expected return while lowering the downside probability of bankruptcy. The increase in expected value directly improves the incentive for investment that appropriability difficulties had reduced.[4]

III. CHALLENGES TO THE EFFECTIVENESS OF PUBLIC FUNDING: HOW THE REQUIREMENTS OF THE VENTURE CAPITAL MARKET CREATE DIFFICULTIES FOR EFFECTIVE PUBLIC FINANCING OF PUBLIC/PRIVATE PARTNERSHIPS

Debt financing will not work for financing risky R&D investments of the sort that may require public funding. There is no up-side to the return to such instruments, and they are suitable for investors who do not want much risk at all. When used to finance risky investment, lenders are exposed to opportunistic behaviour by borrowers because the returns to the lender and to the borrower are asymmetric. The borrower will have an incentive to take big risks, since only the borrower participates in any up-side returns, but both the borrower and the creditor share the downside risk, and the possibility of bankruptcy means that the lender may bear even more downside risk than the borrower. Equity financing then, is the suitable means for financing such risky investment; the investor shares in the up-side profits of the risky venture.

However, equity financing requires a hands-on approach to managing the investment, because if absentee owners place the equity funds in the control of the company investing in R&D, there is an agency problem. The active owners in the firm now must share any gains realised from the upside potential with the absentee owners, and other things being equal will have less incentive to do the best job for the other investors. Whether those who have operating control are entrepreneurs who have obtained venture capital or simply the company's managers, not gaining all of the investment's upside returns, those with operational control have an incentive to undertake less risk than the outside equity owners would prefer; more generally they do not, without some sort of extra incentive mechanism, have an incentive to work in the best interests of the absentee equity investors.

"Venture Capital in OECD Countries" (OECD, 1996) emphasizes the "hands-on" aspect of venture capital for investments in companies in the early stages of development.[5] The survey also emphasizes that venture capital is the key source of long-term funds to small and medium-sized enterprises (SMEs), and it provides a description of the venture capital market and how it works. The extent and success of venture capital markets vary across countries, and there are many government programmes to stimulate venture capital provision. The survey observes that there are differences of opinion about the benefits of government involvement. Some believe that excessive public intervention will lower returns on the early-stage investments to the point where venture capitalists will no longer be attracted. In the context of a limited number of such projects, the public/private partnerships might take the more attractive projects, crowding out private investors. These critics then argue that government should limit its role to assistance in setting up the market infrastructure and in creating an environment conducive to entrepreneurship. However, new technologically intensive firms may not receive sufficient capital, and such capital constraints limit R&D investment especially for small firms (Lerner, 1996).

Lerner (1996) and Gompers and Lerner (1997) observe that the pool of funds committed to venture capital investments has recently grown rapidly. Along with the rapid increase in the venture capital funds, there is the pervasive belief that private venture capital firms will do a better job than the government in monitoring the ventured equity positions in risky companies making R&D investments. The dilemma, however, is that despite a surge in private funds for the venture capital market, and despite the capability of the private market for managing the investment of such funds, because of the appropriability problems and the risk the private sector on its own will typically underinvest in technology and R&D.

For example, the *Financial Times* (Campbell, 1997) reports that there is currently great momentum gathering behind private equity across Europe, observing that: "Private equity encompasses everything from large leveraged buy-out deals to the more traditional venture capital channelled into start-up or early-stage businesses. While there are some signs of a revival of interest in emerging businesses, particularly in the technology sector, today's flood of money is directed primarily towards buy-out opportunities." Detailed evidence on the new interest in venture capital for technology investments emphasizes that the pick-up in interest in providing venture capital to the high-tech sector is starting from a low base because of poor performance in the last decade for venture funds and because of the difficulties of successfully managing such funds (Houlder, 1997; Price, 1997).

Lerner (1996) observes that if the capital constraints literature is correct, then public funding of early-stage high-technology firms would stimulate significant growth for the firms because they would be able to invest in high-return projects that they could not have accepted without the government funding. The question, then, is how to deliver the necessary public funding to provide sufficient investment funds in such a risky environment without losing the monitoring ability of a private venture capital firm and without having to ensure such monitoring with clumsy and costly contracts. Support for the view that public provision of venture capital will not work well is provided by the work of Dyck and Wruck (1996) which studies German government-owned privatisation agencies that own portfolios of eight to ten eastern German firms. Dyck and Wruck hypothesise that private companies are more reliable contracting partners than a government. As a result, governments must use more intricate and hence more costly contracts than private firms would use. The reason that Dyck and Wruck expect governments to be less reliable partners and to require more costly contracts spelling out contingencies and responsibilities is their hypothesis that government organisations as political organisations need to please their diverse constituencies and therefore will be reluctant to make economically painful or controversial decisions.

In his study of the impact of public provision of venture capital in the US Small Business Innovation Research (SBIR) Programme, Lerner (1996) provides evidence in support of a positive view of the prospects for public funding of public/private partnerships. Thus, he tests the hypotheses that the private sector provides too little capital to new firms and that the government can identify companies where investments will yield high social and private returns, and his evidence supports the hypotheses. However, Wallsten (1997) re-examines the SBIR Programme and finds that the SBIR grants crowd out private-firm R&D dollar for dollar. He hypothesises the grants fund research that would have been funded privately because politicians judge the success of technology programmes by the commercial success of the projects they fund, and then of course the managers of the grant programmes choose promising, commercially viable projects that would have been funded privately and needed no subsidy. Wallsten observes (1997, p. 10) that although "Lerner included a control group, he did not deal with the issue of 'picking winners' – the possibility that agencies fund commercially attractive projects that could have been funded privately".

The mechanism for delivering public funding proposed below actually solves this problem, to the extent that it does exist, because for such projects the mechanism results in the private sector completely reimbursing the government for the cost of the publicly funded project. Some transaction costs would remain unreimbursed, but over time, as experience with choosing projects and use of the new financing principle grew, the mechanism would allow identification and weeding out of projects that should not be publicly funded.

Another observation about the venture capital market is also important for the proposal below for a new mechanism for delivering public funds to public/private partnerships. Gompers and Lerner (1997) find a very robust relationship between the valuation of early-stage firms and the volume of venture capital funds that are bidding for the equity of companies seeking venture capital. In particular, a greater volume of commitments of venture capital funds increases the valuation of new investments. Apparently, a larger volume of venture fund commitments translates into more competition for, and hence higher prices for, the type of risky asset provided by entrepreneurs seeking venture funds. There are implications of their finding for the proposed bidding mechanism introduced below. First, evidently, the most propitious time to invite bidding from private venture funds that would bid for the right to manage funds for public/private partnerships would be when outstanding venture capital commitments are high. Second, the need for public funds may be greatest when such commitments are relatively low.

The venture capital literature also emphasizes the importance of a means of "exit" from the venture capital stage. Although exit can be provided by acquisition or merger, anticipated rewards can be increased by the capability of successfully trading the company on an exchange such as the NASDAQ. Several new stock markets for small, fast-growing firms have emerged in Europe recently (*The Economist,* 1997). Gilson and Black (1996) and MacIntosh (1996) emphasize the importance of stock markets as a means for venture capitalists to dispose of their investments. One simple recommendation for technology and innovation policy is then for governments to take steps to increase the availability and ease of use of stock markets for small, rapidly growing firms. Such markets make investment in start-up firms more attractive and, in the context of the mechanism proposed in the next section, reduce the gap between project cost and what firms will bid to be the private partner in the public/private partnerships.

IV.   ENSURING OPTIMAL DESIGN OF PUBLIC FUNDING: A MECHANISM FOR LEVERAGING THE PUBLIC FUNDING

Improving the design of public partnerships raises three fundamental questions: How can the public get the best private partner for each public/private partnership? How to obtain the optimal amount of public funding – not too much, but enough to overcome the underinvestment resulting from market failure? How to overcome the potential for opportunistic behaviour to which both the government and the private partner are exposed?

Premise: the private sector knows more than the government about the investment characteristics of the technology projects – or at least has the resources to take the best guess at the streams of returns and the risk.

Implication: policy should design a mechanism for setting up a public/private partnership that provides the incentive for private parties to determine who is best suited to be the private partner in a public/private partnership.

Premise: the government wants to overcome the underinvestment resulting from market failure and to do so at the least cost to the public.

Implication: policy should design a mechanism that gives the selected private partner for the public/private partnership the incentive to carry out the desired level of investment while providing a proportion of the project's funding that is consistent with a normal expected rate of return for the private firm given the appropriability and risk characteristics of the project.

Premise: both parties want to overcome the potential for opportunistic beha-viour by the other party.

Implication: policy should design a mechanism that gives both the public and the private partners the incentive to participate in the project in a way that max-imises the total value of the project's outcome rather than the value to the individual partner who could of course use opportunistic behaviour to benefit at the expense of the overall results of the project.

General characteristics of the mechanism: what are the general characteris-tics of the optimal mechanism for public/private partnerships that will achieve the desired incentives for the private sector to choose the best private partner, for the private partner to carry out the desired amount of investment at the least cost to the public, and for avoiding opportunistic behaviour by either the public or the private partner?

Consideration of the questions suggests that the optimal mechanism would have the private parties use a contingent valuation method to bid for the right to be the private partner. In particular, the bidding could be a hybrid bidding mecha-nism that combines an up-front bid, a periodic payment bid, and finally a royalty bid: private firms would bid for the right to be the private partner in the public/ private partnership project that the government would fund. Or, instead of bids being accepted directly from the companies that will be performing the R&D, private venture capital companies that would manage the public investments might bid for the rights to manage the projects.

As a simple example of how a bidding process would deliver the public funding to a public/private partnership, consider the following. Suppose that from society's perspective, an R&D investment project would cost 100 now and gener-ate the expectation of 130 in one year and nothing thereafter. Suppose further that the threshold rate of return justifying public funding – society's hurdle rate – is 10 per cent. Thus, the R&D project yields a social rate of return of 30 per cent, which exceeds the hurdle rate of 10 per cent, and of course the net present value of [130/(1.1)] – 100 is greater than zero. Suppose that from a private perspective the project costs 100 and because of incomplete appropriation of returns yields the expectation of just 105 in a year. Suppose further that, given the private risk, the private hurdle rate is 15 per cent. Thus, the private sector would not undertake the project which has an internal rate of return of 5 per cent which is less than the hurdle rate of 15 per cent; and, of course, net present value is then negative.

In the context of the foregoing example, the bidding process would work as follows. The government announces that it will "buy" the R&D project, paying the 100 investment cost.[6] The government then opens the bidding for the right to be the private partner in the public/private partnership. Private firms will bid the amount X such that X (1.15) = 105, implying that X = 91.30. The cost to the public of the project would then be 8.70. With great uncertainty about the future returns, the use of royalty bidding rather than the up-front bidding can yield more to the government. Also, private firms with better capabilities for doing the project would be expected to bid higher than those firms that are less well suited to the project.

There is a large literature describing bidding mechanisms in great detail. McAfee and McMillan (1987) provide a review, and they set out the general hybrid mechanism with the up-front bid as well as the royalty bid. Hansen (1985) and Samuelson (1986) provide analyses of the royalty bidding and bidding for the up-front fee and the royalty rate simultaneously. Just a general overview of a more general bidding mechanism and the bidding mechanism's potential in the context of public/private partnership is provided here.

Broadly, suppose that the government wants to use a public/private partnership to develop a project. The government would announce that it would provide an up-front payment of F to support the R&D investment project to be conducted by the winning bidder in an auction to determine the private partner for the public/private partnership. Further, the government pledges to provide a periodic flow of funds c throughout the project's life to support the flow costs of the R&D project. The fixed cost F and the flow cost c correspond to the typical abstraction of the structure of costs for R&D investment projects (Lee and Wilde, 1980). Bidders then bid for the right to be the private partner in the project by submitting a three-part bid: first, a bid for how much the private firm will pay the government up-front; second, a bid on the periodic flow payment during the life of the R&D project; and, finally, a bid on the royalty rate that it would pay the government on the innovation produced by the public/private partnership and licensed (perhaps exclusively) to the private partner.

As McAfee and McMillan (1987) make clear, in the context of the appropriate combinations of assumptions about the characteristics of the asset being auctioned and the participants in the auction and their beliefs about the value of the asset, there are non-trivial choices to be made about the exact nature of the auction. Apart from the usual choices for auctions in general, there would be choices specific to the new institutional use of auctions to determine the private partner for the public/private partnership. For example, institutional arrangements must be designed to insure that the government's payments of F and c go solely for the purchase of R&D investments; the private partner's profits from the R&D investment project will come after the innovation is introduced. However, for this article, full details of the ideal auction in different circumstances will not be developed. Instead, the article presents the basic idea and observes that the three-part bidding mechanism proposed has the potential for leveraging public funding optimally.

– First, with a well-designed auction, a viable private partner is likely to be chosen. Intuitively, the company that can (or at least *thinks* it can) produce the best results at the least cost will gain more value from winning the bid to be the private partner in the public/private partnership; therefore, it will bid higher and win.

- Second, the government's investment cost will be minimised. Intuitively, that cost is the present value of *i)* the up-front investment *F* minus the up-front bid and *ii)* the flow cost *c* minus the periodic flow payment, and the firm with the best capabilities for producing the research at lowest cost will submit the highest bid for the up-front payment and the periodic flow payment. The government's net costs are reduced further by the royalty payments it will receive. Those royalty payments, however, serve other specific roles in the mechanism design.

- Third, the royalty payments are the contingent payment option that mitigates the effects of uncertainty by tying the actual payment by the private firm to the government to the actual performance of the R&D investment and the innovation it produces. The contingent payment mechanism then increases the willingness of private firms to bid and increases the winning bid and reduces the expected cost to the government. Greater uncertainty about value implies lower expected price at the auction, and using royalty bidding as a type of contingent pricing mechanism gets around that problem, giving in effect *ex post* pricing, whereas without contingency pricing less is bid because no one knows what to pay for the right to be the private partner in the public/private partnership. However, as noted subsequently, with royalties, there is an agency problem that changes the way the winning bidder will exploit the innovation resulting from the public/private partnership, and that issue is addressed below.

- Fourth, the royalty payments give the government an equity stake in the project and reduce the likelihood of opportunistic behaviour on the part of the government.[7] Suppose that the project is one for which public support – funds of course, but also the energy and talents of the government's employees such as those in public laboratories and technology policy departments – will be needed for many fiscal years. The government's equity position in the project may be a way to ensure the credibility of the public's support throughout those early investment years despite changes in administration or changes in public sentiment. The equity position could help to ensure that the government did not abandon a project midstream, and thus make private participation and investment more attractive.

- Fifth, the likelihood of opportunistic behaviour by the private investors is lessened because the private firm or firms will have invested in the project with both up-front and periodic payments, and good faith behaviour would be required to keep the public funds *c* for the flow costs arriving on schedule to protect and sustain the private investment and keep the prospect of the private share of the project's expected earnings.

– Clearly, though, the royalties to the government in return for use of the technology must be low enough so that the problem of reduced incentives for the private firm to promote the innovation does not outweigh the gains because the royalty mechanism mitigates risks and ensures continued public support. With diminishing returns, and hence rising marginal costs of exploiting the innovation, the royalty payments to the government will reduce the private company's use of the innovation below the optimal amount.

The proposed hurdle-lowering auction mechanism, broadly, is that private firms bid for a public/private partnership using a three-part bid reflecting the up-front, fixed costs of the R&D project, its flow costs, and the stream of profits from the resulting innovation. Government wants the right firms to win the bid, and it wants to pay the optimal amount, but not too much, to get the innovations. The three-part bidding mechanism proposed would potentially provide the desired properties. By having private venture capital companies, as contrasted with the early-stage companies performing the government-supported research and technology investment, bid for the contract, the bidding mechanism could even incorporate private venture capital market supervision of the public investments in early-stage firms or joint ventures.[8]

V.   CONCLUSIONS

This article has introduced a simple idea that may be of use for leveraging public funding of investments in technology and innovation. The simple idea is to develop appropriate bidding mechanisms to allow private-market decisions to flexibly tailor the amount and timing and delivery of public funding of public/private partnerships. The article has sketched a prototype three-part bidding mechanism – a hurdle-lowering auction – and explained why it can potentially provide the desired traits for delivering the public funds to public/private partnerships. The approach need not be a radical departure from current practice. The public funding authority can still exercise judgement about which bid to accept, and the process could be seen as an extension of the negotiation process over the exact details and extent of public and private contributions to the project.

Of course, the bidding mechanism, in whatever form it takes, should be evaluated and compared with other mechanisms to ensure that it performed well, especially given the problems of "government failure" that can be just as difficult as problems of "market failure".[9] A good mechanism would have not only the desirable traits – choosing a good private partner, achieving desired investment while minimising the expenditure of public funds, and so forth – that have been associated with the bidding mechanism, but additionally it would have relatively low administrative costs.[10] Bidding mechanisms have the potential to return far more than they cost administratively because they will minimise the public funds needed to support the public/private partnership projects, but that expectation must be tested. Governments should engage in ongoing evaluation and development of the mechanisms for identifying projects for public funding and for delivering the public funds to the public/private partnership.

NOTES

1. Note that public/private partnership more generally need not necessarily involve public and private parties doing research. For example, the public/private partnership could be focused on the provision of appropriate legal infrastructure such as the laws concerning intellectual property, or on the co-ordination of appropriate standards for technologies.

2. Antonelli (1994) provides an overview and details about the economics and policy issues for networked information technology.

3. Scherer (1997) provided a helpful suggestion when asked for his opinion on the question of financing public/private partnerships. He observed: "You might profitably study the experience of the United States in awarding offshore oil tracks by royalty bidding rather than front-end bonus bidding." Following up on his suggestion led to the proposal for the three-part bidding process sketched in this article.

4. Scott (1980) discusses the coefficient of variation as a natural hybrid measure of both return and risk. Tassey (1997) defines risk in terms of the downside potential for project failure; variance in return *per se* is not the key, but the probability of the downside deviations from expected value placing the return so low that the project is deemed a failure. Hence, he implicitly uses a hybrid measure of risk that combines expected return and the variance in the return. Given the variance, a higher expected return can – using the hybrid view of risk – lower risk, because it lowers the probability of failure.

5. Harris and Bovaird (1996, p. 197) also emphasize the need for hands-on management of venture capital investments by studying the successful investments of companies offering funds to young businesses. Rather than simply providing capital, investors need to ensure that early-stage companies address other capability gaps – inadequate management skills, inadequate understanding of the market, inadequate relations with suppliers, and inadequate financial control.

6. Martin and Scott (1998) provide detailed discussion of the circumstances in which market failure and underinvestment would be expected to occur; the discussion is needed to inform the identification of projects that would be funded.

7. Of course, the government is not a profit-maximising firm, and one must be concerned then, that incentive problems will occur because a bureaucrat will be deciding what to do based on his or her own preferences. However, governments do have constituencies to satisfy which can potentially play a role analogous to that of stockholders in a

for-profit firm if a good mechanism for delivering the public funding to the public/private partnership is in place.

8. Clearly the discussion here has only sketched the idea of designing a bidding mechanism to leverage the public financing of public/private partnership projects. Details remain to be developed for actual public/private partnership projects. Such details include the type of auction (for example, English, Dutch, sealed first-bid, or sealed second-bid auctions), the use of a reservation price, and so forth, for various circumstances such as independent or correlated private values, common values or hybrid cases where technological and market uncertainties are subject to different valuation characteristics.

9. Problems with incentives, unintended consequences, interest groups lobbying for concentrated benefits that have diffuse costs, and inconsistencies of group decision making suggest that the makers of technology policy should continually look for ways to remove government-induced obstacles to R&D investment, and ways to make private investment more effective even while implementing new mechanisms to make the government's actions more effective.

10. In the context of their evaluation of alternative tax incentives for R&D, Bozeman and Link (1983) list and critically discuss several criteria by which alternative mechanisms should be evaluated.

BIBLIOGRAPHY

ANTONELLI, C. (guest editor) (1994), *Information Economics and Policy,* Special Issue on "The Economics of Standards", Vol. 6 (3, 4).

BALDWIN, W.L. and J.T. SCOTT (1987), *Market Structure and Technological Change*, in the series *Fundamentals of Pure and Applied Economics,* Vol. 17, Harwood Academic Publishers, London, Paris, New York.

BOZEMAN, B. and A.N. LINK (1984), "Tax Incentives for R&D: A Critical Evaluation", *Research Policy* 13, pp. 21-31.

CAMPBELL, K. (1997), "Funds Flood Across the Channel", *Financial Times Survey* 10 October, p. I.

DYCK, I.J.A. and K.H. WRUCK (1996), "The Government as Venture Capitalist? Organizational Solutions to Contracting Problems in German Privatization", Harvard Business School, Working Paper 97-007, 22 July.

THE ECONOMIST (1997*), "Small-Company Stockmarkets: Europe's Growth Industry",* 15 March, p. 78.

GILSON, R.J. and B.S. BLACK (1996), "Venture Capital and the Structure of Capital Markets: Banks versus Stock Markets", John M. Olin Program in Law and Economics, Stanford Law School, Working Paper No. 135, July.

GOMPERS, P. and J. LERNER (1997), "Money Chasing Deals? The Impact of Fund Inflows on Private Equity Valuations", Harvard University and National Bureau of Economics Research, manuscript, August.

HANSEN, R.G. (1985), "Auctions with Contingent Payments", *The American Economic Review* 74, No. 4, pp. 862-865.

HARRIS, S., and C. BOVAIRD (1996), *Enterprising Capital: A Study of Enterprise Development and the Institutions which Finance It,* Avebury, Brookfield, Vermont.

HOULDER, V. (1997), "The High-Technology Sector: New Funds Focus on IT Companies", *Financial Times Survey*, 10 October, p. V.

LEE, T. and L.L. WILDE (1980), "Market Structure and Innovation: A Reformulation", *Quarterly Journal of Economics* 94, No. 2, pp. 429-436.

LERNER, J. (1996), "The Government as Venture Capitalist: The Long-Run Impact of the SBIR Program", NBER Working Paper 5753, September.

MacINTOSH, J.G. (1996), "Venture Capital Exits in Canada and the US", Faculty of Law, University of Toronto, manuscript, 27 June.

MARTIN, S. and J.T. SCOTT (1998), "Financing and Leveraging Public/Private Partnerships", a report prepared for the Working Group on Technology and Innovation Policy, Division of Science and Technology, OECD, 30 January.

McAFEE, R.P. and J. McMILLAN (1987), "Auctions and Bidding", *The Journal of Economic Literature* 25, No. 2, pp. 699-738.

OECD (1996), "Venture Capital in OECD Countries", Special Features section of *Financial Market Trends* 63, pp. 15-38, based on a paper by M. O'Shea, consultant to the Financial Affairs Division of the OECD.

PRICE, C. (1997), "Early-Stage Investing Across Europe: Fresh Interest in Technology Funds", *Financial Times Survey*, 10 October, p. IV.

SAMUELSON, W.F. (1986), "Bidding for Contracts", *Management Science* 32, No. 12, pp. 1533-1550.

SCHERER, F.M. (1997), Letter to John T. Scott, 29 September.

SCOTT, J.T. (1980), "Corporate Finance and Market Structure", in Richard E. Caves *et al.*, *Competition in the Open Economy: A Model Applied to Canada*, Chapter 13, pp. 325-359, Harvard University Press, Cambridge, Massachusetts.

TASSEY, G. (1997), *The Economics of R&D Policy*, Quorum Books, London.

WALLSTEN, S. (1997), "Can Government-Industry R&D Programs Increase Private R&D? The Case of the Small Business Innovation Research Program", Stanford University, manuscript, November.

OTHER USEFUL REFERENCES

SCOTT, J.T. (1995), "The Damoclean Tax and Innovation", *Journal of Evolutionary Economics* 5, No. 1, pp. 71-89.

LINK, A.N. and J.T. SCOTT (1998) "Assessing the Infrastructural Needs of a Technology-based Service Sector: A New Approach to Technology Policy Planning", *STI Review*, No. 22, OECD, Paris.

An Assessment of the Small Business Innovation Research Program in New England: Fast Track Compared with Non-Fast Track Projects[*]

John T. Scott

Dartmouth College

EXECUTIVE SUMMARY

This paper provides case studies for 14 research and development projects funded in 13 New England companies by the Department of Defense Small Business Innovation Research (SBIR) program. The performance of the six Fast Track projects, each conducted by a different company, is compared with the performance of eight non-Fast Track projects. The primary conclusions from the study of the New England cases are

- The collection of 14 New England SBIR projects studied here exhibited, at the outset of Phase I, high risk—both technical and market risk, high capital costs, and often expectation of a long-time before commercialization of the resulting technology.
- In the absence of the SBIR funding, the research projects would not have been undertaken in the same way or at the same pace. Outside investors, at the outset of Phase I, would have required too high a rate of return to make it possible for the project to proceed with only private financing.
- On the whole, the projects, both Fast Track and non-Fast Track, met both the funding agency's mission and the company's strategy. All fit the general scenario for socially valuable research projects that would have been underfunded in the absence of the SBIR program. In particular, the projects appear to be ones for which the private rates of return in the absence of SBIR funding would have fallen short of the private hurdle

---

[*]This paper was prepared for presentation at the National Academy of Sciences Symposium on the Assessment of the SBIR Fast Track Program, May 5, 1999.

rate required by outside financiers to whom the small businesses would have had to turn for financial support. Yet the social rates of returns to the projects are large and exceed the hurdle rates. The funding from the SBIR program changes the ordering of rates of return anticipated at the outset of Phase I. With the SBIR program providing funds, the expected private return relative to just the private portion of the total project costs is sufficient to move the private rate of return above the hurdle rate, and then the socially valuable research investment is undertaken.

- Taken as a group, the Fast Track projects show higher prospective lower-bound social rates of return—a measure that is based upon expected profits to the innovator and other producers benefiting from the innovation.

- The average duration of additional development beyond Phase II and before commercialization is somewhat less for the Fast Track projects, suggesting that at least on average they are somewhat closer to commercialization at the end of Phase II than the non-Fast Track projects.

- The respondents were unanimous in their appreciation of the SBIR program and in their belief that the program generally works well. They did have several recommendations to improve the working of the program, and those recommendations are listed in this paper. Among other things, the respondents cautioned that the Fast Track program is often simply not useful for companies pursuing socially valuable high-risk research, because at the end of Phase I, such projects often do not yet have the characteristics of projects that allow outside private investors to be attracted.

- In summary, the SBIR program has funded innovative projects with high social rates of return that would not have been undertaken in the absence of the program. Further, the non-Fast Track as well as the Fast Track projects appear to be quite valuable, although the non-Fast Track projects typically do not exhibit private commercial potential as quickly as the Fast Track ones.

INTRODUCTION

As part of a National Academy of Sciences study of the Department of Defense (DoD) Small Business Innovation Research (SBIR) Program, six SBIR Fast Track projects from six companies in New England are studied here along with SBIR non-Fast Track projects from different New England companies matched by similarity of location, size, and project duration. A total of seven projects from six non-Fast Track companies are studied—one project for each of five companies and two for the sixth. Additionally, the study includes a non-Fast Track project of a thirteenth company, Foster-Miller, which is much larger than the other companies in the sample and has been successful with an unusually large number of SBIR awards. In all, the study covers 14 projects at the 13 firms shown in Table 1. All of the SBIR projects studied were awarded both Phase I and Phase II funding. The goal of the study is to describe the SBIR projects and compare the Fast Track projects with the non-Fast Track projects, determining the effect that Fast Track has had on SBIR performance and firm behavior.

The 14 projects are high-risk research projects performed by small businesses, or with Foster-Miller in the sample, what the technology literature calls SMEs—small and medium-sized enterprises. The study finds that these risky SBIR-funded projects have high prospective, expected social rates of return. The social rates of return are calculated as lower bounds based solely on anticipated innovative investment profits for companies rather than on the sum of those profits (producer surplus) and consumer surplus (economists' measure of the value above and beyond what they actually pay that consumers receive from a product or service). Thus, the study's finding that the Fast Track projects as a group have

TABLE 1   The Firms

Company Name	Date Founded	Initial Size[a]
Brock-Rogers Surgical	1995	3
Cape Cod Research	1982	18
Foster-Miller, Inc.	1956	260
Hyperion Catalysis International	1982	20
Lithium Energy Associates, Inc.	1989	3
Materials Technologies Corp.	1986	5
Mide Technology Corp.	1989	3
Optigain, Inc.	1991	8
QSource, Inc.	1982	3
SEA CORP (Systems Engineering Associates Corp.)	1981	93
Spectra Science Corp.	refounded 1997 (originally 1989)	7
Synkinetics, Inc.	1994	8
Yardney Technical Products, Inc.	1940	155

[a]Employees at the time of application for Phase I.

higher social rates of return supports the perception that their prospects for generating profits for innovating firms are especially good. However, some non-Fast Track projects have higher lower-bound expected social rates of return than some Fast Track projects, despite the fact that consumer surplus is not measured. Fast Track and non-Fast Track projects alike have lower-bound social rates of return exceeding the private rates of return in the absence of SBIR funding. Each of the studied projects is the type of research project in which the market would fail to invest in a socially valuable innovation in the absence of SBIR or similar public funding. For the 14 New England SBIR projects studied, the average value of the lower bound for the prospective (i.e., at the start of Phase I) expected social rate of return is estimated to be 60 percent. The estimate would be much higher if consumer surplus could be measured.

HISTORY OF THE FIRMS AND THE PROJECTS

Table 2 provides some background information about the 13 companies as a group. The sampled firms have similar histories in the ways reviewed in the table, except that the Fast Track respondents are less likely to have had a previous SBIR award. Not surprisingly, the companies are not Advanced Technology Program (ATP) award winners; the ATP projects require substantial contributions of private funds from the outset of the projects. As seen in Table 2, the sampled companies are typically small businesses facing severe capital constraints for internal financing of research. Somewhat more than half of the respondents indicated locational advantages. A variety of other competitive advantages were cited; representative examples include "large patent base," "patented core tech-

TABLE 2   History of the Firms. (The number of respondents indicating each category)

Characteristic	Fast Track	Non-Fast Track
Locational advantages		
Near universities	2	3
Near corporate research centers or research parks	1	2
Previous SBIR awards prior to Phase I of current award[*a]		
Yes	3	6
No	3	1
Previous or current ATP Aawards		
Yes	0	0
No	6	7

[a]One company discussed the details of two awards. For purposes of this table, the two awards are considered as one award; their periods of performance are essentially concurrent, and both are non-Fast Track projects.

nologies," "small and lean," "twenty five years experience in the underlying technology," "trade secrets and know-how."

As discussed in detail later, the research projects on the whole are characterized by both high technical risk and high market risk. At the outset of Phase I, there is considerable uncertainty about whether the research will resolve outstanding technical problems. Furthermore, the acquisition plans of DoD are not typically firm at the outset of the research, and although the potential for spillovers to the nonmilitary commercial sector is present, many uncertainties remain about the form of the nonmilitary applications and about the market success of those applications.

Table 3 lists the companies along with the titles of the SBIR projects studied in this paper and their Fast Track status. The following paragraphs are brief overviews of the technologies being created by the sampled SBIR projects, along with discussion about the relationship of the project to the mission of the funding agency and to the strategy of the company.

TABLE 3   The Projects

Company	Project Title	Fast Track Status
Brock-Rogers Surgical	Development of a Force-Reflecting Laparoscopic Telemanipulator	Fast Track
Cape Cod Research, Inc.	Multilayer Capacitors Based on Engineered Conducting Polymers	Non-Fast Track
Foster-Miller, Inc.	Tunable Sting Net	Non-Fast Track
Hyperion Catalysis International	Ultracapacitors Based on Nanofiber Electrodes	Fast Track
Lithium Energy Associates, Inc.	Lithium Copper Chloride Inorganic Electrolyte Battery for More Electric Aircraft Systems	Non-Fast Track
Materials Technology Corp.	Life Prediction of Aging Aircraft Wiring Systems	Non-Fast Track
Mide Technology Corp.	Development of Distributed Area Averaging Sensor	Non-Fast Track
Optigain, Inc.	Single Longitudinal Mode Distributed Feedback Fiber Optics Laser	Non-Fast Track
QSource, Inc.	Multiple Rectangular Discharge CO_2 Laser	Fast Track
SEA CORP (Systems Engineering Associates Corp.)	Rapid Prototype Portable Combat and Launch System	Non-Fast Track
	Second project also discussed: Modular Gas Generator Launch Canister	Non-Fast Track
Spectra Science Corp.	Quantum Dots: Next Generation of Electronic Phosphors	Fast Track
Synkinetics, Inc.	High Precision Gimbal System	Fast Track
Yardney Technical Products, Inc.	Low Cost, Lightweight, Rechargeable Lithium-ion Batteries	Fast Track

Brock-Rogers Surgical. Development of a Force-Reflecting Laparoscopic Telemanipulator. Fast Track. The technology merges electronics, mechanics, computer networking and software to create a telerobot to be used for surgery. The technology allows the surgeon to feel as if he or she were one inch tall and inside the patient. DoD is interested in such computer-augmented remote connections to allow medical personnel to operate on the front lines from remote locations. Beyond the military applications, such technology will change the face of surgery. A deep infrastructure technology is being created—a sophisticated electronic, mechanical, software-networked machine. In that sense, the technology is an enabling one with wide applications outside of medicine. The robot no longer needs to "see"—recognition and reception problems are handled by the human controlling the process.

Cape Cod Research, Inc. Multilayer Capacitors Based on Engineered Conducting Polymers. Non-Fast Track. The technology uses electrically conductive polymers to store energy to power electric cars. The project involves the development of novel and useful materials, and it provides the funding agency with improved energy storage for a variety of applications.

Foster-Miller, Inc. Tunable Sting Net. Non-Fast Track. The technology is the latest in a line of "NETS"—nonlethal entanglement technology systems— developed as SBIR projects by Foster-Miller in response to DoD's interest in funding research about capture mechanics. The family of nets developed by Foster-Miller are compact, light-weight, far-ranging, fast, and can be fired from conventional weapons. The "Sting Net" delivers a remotely controlled electric charge for use with especially aggressive targets and is anticipated to have military applications only. Less physically active versions range from nets that simply entangle to nets using pepper irritant powder to subdue more dangerous targets. The less harsh nets will have use in nonmilitary police operations. The Sting Net project fits with Foster-Miller's highly successful corporate strategy of inventing and licensing patented technologies, and spinning off subsidiary companies to manufacture and market the innovations. Numerous SBIR projects have contributed to that strategy, although the company gets only about 20 to 25 percent of its revenues from the SBIR awards.

Hyperion Catalysis International. Ultracapacitors Based on Nanofiber Electrodes. Fast Track. Electrochemical capacitors, sometimes called ultracapacitors or supercapacitors, are being developed for potential applications in hybrid electric vehicles and other automotive electronic and military systems. To be cost- and weight-effective compared to batteries, these "supercaps" must have adequate energy and power with a long life cycle and must meet cost targets. Hyperion has a proprietary line of nanofibers that have desirable properties and a cost advantage over competing materials. During Phase I, the Hyperion nanofibers showed great promise regarding their power and now in Phase II the nanofibers are being used to design, fabricate, and test electrochemical capacitors. Hyperion would make the nanofiber electrodes and sell them to the manufacturers of supercaps. Beyond the potential for a large commercial market for supercaps and the fact that the military has specialized needs for them that explain the DoD funding of the research, there are other potential applications including uses in boom boxes, electric motor starters, defibrillation medical devices, and in cell phones in combination with batteries where power from a small supercap can allow the use of a smaller battery and a better product than results using a large battery alone.

Lithium Energy Associates, Inc. Lithium Copper Chloride Inorganic Electrolyte Battery for More Electric Aircraft Systems. Non-Fast Track. The batteries developed by Lithium Energy Associates are rechargeable and have high energy density and extraordinary low-temperature performance. They have military applications in small, light-weight, remote-controlled reconnaissance aircraft equipped with TV cameras and in solar planes that fly to high altitudes, charge during the day, and then keep flying at night. The batteries have other military applications as well; for example, after using conventional power to get equipment to a battlefield, the engines could be turned off and the batteries could reposition vehicles quietly and without infrared detection. The batteries will have applications for a variety of military electronics applications such as radios. The low-temperature performance of the batteries also makes them the potential power source for applications in space, such as powering robot stations on the moon or Mars, and research in progress will push the low-temperature capabilities of the batteries into the range making them suitable for lunar or Mars missions. Customers, apart from DoD and NASA, should include original equipment manufacturers of military electronics or civilian police equipment.

Materials Technology Corporation. Life Prediction of Aging Aircraft Wiring Systems. Non-Fast Track. The technology allows safe, accurate, and efficient diagnostic tests of the wiring in airplanes to ensure that the wiring is defect free. With the current technology the inspector opens a panel door and examines bundles of wires with the naked eye. If the 12- to 18-inch section of wire that can be seen looks okay, then the entire wire is judged to be safe. In some cases, the inspector may use a mirror to try to look at the back side of the wires, but because of visibility and space limitations it is rare that the back side is inspected well. The wires themselves are rarely a problem; instead, the insulation on the wires is what degrades; becoming brittle with age, it begins to crack. The plasticizer vaporizes and, over time, the insulation degrades, becomes brittle, and begins to fall apart, exposing bare wire; if two wires are exposed, a short circuit is possible.

The new technology developed by Materials Technology Corporation is the first approach to inspecting for damaged insulation of wiring that allows viewing of all sides of the wiring and does not risk damaging the wires as typically occurs if the wires are bent or disturbed in trying to examine their back side. The technology uses embedded optical sensors in a device that can be put around the bundle of wires and used to get a 360-degree view of the wires. The information gathered by the handheld device is signaled to a computer that pinpoints and displays precisely where on the 360-degree surface a crack is located. New optical imaging technology is used. With the press of a button the image can be recorded and the data transported for use at other sites. It is expected that the system will allow the entire wiring history of the aircraft to be stored on a zip drive that will be carried in the aircraft. Planes will not have to return to a home base to be inspected and repaired. Historical data, supplemented with a visible image, will allow the inspector to see what the wiring looked like at the last inspection and calculate the progression of changes. In addition to examining aircraft wires and cable, the technology can be used to examine the connections and to detect corrosion more generally in aircraft and other objects.

There are many applications beyond those for military and commercial aircraft. The optical scanning procedure is expected to be relevant for dealing with vision problems caused by macular degeneration. And, of course, what is good for aircraft inspection is also good for inspecting bridges and other infrastructure.

Mide Technology Corporation. Development of Distributed Area Averaging Sensor. Non-Fast Track. The technology eliminates harmful vibrations in structures by use of active materials that respond to stimuli; for example, if voltage is applied, the active material expands or contracts. The vibrations of structures have several natural frequencies, and the technology developed by Mide Technology Corporation uses shaped sensors to filter out noise, focusing on a desired frequency to eliminate the associated vibrations. The area averaging sensor simplifies a higher-dimension multi-input/multi-output information problem to a lower-dimension control system that characterizes more simply the necessary information about the natural frequencies causing vibrations, despite a complex set of underlying information. The frequencies that really transmit the noise through the structure of interest can be isolated using a control system with active fiber composite actuators; the smart material is used to simplify the control problem and, ultimately, to allow the elimination of the vibrations from the structure.

The immediate application of the technology is to protect launch satellites from damage from structural vibrations. Alternatively, one could protect the launch satellite with blankets—thin ones to protect against high-frequency noise, and thick ones to protect against lower-frequency noise. The Mide technology is the active way of dealing with the problem. Commercial potential extends beyond the protection from vibration of components in space launch vehicles. The commercial potential comes from using area average sensors with flexible circuitry, and Mide has four commercial products using that technology. The products range from generic technology such as sensors on a flexible circuitry for signal conditioning, a high-voltage amplifier to drive active fiber composites, and sensors connected in various ways on a small matrix board, to a specific application that uses sensors on a the shaft of a golf club to detect club head speed and provide feedback. The generic applications range from military uses such as protecting the launch of a spacecraft or quieting torpedoes in a submarine to nonmilitary commercial uses such as vibration control for the blades of a gas turbine or in air-conditioning ducts. Anything that vibrates and has a dynamics problem with the vibration and noise can potentially benefit from the technology.

Optigain, Inc. Single Longitudinal Mode Distributed-Feedback Fiber Optics Laser. Non-Fast Track. Optigain's technology provides a fiber version of a signal source that is similar to a semiconductor laser. Optigain's fiber laser is a distributed laser induced in a fiber rather than a semiconductor. Transmission systems need a high-quality signal source, and Optigain's technology provides a narrow, high-quality low-noise laser that can potentially capture some of the market for semiconductor lasers used in communications markets. The company's strategy is to develop various fiber-based devices, and the product here is a fiber-based component that can be put into other systems. Several lasers, each a different wavelength, have been developed, and communications markets where Optigain's fiber-based laser will be preferred over the semiconductor lasers are being sought. The superior performance of the fiber-based laser is in the linewidth of the laser and its spectral purity, which should lead to applications in sensor markets as well.

Regarding the relationship between the project and the mission of the funding agency, in this case the agency was quite open about different topics, with awards going to further technology for high-speed communications networks quite generally. The goal of the funding was to enable new technologies for such networks, and the concern was with the overall strength of the solutions rather than a specific set of narrow requirements.

QSource, Inc. Multiple Rectangular Discharge CO_2 Laser. Fast Track. QSource's CO_2 laser technology generates high power and efficiency and has specialized military uses. There are also nonmilitary commercial applications with large market potential. QSource's laser features higher power, smaller size, and an advantage in cost. CO_2 lasers are used in laser radar to bounce a pulse off an object, its high sensitivity allowing detailed information to be obtained about a tank or an aircraft many miles away. The laser system along with a DC battery source can be built in the size of a small suitcase. The CO_2 laser has very high efficiency, transmitting substantial distances with very little power loss; it is compact, uses a simple gas, and is very efficient.

The technology is dual use. For example, the basic transmitter unit in the laser radar has applications for heating, cutting, and trimming, for example, in conjunction with one of the lasers used in eye surgery that was developed initially in another DoD SBIR project trying to track objects at great distance. The laser is inherently sterile, and so, it is ideal for cutting tissue. It can be used for cutting teeth, working on teeth, and as a mechanical drill. It is more expensive than a drill, but it eliminates the risk of transmitting hepatitis or other viruses. A laser dental system has a detachable head in the optical system that delivers the laser and is easy to clean. The surgery is painless; there is no need for anesthesia. The dental market alone over the next 10 years is projected to sell 100,000 dental laser systems once the procedure for hard tissue is approved. A CO_2 laser dental system will sell for about $20,000. The energetic CO_2 lasers that QSource technology improves upon should have a market of $2 billion in the dental market alone. The medical therapeutic uses include the dental applications, skin resurfacing, and microsurgery in the ear. Further markets have been identified for sealed CO_2 lasers in materials processing and various research applications.

There are a large number of CO_2 lasers available and, over the past decade, they have become more functional. The cost of producing them in terms of dollars per watt is not great, but more than half of that cost is in the basic power source needed to energize the laser (i.e., powering the basic laser itself, not the entire system). The big advance provided by QSource technology is to reduce the cost of the power supply. Some of the older technology can achieve the same level of efficiency as the new QSource rectangular discharge laser, but those technologies result in products that are very big and not very sturdy.

SEA CORP (Systems Engineering Associates Corp.). Rapid Prototype Portable Combat and Launch System. Non-Fast Track. The technology is a software based-fire control system that allows a submarine to fire various types of torpedoes. Modern submarine systems are not compatible with all types of torpedoes. SEA CORP has created a system in a suitcase that can be plugged in and will allow the submarine to use different types of torpedoes.

Modular Gas Generator Launch Canister. Non-Fast Track. This second technology developed by SEA CORP is a launcher for torpedoes that uses automotive air-bag technology rather than a conventional gas system. It is modular, environmentally friendly, and uses a commercial off-the-shelf item to meet a specialized military purpose. Other commercial applications of both technologies are being considered, and the technologies will allow SEA CORP to diversify its activities into profitable new lines of business that are very different from its historical focus.

Spectra Science Corporation. Quantum Dots: Next Generation of Electronic Phosphors. Fast Track. The technology centers on better phosphor that results in a brighter image on large-screen projections. The technology combines the three core technologies of Spectra Science. First, the company has laser paint technology using disordered lasers. Conventional lasers use mirrors as the gain source, but laser paints use scatters such as titanium particles. So, a composite system is used to create the gain source; the laser excites the material and the feedback is from materials rather than from mirrors. The laser paint technology is used for identification or authentication, for example, via a label on a fabric or in a document.

The second core technology came from Phase I of this SBIR award. In that research, Spectra developed the ability to make smaller phosphor particles with surfaces for the composite systems that could exhibit gain and could be used in a laser paint. The difficulty to be surmounted was that the surfaces of the particles have a large number of defect sites, which trap light, preventing its emission.

The third core technology is the focus of the SBIR project's Phase II. It is a combination of the first two technologies. Phase I resulted in development of quantum dot phosphors for display applications—better phosphors that could be driven harder with the result of a brighter image. Phase II then shifted gears and focused on developing what had been discovered. Spectra Science has merged its work on display technologies and materials for laser paints to develop a lasing projection system. With previous technologies, large-screen projections can be viewed only in the dark. With Spectra Science's new technology, the phosphors are excited and emit higher energies than previously, overcoming this limitation. DoD's SBIR award here meets their mission in terms of improved images for large-screen projection systems. That goal remained the same even when Phase II was refocused, and the project clearly satisfies Spectra Science's strategic mission of seeking potential applications for its core technologies.

Synkinetics, Inc. High Precision Gimbal System. Fast Track. The Synkinetics technology is an innovative system of gears that provide cost-effective, sturdy, precision devices for positioning and pointing armaments. Such devices are used, for example, in missile control systems. Synkinetics's new speed conversion technology improves current high-precision pointing and positioning transmission equipment at a reasonable cost. The technology features flat-plate cam gears in an in-line mechanism that combines the rolling aspects of bearings with the transmission aspects of gears to obtain a versatile, robust, compact, reduced-weight, high-precision, efficient, and cost-effective drive mechanism. The technology is generic and has countless applications. The transmissions will have uses for pointing and precision positioning of various payloads for industry and the military. Applications of reliable, low-cost, and low-maintenance precision positioners are expected in the medical, electronics, marine, mobile satellite communications, and aerospace industries.

Yardney Technical Products, Inc. Low Cost, Lightweight, Rechargeable Lithium-Ion Batteries. Fast Track. Yardney has developed the battery using the prismatic cell technology identified in Phase I of the project and plans to deliver a prototype to its sponsoring agency. The battery has a 25 percent improvement in capacity compared to the battery that the military now uses and would represent a major jump in performance for the DoD uses for the particular style of battery. The market for the lithium-ion battery has grown rapidly from nothing in 1990 to current sales of $1.2 billion. Currently, the market is growing at 30 percent a year, and there is much opportunity for new technologies. The technology will be useful to other governments; with approval, sales to armies of U.S. allies are expected. Nonmilitary commercial applications are expected as well.

COMPANIES' EXPECTATIONS FOR SBIR PROJECTS AND REASONS THAT SBIR SUPPORT WAS NEEDED

As Table 4 shows, the SBIR awards made possible research that otherwise would not have been undertaken or would have been done on a smaller

TABLE 4   The SBIR Award and the Company's Strategy (The number of respondents indicates the total for the category)

Impact of SBIR Award	Fast Track	Non-Fast Track
Expected an increase in company size (sales or employment) or more diversified product line	6	7
Would the company have undertaken the research without the SBIR award?		
No	5	6
On a lesser scale	1	1
Yes	0	0

scale at a slower pace. The awards are expected to expand the businesses of the SBIR winners.

In answer to the question of whether the company would have undertaken the research without the SBIR award, representative comments included the following ones paraphrased from the interviews.

No. To support our Phase I project, we tried to find support from other companies and venture capitalists. The venture capitalists want too high a rate of return and want returns too quickly. Joint ventures don't work either. You need their money, so they want lots of rights. You must sell your soul to them. These partner companies are providing capital basically and sometimes distribution networks.

No. Working on a particular DoD program enabled us to do further work on our technology and gain insight into commercialization. The SBIR project is an incubation period of sorts to new start-up companies with new technology, an innovative way of approaching a problem. After the SBIR project, the development work that remains is a reorientation of the technology, looking at how to manufacture and commercialize for nonmilitary applications, to come up with a low-cost way to mass produce for less sophisticated requirements. But at the outset, the SBIR award is the lifeblood of new entrepreneurial ventures when new technology is to be advanced. We came up with something worthwhile for DoD, but we also advanced our own technology to another level without going crazy looking for outside investors. The lessons learned in the SBIR project provide the database that allows us to extrapolate intelligently and succeed in nonmilitary, commercial applications of our technology.

We would have devoted some resources to the project, but it is questionable whether we would have gotten this far. We would have sought assistance from other companies and from universities. We would have proceeded on a smaller scale and sought a partner down the road.

No. There is no guarantee that such high-risk research will pan out. And the SBIR program understands that, and it therefore requires not necessarily a commercial product, but instead a good effort. It understands that in many cases the value will be to prove the technological approach taken is *not* the right path. So the [funding agency within DoD] will not go down that path again. In fact, in the case of our award, [the funding agency] gave two awards. So, it spends $1.5 million on two projects running parallel, and the probability of at least one success is increased. We'll have a cookoff . . . with the other company to see which box is the better one to go with.

Probably not. We have no means of acquiring capital except through loans or from investors. But being honest with them, we could not raise the necessary funds—at least not at the outset of the SBIR projects. DoD does not select its highest priority acquisition projects to develop through the SBIR program. Instead, it uses projects that are interesting and have great potential value and the possibility for acquisition. But they are lower priority, high-risk projects. It is difficult to attract outside investment for such projects. These are projects for which we could not show an outside investor definite acquisition plans. If we could, DoD would not use the SBIR program to fund the projects. The SBIR projects are ones for which the acquisition plans are fuzzy.

No. We would not have done the project without the SBIR award. We devote about 6 percent of our income to research. This would not have been a project to get those funds. Without SBIR help, our research would have been more near-term and less challenging.

Table 5 shows the reasons why the SBIR funding was needed. The projects entailed substantial technical and market risks, and the projects required substantial amounts of capital from the perspective of the small businesses doing the research. Clearly, many respondents are concerned about the possibilities for opportunistic behavior by sources of external financing in the early stages of the research that the SBIR program funds. On the other hand, once the small business can finance its early-stage research and has moved beyond the initial research and development (R&D) stage, the company is, on the whole, comfortable with the degree to which it can protect its property rights. Whether from patent protection or from carefully negotiated licensing agreements, despite the fact that the firms typically do not anticipate capturing all of the profits that their research will create, they do expect to capture a sufficient amount of those profits to make their investments worthwhile. Table 5 focuses on the reasons that the companies would not have been able to carry out the research without public funding. Although of course the SBIR program is not expected to change the technical risk or opportunistic behavior, as explained later, it does increase the private expected rate of return above the private hurdle rate. With public funding, despite the risks, the firm will undertake the research.

In addition to their comments accompanying Table 4, respondents offered further insights about their needs for SBIR funding when discussing the list of

TABLE 5   Reasons SBIR Funding Was Needed: Why the Company Would not Have Done the Research, or Would Have Delayed the Research, or Would Have Done It on a Lesser Scale, Without SBIR Funding

Reason[a]	Number of Respondents Indicating the Reason	Rank-Weighted Score[b]
Fast Track Companies		
1. High technical risk	6	43
2. High capital costs	5	35
3. Long time to market	4	27
4. Spillovers to multiple markets	1	1.5
5. Uses technologies in different industries	2	9
6. Property rights	2	8
7. Compatibility and interoperability	1	4.5
8. Opportunistic behavior	2	11
Non-Fast Track Companies		
1. High technical risk	3	23
2. High capital costs	5	35.5
3. Long time to market	4	28.5
4. Spillovers to multiple markets	0	0
5. Uses technologies in different industries	1	7
6. Property rights	2	9
7. Compatibility and interoperability	1	3
8. Opportunistic behavior	4	22

[a]Detailed descriptions for the reasons: (1) High technical risk associated with the underlying research, (2) high capital costs to undertake the underlying research, (3) long time to complete the research and commercialize the resulting technology, (4) underlying research spills over to multiple markets and is not appropriable, (5) market success of the technology depends on technologies in different industries, (6) property rights cannot be assigned to the underlying research, (7) resulting technology must be compatible and interoperable with other technologies, (8) high risk of opportunistic behavior when sharing information about the technology. Reasons are based on Tassey (1997) and Link and Scott (1998).

[b]If a respondent ranks a reason first, that counts for 8 points, second implies 7 points, and so on down to eighth which would count 1 point. However, if a respondent ranks, say, only three reasons, then only those three reasons would receive any rank-weighted score—they would receive 8, 7, and 6 points, respectively, while all other reasons would receive 0 points. Thus, if 10 respondents ranked the first reason most important, and 2 ranked it second, and 1 respondent ranked it fourth, the rank-weighted score for the first reason would be $(8 \times 10) + (7 \times 2) + (5 \times 1) = 99$. Ties split evenly the points assigned for the number of tied reasons. For example, if two reasons tied for first for a respondent, then each would receive scores of 7.5. Finally, note that the rank-weighted scores for the sample of six Fast Track companies should be multiplied by 7/6 to make them comparable with the rank-weighted scores from the sample of seven non-Fast Track companies.

reasons in Table 5. For example, the difficulties faced by small businesses when raising funds from large corporations or venture capitalists are reflected in the following comments that were made when discussing opportunistic behavior.

> In one of our earlier SBIR projects, after we had used Phase I for risk reduction we became convinced that the technology would work, but then only after we had a patent were we willing to approach the large companies for a partnership. A small business needs to have a patent in hand in our area of technology. The big companies, in our area, will say: "We do not sign nondisclosure agreements with small companies."

> The eighth reason, opportunistic behavior is also important. It is what kills Fast Tracks. The outside partner wants to claim rights to the technology. That is what killed our Fast Track. It did not fly because our partner wanted more complete rights. The outside partner would provide one-third of the money but wanted over one-half of the rights.

The second of the two comments is different from the first. The first comment reflects the concern that the outsider will steal the small business's intellectual property and use it for its own purposes. The second comment reflects the fact that because the SBIR projects are high-risk projects, outside investors demand very high expected rates of return. Many comments like the second comment were made when the interviews turned explicitly to discussion of outside finance, and those comments are reported later.

THE COMPANIES' PLANS FOR FUTURE SBIR PROPOSALS

Because of the barriers to complete private funding of small business innovation research that are emphasized in Table 5, all of the small businesses plan to apply for SBIR awards in the future to support additional high-risk research. Table 6 shows that fact and also notes the range of responses to the question of whether previous awards were important for winning the current award. There are two issues here. One is a substantive issue of whether the technology pursued in the present award has evolved from technology developed in previous awards. For some firms, past awards were not directly relevant to the present one, but for others the current award was for further development of technology developed with earlier SBIR awards. A second issue is a procedural one: Would the fact that SBIR awards were won previously have affected the chances, *ceteris paribus,* for winning the current award? There was no general perception among many of the respondents that their chances were affected one way or the other by having won previous awards, apart from the substantive benefits when the technologies were linked and evolving sequentially through time as new SBIR projects were begun. However, a couple of respondents expressed views that previous awards sometimes can reduce a company's chances for winning subsequent awards.

TABLE 6   Plans for SBIR Awards (The number of respondents indicates the number in the category)

	Fast Track	Non-Fast Track
Previous awards were important for winning current award		
Yes	0	2 (reduced chances)
		3 (increased chances)
No	1	1
Planning applications for SBIR awards in future		
Yes	6	7
No	0	0

Responses about the impact of earlier awards include the following comments illustrating views about positive and negative effects.

> Yes. Previous success is a very, very negative factor. Managers of the SBIR program at the highest levels are frustrated by what they perceive as the lack of "success" stories from their program. They have difficulty accepting that their definition of success (commercialization of products from an SBIR program) is an extremely unlikely outcome given the structure of the SBIR program. Thus, there is a built-in bias to award Phase IIs to small companies who already have in place commercial successes not supported by the SBIR program and for which they can take credit. These companies are very rare because they normally do not participate in the SBIR program.

> With the Fast Track Program, there is a two-tier standard favoring firms new to the SBIR program, with 25 percent cost-sharing for a new company and 100 percent cost-sharing for companies like us.

> Previous awards helped us; we learned what the funding agencies' needs were. We learned that to have a successful proposal, we need to understand what is wanted by the agency. Previous SBIR awards helped us learn how to have a successful proposal.

Responses to the question about future applications for SBIR awards (Do you anticipate applying for SBIR awards in the future? Why?) include the following and reflect the reasons that innovative small businesses are enthusiastic about the SBIR program..

> Yes. Although the developments for the military from the SBIR awards will not be directly applicable for nonmilitary, commercial products, indirectly the non-military technology is being advanced. While coming up with something worth-while for DoD, we also advance our own nonmilitary commercial technology to a higher level without going crazy looking for outside investors. The lessons learned in these SBIR projects provide the data base that allows us to extrapolate intelligently. The SBIR program makes it possible for us to learn and develop our technology. The program is fantastic for young vibrant entrepreneurs.

Yes. It's the only way to keep the lights on, given the high risk and high capital costs for the research we are doing as we try to get into a different technology. Our existing line of business generates very little revenue and we cannot fund R&D ourselves. For the type of research we are doing, neither venture capitalists nor large companies will work as sources of outside funding. Both the venture capitalists and the large companies want too high a rate of return—too many rights to the future returns relative to the investment they would make in our company.

Yes, because we have created an efficient infrastructure to generate prototypes in response to requests for Phase I and Phase II proposals.

Yes, selectively. We've got a pilot line now, so we are beyond the SBIR-type project in our current work. Maybe we will find a wrinkle appropriate for another SBIR project in our current technology.

Yes. The SBIR program is the way to get funds for truly innovative high-risk small business projects that cannot effectively be financed by outside private funds, given the opportunistic behavior by companies or lack of understanding of the technology by venture capitalists.

Right now, we're in the midst of Phase II, so no immediate plans. But, yes, because the SBIR program gives us the ability to develop a technology we would not have been able to develop on our own ,given the technical risk and capital costs and the long time from initial research until commercialization.

Yes. We like the challenge and broad scope of the topics.

Yes. Our DoD customers have identified several areas where our technology can be developed further and applied to their needs.

Had it not been for this Phase I, neither we nor the [sponsoring agency] would have been at this stage. We believe we can make similar breakthroughs with future SBIR awards.

Yes. The SBIR awards help us research new technologies, given technical risk and the risk of opportunistic behavior by large companies if we go to them with our ideas before they are developed.

Yes. SBIR awards let us accept the risk of good projects.

Yes. The SBIR program has been very successful for us. It has allowed us to develop a product line for eventual commercialization and growth of our company. The new product line will be more profitable than our existing product lines. We understand the SBIR program is a start-up program, not intended to be used over and over. But it allows us to do high-risk research with commercial potential and to expand our business into new product lines.

THE COMPANIES' COMMERCIALIZATION PLANS

Table 7 shows the ranges of responses about commercialization plans across the projects. Also shown is the range of responses regarding the use of patents

TABLE 7   Commercialization Plans (The number of projects for the indicated category)

Plan	Fast Track (6 projects for 6 firms)	Non-Fast Track (8 projects for 7 firms)
Expected time until commercialization		
≤ 1 year	4	4
> 1 year and ≤ 2 years	1	2
> 2 years and ≤ 3 years	1	0
> 3 years and ≤ 4 years	0	1
> 4 years and ≤ 5 years	0	1
> 5 years	0	0
Anticipating strategic alliances for production		
No	0	4
Yes	5	4
Uncertain	1	0
Patents		
Yes or expected soon	5	5
No	1	3
Scientific papers		
Yes	4	1
No	2	7

and scientific papers that help to disseminate technology as well as protect rights to intellectual property. The patents, of course, can help to create and protect intellectual property rights, while the papers disseminate information and may even bolster the effectiveness of patent rights by making ancillary nonpatented materials common knowledge that cannot be the basis for competing patents. Finally, discussion revealed that the respondents see their SBIR-funded research in a different light from their other technologies with commercial potential. On the whole, the projects are different, entailing more technical and market risk, and they are not generally the sort of research projects that the companies would have pursued without SBIR support. Not surprisingly, then, the respondents report that commercialization plans are different than what would have been the case without SBIR support. On the other hand, given that the SBIR project has proven the commercial potential for what was an extraordinarily risky project at the start of Phase I, the firms often report that with the commercial potential now established, the commercialization plans look very much as they would for any project that had reached the stage of making prototypes and gearing up for production. Nonetheless, it is also true that in many cases the respondents are in the position of needing a "Phase III" to provide the bridge from highly promising technology with great commercial potential to successful development of the manufacturing technology and the final product for the market.

Of course, as seen in Table 4, without the SBIR program, the research projects typically would not have been as close to commercial results, because the projects would not have been undertaken or would have proceeded in a different way. However, here the respondents commented further not only about the delay that might have resulted, but also about the remaining difficulties that they faced as they looked for financial support for additional periods of development before commercializing their technology.

Respondents' comments here about the impact of the SBIR award on commercialization plans included the following.

> I was an academic. I never, never would have done this commercialization research without the SBIR program. The SBIR program spawned a development that would not have happened in the same time frame, and the development will result in commercialization.

> We never would have gotten this far; we would not have taken the $100K look [in Phase I]. We would have put this project aside to work on something else. The SBIR award allowed us to take a six-month look at a promising idea. We got some good results, and we can now justify a million dollar investment ourselves.

> Without the SBIR program, we would have, at a slower pace, tried to bring the technology along so far, to a point, and then we would have tried to generate interest to bring in a partner. But without the SBIR award, we would not have been so far along.

> The SBIR program let us develop our own technology while we created something worthwhile for DoD. We will be able to use the understanding and data we developed in significant ways to further our commercial, nonmilitary technology.

> We would not have done the project without SBIR, but if we had done the project, our commercial plans would be the same.

> The SBIR program put us in a position to develop this new product.

> Assuming that we could have gotten to this point without SBIR, our commercialization plans would have been the same. But we could not have gotten to this point without SBIR. The technology was too unproven. The SBIR program was willing to take the risk when alternative sources of investment funding were not available.

COMPANIES' PERCEPTIONS OF THE RELATIONSHIP BETWEEN THE SBIR AWARD AND PRIVATE THIRD-PARTY FINANCING

Table 8 shows that the Fast Track program *does* address what most respondents see as a difficult period for SBIR projects—namely, the gap between Phase I and Phase II funding. Both Fast Track and non-Fast Track respondents emphasize the difficulties created by the gap: Employees must be paid and the project

TABLE 8   Financing and External Partners (The number of respondents indicating the category.)

	Fast Track	Non-Fast Track
Expressed difficulties bridging a gap in time between Phase I and Phase II		
Yes	0	4
No opinion expressed	6	3
Did the SBIR award facilitate the attraction of outside investors?		
Yes	4	1
No	1	6
No opinion expressed	1	0

kept afloat and progressing from the Phase I stage; yet many small businesses, for the reasons discussed above, find it very difficult to acquire financing while waiting for a Phase II award. The effectiveness of the Fast Track program in this regard is clear from Table 8, because the Fast Track winners did not report "gap" difficulties on their Fast Track projects. Table 8 also shows that winning an SBIR award (for our sample of projects that all won Phase II awards) facilitated the attraction of outside financing to further commercialize the technology developed under the SBIR project, in the perceptions of most Fast Track respondents. With one exception, the non-Fast Track respondents did not find that the SBIR award helped them to secure outside funds. This reflects the difference in prospects for commercialization early in the SBIR-funded research of Fast Track projects as compared with non-Fast Track projects.

Comments of the respondents about the financing issues and their relationship to the SBIR award included the following.

> One Fast Track respondent reported: During Phase I, there was full funding by the government, but beyond that we have had one-to-one matching. Although we did not use the SBIR award as a marketing tool to attract outside funding, when we went to an investor, the award was part of the whole package. The matching funds to go with the outside investor's funds were there, so yes, that helped.

> Another Fast Track respondent said: Yes, the SBIR award was used as leverage, as a marketing tool. That is when it is most helpful. Having the SBIR Fast Track award and the financing that it helped attract served as a bridge between Phase I and Phase II; the gap between Phase I and Phase II was eliminated.

> A non-Fast Track respondent observed: There was an eight-month delay [between Phase I and Phase II]. This allowed our competitors . . . to take our work and get a head start on improvements. This left us in a difficult position when Phase II was eventually awarded.

The same non-Fast Track respondent said: Personal friends seem the best source of outside financing for us. The SBIR award is not a useful marketing tool because most investors do not wish to have copies of proposals, Phase I final reports and Phase II progress reports wandering over the desks of unknown reviewers. Some agencies use outside reviewers who take the best ideas and have their graduate students pursue them. This practice is not supposed to happen, but is the rule rather than the exception.

Another non-Fast Track respondent said: After Phase I ends, you have trained people and your staff is waiting around. You are holding your breath until Phase II begins and the needed funds are available.

Another non-Fast Track respondent commented about the gap between Phase I and Phase II in this way: Considering the public's $750,000 investment, the rights demanded are acceptable; the processing takes a little longer than it should; by the time reports are submitted for Phase I, four months go by. That gap is not a problem for a large corporation, but for us a gap that lasts well over a quarter, and probably six months in the end, is a problem. But overall the process works well.

Another non-Fast Track respondent stated: We used internal funds only. We did not consider using Fast Track. That would have required an outside investor. But the project is a high-risk project and DoD's acquisition plans are not yet clear. It is highly unlikely that we could get the outside investors required for Fast Track. At the end of Phase II, it would be possible to get outside investors, but not at any time prior to that and not even now. Fast Track is a good idea in theory, but in execution there is a problem. At the end of Phase I, a company typically has just a concept. Later when there is a prototype, then you can do something with outside investors.

Another non-Fast Track respondent said: In a small business setting, we are wrapped up in technological issues and production issues and decisions about how to market our product. It would not be productive to get into the specialized activity of fundraising, given the circumstances. There must be somebody willing to put money into the project. Plenty of people will give lip service to the idea and take your time. But the probability of actually getting the money is less than 5 percent. To spend 80 percent of the time for the 5 percent chance of financial support is not a good use of our time.

COMPANIES' VIEWS ABOUT ADMINISTRATION OF THE SBIR PROGRAM

The respondents report that they are highly satisfied with the SBIR program; they are overwhelmingly positive in their overall impressions of the program, as shown in Table 9. The responding companies believe that the SBIR program made it possible for them to do significant research that they otherwise would have been unable to do. They clearly believe that the research has furthered not only their company's strategy but the mission of the sponsoring DoD agency as well.

TABLE 9   SBIR Program Administration: Overall Impressions (The number of respondents indicating the category.)

Impression	Fast Track	Non-Fast Track
Favorable	6	7
Unfavorable	0	0

Nonetheless, the companies offered many suggestions for improving the SBIR program. The suggestions for improvement and the general concerns that were expressed include the following from the Fast Track companies.

> I have no recommendations to improve the program itself, but one recommendation could be made based on the success of my company. I did the technical work, but I brought in others to do the accounting and business administration. The SBIR program could promulgate information about how to proceed: Small business principals should recognize their strengths and weaknesses, and they should bring someone in to do the administrative work rather than having the scientist have to do it all. The SBIR program could encourage small businesses to bring in outside expertise to ensure competence in business administration to go along with the competence in the scientific work.

> I want to promote the SBIR concept. It provides a wonderful opportunity for us to develop our own technology and at the same time do something worthwhile for DoD. SBIRs are the lifeblood of new entrepreneurial ventures when new technology is to be advanced. We are all appreciative and thankful and grateful that there is this highway that allows us the opportunity to develop our technologies. However, one must remember that there is a dichotomy between requirements of the armed forces and requirements of nonmilitary commercialization. Typically, there is very little direct overlap. The military development will often have very costly requirements for high precision, and the results will not often be directly applicable for nonmilitary commercial use, although indirectly the nonmilitary technology is being advanced. One sees a correlation from the program itself into a commercial project, but the commercial project typically will not need to be as sophisticated, as accurate, as costly. It won't need the special materials. One cannot take the thing developed for military use and say it is a commercial product. And, if there are no direct commercialization results, one cannot say the SBIR project failed to pay off. The merits of the SBIR program should not be defined and based on commercialization. There is a gray area here. There may ultimately be commercial products that might not be obvious. The procedure and testing and designing for DoD is a bulwark for the work that follows in the nonmilitary commercial market, work that follows in nonobvious ways. When and where the experience pays off commercially is not always clear.

> The SBIR award did not really help us find our outside financing. We have a sister company that uses the same venture capitalist as the one we have brought

into the project, and the coincidence of the venture capitalist interests in the sister company and the research we are pursing allowed us to attract the third-party investment. So we were lucky getting the Fast Track designation and priority for a Phase II award. The company with equally good research prospects but no luck finding a financial partner will have lower priority. Why should we have priority just because we were lucky finding a partner for third-party investment. The advantage of a Fast Track is that it almost guarantees that you get a Phase II award. Getting a leg up on Phase II is very attractive to us. But there is a problem here if worthwhile projects get low priority because they are either unlucky in seeking outside funding or because they entail research that is not at a stage allowing the small business to attract third-party funds.

I like the SBIR program. It's easy to use. You get early warning on the web. It works. The problems are in the implementation, not the program itself. Some RFPs are so detailed, they are clearly written for one firm. Some RFPs no one can understand. Some are simply silly, asking for something that is not doable. But, overall, there is no real problem with the SBIR program. It works well.

Fast track is a great innovation. One of the lessons, I think, can be discovered by looking at the solicitations. Projects solicited will include at times requests for work on a very specialized technology that already is in existence and for which an upgrade is solicited. I'm not sure why an upgrade should be needed in many of these cases, but in any case why does such a thing appear under the SBIR program? It looks as if the DoD is using SBIR to get little companies to handle what used to be done with routine R&D and procurement at big companies. Now those companies are out of the defense-related business and their former employees are in little companies. It looks like the DoD program solicitation is designed to get the little companies to do what used to be done with DoD procurement. The little companies are perhaps easier to drive a good bargain with, but such projects are not an appropriate use of the SBIR pool of dollars. Fast Track is a great innovation because it takes money out of that pot and puts it into truly innovative small business projects with a high chance of commercialization. The money should be going to finding people with great ideas; lots will crash and burn, but the technology goes into our U.S. technology data bank, and that's where our good jobs come from. Fast Track makes good scientific industrial policy based on innovation and technology. It can find the truly innovative projects. The success here comes from experts reviewing proposals for DoD and making judgments better than cigar-chomping venture capitalists who know nothing about technology. Fast Track takes money out of the general pot of dollars and gets it away from procurement and to truly innovative people. Fast Track helps the SBIR program work as it should.

It is not clear how to structure the Fast Track partnerships so that they fly. A third party is dumping in hundreds of thousands of dollars, and the partnership includes that third party, the government, and us. It becomes very difficult to negotiate the deal. One suggestion might be for the SBIR program to incorporate a Phase III focused on manufacturing technology. When Phase II is successfully completed, there is an interesting product. But it is then up to us to get the money for equipment. A Phase III for developing manufacturing technology, for ramping up for production, might be quite helpful given the difficulties negotiating the third-party investments.

The prospects for commercialization could be improved if the SBIR program provided funding for a Mentor/Consultant as a part of Phase II. The SBIR firm would identify in the Phase II proposal a large corporation or marketing consulting firm that would work with the SBIR firm during Phase II and provide expertise about commercializing the technology. The small firm knows the technology, but the larger firm would act as a mentor during Phase II and would be able to help the small firm understand how to market the technology. The big company with the marketing channels and capabilities needed would look at the small company's innovative device and advise it on how to proceed. It would watch the small company and see what was going on and make recommendations and guide the small company, so that at the end of Phase II the small company is not left wondering what to do next. The funding for the Mentor/Consultant need not be an overly large amount. A cross section of the mentoring company would be needed. Someone from marketing, someone from engineering, someone from administration, finance, and management. Three or four people, maybe 100 hours each, to oversee and mentor the small company so that at the end of Phase II they have a direction and a good feel for the market potential and what to do. The SBIR program is now open ended; it is not realizing the fruits of what the program's projects are developing. Providing the opportunity of mentoring from and consulting with a large corporation could improve the prospects for commercialization of SBIR results.

The critical comments from the non-Fast Track respondents were as follows but, again, these are all comments made in the context of an overwhelmingly favorable impression of the SBIR program. The respondents were simply offering these thoughts as ideas that might be used to make a fine program even better.

We participated in earlier versions of the SBIR program. Fast Track is not useful for us. If we had technology in house during the first few weeks of the Phase I (which we never do), we would not go through the SBIR system at all.

The SBIR program is administered at the top by hard-working and well-meaning people who are really trying to improve our national technology base. As a suggestion, they might rethink how to best go about this task. We need improvements in certain key technology areas and there is widespread agreement as to which areas. However, we do not need uncoordinated Army, Navy, Air Force, DoE, NSF, and NIH SBIR programs, each trying to achieve the same broad goals. These key technology need areas should be assigned a lead agency that should fund all proposals in this area.

Of the 25 pages in the application, only about 5 are needed for technical evaluation. The other 20 could be filed separately, electronically, and be used only in the event the application is being considered for award. This would greatly reduce the complexity of the application process.

The original concept of Phase I followed by Phase II, and then Phase II leading to commercialization is probably flawed. I would recommend revising that concept. The SBIR program could help to complete the process of commercialization. From a successful Phase II project, the SBIR project could go to a stage where the Phase II success is developed further. The SBIR program could support such a bridge to commercialization. The SBIR program now is aimed at establishing technical feasibility, not commercial feasibility. A stage subsequent to Phase II, with government and the company sharing the costs of continuing development work, would be a good policy. Note that it is such sharing of cost for development work that the ATP projects entail. If big companies feel the government needs to help them with such projects, then small businesses need such support too. The Fast Track program is flawed because the end of Phase I is too soon to be ready to establish commercial potential. Fast Track will drive things more toward implementation rather than toward research. Such projects in themselves are fine as long as there is a limit on the amount of the SBIR program that goes to support that sort of effort. I would recommend setting a limited percentage of the SBIR funds that could go to Fast Track projects.

One of the biggest problems we have faced is that our program managers are not able to travel to us because of a lack of funding. Along with the funding, include 30K to 50K for the project monitor to do his job with the specific program for which he is the project manager. It would be easier to interact with the DoD manager if the manager could travel to our location. Also, we can spend the funds for Phase II in two years, but to physically accomplish all of our goals takes time. It would help if there were the latitude to make the Phase II projects three or four years in length rather than just two years.

We thought about Fast Track, but it was not right for us. It was too soon in our research to go to outside investors. We're too inexperienced for Fast Track. To use Fast Track, a company must be in a position to negotiate. Then there is a substantial cost for lawyers.

I recommend that the SBIR program ensure that the technical monitor is involved in the project. When the technical monitor is involved, things go much better than when the technical monitor is not involved.

There is a conceptual problem with Fast Track. The typical SBIR project will not be to the point by the end of Phase I to allow a commitment from an outside investor. Rarely would a venture capitalist think of funding a project unless the research is already done. Such research gets done during Phase II.

Overall the program works very well; things move fairly smoothly.

We did not consider using Fast Track. That would have required an outside investor. But the project is a high-risk project and DoD's acquisition plans are not yet clear. It is highly unlikely that we could get the outside investors required for Fast Track. At the end of Phase II, it would be possible to get outside investors, but not at any time prior to that and not even now. Fast Track is a good idea in theory, but in execution there is a problem. At the end of Phase I, a company typically has just a concept. Later, when there is a prototype, then you can do something with outside investors.

ESTIMATION OF LOWER-BOUND SOCIAL RATES
OF RETURN FOR THE SBIR PROJECTS

The data gathered during the interview with the 13 respondents allowed estimation of the private and social rates of return for the 14 projects discussed. The procedure is explained in much greater detail by Link and Scott (1998, 1999). Here, let me simply emphasize that these are *prospective* expected rates of return, even though the estimates of the investment costs are gathered subsequent to the beginning of Phase I (and arguably reflect what would have been the rational expectations for the costs when the project began). That is, the expected rates of return are, by the logic of the approach used to calculate them, estimations of the expectation of the rates of return *at the time that Phase I began.* At that time the SBIR projects were extraordinarily risky; they had upside potential, but also extraordinary downside risk. That is not only because the projects had great technical risks, and not only because of the market risk—even DoD procurement plans are not clear at the beginning of a Phase I SBIR project, but also because of the issues that make it difficult for small businesses to finance innovative investment. Impacted information, moral hazard, potential for opportunistic behavior on both sides of the financial transaction—all combine to result in a market failure. Indeed, we expect an incomplete market here.

The expected rate of return required by the potential outside investor exceeds the rate that the small business is willing to promise for the project and, as a result, the small businesses in our samples would not have proceeded with their innovative investments without the support of the SBIR program. Regarding the difficulties of raising outside financial capital, the respondents made the following observations.

> We would not agree to sell our souls to the venture capitalists or a large company.

> . . . the project is a high-risk project and DoD's acquisition plans are not yet clear. It is highly unlikely that we could get the outside investors required for Fast Track.

> We would not agree to an arrangement where we would lose control of our company and our intellectual property.

> The outside investors wanted half of the rights to profits in return for providing one-third of the financing.

> For the type of high-risk research funded by the SBIR program, a small company cannot go to the large companies with an interest in the projects because in our area of technology the large companies will not sign nondisclosure agreements with small companies. Only after the technical risk has been reduced and a prototype and a patent are in hand would the small company have the ability to negotiate a partnership.

> We came up with something worthwhile for DoD, but we also advanced our

> own technology to another level without going crazy looking for outside investors.
>
> There must be somebody willing to put money into the project. Plenty of people will give lip service to the idea and take your time. But the probability of actually getting the money is less than 5 percent. To spend 80 percent of the time for the 5 percent chance of financial support is not a good use of our time.
>
> . . ., to support our Phase I project, we tried to find support from other companies and venture capitalists. The venture capitalists want too high a rate of return and want returns too quickly. Joint ventures don't work either. You need their money, so they want lots of rights. You must sell your soul to them. These partner companies are providing capital basically, and sometimes distribution networks.
>
> We cannot use large companies or venture capitalists to fund our research. We protect our intellectual property with trade secrets rather than patents. We must stay out of the grips of the venture capitalists in order to protect our intellectual property.

Thus, at the outset of the SBIR project, the required rate of return for outside financing is not met. Had the expected rate of return exceeded the rate of return required to secure outside financing, the deal for outside financing could have been struck. However, uniformly, the respondents explain that, at the outset of the SBIR, such funding could not be obtained. The SBIR award allows the SBIR project to proceed and ensures that socially valuable research is not lost because of imperfect financial markets, incomplete appropriability, and substantial downside risk. The required rate of return for the outside investors is simply not expected at the *outset* of the project. *Now*, as Phase II draws to an end for the sampled projects, upward of a million dollars or much more has been spent to resolve uncertainties—technical and market uncertainties and also uncertainties about the small business doing the research. Now, after Phase I and Phase II, the logic of our construction of the expected cash flows below would not necessarily hold. *We have estimated prospective rates of return at the outset of Phase I, and these show the market failure and show the reason for the SBIR awards. Without the SBIR funding, socially valuable research would not be undertaken because the required rate of return for outside private investors could not be expected to be achieved, and the small business would not have been able to finance the research itself.*

The calculation of the lower bound for the social rates of return uses the information summarized in Table 10; the information was developed from the interviews that were conducted with the SBIR award winners. Some of the information is also available in the DoD files; however, the information was verified with the respondents and updated to reflect any changes from the DoD files. Variables for duration, total costs, and SBIR funding were combined into one figure for both Phase I and Phase II of the project. Typically, there is an extra

TABLE 10   Definition of Variables for Determining the Prospective Expected Social Rate of Return

Variable	Definition
d	Duration of the SBIR project in years
C	Total cost of the SBIR project
A	SBIR funding
r	Private hurdle rate
z	Duration of the extra period of development beyond Phase II in years
F	Additional cost for the extra period of development
T	Life of the commercialized technology in years
L	Lower bound for average expected annual private return to investing firms
U	Upper bound for average expected annual private return to investing firms
v	Proportion of value appropriated

period of development after Phase II is completed and during which further work with prototypes and initial production lines is done. The length of that additional development period and the extra costs that the company would incur were obtained in the interviews.

Companies cannot expect to appropriate all of the value created by their innovations. First, the innovations will generate consumer surplus that no firm will appropriate, but that society will value. Our estimates of the social rate of return are conservative because we do not attempt to estimate the value of consumer surplus generated by the SBIR projects. Second, some of the profits generated by the innovations will be captured by firms other than the innovators. Larger companies, for example, will observe the innovation and some will successfully imitate it and produce the commercial product in competition with the small business innovator. Respondents were asked to estimate the proportion of the returns generated by their anticipated innovation that they expected to capture. Then, in an extended conversation, other possible applications of the technology developed during the SBIR project were explored. The respondent was then asked to estimate the multiplier to get from the profit stream generated by the immediate applications of the SBIR project's technology to the stream of profits generated in the broader applications' markets that could reasonably be anticipated. Finally, the responding company estimated the proportion of the returns in those broader markets that it anticipated capturing. From the discussion, we were then able to estimate the proportion of value appropriated by the innovating SBIR award winner.

The lower bound L for the average annual private return is found by solving Eq. (1) for L, because that will be the value for L such that the private firm just barely earns the hurdle, or required, rate of return on the portion of the total investment that the private firm must finance. The firm would not invest in the SBIR project unless it expected at least L for the average annual private return.

$$-\int_0^d \left(\frac{C-A}{d}\right)e^{-rt}dt - \int_d^{d+z}\left(\frac{F}{z}\right)e^{-rt}dt + \int_{d+z}^{d+z+T} Le^{-rt}dt = 0$$

$$\Rightarrow -\left(\frac{C-A}{d}\right)\left(\frac{-1}{r}\right)e^{-rt}\Big|_0^d - \left(\frac{F}{z}\right)\left(\frac{-1}{r}\right)e^{-rt}\Big|_d^{d+z} + (L)\left(\frac{-1}{r}\right)e^{-rt}\Big|_{d+z}^{d+z+T} = 0$$

(1)

$$\Rightarrow \left(\frac{C-A}{dr}\right)(e^{-rd}-1) + \left(\frac{F}{zr}\right)(e^{-r(d+z)}-e^{-rd}) - \left(\frac{L}{r}\right)(e^{-r(d+z+T)}-e^{-r(d+z)}) = 0$$

To find the upper bound U for the average annual private return, solve Eq. (2) for U, because any expected annual return greater than U would imply that the rate of return expected by the private firm would be more than its hurdle rate in the absence of SBIR funding, and therefore SBIR funding would not be required for the project.

$$-\int_0^d \left(\frac{C}{d}\right)e^{-rt}dt - \int_d^{d+z}\left(\frac{F}{z}\right)e^{-rt}dt + \int_{d+z}^{d+z+T} Ue^{-rt}dt = 0$$

$$\Rightarrow -\left(\frac{C}{d}\right)\left(\frac{-1}{r}\right)e^{-rt}\Big|_0^d - \left(\frac{F}{z}\right)\left(\frac{-1}{r}\right)e^{-rt}\Big|_d^{d+z} + (U)\left(\frac{-1}{r}\right)e^{-rt}\Big|_{d+z}^{d+z+T} = 0$$

(2)

$$\Rightarrow \left(\frac{C}{dr}\right)(e^{-rd}-1) + \left(\frac{F}{zr}\right)(e^{-r(d+z)}-e^{-rd}) - \left(\frac{U}{r}\right)(e^{-r(d+z+T)}-e^{-r(d+z)}) = 0$$

Our estimate of the average expected annual private return to the firm is $(L + U)/2$. The average expected annual private return to the firm equals v times the average expected annual return that will be captured by all producers using the technology (producer surplus). Knowing the average expected annual private return is $(L + U)/2$ and knowing the portion of producer surplus that is appropriable, v, then we find that the total producer surplus equals $(L + U)/2v$ and hence this value is a lower bound for the average expected annual social return. It is a lower bound because consumer surplus has not been measured.

The private expected rate of return without SBIR funding would be the solution to i in Eq. (3):

$$-\int_0^d \left(\frac{C}{d}\right)e^{-it}dt - \int_d^{d+z}\left(\frac{F}{z}\right)e^{-it}dt + \int_{d+z}^{d+z+T} \left(\frac{L+U}{2}\right)e^{-it}dt = 0$$

$$\Rightarrow \left(\frac{C}{di}\right)(e^{-id}-1) + \left(\frac{F}{zi}\right)(e^{-i(d+z)}-e^{-id}) - \left(\frac{L+U}{2i}\right)(e^{-i(d+z+T)}-e^{-i(d+z)}) = 0$$

(3)

The lower bound on the social rate of return is found by solving Eq. (4) for i:

$$-\int_0^d \left(\frac{C}{d}\right)e^{-it}dt - \int_d^{d+z}\left(\frac{F}{z}\right)e^{-it}dt + \int_{d+z}^{d+z+T} \left(\frac{L+U}{2v}\right)e^{-it}dt = 0$$

$$\Rightarrow \left(\frac{C}{di}\right)(e^{-id}-1) + \left(\frac{F}{zi}\right)(e^{-i(d+z)}-e^{-id}) - \left(\frac{L+U}{2iv}\right)(e^{-i(d+z+T)}-e^{-i(d+z)}) = 0$$

(4)

The private expected rate of return with SBIR funding would be the solution to i in Eq. (5):

$$-\int_0^d \left(\frac{C-A}{d}\right)e^{-it}dt - \int_d^{d+z}\left(\frac{F}{z}\right)e^{-it}dt + \int_{d+z}^{d+z+T}\left(\frac{L+U}{2}\right)e^{-it}dt = 0$$

$$\Rightarrow \left(\frac{C-A}{di}\right)(e^{-id}-1)+\left(\frac{F}{zi}\right)(e^{-i(d+z)}-e^{-id})-\left(\frac{L+U}{2i}\right)(e^{-i(d+z+T)}-e^{-i(d+z)})=0$$

$$(5)$$

Table 11 provides the various prospective expected rates of return for the New England projects as a group and for the Fast Track and the non-Fast Track projects. Tables 12, 13, and 14 provide the summary statistics for the data.

It seems clear that the Fast Track cases are much different from the non-Fast Track cases. Although they begin with a Phase I where a small business needs outside support, they exhibit sufficient commercial potential to attract outside funding quickly, and as a result these are likely to be projects that, relative to non-Fast Track projects, have higher *lower bounds* for social rates of return (recall that the social rates of return measure only producer, not consumer, surplus). Furthermore, because there will be more of the project investment cost paid by private funds, the private rates of return given SBIR support will be lower for the Fast Track projects.

CONCLUSIONS

In all, the collection of 14 New England SBIR projects studied here exhibited high risk at the outset of Phase I—both technical and market risk, high capital costs, and often a long expected time before commercialization of the resulting technology. Comments suggest fairly substantial appropriability problems for some projects, even within the narrower applications of the technology. Appropriability problems typically are greater when broader potential applications are considered. Uniformly, in the absence of the SBIR funding, the research projects would not have been undertaken in the same way or at the same pace.

TABLE 11   Prospective Expected Rates of Return (ROR) for New England SBIR Projects

Region	Number of Cases	Private ROR Without SBIR (prvnosbr)	Social ROR, lower bound (soclwrbd)	Private ROR with SBIR (prvsbr)
New England	14	0.31	0.60	0.58
Fast Track	6	0.33	0.68	0.53
Non-Fast Track	8	0.30	0.55	0.61

TABLE 12   Data for New England Observations (Fast Track and Non-Fast Track)

Variable	Obs	Mean	Std. Dev.	Min	Max
d	14	777,857	0.3833893	2.17	3.5
C	14	1,285,053	692,912.4	717,873	3,450,000
A	14	785,715.6	144,072.6	507,873	1,099,966
T	14	16.32143	8.111263	5	30^a
z	14	1.535714	1.456442	-0.375^b	5
F	14	1,063,929	2,597,688	0	1.00e+07
r^c	7	0.3821429	0.1222312	0.2	0.5
v	14	0.3053929	0.1992511	0.025	0.6
L	14	1,009,056	1,185,032	79,185	4,486,450
U	14	2,370,090	2,174,385	413,400	8,666,330
prvnosbr	14	0.31	0.0689481	0.19	0.43
soclwrbd	14	0.605	0.1754445	0.28	0.82
prvsbr	14	0.5757143	0.2172455	0.21	1.03

[a]One company responded that T would be several decades, and another reported that T would be forever. In both cases, T was conservatively entered as the value 30 years. However, because the relevant discount rates are so high, the difference between 30 years and "forever" is not significant. In the integrals, the term with T entered negatively as an exponent would become zero, but with a large value of T, the term is very small in any case.

[b]This observation has a negative value because commercial returns started before the end of Phase II.

[c]Half of the respondents were uncomfortable estimating the private hurdle rate that outside financiers would apply to their projects at their outset. For those, the average value of r was used in the calculations.

TABLE 13   Data for the New England Fast Track Observations[a]

Variable	Obs	Mean	Std. Dev.	Min	Max
d	6	2.578333	0.3279888	2.17	3.17
C	6	1,659,609	926,636.1	850,000	3,450,000
A	6	855,436.5	170,450.7	598,700	1,099,966
T	6	18.75	9.585145	7.5	30
z	6	1.208333	0.7486098	0.25	2.5
F	6	500,000	411,096.1	100,000	1,000,000
r	3	0.4	0.0901388	0.325	0.5
v	6	0.2379167	0.1296767	0.1575	0.5
L	6	971,784.8	673,530.7	533,085	2,237,640
U	6	1,962,022	654,443.7	1,125,230	3,036,360
prvnosbr	6	0.3266667	0.0388158	0.3	0.4
soclwrbd	6	0.6783333	0.1553598	0.44	0.82
prvsbr	6	0.53	0.1749286	0.35	0.86

[a]See notes to Table 12.

TABLE 14   Data for the New England Non-Fast Track Observations[a]

Variable	Obs	Mean	Std. Dev.	Min	Max
d	8	2.9275	0.3693527	2.5	3.5
C	8	1,004,136	260,581.3	717,873	1,419,895
A	8	733,424.9	102,491.9	507,873	820,000
T	8	14.5	6.907553	5	25
z	8	1.78125	1.838028	-0.375	5
F	8	1,486,875	3,454,596	0	1.00e+07
r	4	0.36875	0.1546165	0.2	0.5
v	8	0.356	0.2342849	0.025	0.6
L	8	1,037,010	1,510,587	79,185	4,486,450
U	8	2,676,142	2,867,886	413,400	8,666,330
prvnosbr	8	0.2975	0.0856488	0.19	0.43
soclwrbd	8	0.55	0.1784857	0.28	0.78
prvsbr	8	0.61	0.2503141	0.21	1.03

[a]See the notes to Table 12.

Not surprisingly, then, respondents reported that outside investors, at the outset of Phase I, would have required too high a rate of return to make it possible for the project to proceed with private financing. For example, one respondent reported that the outside investor wanted one-half of the rights to the profits for contributing one-third of the investment cost. Another reported that the outside financiers wanted so much of the company that he would have lost control of the company and ultimately of its intellectual property. Many other comments along those lines are provided in detail earlier in this paper.

The projects on the whole met both the funding agency's mission and the company's strategy. All fit the general scenario for socially valuable research projects that would have been underfunded in the absence of the SBIR program. In particular, the projects appear to be ones for which the private rates of return in the absence of SBIR funding would have fallen short of the private hurdle rate required by outside financiers to whom the small businesses would have had to turn for financial support. Yet the social rates of returns to the projects are large and exceed the hurdle rates. The funding from the SBIR program changes the ordering of rates of return anticipated at the outset of Phase I. With the SBIR program providing funds, the expected private return relative to just the private portion of the total project costs is sufficient to move the private rate of return above the hurdle rate, and then the socially valuable research investment is undertaken.

In the foregoing ways, the Fast Track and non-Fast Track projects are essentially similar. Nonetheless, taken as a group the Fast Track projects show higher prospective expected lower-bound social rates of return—just as we would expect, because the measure includes only expected profits to the innovator and other producers, rather than including consumer surplus as well. Thus, the Fast Track projects have higher expected private profits, and we expect that to be the case because these are the projects that attracted outside investors at an early stage in the research. Furthermore, the average duration of additional development beyond Phase II is somewhat less for the Fast Track projects, suggesting that at least on average they are somewhat closer to commercialization at the end of Phase II than the non-Fast Track projects.

The respondents and the rate-of-return calculations make clear that although the Fast Track program selects projects that are different from SBIR projects more generally, projects that do not qualify for the Fast Track designation are typically no less deserving of SBIR support, but rather are high-risk projects with potentially great social value that would go unfunded in the absence of the SBIR program. The respondents suggest that, typically, the Fast Track program is simply not useful for companies pursuing socially valuable high-risk research because at the end of Phase I, most such projects do not yet have the characteristics of projects that attract outside private investors.

Finally, two things must be emphasized in conclusion. First, the high social rates of return estimated and reported for the SBIR projects are very conservative, lower-bound estimates because they do not include consumer surplus in the benefit stream. Consider, for example, the non-Fast Track innovation of Materials Technologies that will allow safe, accurate, and efficient diagnostic tests of the wiring in airplanes. The profits that will be generated by the technology are obviously a tiny proper subset of the social benefits that the technology will generate, but the estimation method used measures only the returns in the form of profits to the innovator and to other producers of the technology. Second, some readers will be skeptical about the SBIR award recipients' earnest belief that without SBIR funding the projects would not have been undertaken or at least would not have been undertaken to the same extent or at the same speed. With the SBIR program in place, certainly the pursuit of SBIR funding would perhaps be a path of least resistance. However, if the research would have occurred without the public funding, the estimated upper bound and hence the average of the upper and lower bounds for expected private returns would be too low, and the actual lower bounds for the social rates of return would be even higher than we have estimated. Further, the gap between the social and private rates of return would remain, although that would not in itself justify public funding of the projects.

To summarize in a concise manner, Tables 15 offers a comparison of costs and benefits of Fast Track and non-Fast Track projects over the same time frame.

Other differences between the Fast Track projects and non-Fast Track Projects in the New England comparison groups include the following:

- A smaller proportion of Fast Track companies have had previous SBIR awards (3 of 6 vs. 6 of 7).

TABLE 15   Fast Track and Non-Fast Track Projects: New England Comparison Groups

Variable	Averages for Timeline of Costs and Benefits	
	Fast Track	Non-Fast Track
Total SBIR project cost	$1.7 million	$1.0 million
SBIR funding	$0.9 million	$0.7 million
Additional period of development	1.2 years	1.8 years
Costs for additional development	$0.5 million	$1.5 million
Lower bound rate of return to society (including benefits to SBIR firm and its investors and also to other firms)	68%	55%

- A smaller proportion of Fast Track companies expressed difficulties bridging a gap in time between Phase I and Phase II (0 of 6 vs. 4 of 7).
- A larger proportion of Fast Track companies said that the SBIR award facilitated the attraction of outside investors (4 of 6 vs. 1 of 7).
- Fast Track projects show commercial potential earlier and, by the end of Phase I, outside third-party investors are found.
- Fast Track projects have a higher lower bound for the social rate of return (based on the benefits for the collection of firms using the technology created by the SBIR project).

Similarities between Fast Track and non-Fast Track projects in the New England comparison groups include the following:

- Barriers to investment (such as high technical risk and high capital costs) imply the need for partial public funding to carry out the SBIR projects.
- None of the companies has received ATP awards.
- All of the companies expect long-run strategic benefits from the SBIR award in the form of increased company size (sales or employment) or a more diversified product line.
- The SBIR projects are socially valuable: The social rate of return is greater than the rate of return needed for a worthwhile project.

Respondents in the New England comparison groups expressed concerns about and recommendations for improving the SBIR program. From the Fast Track project respondents came the following:

- Small businesses should be encouraged to acquire expertise to ensure proper business administration to go along with the competence in scientific work.

- Nonmilitary commercialization should not be the defining basis for the merits of the SBIR program because many valuable projects develop information with narrow applications within DoD.
- The Fast Track program may cause worthwhile projects to have a low priority for Phase II awards simply because they entail research that does not by the end of Phase I reach the stage that attracts outside funding.
- Some SBIR projects appear to be the sort of routine R&D and procurement that used to be done at large companies. Fast Track is a great innovation because it puts money into truly innovative small business projects with a high chance of commercialization.
- A Phase III for developing manufacturing technology, for ramping up production, might be quite helpful given the difficulties in negotiating the third-party investments.
- Funding should be provided for a Mentor/Consultant as a part of Phase II, with the SBIR firm identifying in the Phase II proposal a large corporation or marketing consulting firm that would work with the SBIR firm during Phase II and provide expertise about commercializing the technology.

From non-Fast Track project respondents came these observations:

- Fast Track is not useful when the SBIR funding is needed to support high-risk research that does not result in a commercially viable technology before Phase II. Without having such an early result, attraction of outside funding is not possible in time for a Fast Track award.
- Key technology areas should be assigned to a lead agency, which would fund all proposals in that area. There is agreement that improvements are needed in certain key technology areas. However, better coordination of the efforts of various agencies administering SBIR awards, each trying to achieve the same broad goals, is needed.
- Of the 25 pages in the application, only about 5 are needed for technical evaluation. The other 20 could be filed separately, electronically, and would be used only in the event the application is being considered for an award.
- The SBIR program could help to complete the process of commercialization. Continuing support for a successful Phase II project, the SBIR program could support a bridge to commercialization. The SBIR program now is aimed at establishing technical feasibility, not commercial feasibility.
- Phase II funding for the DoD project monitor to travel to our location and interact with us should be provided. This would ensure that the technical monitor is actively involved in the project.
- Phase II awardeed should be allowed to spend funds over three or four years instead of just two years.

TABLE 16   Fast Track and BMDO-Matching Projects Compared with Others in the New England Sample[a]

Type of Project[b]	Averages		
	d (years)[c]	z (years)[d]	soclwrbd (%)[e]
F	2.43	1.00	69
B	2.72	2.04	67
Both F & B	2.72	1.42	67
Neither	3.05	1.62	48

[a]Sample consists of 14 New England projects; 3 F, 3 B, 3 F & B, 5 neither F nor B.

[b]F denotes Fast Track and B denotes BMDO-matching.

[c]d is the duration of the SBIR project (Phase I + Phase II) without including the gap between the two phases and hence d is the duration of performance.

[d]z is the length of the additional period of development beyond the end of Phase II and until commercialization.

[e]soclwrbd is the lower bound rate of return to society, including benefits to the SBIR firm and its investors as well as to other firms.

Table 16 provides additional insight by distinguishing the projects of the Ballistic Missile Defense Office (BMDO), where matching funds are required although, unlike Fast Track, the matching funds can come from the SBIR company itself. Fast-Track and BMDO-Matching SBIR projects are of shorter duration than other projects, even ignoring the gap between Phase I and Phase II. The additional period of development beyond the end of Phase II and until commercialization is less for Fast Track projects than for BMDO-matching projects. The lower-bound rate of return to society (including benefits to the SBIR firm and its investors and also to other firms) is greater for Fast Track and BMDO-matching projects. In sum, Fast Track Projects take less time to reach commercialization; both Fast Track and BMDO-matching projects have more commercial potential in the sense that they are expected to generate greater returns to the SBIR firm and its investors and also to other firms. Further investigation, available on request from the author, showed that the qualitative differences among the projects remain the same when controls for technology categories are added in a regression model.

The conclusion is that the SBIR program has funded innovative projects with high social rates of return that would not have been undertaken in the absence of the program. Further, the non-Fast Track as well as the Fast Track projects appear to be quite valuable, although the non-Fast Track projects typically do not exhibit private commercial potential as quickly as the Fast Track projects.

ACKNOWLEDGMENTS

I would like to thank the following individuals for generously giving of their time for the interviews underlying the study. David Brock of Brock-Rogers Surgical; Myles Walsh of Cape Cod Research; Adi Guzdar of Foster-Miller, Inc.; Bob Hoch of Hyperion Catalysis International; Frederick Dampier of Lithium Energy Associates, Inc.; Yogesh Mehrotra of Materials Technologies Corporation; Marthinus C. van Schoor of Mide Technology Corporation; Steven P. Bastien of Optigain, Inc.; Peter Chenausky of QSource, Inc.; David Miller, Larry Willner, and Gregory Lane of SEA CORP (Systems Engineering Associates Corp.); Timothy J. Driscoll of Spectra Science Corp.; Frank Folino of Synkinetics, Inc.; and Grant M. Ehrlich of Yardney Technical Products, Inc. I am grateful to David B. Audretsch, William L. Baldwin, Albert N. Link, and Nancy A. Scott for helpful comments and suggestions.

REFERENCES

Link, Albert N., and John T. Scott. 1998. *Overcoming Market Failure: A Case Study of the ATP Focused Program on Technologies for the Integration of Manufacturing Applications (TIMA).* Draft final report submitted to the Advanced Technology Program. Gaithersburg, MD: National Institute of Technology. October.

Link, Albert N., and John T. Scott. 1999. "Estimates of the Social Returns to SBIR-supported Projects," this volume.

Tassey, Gregory. 1997. *The Economics of R&D Policy* (Westport, Conn., and London: Quorum Books.

[8]

An Assessment of the Small Business Innovation Research Fast Track Program in Southeastern States

Albert N. Link

University of North Carolina at Greensboro

EXECUTIVE SUMMARY

This paper presents descriptive findings from 12 case studies of Small Business Innovation Research (SBIR) award recipients in southeastern states. The focus of the case studies was to determine, to the extent possible, if the Fast Track Initiative encourages more rapid commercialization of research results through the acquisition of private investment capital, and if Fast Track projects progress more rapidly than standard SBIR awards. The key findings from the sample of 12 firms indicate that:

- Fast Track projects proceed to Phase II research faster than non-Fast Track projects;
- Fast Track projects develop a commercialization strategy sooner than non-Fast Track projects, but those Fast Track projects do not anticipate having commercial products sooner than non-Fast Track projects; and
- the post-Phase II funding expected to be needed to commercialize Fast Track projects is greater than is expected to commercialize non-Fast Track projects.

INTRODUCTION

The U.S. Department of Defense (DoD) requested that the National Academy of Sciences (NAS) review its Small Business Innovation Research (SBIR) Fast Track program to determine, to the extent possible,

- if the Fast Track Initiative encourages more rapid commercialization of research results through the acquisition of private investment capital, and
- if Fast Track projects progress more rapidly than do the standard SBIR awards.

To accomplish this, NAS undertook a multifaceted research strategy that included both a broad-based mail survey to a representative sample of SBIR awardees and focused regional case studies from that sample.

This descriptive paper presents the findings from 12 case studies of award recipients in southeastern states. It will join other researchers' papers that focus on various regions of the United States. In the second section, the overall NAS strategy for the collection of information related to the above two questions is described. Then, In the third section, the process for selecting these 12 southeastern firms is presented. In the fourth section, observations about the commercialization impacts realized to date from the Fast Track Initiative are offered. In the fifth section, observations about other project impacts are discussed. In the sixth section, estimates of the social benefits associated with the SBIR program, and the Fast Track Initiative in particular, are presented.[1] Concluding remarks are presented in the last section. The Appendix to the paper contains brief summaries of each of the 12 projects studied.

NAS STRATEGY FOR COLLECTION OF INFORMATION

NAS was asked by DoD to determine, to the extent possible,

- if the Fast Track Initiative encourages more rapid commercialization of research results through the acquisition of private investment capital, and
- if Fast Track projects progress more rapidly than do the standard SBIR awards.

Toward that end, a team of researchers was assembled, and each was assigned a different region of the country from which to identify a sample of Fast Track program awardees and non-Fast Track program awardees. Each researcher was given latitude with regard to how he/she approached the questions during the interview data collection process; however, certain crosscutting issues were common to each. These crosscutting issues related to information about the background of each firm being interviewed, information about how the SBIR award is affecting the firm's research and commercialization strategy, and each firm's general opinion about the administration of the SBIR awards program.

---

[1] A more detailed analysis is provided by Link and Scott, "Estimates of the Social Returns to Small Business Innovation Research Projects" in this volume.

SELECTION OF THE CASE STUDY FIRMS

As requested by NAS, the geographic focus for this paper is southeastern states. An inspection of background information provided by DoD and NAS shows that there have been 31 SBIR awards to firms in southeastern states over the period from 1993 to 1996.[2] Of these 31, six firms received Phase II awards through the Fast Track Initiative. These six firms are shown in the upper portion of Table 1. NAS requested that 12 case studies be conducted in southeastern states, six non-Fast Track firms were thus selected for the purpose of comparison.

Several factors were considered in the selection of the six non-Fast Track firms, including state, duration of the Phase II project, and number of employees in the firms. The six non-Fast Track firms are shown in the lower portion of Table 1. Also shown in Table 1 are selected characteristics of the firms and their projects. Because of the small size of the defined population of regional firms, comparability of firms and projects between the Fast Track and non-Fast Track groups is not defined on the basis of a statistical criterion.

DoD provided the name and telephone number of the principal investigator (PI) for each Phase II project in each of the firms in Table 1, based on information from the Phase II application. In most cases, the PI's name was correct, but more often than not the firm had moved or changed its telephone number. However, each noted PI was eventually located and contacted by telephone. During the initial conversation, the nature of the study was described, confidentiality issues were discussed, and an overiew of the type of information being requested was given. After that initial conversation, a subsequent telephone interview time was arranged. In three instances, the PI was not interested in participating in the telephone interview. In those three instances, the DoD technical monitor on the project was located and contacted; he intervened and reinforced to each of the three PIs the importance of the study to DoD and assuaged confidentiality concerns. Subsequently, each of these three individuals agreed to participate in a telephone interview, although two of the three (both Fast Track) agreed to answer only a limited number of telephone interview questions. The focus of these two limited interviews was the importance of the Fast Track program in closing the funding gap between Phase I research and Phase II research. Each of the other 10 full telephone interviews focused on this issue as well as other issues related to commercialization.

As seen from Table 1, the group of Fast Track projects and the group of non-Fast Track projects are similar in the following dimensions: Each Phase II project was proposed to last approximately 24 months; the average number of employees in the company that was specific to the Phase II project was nine; and the companies themselves had been in operation for approximately eight years prior to the Phase II research.

Each complete interview averaged just over 60 minutes.

---

[2]These firms are located in Alabama, Georgia, Florida, North Carolina, and Tennessee.

TABLE 1   Selected Characteristics of the Sample of Firms Interviewed

Firm	State	Fast Track (F)	Project Duration (months)[a]	Number of Employees[b]	Year Founded
Matis, Inc.	GA	F	24	5	1990
OPTS, Inc.	AL	F	24	5	1994
CG2, Inc.	AL	F	24	15	1995
Power Technology Services, Inc.	NC	F	12[c]	5	1984
Summitec Corporation	TN	F	30	19	1987
Bevilacqua Research Corporation	AL	F	24	7	1992
System Design and Analysis Corporation	AL		24	3	1996
Accurate Automation Corporation	TN		24	17	1989
MicroCoating Technologies[d]	GA		24	8	1993
Optimization Technology, Inc.	AL		24	21	1983
Optical E.T.C., Inc.	AL		24	5	1990
Intelligent Investments	NC		24	3	1995

[a]Proposed project duration.

[b]Number of full-time-equivalent employees at the time the project was funded; two part-time employees equal one full-time employee.

[c]As discussed in the Appendix, this company originally was funded for a basic Phase II but has received additional Phase II funding, thus extending the duration to 2 years.

[d]Formerly CCVD, Inc.

INDICATIONS OF COMMERCIAL IMPACTS ASSOCIATED WITH FAST TRACK PROJECTS

None of the firms interviewed has commercialized a product or process that was associated with the Phase II award under study. This absence of direct commercialization success was expected *a priori* because the Fast Track Initiative is a relatively young program and there are few firms that have even completed their Phase II study. In fact, from the 12 firms interviewed, only 2 are just now (in 1999) at the end of their Phase II research. However, other information was obtained during the interviews in an effort to glean some preliminary insight into the possible commercialization impacts associated with the Fast Track program. This other information is described in the Appendix. Because the sample size is small, the technologies differ across firms, and the research and commercialization expertise is unique to each firm, care should be exercised in generalizing beyond this sample of 12 firms/projects about the possible commercial impacts associated with the Fast Track program.

Before proceeding to discuss issues related to commercialization, it was the case in each of the 12 firms that the Phase II research was related to the research background of the PI or the firm. It was also the case in each of the 12 firms that this Phase II research would form the foundation for subsequent research—which may or may not be SBIR funded. In other words, there is no indication among the

TABLE 2   Average Funding Gap Between Phase I and
Phase II Research

Status	Funding Gap (months)
Fast Track firms	< 1
Non-Fast Track firms	4.3

group of 12 firms that the Phase II research under study was sought in a one-time opportunistic fashion; it is part of each firm's long-term technology strategy.

Length of the Funding Gap

Each of the 12 interviewees was asked, as background information, if Fast Track facilitated continuous funding from Phase I into Phase II. That is, each was asked if there was a funding gap between these two milestones. Among the Fast Track projects, five firms reported no funding gap at all, and one firm reported a four-month funding gap. In this latter situation, the Phase II project was approved in a timely manner, although funding was not immediately available from DoD. Among the non-Fast Track projects, the average funding gap was 4.3 months, with a range from 0 months to 12 months. (See Table 2.)

If commercialization is enhanced by a reduction of time between Phase I and Phase II, then these descriptive findings, as summarized by the data in Table 2, are suggestive of one aspect of the benefits associated with the Fast Track Initiative.

Time to Commercialization

Each interviewee was asked how soon after the Phase II project's completion will the technology(ies) being developed be commercialized. Six of the Fast Track firms that responded to this question, expected the mean time period to be nine months. The six non-Fast Track firms also expected the mean time period to be nine months. See (Table 3.)

Based on the data in Table 3, it appears that the reduced funding gap associated with Fast Track firms is not related to the expected duration from the end of Phase II to commercialization. Hence, one cannot conclude that these Fast Track firms expect to commercialize faster than the non-Fast Track firms.

Commercialization Strategy

Four of the six Fast Track PIs stated that their commercialization strategy was currently in place as a result of working with their third-party private-sector investor. Each of the PIs in these four firms went on to say that the Fast Track Initiative was instrumental in their receiving third-party funding. One respondent

TABLE 3   Average Expected Duration from End of
Phase II to Commercialization

Status	Time to Commercialization (months)
Fast Track firms	9
Non-Fast Track firms	9

referred to Fast Track as being "critical" for his obtaining an outside investor, and
another respondent stated that SBIR's support gave his project "instant credibility" to the outside investor.[3] Two of the Fast Track firms are receiving third-
party funding from other government sources and neither thought of their research as having a commercialization strategy.

All of the non-Fast Track firms eventually expect to obtain third-party funding. Two of these six firms reported that they do not yet have a commercialization strategy, but anticipate developing one when outside funding is obtained.
These two firms anticipate finding outside funding through a joint venture ar-
rangement with already identified but not yet contacted private-sector firms. A
third firm has found a local investor, and a commercialization plan is being developed. The other three firms hope to be able to commercialize but are unsure of
their ability to acquire additional private-sector funds and/or unsure of how to
commercialize a product. No firm mentioned that its geographic location gave it
any advantage in attracting third-party funding.

The above two findings are not necessarily at odds with one another. The
fact that Fast Track firms develop a commercialization strategy sooner than non-
Fast Track firms perhaps may say more about the expected success of their commercialization efforts than about the timing of their commercialization efforts.

Post-Phase II Precommercialization Funding Requirements

Each interviewee was asked the approximate level of additional funding that
will be required to commercialize its technology(ies) between the end of Phase II
research and the expected date of commercialization. Mean responses are in Table 4.

The expected funding needs in Table 4 are the averages for four Fast Track
firms and for six non-Fast Track firms. Based on these statistics, Fast Track projects
are expected to require more than twice the additional funds of non-Fast Track
projects. To reemphasize, the type of project and the related technology differ between these two broad groups, as seen from the project summaries in the Appendix.

---

[3]Each of these respondents was emphatic about the confidentiality of the interview information,
and each was very uncomfortable about a subsequent discussion with the third-party investor, although the names of all third-party investors are public information. Accordingly, no interviews
were conducted with any third-party investors.

TABLE 4   Average Additional Non-SBIR Funding
Expected for Commercialization

Status	Required Funding
Fast Track firms	$744,000
Non-Fast Track firms	$354,000

Total Research from Concept to Commercialization

Related to the additional non-SBIR funding expected to be needed for commercialization of the Phase II technology(ies), as discussed in the preceding section, Table 5 shows the average total cost to conduct Phase I research and Phase II research, from all sources, plus the additional funding expected to be needed for commercialization.

On the basis of the dollar amounts in Table 5, Fast Track projects will cost approximately 54 percent more than non-Fast Track projects, on average.

OBSERVATIONS ABOUT OTHER PROJECT IMPACTS

Other characteristics of the 12 Phase II research projects studied, as well as differences in those characteristics between the group of Fast Track projects and non-Fast Track projects, are described in this section.

Employment Growth

The number of employees in each firm at the time that the Phase II award was made is shown in Table 1 above.[4] Each PI was asked how many additional employees were added to the firm during the Phase II research. Using the algorithm that two part-time employees equals one full-time-equivalent employee, the average growth in employees among the six Fast Track firms and among the six non-Fast Track firms is shown in Table 6.

Three of the six non-Fast Track PIs reported that the number of new employees hired during Phase II would be reduced once the research was completed; in fact, two of the three PIs that reported a post-Phase II decline in employment are in the two firms with the greatest growth in numbers of employees (180 percent and 133 percent) during the Phase II research. None of the six Fast Track PIs made such a statement; in fact, all Fast Track PIs were of the opinion that employment growth due specifically to the Phase II project would be permanent.

---

[4]One should not generalize about the average employment size of an SBIR Fast Track firm compared to a non-Fast Track firm on the basis of the employment data in Table 1 because the comparable six non-Fast Track firms included in this study were selected, in part, on the basis of the number of employees.

TABLE 5 Average Total Research Cost from Concept to Expected Commercialization

Status	Research Costs
Fast Track firms	$1,894,000
Non-Fast Track firms	$1,233,000

Fast Track Versus Non-Fast Track Applications

Previous funding relationships between each of the 12 firms and SBIR is shown in Table 7. Both Fast Track and non-Fast Track firms have had previous award experience with the SBIR program.[5]

All six of the non-Fast Track PIs stated that they were aware of the Fast Track program, but each PI stated that his/her firm did not pursue that funding avenue primarily because of lack of time and experience in identifying a potential third-party investor.

SBIR Administration

Each PI was queried about his/her experience with the SBIR on this Phase II project. The six Fast Track firms reported complete satisfaction with the Fast Track process and had no suggestions for changes. Noteworthy is the fact that three of the six Fast Track PIs stated that they had previous investment dealings with the company that invested in their Phase II project. Two of the non-Fast Track firms did offer constructive suggestions. One PI recommended that SBIR provide assistance to firms, especially the very small ones, regardless of their previous relationship with SBIR, about how to market and how to commercialize products. Another PI noted that the six-month Phase I period is too short a time for a small firm with no or little commercialization experience to identify a potential investor, much less to establish a relationship and attract outside funding. All 12 interviewed firms expected to seek additional SBIR research support in the future. The six Fast Track firms anticipated applying again through the Fast Track program, and the six non-Fast Track firms were uncertain about their future use of Fast Track.

Intellectual Property Protection

None of the 12 interviewed PIs reported any patent activity related to their current Phase II project. Only one, a non-Fast Track firm, expected to file a

---

[5]Respondents also were asked if they have sought or expect to seek funding from the Advanced Technology Program at the National Institute of Standards and Technology. None knew about the program.

TABLE 6   Employment Growth During Phase II

Status	Employment Growth (%)
Fast Track firms	82
Non-Fast Track firms	74

patent at the completion of the Phase II research. The dominant reasons offered for the lack of patenting activity were the cost of filing and the cost of patent protection after the fact.

PRELIMINARY ESTIMATES OF THE SOCIAL RETURN TO SBIR FUNDING

As discussed in Link and Scott's contribution to this volume, as part of this NAS review of DoD's Fast Track Initiative, a model was formulated for estimating the social rate of return attributable to SBIR-sponsored research projects. Only the findings from the application of this model to the projects studied are described here.

All firms, Fast Track as well as non-Fast Track, reported that they would not have undertaken the entire research project absent SBIR support (one Fast Track PI reported that his firm would have undertaken a small portion of the research absent SBIR funding). For each project, two rates of return are shown in Table 8: a private rate of return absent SBIR support under the counterfactual situation in which the research was undertaken, and a lower bound on the social rate of return associated with the SBIR-sponsored project.

TABLE 7   Previous Funding Relationships Between Sample Firms and SBIR

Firm	Fast Track (F)	Previous SBIR Awards
Matis, Inc.	F	Phase 1
OPTS, Inc.	F	Phase 2
CG2, Inc.	F	none
Power Technology Services, Inc.	F	Phase 2
Summitec Corporation	F	Phase 2
Bevilacqua Research Corporation	F	Phase 2
System Design and Analysis Corporation		none
Accurate Automation Corporation		Phase 2
MicroCoating Technologies[a]		Phase 2
Optimization Technology, Inc.		Phase 2
Optical E.T.C., Inc.		Phase 1
Intelligent Investments		none

[a]Formerly CCVD, Inc.

TABLE 8   Private and Social Rates of Return

Status	Rate of Return (%)	
	Private	Social
Fast Track firms	28	132
Non-Fast Track firms	21	104

A more complete economic interpretation of the findings reported in Table 8, as well as cross-project differences in the net social rates of return are discussed by Link and Scott (1999). Also in Link and Scott (1999) is a detailed discussion of the elements of market failure associated with the projects studied and the related markets on which the technologies are focused. These aspects of market failure are noted, but are not discussed, in each project summary in the Appendix. It is sufficient for this descriptive paper simply to note that SBIR is providing a socially desirable role in funding both Fast Track and non-Fast Track projects; however, the estimated social rate of return (actually a lower bound on the social rate of return) for Fast Track projects is greater than for non-Fast Track projects. This finding is discussed in detail by Link and Scott (1999).

CONCLUDING OBSERVATIONS

The descriptive information presented in this paper indicates that in some dimensions Fast Track firms and programs are different from non-Fast Track firms and programs. However, the southeastern states sample studied and summarized herein is too small to infer more definite conclusions. A comparison of the case study results from other regions in the United States will confirm or not confirm the propositions stated in this paper. Also, and perhaps more importantly, a case comparison of Fast Track and non-Fast Track projects after Phase II research is completed and after sufficient time has passed to evaluate the commercialization results from the projects seems warranted.

ACKNOWLEDGMENTS

This paper has benefited from the comments and suggestions of David Audretsch and John Scott.

REFERENCE

Link, Albert N. and John T. Scott, 1999. "Estimates of the Social Returns to Small Business Innovation Research Projects," this volume.

———————————— APPENDIX ————————————

Research Summary of Phase II Projects

Matis, Inc., Atlanta, Georgia

COMPANY ORIGIN: Founded in 1990 in Georgia.

PROJECT: A Novel Computational System for Real-Time Analysis and Prediction of Antenna-to-Aircraft and Antenna-to-Antenna Interactions.

PRINCIPAL INVESTIGATOR: Vladimir Oliker, Vice President of the company; Engineer.

PROJECT SUMMARY: There is a major problem with communication systems in general, and with antenna systems in particular. If antennas have no obstructions, then signals are transmitted and received clearly. However, such an environment rarely exists. On aircraft and ships, there often are obstructions of one form or another. These obstructions could be communications hardware or parts of the vehicle on which the communications are mounted. It is therefore critical to the quality of the communication system that the antennas be in an optimal position to minimize interference. Matis is developing software to simulate the antenna's environment and to measure the communication quality of alternative antenna placements. Given simulated information on alternative placements, it is the responsibility of engineers to trade off communication efficiency with engineering feasibility. The technology to develop this software comes from previous research projects.

COMMENT: Absent SBIR funding, Matis likely would have taken on this project on a limited scale. Although the capital and labor costs to undertake this research are extraordinarily high, Matis has previous investment relationships with companies and could acquire partial funding.

OPTS, Inc., Huntsville, Alabama

COMPANY ORIGINS: Founded in 1994 in Alabama.

PROJECT: Imaging Automatic Gain Control for Target Acquisition, Automatic Target Recognition, and Tracking.

PRINCIPAL INVESTIGATOR: Charles Hester, President of the company; Industrial Scientist.

PROJECT SUMMARY: It is important for a missile to know what it is going to hit as opposed to where it is going to hit. For example, a missile might see two vehicles, a tank and a truck, at a predetermined location. To be most effective, the missile should be able to distinguish between vehicles and hit the most militarily important one. To be able to do this, the missile guidance system must be able to process infrared images into a pattern recognition program; however, there is tremendous noise in infrared imaging. Existing technology relies on what is called simple gain, meaning that the sited image is enlarged in all dimensions. OPTS is developing hardware to install on missiles that will enhance images selectively, or apply gain selectively, so as to improve recognition. This will take place in real time on the missile.

COMMENT: Absent the SBIR award, the firm would not have undertaken this research. The reason is that the capital costs are high and there are few investment sources. Also, there is a very limited commercial market for this technology; hence, finding a commercial investor was extremely difficult.

CG2, Inc., Huntsville, Alabama

COMPANY ORIGINS: Founded in 1995 in Alabama.

PROJECT: Virtual Reality Scene Generation by Means of Open Standards.

PRINCIPAL INVESTIGATOR: David King, President of the company; Engineer.

PROJECT SUMMARY: To test a missile, it has to be developed, tested under controlled conditions, and then fired. The model must be fired a significant number of times to verify its capabilities. The cost for each firing is between $10 million and $15 million. CG2 is investigating a lower-cost process for verifying the capabilities of a missile under development. The software that is being developed is designed to run a hardware-in-loop process. After a missile is launched once, all of the information from that launch is stored in a simulation computer. The simulation computer is then connected to the circuitry of a new missile, and to an image scene generator. Then the image scene generator is connected to the missile, completing the loop. The loop first repeats for the new missile the flight of the tested missile. Then, there is what is called a validated simulation. Once the simulation is validated, the missile can be tested in various environments that are created by the image scene generator. For example, the image scene generator can tell the missile that it is seeing various things (e.g., a mountain) and it will measure how the missile reacts. The missile's reaction is stored in the simulation computer. Once completed, this technology can save the DoD billions of dollars per year in unneeded missile firings.

COMMENT: Because of the high capital costs for this research and the lack of available funding sources, this research would not have been undertaken in the absence of the SBIR award. Outside investors would not have been interested because the market is so small, and the technology can be imitated quickly. Accordingly, CG2's outside investor is the government.

Power Technology Services (PTS), Inc., Raleigh, North Carolina

COMPANY ORIGINS: Founded in 1984 in North Carolina.

PROJECT: A New Dual-Gated Motion Control Technology for Hybrid Electric Power Systems.

PRINCIPAL INVESTIGATOR: John Driscoll, President of the company; Engineer.

PROJECT SUMMARY: Motion control motors use approximately 70 percent of all electricity in the United States. About half of them are used in industry. These motors currently are controlled by insulated gate bipolar transistor (IGBT) technology. These IGBT chips are very expensive and need to be imported from Japan. PTS is developing a double-sided flip chip that is smaller and will be less expensive than Japan's IGBT chip. In addition, these chips will be made domestically. The chips have an immediate use in military electric tanks. Driscoll was previously a scientist at General Electric, and he holds patents from that tenure. It is these patents that are forming the technological base for the research.

COMMENT: Absent the SBIR award, this research would not have taken place. The reason is the high capital cost of obtaining access to a fabrication facility to produce the chips. Efforts were made to acquire funds for this project before applying to SBIR, but no investors would incur the cost.

Summitec Corporation, Oak Ridge, Tennessee

COMPANY ORIGINS: Founded in 1987 in Tennessee.

PROJECT: Very-Low-Bit-Rate-Error-Resilient Video Communication.

PRINCIPAL INVESTIGATOR: Andrew Yin, President of the company; Researcher.

PROJECT SUMMARY: The lack of available bandwidth is the technical constraint on video imaging, especially wireless video imaging. With limited bandwidth, transmission of pictures is difficult and slow and video is nearly impossible. Summitec is developing a compression-like software that will select only the important pieces of information to transmit over a narrow bandwidth so that video images will be clear. As the technical monitor explained, this software is like getting 10 pounds of potatoes into a 5 pound bag. The primary use of the software is in surveillance. Video information can be transmitted to planes to assist them in locational bombing.

COMMENT: Outside investors are very difficult to locate because the commercial return to this technology will not occur quickly. The long-time to market is the hurdle that investors see.

Bevilacqua Research Corporation, Huntsville, Alabama

COMPANY ORIGINS: Founded in 1992 in Alabama.

PROJECT: A Dialectic Approach to Intelligence Data Fusion for Threat Identification.

PRINCIPAL INVESTIGATOR: Andy Bevilacqua, President of the company; Engineer.

PROJECT SUMMARY: The goal of this project is to produce a software architecture that will make computers think more like people think. DoD has a strong desire to be able to do intelligent programming. It has attempted this in the past through what was called "role-based expert systems." That technology worked fine in a FORTRAN world of "if this, then that." However, the needs of DoD are more complex, and alternative technology is needed. The software being developed will take systematic concepts and translate them into numbers so that the computer can process them. For example, when people think of a concept, they do so in terms of a vector of characteristics of the concept. However, if two concepts are combined, then the vector of characteristics of the combined concepts is not necessarily a linear combination of the individual concept vectors. Bevilacqua calls this architecture a "cognitive reasoning engine."

COMMENT: The company would not have undertaken this concept absent SBIR funding for two reasons. One, it did not have access to sufficient funding and the commercial applications of the technology would not have been readily understood by investors. Two, the architecture can be imitated quickly once commercialized. The third-party investor in this project is the government.

System Design and Analysis Corporation (SDAC), Huntsville, Alabama

COMPANY ORIGINS: Founded in 1996 in Alabama.
PROJECT: A Generic Ducted Rocket Test Facility Setup and Simulation Program.
PRINCIPAL INVESTIGATOR: Gary Kirkham, Partner in the company; Computer Science.
PROJECT SUMMARY: The company is developing a software tool specific to ducted rockets. When designing a facility to test rockets, there are cost reasons for being able to test the facility prior to testing the rockets. There are software packages on the market to assist in the design of test facilities, but they are generic in their abilities and thus are not sophisticated enough to meet the needs of ducted rocket facilities.
COMMENT: The company considered applying to the Fast Track program but could not find investors. The reason was that the research takes a long time to complete and commercialize. Hence, sources of capital were not available for such high-market-risk projects.

Accurate Automation Corporation, Chattanooga, Tennessee

COMPANY ORIGINS: Founded in 1989 in Tennessee.
PROJECT: Neural Network Figure of Merit Subsystem.
PRINCIPAL INVESTIGATOR: Alianna Maren, Researcher.
PROJECT SUMMARY: Many military vehicles use radar. Each vehicle can have multiple radar units, and radar can be located away from the vehicles as well. It is likely that radar in both locations might be tracking the same signal. Each radar

will produce its own information but, because each is in a different position at different times, each will have periods of locational advantage, but there will be overlapping information. To be precise in tracking, what is needed is a total combined or "fused" picture of what is being tracked. Although it is technologically possible to fuse overlapping information, the question then becomes one of how good or accurate the fused picture is. The answer to that question required a definition of "good." This research project deals with the development of a proof of concept that algorithms can be developed to define good. The output of the Phase II research is a commercializable software package that incorporates the algorithms developed.

COMMENT: Commercial potential is far off and there could not be investors or borrowed money absent SBIR.

MicroCoating Technologies (formally CCVD, Inc.),Atlanta, Georgia

COMPANY ORIGINS: Founded in 1993 in Georgia.

PROJECT: Non-Chromate Combustion Chemical Vapor Deposition (CCVD) Coating for Naval Engine Components.

PRINCIPAL INVESTIGATOR: Andrew Hunt, President of the company; Materials Science.

PROJECT SUMMARY: Hexavalent chrome is widely used in the Navy as well as in industry. However, it is a known carcinogen, and thus its use creates a toxic waste problem. The U.S. Environmental Protection Agency (EPA) knows of the problems associated with hexavalent chrome, but it has not yet mandated that it cease being used because no replacement is yet available (EPA practice). Congress has given DoD an internal directive to find a replacement material, and so, MicroCoating is developing such a material. It is based on a thin-film oxide that can be applied to metal during a CCVD process. During that process, the thin film is sprayed on metal with a flame, and the residual gas contains a replacement molecular coating that performs like hexavalent chrome but has more environmentally friendly properties.

COMMENT: This project would not have occurred absent SBIR. In fact, the company would not be in business. Hunt did try to find venture funding but it was simply not available. Venture capitalists are not interested in materials science. Industry eventually will need to use this process, but until EPA mandates a replacement, industry will not invest. His process can very easily be imitated, but he holds a flame deposition patent that will protect it.

Optimization Technology, Inc., Huntsville, Alabama

COMPANY ORIGINS: Founded in 1983 in California. Branch located in Auburn and that is how McGraw became involved. California branch could not make it but the Auburn branch did.

PROJECT: C41 Distributed Performance Simulation Environment.

Principal Investigator: Chris McGraw, President of the company; Computer Science.

PROJECT SUMMARY: As computers have moved from a supercomputer main-frame environment to a "distributed paradigm" where desktop computers are net-worked, a problem has arisen as to how best to share the processing loads across components in the network so as to maximize the efficiency of the network. This is not an interoperability problem; it is an ex post workload problem. Powerful desktop computers are being purchased but, depending on where the software resides and how the processing load is spread across machines, it could well be that the whole operates less efficiently than the potential sum of the parts. It is impossible to predict a priori how best to distribute workload. One needs trial and error to see what network configuration degrades the system the least. C4D is a software package that simulates various office systems before systems are purchased. The user can determine how to distribute software and workload efficiently.

COMMENT: There seem to be two aspects of market failure here, according to McGraw: (1) The work is very theoretical and outside investors have a hard time understanding it; and (2) it is hard to identify investors. McGraw claims that it is not so much that the outside funding market is thin as it is that it is hard to know how to find investors.

Optical E.T.C., Inc., Huntsville, Alabama

COMPANY: Founded in 1990 in Alabama.

PROJECT: High-G Microelectromechanical Accelerometer.

Principal Investigator: Arthur Werkheiser, Vice President (partner) of the company; Engineer.

PROJECT SUMMARY: The Air Force uses light gas guns for testing the air dynamics of various devices. These guns are 300-500 ft long. Artillery shells or small missiles are shot through these guns and pictures are taken of events such as ionization, tumbling, and other aerodynamic properties. When these pictures are taken, the acceleration of the object must be known. Acceleration needs to be measured up to 120,000 Gs (humans black out at 8-10 Gs. A sensor was needed that could be mounted on the object to measure acceleration in such an environ-ment. The company is building such a sensor on silicon chips, using infrared devices that can withstand the acceleration. The technology underlying this project is known as microelectromechanical systems.

COMMENT: The technical risk associated with this project is large because the sensor needs to be so small (0.33 in.^{3}). It also will be very hard to appropriate property rights once it is commercialized.

Intelligent Investments, Greensboro, North Carolina

COMPANY ORIGINS: Founded in 1995 in North Carolina.

PROJECT: Multiagent Tool for Effective Network-Based Training Systems.

PRINCIPAL INVESTIGATOR: David Goldstein, President of the company; Computer Science.

PROJECT SUMMARY: Software is being developed in an interactive way to develop Web pages. Multiple individuals in different locations can work on the development of the page simultaneously.

COMMENT: The software can be partially imitated, but not totally, since he claims to have greater technical experience than others.

PART III

OTHER EVALUATION METHODS

J Technol Transf (2009) 34:525–559
DOI 10.1007/s10961-009-9120-8

Cost-benefit analysis for global public–private partnerships: an evaluation of the desirability of intergovernmental organizations entering into public–private partnerships

John T. Scott

Published online: 28 April 2009
© Springer Science+Business Media, LLC 2009

Abstract This paper explains the use of cost-benefit analysis for the evaluation of global public–private partnerships that combine international intergovernmental organizations with national governments, businesses, and the non-profit organizations of civil society. The partnerships allocate resources to projects that are socially desirable from an international perspective, yet without the global partnerships will not be performed. Cost-benefit analysis can identify and compare the social and the private costs and benefits of the projects, thereby identifying cases where global public–private partnerships will provide socially desirable results when markets alone will not. Cost-benefit analysis can assess the necessity and the sufficiency of strategies proposed by the partnerships. The paper discusses modifications to cost-benefit analysis required for its use in evaluations of the global public–private partnerships, explaining the need for market-centered valuations, but also explaining the role of alternative social valuations.

Keywords Cost-benefit analysis · Global public–private partnerships ·
Intergovernmental organizations · International organizations · Market failure ·
Program evaluation · Social opportunity costs

JEL Classification H420 · H430 · H870 · O190 · O220 · O380

1 Introduction

The purpose of this paper is to discuss how cost-benefit analysis can be used by international intergovernmental organizations to evaluate the desirability of entering into global public–private partnerships with combinations of national governments, businesses, and the non-profit organizations of civil society. The partnerships address economic problems that are not solved by reliance on markets alone. The partnerships strive to achieve allocation of resources to programs and projects that are socially desirable from an

J. T. Scott (✉)
Department of Economics, Dartmouth College, Hanover, NH 03755, USA
e-mail: john.t.scott@dartmouth.edu

 Springer

international perspective, yet without the global partnerships will not be performed by the private sector alone. Cost-benefit analysis can be used to identify and compare both the social and the private costs and benefits, thereby identifying cases where markets alone will not provide socially desirable results and where global public–private partnerships can achieve the desired results.

For an example of a global public–private partnership, consider Kaul's discussion of the Medicines for Malaria Venture (Kaul 2006, p. 256):

> Malaria kills more than 1 million people each year. Some 300–500 million new clinical cases occur annually, mainly among poor people and mainly among children and pregnant women. More than 90 percent of the malaria burden falls on Sub-Saharan Africa. Drug resistance is a serious challenge, calling for continuous research and development (R&D) and requiring a new antimalarial drug to be commercialized every five years on average.

> But because most people threatened by malaria are poor, market incentives for R&D are weak.

The social desirability of public support of investments in innovative antimalarial drugs can be established with cost-benefit analysis. One might expect that social benefits exceed social costs while the private benefits fall short of the private costs, but the formal cost-benefit analysis heightens awareness of the market failure and compares the benefits with the opportunity costs—the value of the best alternative uses for the R&D resources. The cost-benefit analysis can identify the market failure and present the case for action by a public–private partnership. The private sector alone cannot provide the socially desirable R&D investments if, as expected and as cost-benefit analysis would determine, the private benefits—the returns appropriated by the companies investing in R&D—fall short of the private costs.

As Kaul explains, the global public private partnership can correct the market failure of underinvestment in the socially desirable R&D (Kaul 2006, p. 256):

> ... The Medicines for Malaria Venture (MMV) ... seeks to provide the missing incentives to encourage the private pharmaceutical industry to focus on affordable antimalarial drugs.

> MMV has a two-part strategy for building new incentives. First, it uses the financial contributions of its donor group (private foundations, intergovernmental organizations, national aid agencies, and the International Federation of Pharmaceutical Manufacturers Associations) and the in-kind contributions (such as free use of laboratory facilities) of its business partners to support research by private companies. Second, MMV negotiates differential patenting agreements with its private sector partners. The MMV's intellectual property rights usually cover the disease-endemic countries and its private partners, the richer, industrial countries (the "travelers' market").

I shall explain that cost-benefit analysis allows evaluation of whether the strategy of a global public–private partnership will be sufficient to correct the market failure—in the foregoing example, the underinvestment in R&D for the continual development of new antimalarial drugs that defeat the evolving drug resistance of new strains of malaria.

Further, I shall explain that cost-benefit analysis can address the question of whether the donor group's financial contributions are not only sufficient but necessary as well. Conceição et al. (2006) describe new approaches for financing global public–private partnerships, and Conceição (2006) documents the growth in the number of new financing mechanisms for international cooperation in global public–private partnerships. Cost-benefit analysis, with its emphasis on comparing private and public benefits and costs and the associated private and public rates of return on investments, can contribute to the analysis of the appropriate financing technologies and the *necessary* combination of public and private finance used to support the partnerships.

Conceição et al. (2006) explain that the use of the new financing technologies will require "a new perspective on financing international cooperation" (paraphrasing from Table 1, Conceição et al. 2006, p. 285):

> The focus for financing international cooperation must shift from public revenue to private finance, from direct spending by governments and intergovernmental agencies to the provision of public–policy incentives to private investors, from payment now and in full to payment for services when they become available, from international cooperation as charity to international cooperation as an investment.

Cost-benefit analysis, as I shall explain in this paper—with its identification of the private and social benefits and costs and the associated private and social rates of return—provides a pragmatic theoretical foundation for the shifts in perspective identified by Conceição et al. (2006). Further, cost-benefit analysis provides a pragmatic evaluation tool that intergovernmental organizations can use to assess the desirability of entering into global public–private partnerships. Moreover, the cost-benefit analysis can be used to assess the sufficiency and the necessity of the strategies proposed by the global public–private partnership.

Individual nations have used various public policies to confront the failure of markets to provide socially desirable outcomes. A national government develops and carries out such policies. The policies could leave the market mechanism to work alone after hands-off, arms-length adjustments to private incentives. A tax credit for investment in research and development (R&D) is an example of such an adjustment to incentives. The credit can stimulate socially desirable investment when without the special incentive the market would fail, resulting in underinvestment in R&D. However, hands-off adjustments—with the government keeping a distance between itself and the market's actions and not becoming actively involved with the economic activity itself—will not always suffice to correct market failure.[1] In some of those cases that require more active intervention by government, national governments have turned to public–private partnerships. Link (1999) describes the use of public–private partnerships in the United States, with a focus on the partnerships of the last 25 years that have been designed to promote R&D and technological competitiveness of US companies.

Kaul (2006) describes the growing use of global public–private partnerships as intergovernmental organizations combine their resources with the resources of national governments, businesses in the private sector, and civil society to address international issues that have not been adequately addressed by markets. Witte and Reinicke (2005) describe the need for and the upsurge in the United Nations partnerships with business and civil society to advocate causes of international importance, develop codes of conduct and

---

[1] Focusing on government policy to correct markets' underinvestment in research and development and innovation, Martin and Scott (2000) develop a taxonomy of innovation modes and associated market failures and appropriate policy responses. Focusing on technology policy in a national context, Tassey (1997) explains how technology policy addresses market failures resulting from barriers to the private sector's development of new technologies. Conceição and Mendoza (2006) provide a taxonomy of global public goods focused on the problems that hinder successful provision of the goods.

standards for international business behavior, share and coordinate resources to promote international development, and create incentives for business activity when—in the absence of the partnerships—markets would fail to provide socially desirable investments and products.

Witte and Reinicke (2005, p. xii) emphasize that "the lack of systematic and comparable impact assessment" is an impediment to more effective partnering between the United Nations and businesses and civil society:

> ... Though individual partnership projects may be assessed as part of standard evaluation practices, these evaluations are usually not comparative. For the United Nations, impact assessment is not only important for accountability purposes—a comparative review of partnership engagements also forms the basis for higher level strategy development and appropriate resource allocation as well as for learning.

I shall discuss, then, how the emerging and increasingly important global public–private partnerships can be evaluated using cost-benefit analysis. Such analysis has been used to evaluate public–private partnerships in individual nations where the partnerships have addressed the failure of markets to provide socially desirable outcomes.[2] Now, increasingly global public–private partnerships are using world-wide combinations of resources to confront market-failures that threaten international stability.

Although this paper strives to be pragmatic, it will not ignore theoretical foundations. To the contrary, pragmatic approaches are grounded in theory because the theory explains why the pragmatic approaches are expected to have desired effects. That is, the theoretical grounding explains why the approaches have various positive and normative qualities and effects. The theory links public policy to the costs and benefits of economic activity and implies that socially valuable business behavior—that in the absence of appropriate public policy would not occur—can be induced by public policies. For an example, the theory provides the appropriate framework for discussing and determining the appropriateness of intergovernmental organizations allowing their reputation and legitimacy to be associated with the behavior of private economic actors. Such associations—of intergovernmental organizations with privately performed economic activities—occur often in prominent global public–private partnerships.

This paper will explore the following topics:

- The reasons that public actors, including international intergovernmental organizations, might want to enter into global public–private partnerships;
- Methodologies used within the national context for determining the desirability of governments entering into various types of public–private partnerships and the lessons learned about the evaluation methodologies in the national context;
- The applicability of the foregoing methodologies and the modifications of those methodologies that may be required for their use in evaluations of the global public–private partnerships of international intergovernmental organizations;
- Conceptual and methodological issues that need further research.

In the context of social versus private costs and benefits, Sect. 2 discusses market failure as an explanation for why intergovernmental agencies might want to enter global public–private partnerships. Section 3 provides an overview of cost-benefit evaluation, and then Sect. 4 considers the alternative conceptual measures of costs and benefits. In particular, Sect. 4 explains the need for and the use of market-centered valuations, but it also explains

---

[2] See, for example, Link and Scott (1998a, b, 2000, 2001, 2005a, b, 2006, forthcoming).

 Springer

the role of alternative social valuations needed for the successful use of cost-benefit methodologies in the evaluation of global public–private partnerships. Section 5 enumerates lessons learned that inform the application of cost-benefit analysis to global public–private partnerships. Section 6 provides the conclusions of the paper. The Appendix identifies important topics for future research and development of cost-benefit analysis for the evaluation of global public–private partnerships.

2 Market failure and the economic role of intergovernmental organizations

This section of the paper will develop the idea that international intergovernmental organizations use global public–private partnerships to address economic problems that have not been adequately solved by markets, national governments, and the philanthropic organizations of civil society.

Private costs and benefits govern actions in markets. By private costs and benefits, I mean the costs and benefits faced by the private actors—the business firms supplying goods and services and then the households purchasing and consuming those goods and services—in markets. When those private costs and benefits of actions diverge from their social valuations, markets typically fail to produce socially desirable results. Absent corrective policy, a market failure results in a situation where the marginal social benefit of an economic activity differs from its marginal social cost. For example, if a company cannot appropriate the full social value from its investments (there are then "externalities"— benefits from the investments that are not captured by the investor), then at the level of investment that it finds to be most profitable—where its marginal private benefit from additional investment equals its marginal cost—society might find that the marginal social benefit of more investment exceeds the marginal cost. From a social standpoint, there would be underinvestment, and the market would have failed. The market's result would be inefficient because more net social value could be had with the application of additional resources to the economic activity in question. From the perspective of economics, important roles for government include provision of an institutional setting within which markets can work well and then provision of policies to address inefficiencies and inequities left in the wake of market forces. Cost-benefit analyses are often used to evaluate, both prospectively and retrospectively, the programs and projects that are used in policies addressing inefficiencies.

Government policies that address inequities typically redistribute income and wealth. In addition to addressing inefficiencies and inequities, governments typically provide "merit goods" and prohibit "merit bads." Stiglitz and Walsh (2002, p. 319) summarize the role of government:

> There are three basic reasons why the government intervenes in the economy: (1) to improve economic efficiency by correcting market failures; (2) to pursue social values of fairness, or equity, by altering market outcomes; and (3) to pursue other social values by mandating the consumption of some goods, called merit goods, and prohibiting the consumption of other goods, called merit bads.

Regarding the inefficiencies associated with market failure, the government's policies address inefficiencies caused by imperfect competition, by imperfect information, by externalities in production and consumption, and by the need for public goods that markets

 Springer

do not provide because they are non-rivalrous and non-excludable in consumption.[3] For example, government might support public art such as a towering memorial sculpture overlooking a capital city because the public art has attributes of a public good—it is non-rivalrous in consumption (I can enjoy it, and it is still there for you to enjoy) and it is non-excludable in consumption (I can enjoy it as I visit in the city, even if I did not pay toward its creation). Or the government might subsidize an art museum or a symphony because it believes there are positive externalities—benefits to others, associated with the creation and consumption of the art and music, for which the creators will not be paid if markets alone are used to reward the artists' efforts.

Regarding inequities, a national government's policies address redistribution of income and wealth. Even if a country's market system succeeds in achieving adequate levels of efficiency, the efficient economic outcomes may be associated with great income and wealth inequality that the nation's society as a whole considers inequitable. Some households that are not highly rewarded by the market system will not be able to afford adequate nutrition, housing, or clothing, while others will enjoy the best restaurants, numerous luxurious homes, and designer clothing. Government can mitigate those inequities through its policies that redistribute income and wealth.

Merit goods have included education. Merit bads have included drinking or smoking. Although policies aimed at reducing inequities or mandating consumption of a merit good or prohibiting consumption of a merit bad could be evaluated with cost-benefit analyses, the policies are not always studied in that way. They are motivated by an innate sense of what is appropriate or inappropriate that for many transcends an accounting of the benefits versus the costs. Moreover, it is especially difficult to place valuations on the benefits for policies that redistribute income or provide or prohibit goods based on a paternalistic society's sense of merit.

A key point that I emphasize throughout this paper is that the usual sharp distinction between the efficiency enhancing versus equity enhancing roles for government is overstated. I shall argue that there is far less distinction than typically drawn between government actions to promote efficiency and those actions to redistribute income and thereby promote equity or actions simply to promote what the government considers right by mandating certain types of consumption and forbidding other types. The reason is that the set of efficient solutions is not at all independent of a government's policies regarding equity or merit goods and merit bads.

Understanding the interdependence among efficient solutions and policies toward equity and merit goods and bads is important for understanding the use of cost-benefit analysis. Hence, the understanding is necessary for the topic of this paper—that is, for the use of cost-benefit analysis in the evaluation of the desirability of an intergovernmental organization entering into a global public–private partnership. I shall develop the idea of interdependence between policy and the set of efficient solutions as I explain cost-benefit analysis in Sects. 3 and 4. Here, in Sect. 2, I shall develop an extension of the analysis of the role of government in a national economy to explain the economic role of intergovernmental organizations and global public–private partnerships.

Seeing government as establishing the appropriate setting for markets to operate well and then using government policies to reduce remaining inefficiencies and inequities is a conventional, commonly held view of the government's role. In that context, the role of intergovernmental organizations such as the United Nations or the World Bank can be seen as developing and coordinating international policies to address the international

---

[3] For an accessible yet thorough discussion, see Stiglitz and Walsh (2002, Chap. 11).

 Springer

community's perspective about specific inadequacies in national government policies toward those inefficiencies and inequities that remain after markets have provided their solution for the allocation of resources to various activities.[4]

Many government policies to address inefficiencies that are not resolved by market processes may not solve the problems satisfactorily. Unsatisfactory government solutions to inefficiencies are attributed to many things, but perhaps the most fundamental is that the values and costs of economic activities that shape the government's perceptions of inefficiencies (to be addressed with policies) are often market-centered ones that reflect the current distribution of income and wealth and hence the preferences—expressed as willingness to pay—implicit in that distribution. The preferences of "alternative economic majorities" are not expressed and were they expressed might well imply a very different agenda for government policies to address inefficiencies.[5]

Whether social valuations are market-centered or not, government provision of public goods and subsidies for activities that are under-rewarded by markets will necessarily be imperfect from the perspectives of some whose preferences are not reflected fully in the government's policies. The issue is more than the hard fact that some people are in the majority while others are not. There are inconsistencies in the collective rationality as determined by the political process. Arrow's (1963) reasoning implies that collective judgments, reached through the political process to provide through government various services, need not adequately reflect the range of individuals' values.[6] As he observes (1963, p. 60): "If consumers' values can be represented by a wide range of individual orderings, the doctrine of voters' sovereignty is incompatible with that of collective rationality." With reasonable conditions required for collective rationality, the desire to use the values of all individuals in the making of collectively rational social welfare judgments is not typically met as judgments are imposed that do not reflect the full range of individuals' values.[7]

One role for the philanthropic organizations of civil society is to allow mobilization of funds to activities supported by those whose preferences are not adequately reflected in the

---

[4] Following the conventional view of the government's role, I am portraying the government as the primary vehicle for joint action, with civil society and its various philanthropic organizations—in both the national and international contexts—filling needs not adequately addressed by government. In discussions with me, Meir Kohn has made the following observations that I paraphrase in this note. He observes that while in descriptive terms my portrayal may be accurate today, historically it is not accurate. Both government and the philanthropic organizations of civil society offer frameworks for joint action when market (individualistic) solutions are unsatisfactory. The basic difference between them is that government relies on coercion while civil society relies on voluntary efforts. The ideal division of labor between government and civil society is an open and important question. It is also, of course, a difficult one.

[5] See Scott (2000b). The set of efficient outcomes (regarding the mix of goods and services and the investment projects undertaken) would differ because the distribution of income determines whose preferences count in the markets where consumers cast their dollar votes for the various goods and services. A different distribution of income implies a different set of preferences will determine the values of goods and services as reflected by the demands for them. The optimal set of goods and services (the efficient mix of output) and the optimal set of investment projects will vary with the differing relative demands.

[6] Arrow established the result formally with his "impossibility theorem." As Stiglitz and Walsh (2002, pp. 333–334) point up, the result is a more general statement of the problem identified by Condorcet's "voting paradox" regarding majority voting. Arrow's impossibility theorem shows that no voting system can avoid inconsistencies which are inherent in the decision-making process of any democratic government.

[7] The term "social welfare" covers a wide range of views about what is good for society as a whole. For example, economists often use the term "social economic welfare" to denote the total net value (value in excess of the opportunity costs of the resources used) produced by scarce economic resources in a particular use. Social philosophers might equate "social welfare" with fairness or social justice.

 Springer

government's valuations of activities under-rewarded by markets. In this context of the economic role of government and civil society, international intergovernmental organizations such as the United Nations—that are working in global public–private partnerships with national governments, civil society, and businesses in the private sector—address issues requiring the allocation of resources for socially valuable projects that would not be done by international markets, national governments, or civil society acting in various combinations but without the authority and participation of international intergovernmental organizations. At the international level, intergovernmental organizations are addressing problems that, from the perspective of the international community, have not been adequately addressed by either markets or nations' governments and civil society. As Kaul (2006) documents, intergovernmental organizations are increasingly addressing such problems in prominent global public–private partnerships by combining and marshaling the resources of national governments and civil society in concert with their own expertise and resources.

Even apart from the disagreements that may remain about the socially desirable policies that are chosen for government action, governments may fail to perform well. One way to reduce the possibilities for government failure is to take advantage of the private sector's ability to mobilize and apply resources and have private performance rather than public performance of a project. That is, the government would focus on the provision of appropriate incentives for good private performance, and then the private sector—given the appropriate incentives—would carry out the provision of the socially desirable goods and services rather than the government. As Kaul (2006) and Conceição et al. (2006) explain, public–private partnerships, both in a national context and in the international context of global public–private partnerships, provide one approach for combining the resources and complementary strengths of both the public and the private sectors. Such partnerships represent much more than arm's length policy by governments, even when the private sector carries out the actual performance of the resource allocations for the task—such as producing and delivering medicines to those who could not otherwise afford them—at hand.

The partnerships can ensure appropriate incentives for private performance of actions that are in the public interest in situations when the market alone would not provide those socially desirable actions. Conceição et al. (2006) catalog and explain numerous ways that governments or intergovernmental organizations can provide sufficient incentives while leaving the actual provision of the socially desirable investments and substantial amounts of the financing to the private sector. For example, governments or intergovernmental organizations might provide purchase commitments needed to assure the private sector's companies that they could indeed sell the goods that they would produce and deliver to those with uncertain prospects regarding their ability to pay. Or, governments or intergovernmental organizations could provide guarantees for the loans needed to assure private-sector lenders that they could finance the small business enterprises of a developing economy when without the loan guarantees the loans would be too risky to make. Conceição et al. (2006) explain and describe complex financing arrangements that are being used to fund global public–private partnerships.

Why would market failure necessitate global public–private partnerships? Why not simply rely on public–private partnerships in national contexts to correct market failure? Intergovernmental organizations in global public–private partnerships might be much more effective than public–private partnerships at the national level—especially when the set of issues that are not addressed adequately by markets are international in their scope, requiring coordination among nations. Concerns about climate instability caused by

 Springer

pollution—or about the adverse environmental effects of pollution more generally—require coordination among nations because the pollution occurring in one nation can have an impact on other nations. Crises in the health of one nation's population become crises for the health of those in other nations. For example, a world-wide health crisis could be precipitated by migratory birds carrying the source of avian flu from one nation to another or by the international travels of infected people. The problem of extreme poverty in one nation becomes the problem of all nations not only because of moral imperatives but as well for the very pragmatic reason that hunger and homelessness and deprivation more generally can generate national political instability and even terrorism that can become international in scope just a surely as crises of disease can become international crises.

In the following sections, I turn to a discussion of cost-benefit analysis as a methodology for identifying market failure and the situations where intergovernmental organizations would want to enter into public–private partnerships with the goal of correcting the market failure. In the context of its ongoing study—featured in Kaul and Conceição (2006)—of the role of intergovernmental organizations in the response to global challenges, the Office of Development Studies at the United Nations Development Programme has identified three broad situations where intergovernmental organizations address market failures[8]:

- Global market failure (a situation where the market fails to adequately provide a public good in which all nations have a strong interest);
- Market failure and international cooperation failure (a situation where the market fails to provide a public good in which only some countries have a strong interest but perhaps lack the ability to pay);
- Individual-country market failure (a situation where market failure has a national reason and the intergovernmental organization supports the national government in addressing the market failure).

The present paper's discussion of the desirability of intergovernmental organizations entering into public–private partnerships is grounded in the concept of market failure and in the idea that intergovernmental organizations working through global public–private partnerships can correct such failures—occurring in the three types of situations identified by the Office of Development Studies—or, at least, ameliorate them.

3 Social versus private costs and benefits, market failure, and global public–private partnerships

Cost-benefit analysis provides a way to evaluate the desirability of intergovernmental organizations entering into global public–private partnerships. Such analysis can be used both to identify situations where markets will fail to provide socially desirable economic actions and also to distinguish likely cases where global public–private partnerships will be needed rather than some other approach. The global partnerships with intergovernmental organizations coordinating efforts and resources of national governments, businesses, and civil society may be needed because it will not suffice to rely on the hands-off, arms-length

---

[8] These three situations for market failures to be addressed by intergovernmental organizations are set forth in the terms of reference, prepared by the Office of Development Studies at the United Nations Development Programme, for Scott (2006).

policies by national governments or intergovernmental organizations. Further, the other efforts—including public–private partnerships—within nations by governments, civil society, and businesses may not suffice to assure the provision of international public goods or other international actions to correct market failures.

As a methodology for assessing the desirability of intergovernmental organizations entering global public–private partnerships, cost-benefit analysis allows a focus on some of the consequences of the actions or lack of action by intergovernmental organizations. Social costs are opportunity costs—the value of the best foregone use of the scarce economic resources used in the program or project. If a project yields private benefits exceeding or equaling the private costs, one expects that markets will perform the project. However, many projects that would be considered socially desirable from the perspective of the international community may not yield private benefits as great as the private costs. For example, the international community could identify a need for the provision of medical supplies to large numbers of individuals without the means to pay for them. The private sector alone through the market system would not typically provide those supplies because the costs of doing so would not be met by the revenues from sales. Yet from the social perspective of the international community, benefits would exceed the costs. Or, for another example, the international community could identify a need for investments in the infrastructures of developing nations, or investments in the emerging businesses of those sectors. Given the prospect for appropriating the value of the investments, the private sector might find that the expected benefits fall short of the costs, and the market system alone would not carry out the investments. Yet, from a social perspective, the benefits created by the investments would exceed the costs.

Benefits and costs typically occur over time, and the present values of those streams of returns from a project depend on the discount rates used to convert future returns to current values.[9] Thus, benefits and costs are each a function—benefits(r) and costs(r)—of the discount rate r.[10] The difference between the present value of the benefits and the present value of the costs is the "net present value" often presented in cost-benefit studies; the ratio of the present values of the benefits and costs is presented as a benefit-to-cost ratio. Also useful is the concept of the internal rate of return, i (also called simply the rate of return) for a project. The internal rate of return denotes the rate at which the investments in the project grow to reach the stream of benefits. For a simple case where all costs are incurred at the outset of the project and then the benefits follow, the internal rate of return is the rate that discounts the future benefits back to those costs. Hence, the internal rate of return is i such that costs equal benefits(i). More generally, with a stream of costs as well as benefits, the internal rate of return is the growth rate—interest rate—for the

---

[9] The streams of returns can be discrete—that is, the returns occur at discrete points in time—or continuous, flowing at a rate per unit of time. Whether discrete at varying intervals or continuous, the substance of the idea of present value is the same. For illustrations of cost-benefit analyses using discrete flows, see Link and Scott (2005b); Link and Scott (2001) provides examples using continuous flows. Link and Scott (1998b) provide detailed discussion of the various cost-benefit metrics such as the benefit-to-cost ratio and the net present value and the internal rate of return. Typically—Link and Scott (2005b) provides many examples—the cash flows are "real" and the rates of return are "real"—that is, appropriate adjustments are used to keep the purchasing power of the monetary unit (that measures the cash flows) constant despite inflation.

[10] Different discount rates could in principle be appropriate for flows of different kinds, including flows at different times. The simple single-discount rate case is useful for exposition of concepts and also in practice.

🔊 Springer

investments such that the discounted benefits just equal the discounted costs—costs(i) equal benefits(i).[11]

For clarity in exposition (avoiding the more complicated exposition referred to in the footnotes), consider a project with all costs incurred at the outset of the project. The benefit stream has a present value denoted benefits and equal to benefits(r), and the internal rate of return i is such that costs equal benefits(i). Therefore, if the benefits—the present value, benefits(r), of the benefit stream—exceed the project's costs, then equivalently the project's internal rate of return i exceeds the discount rate r, since the internal rate of return is just high enough to discount the benefit stream back to costs, while the discount rate discounts the benefit stream back to an amount more than those costs. Thus, the investment in the project is growing at a rate greater than the discount rate. That discount rate is therefore called a required rate of return or a hurdle rate, because to invest in a project the present value of benefits must equal or exceed the project's costs, and that occurs when the internal rate of return or yield on the project meets or exceeds the discount or hurdle rate. If the benefits fall short of the costs, then the internal rate of return is less than the discount rate—also called the hurdle rate or the required rate of return—because the internal rate of return discounts the benefit stream to equal the costs, while the discount rate discounts the benefits to less than the costs.

With the foregoing concepts in hand, Fig. 1 illustrates the use of cost-benefit analysis in an intergovernmental organization's evaluation of the desirability of entering a global public–private partnership.[12] The diagram illustrates three projects—A, B, and C—with the point A denoting the private rate of return—measured on the horizontal axis—and the social rate of return—measured on the vertical axis—for project A. The private and social rates of return for projects B and C are denoted analogously by the points labeled B and C. Also, the diagram shows the private and the social hurdle rate. Society's hurdle rate for a project is expected to be less than the private hurdle rate, because, as compared to private investors, society as a whole may be more patient—having a lower rate of time preference—and less risk averse—having less divergence between the weight placed on the disutility from results that are less than expected and the weight placed on the utility from greater than expected results. A hurdle rate—alternatively called the required rate of return—reflects the opportunity cost of the investment funds. In general, society will not perceive the same opportunity costs as private investors. As Link and Scott (2005b, pp. 107–108) explain:

> ... when we evaluate public investment projects, we are invariably looking at cases where there has been some sort of market failure. To improve upon the market solution, the government has become involved (in a variety of ways, in practice) with an investment project. Just as market solutions for the prices of goods may not reflect

---

[11] For the archetypal illustrative case to explain the concept, the net cash flows of benefits minus the costs begin as negative and then become positive, with just a single reversal in the sign for the series of flows. There is then at most a single real solution for the internal rate of return. Of course, for actual investment projects there can be multiple reversals in the signs for the net cash flows, and then using the internal rate of return concept for a cost-benefit analysis requires some additional work with the time series of benefits and costs. For an actual example with an explanation of how to treat the issue, see Link and Scott (1998b, p. 46).

[12] Kaul (2006, p. 246) adapts the figure from the ones in Link and Scott (2001) and in Audretsch et al. (2002). Jaffe (1998, p. 16) introduced the basic diagram in the discussion of the role of the Advanced Technology Program—a public-private partnership at the US National Institute of Standards and Technology; Link and Scott (1998a) adapted that figure to illustrate their analysis of the desirability of a particular public-private partnership in a national context, an analysis that is reprised in Link and Scott (2001, forthcoming) and Audretsch et al. (2002).

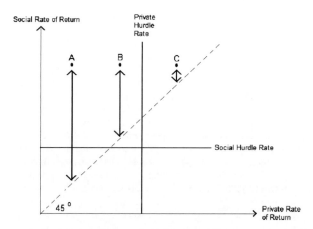

Fig. 1 The gap between social and private rates of return: Cost-benefit analysis and the desirability of public–private partnering. *Source:* Based on Jaffe (1998), Link and Scott (2001), Audretsch et al. (2002), Kaul (2006, pp. 245–246), and Link and Scott (forthcoming)

the social costs for the goods (because of market failure stemming from market power, imperfect information, externalities, or public goods), the private hurdle rates that reflect market solutions for the price of funds—the opportunity cost of funds to the private firms—may not reflect the social cost of the funds. The government may decide that the appropriate social cost—the opportunity cost for the public funds to be invested—differs from the market solution. Typically, in practice, the government believes that it faces less risk than the private sector firms doing similar investments; hence it will believe a lower yield is satisfactory since the public is bearing less risk than the private sector firm going it alone with a similar investment. More generally, government must decide what the opportunity costs of its public funds will be in various uses, and in general that will not be the same as the market rate. However, all that said, Arrow's thinking about social choice teaches us that the government's decision about what the rate should be cannot possibly reflect the diversity of opinion in the private sector regarding the decision (Arrow 1963). Consequently, as a logical matter, one could not prove the government's choice of the right hurdle rate is obviously correct because diversity of opinion about the correct rate will not be reflected in the government's choice.

Summarizing the arguments in Link and Scott (2001) and Audretsch et al. (2002), for all three of the projects shown—projects A, B, and C—the social rate of return exceeds the social hurdle rate (hence, as explained above, social benefits exceed social costs) and from a social standpoint the projects are worth doing. Only project C would be provided by the private sector in a market economy; for projects A and B the private rate of return falls short of the private hurdle rate, and for those projects, then, the private benefit falls short of costs. The market will therefore not provide projects A and B. However, with project B, the private rate of return is relatively close to the private hurdle rate; consequently, a hands-off or arms-length public policy such as a tax credit for the investment may suffice to increase the private rate of return for project B above the private hurdle rate. With such a public policy, the market would then provide project B. For project A, the private rate of return

 Springer

falls so far short of the private hurdle rate that something more than an arms-length public policy may be needed. A public–private partnership may be able to create a situation in which the private sector, with government support, will provide the project A because the government support essentially transforms the A-type project into a C-type project.

Audretsch et al. (2002, p. 153) conjecture:

> ... For projects like project B, a tax credit may be sufficient to increase the expected return so that the firm views the post-tax credit private return to be sufficient for the project to be funded.
>
> However, for projects like project A, a tax credit may be insufficient to increase the expected return enough to induce the private firm to undertake the project. Such projects could include for example projects expected to yield an innovative product that would be part of a larger system of products. Even if technically successful there might be substantial risk that the product would not interoperate or be compatible with other emerging products ....

They suggest that a public–private partnership might be used to stimulate socially desirable investment in such cases. Link and Scott (2000, 2001) provide actual examples showing how public–private partnerships can essentially change A-type projects into C-type projects that the private sector will perform.

Kaul (2006, p. 245) reinterprets the figure and its cases in the context of intergovernmental organizations evaluating the desirability of entering global public–private partnerships, observing:

> ... For project B, an arm's–length intervention might suffice. In the national context this could mean a tax credit or subsidy. In the international context, where such instruments are unavailable, a simple partnership may be required, along the lines, say, [of brokering affordable price deals or leveraging research and development]. For project A, however, where large or multiple incentive gaps have to be overcome, [the situation may warrant global public–private partnerships managing for strategic results—by assembling inputs from many economic sectors and increasing the problem-solving capacity of the international community—when the international challenges require multisectoral, multilevel, multiactor interventions].

The theoretical and empirical fact that the simplest arms-length public policies may not suffice to correct underinvestment in socially valuable projects has been prominently discussed in the contexts of national technology policy. Scott (1995) uses a well-known model of R&D investment (that reflects the complex cost structure of such investment as well as the investment's technological and market uncertainty) to simulate an example where R&D tax credits would not correct the R&D underinvestment resulting because of market failure, observing (Scott 1995, p. 80):

> R&D tax credits have often been found to provide only weak stimulus to R&D investment. To illustrate, ... our model ... simulates the effect of a tax credit similar to the U.S. R&D tax credit ....
>
> ... The simulation suggests that the empirical findings of modest effects of the tax credit for R&D spending have a sound theoretical explanation. The simulation certainly provides theoretical support for the U.S. Congressional Budget Office's summary ... of the position of critics of the U.S. tax credit for R&D: "Critics contend that the credit encourages little additional R&D, and so provides a subsidy to

firms that would undertake the R&D anyway." The simulation shows that the problem need not be attempts to gain the tax credit by the reclassification of existing expenditures as R&D. Instead, the fundamental problem is that the credit does not provide a strong incentive to increase R&D at the margin even though the credit does increase profits. Basically, the problem is a lack of appropriation on the demand side. Even if we cut R&D costs by 20%, to add another [R&D] trial implies a big jump in R&D costs, and we have done nothing for improving the appropriating of the benefits.

The problem here is quite general, if private firms have substantial difficulty appropriating the returns from their efforts to supply goods and services or to do R&D to develop new products and new processes, something more substantial for incentives is needed—something beyond the usual reductions in taxes from credits for costs. In the international context, as Kaul (2006, p. 245) explains, even the usual simpler arms-length mechanisms available in the national context may not be available to intergovernmental organizations, and addressing market failure in an international context may require the use of global public–private partnerships for Case-B as well as Case-A projects.

For an example of the way that a partnership can ensure the appropriation of returns needed for the provision of socially desirable products, Kaul (2006, p. 235) describes partnerships that broker affordable price deals and thereby:

> ... facilitate market transactions in which developing country governments are the purchaser and private firms the supplier. Brokers weave a partnership between the two sides. The main tool is the political clout and persuasiveness of the key mediator. The outcome is ... to make critical goods affordable for poor countries and poor people.

> An example ... is the agreement negotiated by the Clinton Foundation, in collaboration with the Global Fund to Fight AIDS, Tuberculosis, and Malaria, the World Bank, and the United Nations Children Fund, under which developing country governments purchasing AIDS drugs and diagnostics commit themselves to longer term purchase contracts. In return, pharmaceutical companies offer the goods at their lowest possible price .... The multilateral agencies provide financing guarantees, while the Clinton Foundation bundles demand.

The R&D projects of interest to intergovernmental agencies also present private firms with appropriability difficulties that global public–private partnerships may be able to overcome. Kaul (2006, pp. 236–237) observes that global public–private partnerships can leverage research and development (R&D). Explaining that knowledge is a key to development, Kaul observes that the private firms with a major role in the R&D need the expectation of a high market value for the products they develop with their R&D investments. Yet, Kaul (2006, pp. 236–237) observes:

> Products that respond to the needs of poor people do not hold this ...promise, so R&D and product-development initiatives are often stunted. Especially neglected is pro-poor knowledge that is completely noncommercial, such as knowledge about hygiene and nutrition. ...[G]lobal public–private partnerships try to correct these shortcomings by targeting incentives, mostly financial support, to R&D providers.

> Given the many health challenges facing the poor and, through spillover effects, the world as a whole, several health-related pro-poor R&D and product development

 Springer

partnerships have sprung up, including Aeras Global TB Vaccine Foundation, Global Alliance for Tuberculosis Drug Development, Hookworm Vaccine Initiative, International AIDS Vaccine Initiative, Medicines for Malaria Venture …, and Institute for OneWorld Health. Other … partnerships foster knowledge generation on critical environment issues, such as the Global Climate and Energy Project and the Global Water Partnership.

Some of these global public–private partnerships are akin in their functioning to the public–private R&D partnerships that have become common in the national context. Such partnerships began to emerge as governments found that R&D promotion often requires going beyond an arm's-length approach—going beyond tax credits, subsidies, or prizes. To ensure that public policy incentives generate more than company-specific private gains and benefit society more broadly, close interaction between researchers and their sponsors may be needed. This realization has given rise to several national public–private research partnerships (Audretsch et al. 2002). Global R&D partnerships are similar, emerging in particular where there is a need to incentivize private industry to explore urgently needed knowledge products for which there is no readily available market and to ensure, through close public–private interaction, that the end product is of high quality and appropriately priced.

In the following section, I shall consider the appropriate measure for costs and benefits. Precisely because global partnerships need to provide incentives for private industry to provide goods and services as well as R&D in circumstances where markets alone will not suffice, traditional "market-centered" cost-benefit analysis is crucial to successful evaluation of the partnerships' strategies. I turn first to the conceptual foundation, and then subsequently to several examples from the global public–private partnerships that are profiled in Kaul (2006).

4 The appropriate measure of costs and benefits: market-centered versus broader social valuations

Section 3 describes market failures to be addressed by public–private partnerships when social benefits exceed social costs for a project, yet markets will not carry out the project because private benefits are less than private costs. Equivalently (as explained in Sect. 3), in terms of Fig. 1, the social rate of return exceeds the social hurdle rate, yet markets do not accept the project because the private rate of return is less than the private hurdle rate. A key question for the usefulness of the cost-benefit analysis remains unanswered. For intergovernmental organizations to be able to use cost-benefit analysis in evaluations of the desirability of global public–private partnerships, the measure of the costs and benefits must be specified.

Sen (2000, p. 952) observes:

When all the requirements of ubiquitous market-centered evaluation have been incorporated into the procedures of cost-benefit analysis, it is not so much a discipline as a daydream. … Sensible cost-benefit analysis demands something beyond the mainstream method, in particular, the invoking of explicit social choice judgments that take us beyond market-centered valuation.

 Springer

This section must address Sen's challenge, because in the many cost-benefit evaluations of the publicly supported projects in national contexts, such as those of US public–private partnerships, typically market-centered valuations have been used. This section will explain why the market-centered valuations are appropriate in the typical cost-benefit analysis of a public project. Making the argument, however, points to the need for more general analyses of the social valuations to ensure that cost-benefit evaluations can be appropriately and usefully applied to evaluate the work of global public–private partnerships. The discussion in this section will explain that cost-benefit analyses as described in Sect. 3 and in the discussion of Fig. 1 are applicable for evaluating the projects of global public–private partnerships, but for many of those projects, in addition to market-centered social valuations, other social valuations will be useful as well.

When explicit cost-benefit analyses are used to evaluate a government's public programs and projects, the costs and benefits are typically market-centered valuations—that is, not only do the *private* costs and benefits reflect what people and businesses are paying for goods and services, but as well the *social* costs and benefits reflect what is paid and what people would be willing to pay given the extant distribution of income and wealth. For example, the R&D efforts of a private company will typically generate market-centered benefits for other producers, who use the results of the R&D for their own production and products, and also market-centered benefits for consumers, who realize consumer surplus on their purchases of the products. Markets fail to provide the appropriate amount of R&D and fail, therefore, to provide the products that that R&D would have developed because private benefits for the providing firms fall short of the firms' costs, yet there are social market-centered benefits that are not captured by the providing firms. The result is that social market-centered benefits exceed social costs, and society as a whole would benefit from the provision of the goods even though markets alone will not provide them.

Of course, in its role to address situations society perceives to be inequitable, a government may provide goods and services that address needs that markets do not address because those needing the goods have no ability to pay for them. Why, then, would a "market-centered" value be appropriate to assess the benefits? This section develops the idea that market-centered valuations of costs and benefits can be appropriate in both the national and the international context, where intergovernmental organizations evaluate the desirability of entering into global public–private partnerships. Nonetheless, a complete analysis requires that alternative social valuations of costs and benefits be used in addition to market-centered ones, and that will be especially important in the context of international cooperation in global partnerships.

The issue here is about the measure of the *social* costs and benefits rather than the private costs and benefits. With regard to the actions of businesses, one expects that the private costs and benefits are market-centered. That is, they are determined by what people and businesses are willing to pay for the scarce resources and the goods and services produced with those scarce resources. For understanding the private behavior addressed with cost-benefit analysis, market-centered valuations of private costs and benefits (and hence private rate of return and private hurdle rate of Fig. 1) are the measures needed whether the evaluation is for a national or a global public–private partnership. What then is the appropriate measure of *social* costs and benefits? Why would market-centered valuations of the social costs and benefits be appropriate?

Market-centered valuations—for social as well as private benefits and costs—are used in the evaluations of government programs and projects in which I have participated, including, among others, Link and Scott (1998a, b, 2000, 2001, 2005a, b, 2006, forthcoming) and Scott (2000a). There are many reasons why market-centered social valuations

 Springer

can be appropriate in the evaluations of government programs and projects in a national context; these reasons explain the use of the market-centered valuations in the foregoing examples. The reasons include: (1) commercialization of technology is an important goal of the programs and projects being evaluated; (2) political and social acceptance and support for the programs and projects is crucial; and (3) in the national context, there is a well-defined sense that market-centered valuations are the society's valuations, although the valuations will reflect only imperfectly the differing opinions of society's members in the sense that collective rationality as generated by the political process will not completely reflect the range of individuals' values.

For the US National Institute of Standards and Technology and its Advanced Technology Program as well as for the US. Small Business Innovation Research Program, commercialization of technology is at the heart of the goals for the programs.[13] Therefore, the commercial value of the results of the programs and projects is central to evaluation. Obviously, commercial value determines the private costs and benefits that affect the behavior of the companies benefiting from research in government laboratories or performing the research and using the results. Beyond that the public through these programs wants to develop commercial value—value that is reflected in the streams of producer surplus and consumer surplus that together determine benefits in a market-centered model of valuation.[14] Social costs are opportunity costs in the context of that market-centered model—the commercial value in their best alternative use of the scarce resources used in the program or project.

Within a nation, the market-centered social valuations of goods and services and scarce resources reflect public choice regarding the legal framework, provision of infrastructure, fiscal and various other policies, and therefore ultimately the distribution of income and wealth and hence the ability of individuals to express their preferences with purchases. The political consensus about choices determining market-value comes from the citizens who will or will not support the programs and projects. Therefore, the effective political support—that will reflect the opinions of those same citizens who formed the political consensus about the choices determining market value—for a program or project is expected to be stronger when evaluations and decisions are based on market-centered social valuations.

In a national context where the public has accepted a mixed economy, are market-centered values really different from social values? The answer is not obviously yes because market-centered valuation is not independent of public choice regarding policies. National governments influence the total economic surplus resulting from the market's allocation of scarce resources in a mixed economy—that is, one where government takes an active role in shaping the market forces and also in performing some economic tasks itself. Government influences total surplus because the institutional setting created by government—including the legal framework and property rights and the public's investments in infrastructure, health, education, research and development, direct redistributions of income and wealth, and so forth—determines the distribution of income and wealth and therefore determines whose preferences are expressed in the market valuations of scarce

---

[13] For details about the mandate and purposes for the US National Institute of Standards and Technology, see Link and Scott (1998b). For the description of the mandate and purposes for the Advanced Technology Program, see Link and Scott (2005b). Audretsch et al. (2002) provide a description of the mandate and goals for the US Small Business Innovation Research Program.

[14] See Link and Scott (1998b) for discussion, in the context of institutional evaluations, of the traditional models based on the work of Griliches (1958) and Mansfield et al. (1977) in which benefits are measured by the stream of total economic surplus, itself the sum of consumer and producer surplus.

 Springer

resources and the goods and services provided with those resources. For an obvious example, if the institutional setting resulted in a more equal distribution of income, presumably there would be less demand for second homes for extremely wealthy families and more demand for modest, "affordable" housing from those who currently do not have dollar votes to cast for even modest housing.

Even given the distribution of income and wealth, by setting standards for business behavior and performance, government can also influence the pattern of demands and hence market values. For example, clear standards for the environmental performance of industry can channel industrial R&D toward innovations that reduce emissions that damage the environment (Scott 2003; 2005a, b). Government policy can make "green"—that is, environmentally friendly—behavior and performance commercially valuable when otherwise it would not be. The standards for the environment will imply new demand for innovative talent and outputs that would not be present in the absence of the government's policies. The new demand is not simply a matter of innovations to satisfy government demand expressed with government expenditures, but as well consumers may have greater demand for products produced in environmentally friendly ways. The government with its information about the problems and about the "green" behavior of companies can create a situation where consumers reward the companies with environmentally friendly practices.[15]

More generally, governments can inform the public about socially desirable behavior and performance and thereby shift market demands toward companies that demonstrate socially desirable behavior that would go unrewarded in the market without the government's leadership in setting standards for behavior and performance and in recognizing the socially responsible companies. At the global level, such leadership is what is occurring when an intergovernmental organization allows private corporations to advertise their association with the organization in conjunction with activities that are socially desirable. Thus, providing such leadership and its effects on market demands that increase the market value of socially responsible corporate behavior is the rationale for "selling" the reputation and legitimacy of the intergovernmental organization.

For example, among the global public–private partnerships, profiled as a part of the overall and ongoing study described by Kaul (2006), is "British Petroleum Social Responsibility Initiatives." The major funding for the partnership comes from British Petroleum, and the partners other than British Petroleum include the United Nations Development Programme (UNDP), the United Nations Environment Programme (UNEPO) and also, in addition to the foregoing intergovernmental organizations, various local government agencies. Also, there are many civil society partners in the environmental field covering a broad spectrum of non-profit partners. Discussing the motivation for its funding of the global public–private partnership, British Petroleum states [Source: Quoted from material at http://www.bp.com as reported in the website http://www.thenewpublic

---

[15] There are many examples of companies responding to public concerns about the environment by adopting environmentally friendly behavior and then advertising that behavior because it is expected to increase sales and profits. One example, as reported in Sneyd (2005), is for McDonald's, the world's largest fast-food chain. Sneyd reports that McDonald's introduced to its New England and up-state New York outlets a new organic coffee certified as "Fair Trade." That is, the coffee is certified to have been made from coffee beans produced by farmers who receive a guaranteed basic minimum wage and who practice organic and sustainable cultivation. McDonald's promotes the new coffee as "Good for you. ...Good for the environment. ...Good for the world." Sneyd (2005, p. A3) reports that "McDonald's will be promoting the new brew heavily and will be emphasizing the organic and Fair Trade angles. ...A trade association that promotes Fair Trade products said the move makes great business sense for McDonald's and could further enhance the market for such goods."

 Springer

finance.org/ for Kaul and Conceição (2006) where the Office of Development Studies, United Nations Development Programme, has posted a database of global public–private partnerships.]:

> Partnering with these groups is essential if [British Petroleum is] to sustain a mutually beneficial business. … These partnerships allow BP to hand their social responsibility initiatives over to organizations better suited to undertake them and also allow BP to advertise its cooperation with agencies with a respected name in the social responsibility field. These partnerships can take the form of research initiatives or service provision agreements but often involve funding arrangements in exchange for recognition of BP's involvement.

Observe that British Petroleum clearly sees as profitable business its sponsorship of partnerships pursuing socially responsible behavior. The company says the socially responsible corporate behavior is essential for sustaining business; thus, socially responsible behavior is not charity, it is instead good business given the association with the United Nations. British Petroleum considers important the association with the respected United Nations intergovernmental organization, and the company believes that it needs the recognition of its work that comes from association with such a respected organization in the area of social responsibility. That association makes profitable the socially responsible behavior that might otherwise be unprofitable. Corporate social responsibility (CSR) can be profitable, as explained by McWilliams and Siegel (2001, p. 125):

> … [T]here is some level of CSR that will maximize profits while satisfying the demand for CSR from multiple stakeholders. … To maximize profit, the firm should offer precisely that level of CSR for which the increased revenue (from increased demand) equals the higher cost (of using resources to provide CSR) [for the marginal dollar of spending on CSR]. By doing so, the firm meets the demands of relevant stakeholders—both those that demand CSR (consumers, employees, community) and those that "own" the firm (shareholders).

The point is that when a respected intergovernmental organization such as the United Nations Development Programme joins with a private company such as British Petroleum in a global public–private partnership, the intergovernmental organization provides a credible signal announcing and establishing as socially responsible the behavior of the private company with its investments through the partnership. That credible signal makes the behavior commercially valuable for the private company; with the signal the behavior can be profitable even when without the credible signal from a respected organization promoting social responsibility it would be an unprofitable investment.

Thus, for a nation with an economy that can be affected by the government's policies, those policies shape and change the sums of consumer and producer surplus that are together the total economic surplus that constitutes market-centered valuations of cost-benefit analysis. At the national level, then, there is a well-defined sense in which market-centered valuations are the society's valuations; the two are not unambiguously different. However, because the political consensus about public choices cannot fully reflect the diversity of opinion among a nation's citizens, one could introduce social valuations other than the market-centered ones—that are to be sure a result of public policies reflecting a political consensus and hence an expression of social valuations—as a way of encouraging a society to think about the differences in perspective and valuation that would remain given the market-centered valuations. Those market-centered valuations—decided by a political consensus about a nation's policies that, in a sense, rendered them "the society's"

 Springer

valuations—will not reflect the diversity of opinion, and invoking social valuations other than market-centered ones can be another way to reflect and discuss the different opinions.

For that reason, when discussing the use of cost-benefit analysis for national policy toward publicly supported R&D projects, Scott (2000b, p. 12) suggests that it would be good to explore how costs and benefits might change if the market valuations used to evaluate a project were determined by alternative distributions of the ability to purchase goods and services:

> Following Griliches (1958) and Mansfield et al. (1977), the social and private rates of return that we have described are based on the concept of total economic surplus and its components, producer and consumer surplus. ... [The] surplus measures and associated rates of return are based on the current distribution of income and wealth and the choices that consumers make given that distribution. Our surplus measures and choices among projects then reflect what could be called the current economic majority that would cast the dollar votes for various products and services. There are other hidden economic majorities—economic majorities associated with other income and wealth distributions—that a government should take into account. Indeed, the political process is one way that a "hidden" economic majority could use the government process to choose a direction for technological change that would not be the choice of the current economic majority. For example, even if the current economic majority would prefer to devote R&D resources to an R&D project in the entertainment industry yielding a social return of 80% as compared to the best alternative use of let us say an R&D project to develop low-income housing and medical care that has a social rate of return considerably less than 80%, for some hidden economic majority the inequality [that is, the comparison showing that one rate of return is greater than the other] might well be reversed.

Imagine, for example, that instead of the great inequality in the distribution of income and wealth that generated the market-centered values favoring the entertainment industry's innovation, there were virtual equality in the distribution of purchasing power across the nation's populace. With that alternative distribution, the project for low-income housing and medical care might have a greater return than the project in the entertainment industry. Thus, observing that the arguments can be made not only for the evaluation of R&D projects, but as well for any projects using economic resources, Scott (2000b, p. 14, p. 12) concludes:

> The conventional finding of a social rate of return exceeding the private hurdle rate for a project, although important and useful information about social value, is neither necessary nor sufficient as an indicator of the social usefulness of an R&D project .... Economists can help to identify other applications of the resources with even higher social returns, and some of those applications may reflect the economic surpluses associated with different economic majorities than the current one.

> ... [G]overnments can rationally choose to deploy R&D resources using an evaluation metric other than the total economic surplus of the current economic majority.

Although the foregoing arguments were developed for the evaluation of public–private partnerships in a national context, the arguments seem especially pertinent for the evaluation of global partnerships. With global public–private partnerships led by intergovernmental organizations, certainly we do not have the argument that a single, world-wide public policy—reached through a supra-national political process analogous to a nation's political process—has determined the market-centered valuations measured as consumer and producer economic surpluses and hence the total economic surpluses of the traditional, market-centered cost-benefit analysis. The world does not have an international government, but rather intergovernmental organizations striving to get nations to cooperate. There is no political consensus across the nations about the set of national public policies that determine international market values.

Furthermore, although each nation will have decided on its own public policies to shape to whatever extent possible the market outcomes the nation's political process finds desirable, nations' governments will differ in their abilities to shape market forces and nations' populations will differ in their overall purchasing power and will therefore have different amounts of influence on the market-centered valuations that determine the streams of benefits and costs associated with programs and projects being evaluated by global partnerships. Therefore, market-centered valuations given the world's current distribution of income and wealth do not reflect a world society's valuations in the sense that within a nation the market-centered valuations—that are influenced by the nation's public policies that at least reflect a political consensus within the nation—reflect the nation's valuations.

To reflect nations' diversity in opinion about values, the evaluation of the desirability of global public–private partnerships, then, will require identifying the different national valuations. One approach to developing international understanding is for the international community to think about how the valuations of wealthy nations would change if they were less wealthy. The counterfactual experiment would ask the wealthy nations to put themselves in the circumstances of the less wealthy nations, thereby identifying the different assessments of costs and benefits if the world-wide distribution of income and wealth across nations were very different from what it is currently. Identifying those differences seems important and logical even if one were willing to accept market-centered valuations as society's valuations within a given nation. Exploration to identify differences in costs and benefits for alternative distributions of income and wealth can be important even within a nation, as argued in Scott (2000b), but in the evaluation by intergovernmental organizations of the desirability of global public–private partnerships, developing understanding of different perspectives is of paramount importance because those organizations operate without a world government.

I return then to the wisdom of Sen's observation, an observation that seems especially important in the context of the evaluation of global public–private partnerships (Sen 2000, p. 952):

> Sensible cost-benefit analysis demands something beyond the mainstream method, in particular, the invoking of explicit social choice judgments that take us beyond market-centered valuation.

One way to accomplish such judgments is to imagine what the market-centered valuations would have been if the distribution of income and wealth across individuals and across nations was very different from what it is currently. In the context of the set of global public–private partnerships—with their emphasis on providing benefits to those without the ability to pay—as profiled by the United Nations Development Programme as described in Kaul (2006), an especially useful alternative distribution to imagine is one with equality in the distribution of income and wealth across and within nations.

Global public–private partnerships largely focus on projects for beneficiaries who do not have the ability to pay fully for the goods and services received; and therefore, the partnerships have their own unique character as compared to many national public–private

 Springer

partnerships. Yet, many global public–private partnerships are in some ways quite similar to the partnerships funded in part by the US. Small Business Innovation Research (SBIR) Program or the US. National Institute of Standards and Technology (NIST) and by its Advanced Technology Program (ATP). The SBIR, NIST, and ATP projects have been evaluated with market-centered cost-benefit analysis, and can in part serve as examples for the evaluation of global public–private partnerships. For the reasons I am discussing in this paper, the evaluation of the global partnerships requires the market-centered analysis, but can benefit as well from the use of other social valuations for costs and benefits since market-centered valuations will not reflect all social valuations—especially from the international perspective. The evaluation of global partnerships requires market-centered analysis given the current distribution of income because: (1) in many cases commercialization is itself a goal; (2) private, rather than public, performance of the investments or provision of goods and services is desired; and (3) political support for the partnership will be correlated with the market-centered analysis given the current distribution of income.

For an example a global partnership with activities closely related to those at NIST, consider the International Organization for Standardization (ISO). As discussed by Kaul (2006, p. 253), to facilitate the development of technical standards, the ISO brings together the national standards institutes for countries world-wide along with private sector agencies representing industry. The development of technical standards by the ISO fosters commercialization, but the ISO is focused as well on how the standards affect the environment and social responsibility. Link and Scott (1998b) use cost-benefit analysis to evaluate many NIST projects that have developed standards. In addition to the focus on supporting commercial activities, these projects at NIST often have an international dimension as well as concern about the environment and social responsibility. For example, as described in Link and Scott (1998b, pp. 91–102), the Alternative Refrigerant Research Program used NIST's technical expertise to support industry's response to the international environmental problem of ozone depletion and the Montreal Protocol of 1987.

For another example, the global public–private partnership Small Enterprise Assistance Funds provides funds to finance enterprise development, supporting the growth of small businesses. Similarly, ACCION International supports the development of small businesses by poor women and men who have not previously had business experience.[16] These and many other global partnerships with similar goals and methods could be evaluated using cost-benefit methodology similar to that used to evaluate the projects in the SBIR Program (Link and Scott 2000; Scott 2000a). In the SBIR Program, government has redirected R&D resources toward small businesses, supporting R&D in technologies and in parts of the country that the private sector was unlikely to support and providing funds for inexperienced businesses and for minority-owned businesses when the private sector would not provide the funds (Scott 2000b).

For another example, the Internet Corporation for Assigned Names and Numbers (ICANN) is a global public–private partnership focused on Internet Protocol issues and services [Excerpted from http://www.icann.org/general/ as reported in the website http://www.thenewpublicfinance.org/ for Kaul and Conceição (2006) where the Office of Development Studies, United Nations Development Programme, has posted a database of global public–private partnerships.]:

---

[16] These partnerships are profiled in the website http://www.thenewpublicfinance.org/ for Kaul and Conceição (2006) where the Office of Development Studies, United Nations Development Programme, has posted a database of global public-private partnerships.

As a private–public partnership, ICANN is dedicated to preserving the operational stability of the Internet; to promoting competition; to achieving broad representation of global Internet communities; and to developing policy appropriate to its mission through bottom-up consensus-based processes.

The ICANN global public–private partnership and other global partnerships focused on world-wide use of information technology are similar to partnerships in a national context that promote the development and use of infrastructure technology to increase the productivity of information technology. An analysis of the US experience with infrastructure for information technology and its affects on productivity is provided in Scott (1999). Cost-benefit analysis applied to public–private partnerships to develop information technology is provided in Link and Scott (1998a, 2001).

In such cases, where the projects to be evaluated have commercialization as a key objective, the conventional market-centered valuations using the current distribution of income and wealth will provide especially important information for the evaluation. Nonetheless, other social valuations will be of interest as well to provide complete understanding of the social benefits. Market-centered evaluations explain the private sector's behavior, provide an indication of the political support for a project, and reflect the social valuations that emerge from the political process that shapes the distribution of income and wealth. Yet, as I have emphasized, there is no international government with an international political process in the same sense that there are national governments and national political processes. Consequently, full understanding of the social benefits and costs requires the use of other social valuations for costs and benefits in addition to the market-centered ones. That will be true even in a national context, but it is especially important in the international context.

With projects –such as the Medicines for Malaria Venture discussed in Sect. 1 or the Clinton Foundation's AIDS Initiative discussed in Kaul (2006, p. 255)—providing research or goods and services when there would be no market because the direct beneficiaries do not have the ability to pay, then the market-centered valuations (even including the market-centered values—not appropriated by the firms that invest in the project—in consumer surplus or the producer surplus of firms benefiting from spillovers of value) cannot possibly be the whole story about social valuations of the work of the global public private partnership. The market-centered valuations are important to understand the behavior of the private sector and to understand how the global public–private partnership can create incentives to redirect the private behavior in socially desirable ways. The traditional market-centered valuations are useful for developing the value of the partnership's work that may accrue to those—including both businesses and donors and the public more generally—other than the direct beneficiaries. To fully understand the social benefits, however, one needs to look beyond the streams of consumer and producer surplus that would result from the project given the current distribution of income and wealth.

The market-centered valuations can show how those with the ability to pay value the work—and that value could of course be substantial whether because the donors value helping others or realize and appreciate that they are investing in their own welfare when they reduce poverty and improve world-wide health. Thus, these market-centered benefits would reflect market-centered costs avoided if a global project reduced the problem of extreme poverty in one nation that would have become the problem of all nations when the deprivation generated instability that became international in scope, or market-centered costs avoided if the global partnership stopped a disease that would have spread and created an international crises. Nonetheless, for complete analysis of the social benefits,

 Springer

analysts need to develop a measure of the value that reflects the benefits to those who have no ability to pay for the results of the partnership's work yet are the direct beneficiaries of that work. Designing convincing ways to develop understanding of those social benefits is an important and difficult task for future research that will develop cost-benefit analysis for the evaluation of global public–private partnerships.

5 Pragmatic evaluation of the desirability of global public–private partnerships: lessons learned about costs and benefits and the evaluation of public–private partnerships

This section identifies lessons learned about the estimation of costs and benefits. In many cases, the lessons are based on experience evaluating public–private partnerships in a national context.

Lesson 1. Different distributions for income and wealth imply different benefits and costs; hence, valuations for counterfactual income distributions can usefully inform cost-benefit analyses of global partnerships providing benefits for those without the ability to pay. The locations of projects A, B, and C in Fig. 1—that is, their combinations of private and social rates of return—will in general vary with different distributions of income and wealth. For many of the goods and services provided by global public–private partnerships, market valuations corresponding to the direct use of the goods will provide an incomplete picture of social valuation because they are provided by the government to those in need who have no ability to pay. With the current distribution of income and wealth, the preferences of these people in the lower end of the distribution do not receive much weight in the market forces determining market prices. Although as I have explained in Sect. 4 the conventional market-centered social valuations are important and useful, for a complete analysis of benefits it will be necessary to invoke "explicit social choice judgments that take us beyond market-centered valuation" as Sen (2000, p. 952) has stated.

One possibility for developing additional perspectives about costs and benefits—perspectives in addition to the one provided by analysis of market-centered costs and benefits—for such projects is suggested by the discussion in Sect. 4 comparing, for unequal versus equal distributions of income, the relative preferences for innovation in the entertainment industry versus innovation in low-income housing. Namely, imagining what Fig. 1 would look like if there were equality in the distributions of income and wealth across countries and across their populations is a counterfactual exercise that could be used to generate non-market-centered valuations of the costs and benefits of a global public–private partnership being evaluated by an intergovernmental agency. Interestingly, the non-market-centered valuations thereby generated are in a sense "market-centered," because they would reflect what the market-centered valuations would have been if the distribution of income and wealth were equal rather than extremely unequal.

One way to develop non-market-centered valuations, then, is to pose the questions about value conditional on the counterfactual circumstances of equality in the distribution of income and wealth.[17] Counterfactual analysis based on market-centered valuations has

---

[17] Note the distinction between the question that we are asking and the fundamental question posed by Rawls (1971) about what individuals would choose as a just society. The typical discussion of fairness in the distribution of income asks for assessment of whether less inequality in the distribution is desirable. Rawls considers what individuals in a hypothetical "original position"—that is, without knowledge of their subsequent positions in society—would unanimously choose for a society's approach to justice. In the original position they might be more disposed toward the virtues of equality in the distribution of income than

 Springer

been used by Link and Scott (1998b) to evaluate R&D and technology projects with the goal of commercialization. The methodology, as explained in Link and Scott (1998b) and then illustrated with several case studies, asks knowledgeable people about market valuations in the counterfactual circumstances where the private sector rather than the public sector performs the research and technology development. In the case of global public–private partnerships, cost-benefit analysis would require that knowledgeable people be identified who could provide estimates of market valuations in the counterfactual circumstance of equality—or some stated reduction in the inequality—in the distribution of income and wealth. One approach would be the development of sophisticated surveys asking samples of potential consumers across many nations (and with control for selection into the samples) about their preferences in a variety of counterfactual circumstances. Another approach would use samples of people within and across countries to develop applicable models of income-constrained consumption behavior. The models could become the material for predicting behavior and thereby reveal preferences in somewhat different circumstances regarding the distribution of income and wealth.

Lesson 2. Benefits and costs are not uniformly distributed across nations and individuals; hence, cost-benefit evaluations of global partnerships should address distributional impacts. The costs and benefits, and therefore the associated rates of return in Fig. 1, reflecting the current distribution of income and wealth and typically used in cost-benefit analysis do not in themselves address the varying impacts—across different nations or individuals—for the project being evaluated. That is, the costs and the benefits are total costs and benefits; the distribution of those costs and benefits is often not addressed in conventional cost-benefit studies. The assumption is that if the total benefits exceed the total costs, then there are gains from the project, and those gains can be redistributed to ensure that the project achieves improvements in well-being. Of course, such redistribution is not typically actually carried out; therefore, the possibility of redistribution should not be used to ignore the potential problems that variation—across nations and individuals—in the impacts of the project might cause.

As Conceição and Mendoza (2006) explain, distributional impacts cannot be ignored in the evaluation of global partnerships. They emphasize that the success of global public–private partnerships requires careful attention to the variance in the impacts of the projects' benefits and costs across nations. They offer pragmatic methodology for identifying those distributional effects of a global public–private partnership and for using the information in the evaluation of the partnership's projects.

Lesson 3. Market-centered costs and benefits and the associated private and social rates of return are not independent of public policies; hence, public policy can redirect private economic resources toward socially desirable activity. Effective cost-benefit analysis and effective policy require an understanding of the links from public policy to market-centered costs and benefits. Therefore, an important part of the cost-benefit evaluation of a global public–private partnership will be cost-benefit analysis using market-centered valuations.

Footnote 17 continued
society in general seems to be. In any case, here we are not asking what people think about more or less equality in the distribution of income. Rather, we are asking them to think about how the valuations of various goods and services would change if the distribution of income were equal rather than its actual distribution. The market values of goods and services have been determined by that actual distribution, and we would like to know what the market values would be given the hypothetical situation of equality in the distribution of income.

Whether in a national context or in the international context where intergovernmental organizations coordinate public–private partnerships, public policies can redirect private economic activity and resources toward socially desirable economic activity. Based on studies of public–private partnerships in a national context, the evidence supports the belief that socially desirable redirection of resources can be achieved by global public–private partnerships combining the relative strengths of intergovernmental organizations, national governments, businesses, and civil society. For example, Scott (2005b) estimates that large and significant redirection of resources toward environmental R&D—investments in research and development with the goal of introducing innovations to reduce harmful industrial emissions—can be achieved with more stringent regulations of industrial emissions, with diplomacy to make such emissions regulation more uniformly stringent world-wide, with facilitation of financing of industrial R&D, with support for cooperative R&D, and with facilitation of the dissemination of knowledge.

When market-centered valuations are used for cost-benefit analysis, the costs and benefits—and hence the private and social rates of return in Fig. 1—are not independent of the public policies. The actions of governments and of intergovernmental agencies affect the costs and benefits and the associated private and social rates of return. The traditional cost-benefit analysis of Griliches (1958) and Mansfield et al. (1977), with consideration of private and social rates of return, uses the market-centered values for the streams of producer and consumer surplus resulting from a project. Those surplus streams are "market-centered" because they reflect the values (of the products and services and the resources used to make them) in a market system given the distribution of income and wealth and therefore given the distribution of the ability to express preferences in markets and as well, because of the distribution and individuals' places within it, given the preferences themselves.

Moreover, the traditional method uses market values given not only the distribution of income and wealth, but given the rules of the market game, including standards and regulations regarding the environment and health, income redistribution and income support programs such as government supported retirement and health plans, and so forth. All of these things under government control condition and help determine the market values. Consumer surplus or producer surplus appropriated by producers other than those doing the investments are not in the market values received by the investing firms. Nonetheless they are "market-centered" values, based ultimately on the ability to pay for goods and services that itself comes from the command of scarce resources valued in the market system of a mixed economy. The political process of choosing the income redistribution, the environmental regulations, and so forth, then influences the market outcomes—the market values for the resources and the goods and services made with the resources.

For the evaluation of the projects of a global public–private partnership, the implication is that market-centered cost-benefit evaluation is important not only because the commercial success of a project must be understood, but because market values and commercial success will be affected by the policies of the partnership. To use one of the examples discussed earlier, if an intergovernmental organization associates its reputation and authority with a partnership's efforts through its business partners to engage in socially responsible corporate behavior, then that behavior can become commercially valuable even though without the intergovernmental organization's "stamp of approval," the behavior would not have market value.

The most obvious and direct effects of policies are on private benefits and costs, but also because of spillovers, policies will also affect social benefits and costs beyond those

 Springer

captured in private benefits and costs of the companies doing the investments or providing the goods and services associated with a public–private partnership. Link and Scott (2000, 2001) and Scott (2000a) provide actual examples of estimates of spillovers captured as producer surplus, and Link and Scott (2005a) provide an example of an estimate of consumer surplus resulting from a project. As discussed earlier, in general not just investment programs, but also programs that redistribute income will affect market values and change both producer and consumer surplus associated with markets.

The interdependence of policies and the market-centered private and social valuations of market outcomes implies that market-centered values are useful for evaluation of global public–private partnerships. For policies to provide incentives for the private performance that is often desired, there is a need to understand private costs and benefits and hence the commercialization potential. Whether purchase commitments, loan guarantees, or simply lending of the good name of an intergovernmental agency to a project, the actions of the public–private partnerships influence market values and private behavior. The partnerships bring the private and public sectors together and with the appropriate incentives make the projects commercializable when they would not be performed by the private sector in the absence of the partnerships.

Lesson 4. Even for projects where markets or national governments would provide the socially desired investments or goods and services, a global public–private partnership to carry out an initiative of an intergovernmental organization in cooperation with businesses, civil society and national governments may be the most efficient way to achieve the partnership's goals. In such cases, the cost-benefit analysis would focus on the gains from the global partnership as contrasted with relying on markets and individual national governments without global cooperation. Kaul (2006) and Conceição et al. (2006) emphasize global partnerships bringing together the resources and combining the strengths of the public and private sectors to have a more efficient way of delivering the desired output for the projects. In these cases where global public–private partnerships are hypothesized to increase the efficiency with which the economic activities are done, the counterfactual method described and applied in Link and Scott (1998b) would be useful. In the national context, the method allows estimation of the benefits of using the partnership as compared with relying on markets alone. In the international context of global partnerships, the method would allow estimating the benefits of using the global partnership as compared to relying on markets and national governments alone.

Lesson 5. The literature about cost-benefit analysis provides many different approaches for collecting both market-centered and non-market measures of value.

Conceição and Mendoza (2006) provide a broad overview of sensible steps for cost-benefit analysis of global public–private partnerships, setting out pragmatic guidelines for identifying high-return investments for the partnerships and identifying the distribution of the costs and benefits across countries. The Conceição and Mendoza methodological guidelines for cost-benefit analysis of global partnerships pay attention to countries having different consumption preferences and realizing different benefits and costs from the projects of global partnerships. The literature applying cost-benefit analysis to public–private partnerships in a national context offers many useful ways to gather information about the benefits and the costs to use within the broad methodological steps outlined by Conceição and Mendoza (2006).

As I have explained, estimates of market-centered costs and benefits are useful for the evaluation of global partnerships. A variety of approaches have been used to obtain such estimates. Experts in industry can be asked directly about the benefits from a partnership's investments. For an example that uses expert opinion in the context of the traditional, market-centered model of Griliches (1958) and Mansfield et al. (1977) to analyze the costs and benefits and social rate of return for a project at the US National Institute of Standards and Technology, see Link and Scott (2005a). For several examples of project evaluations that use expert opinion about counterfactual, market-centered benefits—the counterfactual costs avoided because of the project as compared to the results if there were only the market solution without the public–private partnership—see Link and Scott (1998b).

In circumstances where direct estimates of benefits by experts are difficult, the literature has examples of successful application of a different approach. In particular, when it would be difficult to obtain direct estimates of the flows of benefits and costs, it is sometimes possible to ask the experts a set of questions about a small set of key parameters about which they are well informed. Then, those parameters are used by the analysts in the context of an investment model to estimate the flows of benefits and the private and social rates of return from the project. The approach is especially useful for prospective analyses, where the future flows of benefits are predicted, as contrasted with retrospective analyses where experts make estimates of realized flows. Examples of this approach of obtaining the estimates of benefits and rates of return indirectly, through the acquisition from experts of a few key parameters of the investment model, are provided in Link and Scott (1998a, 2000, 2001) and Scott (2000a).

For examples of non-market-centered valuations, Conceição and Mendoza (2006) not only offer many examples for global partnerships—such as direct evidence about the output provided by the global partnerships, whether lives saved or percentage reduction in a disease or the percentage of a pollution problem that is cleaned up—but also place such non-market measures in the context of pragmatic steps for analyzing the costs and benefits of partnerships' projects and compare their pragmatic approach to the more traditional market-centered approach. For examples of non-market valuations in the context of evaluating public–private partnerships in a national context, Link and Scott (2005b) survey knowledgeable individuals about research project outcomes such as the numbers of publications, presentations, or patents resulting. Link and Scott (2005b) use both models of response to the survey and models of the substantive measures of project performance. In that way, they provide estimation of performance with control for selection into the sample.

Lesson 6. The public, whether through national governments or through intergovernmental organizations, does not need to pay all of the costs for global public–private partnerships; instead, the necessary and sufficient subsidy will be the amount that raises the private rate of return to the private hurdle rate. Typically the public pays more than it has to pay to ensure private performance of a project sponsored by a public–private partnership. The public needs only to fund enough of the project to change a type-A project in Fig. 1 to a project with its private rate of return as high as the private hurdle rate. Scott (1998, p. 76) describes a bidding process that could provide one way to use the needed amount of public funding, yet not have the public paying more than necessary to get the private sector to perform the project. The goal is to have a:

> … mechanism for public/private partnerships that will achieve the desired incentives for the private sector to choose the best private partner, for the private partner to carry out the desired amount of investment at the least cost to the public, and for avoiding opportunistic behaviour by either the public or the private partner.

There are many details of the proposed bidding mechanism, but the following simple example explains the essential idea (Scott 1998, pp. 76–77):

 Springer

Suppose that from society's perspective, an R&D investment project would cost 100 now and generate the expectation of 130 in one year and nothing thereafter. Suppose further that the threshold rate of return justifying public funding—society's hurdle rate—is 10 per cent. Thus, the R&D project yields a social rate of return of 30 per cent, which exceeds the hurdle rate of 10 per cent, and of course the net present value of $[130/(1.1)] - 100$ is greater than zero. Suppose that from a private perspective the project costs 100 and because of incomplete appropriation of returns yields the expectation of just 105 in a year. Suppose further that, given the private risk, the private hurdle rate is 15 per cent. Thus, the private sector would not undertake the project which has an internal rate of return of 5 per cent which is less than the hurdle rate of 15 per cent; and, of course, net present value is then negative.

In the context of the foregoing example, the bidding process would work as follows. The government announces that it will "buy" the R&D project, [committing to stand behind the project and see it through, ensuring] paying the 100 investment cost. The government then opens the bidding for the right to be the private partner in the public/private partnership. Private firms will bid the amount X such that $X(1.15) = 105$, implying that $X = 91.30$. The cost to the public of the project would then be 8.70. With great uncertainty about the future returns, the use of royalty bidding rather than the up-front bidding can yield more to the government. Also, private firms with better capabilities for doing the project would be expected to bid higher than those firms that are less well suited to the project.

Placing the foregoing example in the context of Fig. 1, just the right amount of public funding has been provided to change a type-A project—with social rate of return of 30% exceeding the social hurdle rate of 10%, yet a private rate of return of 5% falling short of the private hurdle rate of 15%—into a project that is acceptable to the private sector, because after the partial public funding, the private hurdle rate is met. The point depicting the private and social rates of return for the project has been shifted from point A to the point at the intersection of the horizontal line through point A and the vertical line depicting the private hurdle rate.[18]

6 Conclusions

There are within the foregoing discussion many conclusions; some of them are restated and emphasized in this concluding section, including the following.

- Public policies—policies of a national government and also the policies of international intergovernmental organizations working through global public–private partnerships—and market-centered social valuations—the present values of the streams of consumer surplus and producer surplus generated by the market system—are not independent; thus, public policies can redirect economic resources to promote socially desirable economic activity.

---

[18] A detailed description of the way that appropriability difficulties and risk interact to make a project like project A unacceptable to the private sector, and then a description of how the partial public funding overcomes the problems, is provided in Scott (1998, p. 71). Additional detailed description including a diagrammatic presentation of risk and return is provided in Link and Scott (2001) in the context of actual projects for public-private partnerships.

 Springer

Stated differently, the combination of private and public rates of return from an investment project are not independent of the governmental or inter-governmental policies. In terms of Fig. 1, the point A, B, or C will be at different places for different public policies. Policies directly focused on a project of course affect the rate of return for the members of a partnership. For example, as illustrated with actual investments in Link and Scott (2001), greater amounts of public funding will increase the private rates of return from the investment projects of public–private partnerships. Moreover, public policies will in general affect the rates of return. For example, when a government identifies socially responsible corporate behavior, the public support for such behavior can itself make the behavior commercially profitable. Clear standards for the environmental performance of industry has redirected industrial R&D toward innovations that reduce emissions that damage the environment, as illustrated in Scott (2003, 2005a, b). For another example, the public investments in laboratories to develop infrastructure technology increase the productivity of private investments, as illustrated in Link and Scott (1998b, 2005a) for just a few of the documented examples. Even when the governmental or intergovernmental policies are focused on issues of equity, rather than directly on improvements in efficiency, there can be an indirect effect on the public and private rates of return (the positions in the plane of points A, B, and C in Fig. 1) for investment projects. For example, using the discussion in Sect. 4, with a more equal distribution of income and wealth a project for low-income housing and universal-access medical care might have a greater market-centered social rate of return than a project in the entertainment industry, even though with the present state of great inequality in the distribution of income and wealth, the investment project in the entertainment industry had the higher market-centered social rate of return.

From the foregoing interdependence of market-centered social values and the policies of governments and intergovernmental organizations, and in the context of our discussion of cost-benefit analysis in this paper, other conclusions follow. These include:

- Cost-benefit analyses are useful to inform the choice of appropriate policies. The evaluations provided by the analyses are useful not only for the choice of the socially appropriate projects, but as well for the choice of the appropriate extent of public financing. The analyses identify cases of market failure, point to the cases that global public–private partnerships can usefully address, and provide tools for both prospective and retrospective evaluation of projects. The theory underlying cost-benefit analysis explains the reasons for and the need for the new perspectives about the organization and financing of global public–private partnerships that have been emphasized and documented in Kaul and Conceição (2006).
- Market-centered valuations are useful for the measures of costs and benefits for several reasons. For one, the market-centered valuations are appropriate because commercialization of a project's outputs is often an important goal. Understanding the market-centered valuations will be important as well when commercialization is necessary because the private sector is expected to perform the project's investments or produce and deliver the goods and services the project will provide. Also, the market-centered valuations are needed to understand more generally the impact of a project on the behavior of businesses and consumers. Further, even when the project's goals are investments or the delivery of goods and services where the direct benefits are for those who cannot pay for them, there are indirect effects—apart from the direct value received by the recipients of the project's output. For example, providing food for the hungry may avoid costs of international political instability or international health

 Springer

crises—costs for which market-centered valuations are appropriate. Market-centered valuations are also useful for understanding the political support for a project.
- Non-market valuations are important as well because often the goal of a global public–private partnership will be investments or delivery of goods and services for those without the means to pay. Examples of non-market valuations range from enumeration of a project's outputs—such as the numbers of hungry people fed, the reduction in cases of a disease, the reduction in pollution—to "market-centered" valuations in the counterfactual case of equality in the distribution of income across and within nations.
- Consideration of what "market-centered" valuations would be for counterfactual circumstances with alternative distributions of income and wealth will be useful. With such consideration, society's discussion of the costs and benefits of policy will at least be informed by an understanding of how those values would differ if the ability to pay for goods and services were more equally distributed, and that knowledge will help those with economic and political power see value from the perspective of those without such power.
- With market-centered private values, cost-benefit analysis—as I have discussed it in terms of the theory of market failure and its correction by appropriate policies— provides the rationale for "selling" the reputation and legitimacy of the intergovernmental organization as a part of its contribution to a global public–private partnership. The mere presence of a respected international intergovernmental organization in a global partnership with private businesses can increase the market value of socially responsible corporate behavior and make such behavior profitable. The presence of the intergovernmental organization signals that the behavior is laudable from society's perspective, and what would be a type A or B project can become a type C project if consumers purchase the project's output to reward the socially responsible corporate behavior. The presence of the intergovernmental organization as a member of the global public–private partnership then literally increases the contributions of the private sector to the partnership, and "selling" the intergovernmental organization's reputation has a very literal interpretation and as well the implication that the public pays less to accomplish the socially desirable objectives of the partnership.
- The usual distinction between a policy to promote efficiency and a policy to promote equity or merit goods is not a sharp, clear one. Policies that change the distribution of income and wealth will in general change the pattern of demands for goods and services; prices, costs, and outputs of goods and services will be affected. Therefore, the policies will in general change both the actual mix of goods and services and the socially efficient mix. Cost-benefit analyses can usefully help understand and anticipate those changes, especially for global public–private partnerships addressing issues affecting world-wide stability. However, developing pragmatic ways to identify and measure the interdependencies between policies to promote efficiency and policies to promote equity or merit goods is an additional topic for future research that can usefully be added to the topics listed in the Appendix.
- Cost-benefit analyses are useful for all types of policies—for efficiency, for equity, for merit goods—used by governments or intergovernmental organizations. The usual market-centered analysis would show the net market-centered benefits—including the benefits not captured by the private investors but nonetheless valued using market-centered measures—of an investment project. Or, a policy to redistribute income could be analyzed in terms market-centered values for a reduction in the costs of treating the health problems of people who would live in poverty in the absence of the policy. Yet non-traditional metrics for the benefits and costs of projects will also be useful. For

 Springer

example, returning to Sect. 4's contrasting of the investment in low-income housing and medical care versus investment in entertainment, a useful social valuation for effects of an investment project would be the counterfactual "market-centered" valuations that would emerge if the distribution of income and wealth were equal. The value of avoiding the costs of treating the health problems of the poor—and hence the benefits of the policy to redistribute income and wealth above—is expected to look quite different if evaluated by a population with equality in the distribution of income. Such counterfactual analysis is needed, as a complement to the traditional market-centered analysis, for a more complete understanding of the value of a project focused on benefits for people who do not have the ability to pay for them.

The foregoing conclusions are relevant for evaluating public–private partnerships both within a national context where the nation's government is the public partner and for the global context where international intergovernmental organizations are among the members of the partnership. The conclusions are especially relevant in the global context, however, because the several nations affected by the work of a global public–private partnership will have different perspectives on social valuations, whether or not they are market-centered valuations.

Acknowledgments This paper is a revision of a report, Scott (2006), prepared for the United Nations Development Programme's Office of Development Studies. For helpful comments, I thank Pedro Conceição, Inge Kaul, and Albert N. Link.

Appendix: Topics for additional research

In this appendix, several topics for future research are discussed.

Topic 1. Practical methods for identifying the opportunity costs of public funds. We can get the private sector's opportunity cost of funds—the private hurdle rates—for various types of projects. The concept of the required rates of return for the private sector's investments in various types of projects is well-developed in the literature of corporate finance. Experts in industry are able to discuss and provide appropriate private hurdle rates as they did for evaluations in Link and Scott (2000, 2001) and Scott (2000a), and the corporate finance literature provides several approaches for estimating private hurdle rates. However, appropriate opportunity costs for public funds—the appropriate social hurdle rates for particular types of projects—are not so readily found. For the evaluations in Link and Scott (1998a, b, 2000, 2001, 2005a, b, 2006, forthcoming), the social hurdle rate used was mandated by the national government. The government came up with the official number, but there are many questions about how the decision is made and how well it reflects the opportunity cost of the public funds. In Sect. 3 above, I discussed the theory of why the social and private hurdle rates are expected to differ. Additional research should be done to inform the public's choice about the opportunity cost for public funds; those costs should differ for projects with different risk characteristics, and research to systematize the choice for appropriate social hurdle rates is needed. As observed in Scott (2000b), social opportunity costs are not readily known; even projects with high social rates of return when evaluated with conventional cost-benefit analysis might find better uses for their resources (Scott 2000b, p. 12, italics in original):

> ... [T]here are two sensible reasons that governments might direct the use of economic resources away from uses with high social rates of return. First, there may be ... projects with even higher rates of return conventionally defined—that is, defined

using actual ... expenditures and the present value of total economic surplus given the current distribution of income and wealth. Especially in the redirection of R&D resources that can shape the path of technological change for better or for worse, government needs to address such alternatives explicitly rather than setting a rather arbitrary hurdle rate. Second, governments can rationally choose to deploy ... resources using an evaluation metric other than the total economic surplus of the current economic majority.

Future research could usefully address how to identify alternative uses of resources rather than just using a rather arbitrary social hurdle rate that is same for all projects.

Topic 2. Practical methods for determining public contributions versus private contributions to funding. The "hurdle lowering auction" described in Scott (1998) is in principle a way to ensure that the public pays no more than necessary to achieve the socially desirable results of a public–private partnership. The mechanism lowers the hurdle faced by the private sector—the private rate of return is raised to the private hurdle rate but no more, and then the investment can be made by the private sector. The bidding mechanism suggested is, however, quite complex and awaits development in actual applications if it is to be a useful approach to leveraging the public financing of public–private partnerships. Despite the innovations—documented and reviewed in Conceição (2006) and in Conceição et al. (2006)—in the financing of global partnerships, there is room for applying Lesson 6 above to the refinement of the financing mechanisms to ensure that the public does not pay more than necessary to achieve the goals of the partnerships.

Topic 3. Practical methods for measuring the social value of benefits for those without the ability to pay. As observed earlier, a complete analysis of the social benefits of the work of a global public–private partnership would require a measure of the value that reflects the benefits to those who have no ability to pay for the results of the partnership's work yet are the direct beneficiaries of that work. Future research to develop understanding of those social benefits is needed. The approaches set out in Lesson 5 above for forming non-market measures of social value provide a useful starting point. Clearly, however, those practical non-market measures at best only indirectly capture value for the direct beneficiaries. Sophisticated surveys with responses about preferences conditioned on counterfactual situations regarding the ability to pay and with control for sample selection are one possibility. For another, researchers could use samples of people within and across countries to develop models of income-constrained consumption behavior. Possibly, the models could be used to predict consumption behavior and thereby reveal preferences and value in different circumstances regarding the distribution of income and wealth.

Topic 4. Hypothesis tests using the UNDP/ODS global public–private partnership data set. The website http://www.thenewpublicfinance.org/ for Kaul and Conceição (2006) has posted a dataset of global public–private partnerships. The sets of partnerships and data about them posted at the website have been assembled by the Office of Development Studies (ODS) of the United Nations Development Programme (UNDP). These posted inventories of global public–private partnerships include the links to the websites for the partnerships and systematic descriptions of the partnerships that ODS has developed by studying the information available about each partnership. Future research can use the UNDP/ODS data about global public–private partnerships, developing the data and putting it in a form suitable for using econometrics to test hypotheses about the behavior and performance of the partnerships, and then carrying out the hypothesis tests.

The econometric hypothesis tests will develop understanding about the circumstances in which the private sector will, absent special policies, provide finance to support

 Springer

government or intergovernmental-organization funded investments to be performed in the private sector—analogous to the evidence developed in Scott (2000b) about third-party private finance of Small Business Innovation Research projects. Further, the hypothesis tests will develop understanding about the ways that government or intergovernmental-organization support of a variety of policies can make socially desirable projects commercially attractive for private business—analogous to the evidence developed in Scott (2005a, b) about corporations' socially responsible investments in environmental R&D in response to various public policies. The UNDP/ODS data sets as well as the websites for the partnerships provide the names of the members of the partnerships. Analogous to the evidence developed in Link and Scott (2005c) about the presence of universities as partners in research joint ventures, econometric study of the circumstances in which particular types of partners—such as universities—are among the organizations participating in a global partnership can provide insights about economics of the partnership—the appropriability conditions faced by the business partners and the importance of scale and scope for the realization of efficiencies and synergies.

The knowledge generated by the hypothesis tests will inform policies to encourage corporate social responsibility and help intergovernmental organizations design effective projects to combat crucial world-wide problems including poverty and hunger and disease, pollution and climate instability, and terrorism. These and other world-wide problems are the focus of a burgeoning array of global public–private partnerships, and econometric hypothesis testing grounded in the theoretical framework exposited in the present paper will help in the development of practical ways to improve the performance of the partnerships.

References

Arrow, K. J. (1963). *Social choice and individual values* (2nd ed.). New Haven and London: Yale University Press.

Audretsch, D. B., Link, A. N., & Scott, J. T. (2002). Public/private technology partnerships: Evaluating SBIR-supported research. *Research Policy, 31*(1), 145–158.

Conceição, P. (2006). Accommodating new actors and new purposes in international cooperation: The growing diversification of financing mechanisms. In I. Kaul & P. Conceição (Eds.), *The new public finance: Responding to global challenges* (pp. 269–280). New York; Oxford: Oxford University Press.

Conceição, P., & Mendoza, R. U. (2006). Identifying high-return investments: A methodology for assessing when international cooperation pays–and for whom. In I. Kaul & P. Conceição (Eds.), *The new public finance: Responding to global challenges* (pp. 327–356). New York; Oxford: Oxford University Press.

Conceição, P., Rajan, H., & Shah, R. (2006). Making the right money available at the right time for international cooperation: New financing technologies. In I. Kaul & P. Conceição (Eds.), *The new public finance: Responding to global challenges* (pp. 281–303). New York; Oxford: Oxford University Press.

Griliches, Z. (1958). Research costs and social returns: Hybrid corn and related innovations. *The Journal of Political Economy, 66*(5), 419–431. doi:10.1086/258077.

Jaffe, A. B. (1998). The importance of 'Spillovers' in the policy mission of the advanced technology program. *The Journal of Technology Transfer, 23*(2), 11–19. doi:10.1007/BF02509888.

Kaul, I. (2006). Exploring the policy space between markets and states: Global public–private partnerships. In I. Kaul & P. Conceição (Eds.), *The new public finance: Responding to global challenges* (pp. 219–268). New York; Oxford: Oxford University Press.

Kaul, I., & Conceição, P. (Eds.). (2006). *The new public finance: Responding to global challenges.* New York; Oxford: Oxford University Press.

Link, A. N. (1999). Public/private partnerships in the United States. *Industry and Innovation, 6*(2), 191–217. doi:10.1080/13662719900000011.

 Springer

Link, A. N., & Scott, J. T. (forthcoming). *Public goods, public gains: Calculating the social benefits of public R&D*. Oxford: Oxford University Press.

Link, A. N., & Scott, J. T. (1998a). *Overcoming market failure: A case study of the ATP focused program on technologies for the integration of manufacturing applications (TIMA)*, a report to the advanced technology program, National Institute of Standards and Technology, October.

Link, A. N., & Scott, J. T. (1998b). *Public accountability: Evaluating technology-based public institutions*. Boston, Massachusetts: Kluwer Academic Publishers.

Link, A. N., & Scott, J. T. (2000). Estimates of the social returns to small business innovation research projects. In C. W. Wessner (Ed.), *The small business innovation research program: An assessment of the department of defense fast track initiative* (pp. 275–290). Washington, DC: National Academy Press.

Link, A. N., & Scott, J. T. (2001). Public/private partnerships: Stimulating competition in a dynamic market. *International Journal of Industrial Organization, 19*(5), 763–794.

Link, A. N., & Scott, J. T. (2005a). Evaluating public sector R&D programs: The advanced technology program's investment in wavelength references for optical fiber communications. *The Journal of Technology Transfer, 30*(1–2), 241–251.

Link, A. N., & Scott, J. T. (2005b). *Evaluating public research institutions: The US advanced technology program's intramural research initiative*. London; New York: Routledge.

Link, A. N., & Scott, J. T. (2005c). Universities as partners in US. Research joint ventures. *Research Policy, 34*(3), 385–393.

Link, A. N., & Scott, J. T. (2006). An economic evaluation of the Baldrige national quality program. *Economics of Innovation and New Technology, 15*(1), 83–100.

Mansfield, E., Rapoport, J., Romeo, A., Wagner, S., & Beardsley, G. (1977). Social and private rates of return from industrial innovations. *The Quarterly Journal of Economics, 91*(2), 221–240. doi:10.2307/1885415.

Martin, S., & Scott, J. T. (2000). The nature of innovation market failure and the design of public support for private innovation. *Research Policy, 29*(4–5), 437–447.

McWilliams, A., & Siegel, D. (2001). Corporate social responsibility: A theory of the firm perspective. *Academy of Management Review, 26*(1), 117–127.

Rawls, J. (1971). *A theory of justice*. Cambridge: Harvard University Press.

Scott, J. T. (1995). The damoclean tax and innovation. *Journal of Evolutionary Economics, 5*(1), 71–89. doi:10.1007/BF01199671.

Scott, J. T. (1998). Financing and leveraging public/private partnerships: The hurdle-lowering auction. *STI (Science, Technology, Industry) Review*, Number 23, Paris, OECD, 67–84.

Scott, J. T. (1999). The service sector's acquisition and development of information technology: Infrastructure and productivity. *The Journal of Technology Transfer, 24*(1), 37–54. doi:10.1023/A:1007764518400.

Scott, J. T. (2000a). An assessment of the small business innovation research program in New England: Fast track compared with non-fast track projects. In C. W. Wessner (Ed.), *The small business innovation research program: An assessment of the department of defense fast track initiative* (pp. 104–140). Washington, DC: National Academy Press.

Scott, J. T. (2000b). The directions for technological change: Alternative economic majorities and opportunity costs. *Review of Industrial Organization, 17*(1), 1–16. doi:10.1023/A:1007875415472.

Scott, J. T. (2003). *Environmental research and development: US industrial research, the clean air act and environmental damage*. Cheltenham, UK; Northampton, Massachusetts: Edward Elgar Publishing.

Scott, J. T. (2005a). Corporate social responsibility and environmental research and development. *Structural Change and Economic Dynamics, 16*(3), 313–331.

Scott, J. T. (2005b). Public policy and environmental research and development. In A. N. Link & F. M. Scherer (Eds.), *Essays in honor of Edwin Mansfield: The economics of R&D, innovation, and technological change* (pp. 109–127). New York: Springer Science.

Scott, J. T. (2006). Cost-benefit analysis for global public–private partnerships: Determining the desirability of intergovernmental organizations entering into public–private partnerships, a report to the United Nations Development Programme's Office of Development Studies, February 10.

Sen, A. (2000). The discipline of cost-benefit analysis. *The Journal of Legal Studies, 29*(2), 931–952. doi:10.1086/468100.

Sneyd, R. (2005). Organic Java? Try McDonalds's. *Valley News, 54*(142), A1–A3.

Stiglitz, J. E., & Walsh, C. E. (2002). *Principles of microeconomics* (3rd ed.). New York: W. W. Norton.

Tassey, G. (1997). *The economics of R&D policy*. Westport, Connecticut: Quorum Books.

Witte, J. M., & Reinicke, W. (2005). *Business UNusual: Facilitating United Nations reform through partnerships*. New York: United Nations Global Compact Office.

 Springer

[10]

Evaluating Public Sector R&D Programs: The Advanced Technology Program's Investment in Wavelength References for Optical Fiber Communications

Albert N. Link[1]
John T. Scott[2]

ABSTRACT. Griliches (1958) [*Journal of Political Economy*, 66: 419–431] and Mansfield *et al.* (1977) [*Quarterly Journal of Economics*, 91: 221–240] pioneered the application of fundamental economic insight to the development of measurements of private and social rates of return to innovative investments. This paper illustrates field-based methods for measuring the social rates of return to innovative investments by the public sector. The case study described herein relates to the development of an improved standard reference material for the measurement of the wavelength of light in an optical fiber network.

Key words: social rate of return, benefit-cost analysis, internal rate of return, net present value, program evaluation, innovation

JEL Classification: O33, H54

1. Introduction

Fundamental to an evaluation of any federal program, research program or otherwise, is that the program is accountable to the public. For research programs, such accountability refers to being able to document and evaluate research performance using metrics that are meaningful to

the institutions' stakeholders—the public, including the taxpayers.[1] Metrics developed for assessing returns to private investment have been adapted to public investments using case-study techniques that emphasize analysis of public benefits to research users and taxpayers.

With any performance evaluation, it is generally assumed that the government has an economically justifiable role in supporting innovation because of market failures stemming from, among other things, the private sector's inability to appropriate returns to investments, the public-good nature of the research focus, or the riskiness of those investments.[2] Ignoring such an assumption may imply that any evaluation of a public research program is wanting in the sense that the program should initially be scrutinized on first principles as to why it is even undertaking research.

Griliches (1958) and Mansfield *et al.* (1977) pioneered the application of fundamental economic insight to the development of measurements of private and social rates of return to innovative investments. Streams of investment costs generate streams of economic benefits over time. Once identified and measured, these streams of costs and benefits are used to calculate such performance metrics as social rates of return and benefit-to-cost ratios.

For example, for a process innovation adopted in a competitive market, using the traditional framework, the publicly-funded innovation being

[1] *Department of Economics*
University of North Carolina at Greensboro
Greensboro, NC 27412
and Max Planck Institute, Jena, Germany
E-mail:al_link@uncg.edu
[2] *Department of Economics*
Dartmouth College
Hanover, NH 03755
E-mail: john.t.scott@dartmouth.edu

Journal of Technology Transfer, 30 1/2, 241–251, 2005
© *2005 Springer Science+Business Media, Inc. Manufactured in The Netherlands.*

evaluated is thought to lower the cost of producing a product to be sold in a competitive market. As the innovation lowers the unit cost of production, consumers will actually pay less for the product than they paid before the innovation and less than they would have been willing to pay—a gain in consumer surplus. The social benefits from the innovation include the total savings that all consumers and producers receive as a result of producers adopting the cost-reducing innovation. Depending on the extent to which reduced costs are reflected in the price charged to consumers, social benefits are shared by producers who adopt the innovation and consumers of their products. Thus, the evaluation question that can be answered from this traditional approach is: Given the investment costs and the social benefits, what is the social rate of return to the innovation?

This paper, written in honor of Ed Mansfield, illustrates—in the context of a public sector investment—the Griliches/Mansfield pioneering field-based methods for measuring the social rates of return to innovative investments. The case study described herein relates to the development of an improved standard reference material (SRM) for the measurement of the wavelength of light in an optical fiber network. That research, which was conducted at the National Institute of Standards and Technology (NIST), was funded by an intramural grant through NIST's Advanced Technology Program (ATP).

The following Section 2 briefly describes ATP's intramural research program. Section 3 overviews the case study, and relevant social rate of return metrics are presented in Section 4. Section 5 concludes the paper with general observations about the evaluation of public sector R&D.

2. ATP's intramural research program

Since its inception in 1990, ATP has stimulated economic growth through the development of innovative technologies that are high in technical risk and enabling in the sense of having the potential to provide significant, broad-based economic benefits.[3] Industry proposes research projects to ATP in competitions in which proposed projects are selected for funding based upon both their technical and economic or business merits.

The ATP intramural research program provides funding to NIST laboratories to conduct research to advance the U.S. technology infrastructure in order to assist industry in continually improving products and services. Under the statute governing ATP, up to 10% of ATP's budget could be allocated for this research. Since 1997, ATP required that these intramural projects:

- emphasize generic basic research,
- relate to groups of ATP extramural projects, and
- focus on measurement and standards that would facilitate the deployment and diffusion of technologies developed in ATP extramurally-funded projects.

3. Case study of wavelength references for optical fiber communications

The goal of this research project was to develop an improved SRM for the measurement of the wavelength of light in an optical fiber network.

The Optoelectronics Division of the Electronics and Electrical Engineering Laboratory began research on optical communications in the mid-1970s and expanded its research program substantially in the late 1980s. The Optical Fiber and Components Group of the Division began research on SRMs in 1991. The Group's first SRM became available in 1993; with SRM 2520, an optical fiber diameter standard. Since then the Group has produced a number of optoelectronic standards. SRM 2517 was issued in 1997; it was intended for use in calibrating the wavelength scale of wavelength measuring equipment in the spectral region from 1510 to 1540 nm.

In 1998, Dr. Sarah Gilbert in the Optical Fiber and Components Group began a two-year ATP intramural project to develop a more accurate version of SRM 2517. Dr. Gilbert received $145,000 over two years—$70,000 in fiscal year 1998 and $75,000 in fiscal year 1999. The project produced the new SRM for calibration of wavelengths in the spectral region from 1510 to 1540 nm. The references in the 1500 nm region are important to support wavelength division multiplexed (WDM) optical fiber communications systems. In a WDM system, many channels, each associated with a different wavelength, of communication information are sent down the same fiber. Thus, WDM in effect increases the bandwidth of the communications system, because any given spectral region will support more channels through which communications information can be sent. A WDM system requires stable wavelengths throughout the components of the system, and equipment must be calibrated to measure those wavelengths. The wavelength references provided by NIST are needed to calibrate the instruments—such as optical spectrum analyzers, tunable lasers, and wavelength meters—that are used to characterize the components of WDM optical fiber communications systems. The wavelength references are also used to monitor the wavelengths of the channels while the system is in use, because if one channel's wavelength were to shift, crosstalk could occur between it and a neighboring channel, thus disrupting the accurate flow of communications information through the channels of the system.

The output of Dr. Gilbert's ATP-funded NIST research with William Swann was Standard Reference Material 2517a, High Resolution Wavelength Calibration Reference for 1510—1540 nm Acetylene ($^{12}C_2H_2$). Quoting NIST's description of the new SRM provides an exact description of the artifact—an "absorption cell" filled with acetylene gas that produces characteristic "absorption lines" in the readouts resulting when lasers project light of various wavelengths through the gas-filled cell. The absorption lines observed can then be used to identify the wavelengths for the laser emitting device being calibrated.[4] NIST's description of the artifact is as follows.[5]

"Standard Reference Material 2517a is intended for wavelength calibration in the spectral region from 1510 nm to 1540 nm. It is a single-mode optical-fiber-coupled absorption cell containing acetylene ($^{12}C_2H_2$) gas at a pressure of 6.7 kPa (50 Torr). The absorption path length is 5 cm and the absorption lines are about 7 pm wide. The cell is packaged in a small instrument box (approximately 24 cm long × 12.5 cm wide × 9 cm high) with two FC/PC fiber connectors for the input and output of a user-supplied light source. Acetylene has more than 50 accurately measured absorption lines in the 1500 nm wavelength region. This SRM can be used for high resolution applications, such as calibrating a narrow-band tunable laser, or lower resolution applications, such as calibrating an optical spectrum analyzer."

The primary difference between the new wavelength calibration standard, SRM 2517a, and its predecessor, SRM 2517, is the use of lower pressure in the acetylene cell to produce narrower lines. Because of that difference, SRM 2517a can be used in higher resolution and higher accuracy applications.

This ATP intramural project complemented the SRM-related research of the Optical Fiber and Components Group and was a natural extension of previous research related to SRM 2517. While research on SRM 2517a would have occurred in the absence of ATP's support, it would not have progressed as rapidly. According to Dr. Gilbert: "The ATP funding accelerated this project and enabled us to complete the development of a new wavelength calibration SRM about 1 year faster that we would have without this funding."

Thus, if ATP had not funded the project, in the course of its ongoing operations, the NIST laboratory would have invested a similar amount, but the streams of costs and benefits would have begun roughly a year later. In this paper, we evaluate the social rate of return from the investment in the project. We do not try to identify the incremental gain from having the project funded by ATP rather than the NIST laboratory that performed the research. NIST has been selling SRM 2517a at a rate of two to three per month since it was introduced in late 2000.[6]

4. Estimating the social rate of return

The traditional evaluation method pioneered by Griliches and Mansfield is used in this case study to estimate the social rate of return to ATP's (i.e. the public sector's) investments in SRM 2517a.[7] To implement that method, two general data series are needed. One data series is related to investment costs, and in the case of this study the relevant investment costs are those associated with the ATP intramural project.[8] The other data series is related to the benefits realized by society, net of society's costs to use the innovation (i.e. pull costs). Society includes both private sector companies and consumers. ATP's investment costs are known.

Benefit data have to be collected, and these data can be of two types. Benefit data can be retrospective in nature, meaning that the company or consumer who has benefited from the ATP project has already realized benefits; or benefit data can be prospective in nature, meaning that the company or consumer who will benefit in the future from the ATP project can estimate when and to what degree benefits will be realized.[9] Both types of benefit data were collected in this study.

Benefit and cost information[10]

Detailed descriptions of the uses of SRM 2517a are provided below, but in overview NIST's experience suggests that most of the test equipment manufacturers in industry use the SRM units to conduct periodic calibration checks on their equipment. The calibration checks with the SRM are not typically in the production line where various intermediate standards are used for routine calibration checks. Rather, the SRM is used to check these intermediate standards. Some of these test equipment manufacturers make absorption cells—commercial versions of the SRM 2517a artifact described above—to incorporate into their products. In those situations where the absorption cells are purchased, discussions with industry experts reveal that SRM 2517a is used both to check the commercial versions of the absorption cells and for study as a manufacturing guide in the production of the commercial high-volume versions of the cell. Discussions with industry show that the component manufacturers often integrate the SRM 2517a into their production lines to continuously calibrate their equipment. Network systems providers use the SRMs to calibrate their test equipment.

The industry costs and benefits for SRM 2517a are based on estimates—obtained through detailed telephone interviews—from industry respondents that collectively have purchased about 30% of the SRM 2517a cells.[11]

Discussions with industry identified several types of benefits and costs associated with SRM 2517a. Benefits fall within five general categories: production related engineering experimentation cost savings, calibration cost savings, yield, negotiation, and marketing. Costs are the ATP development costs plus the pull costs associated with using the SRM purchased from NIST.

Separating the benefits from SRM 2517a from the benefits from other SRMs in the 25xx family was often difficult for industry respondents.[12] Some use the entire set of SRM 25xx artifacts; those respondents sometimes think of the set of artifacts as an integrated whole, covering different parts of the spectrum of wavelengths to which equipment must be calibrated. Thus, to some extent the benefit estimates below reflect a joint benefit from the set of NIST SRM 25xx artifacts. However, there are also major sources of unmeasured industrial benefits from SRM 2517a. As a result, the benefit estimates used are, on balance, conservative for at least three reasons. First, the estimates are truncated after 10 future years, even though some respondents believed that the commercial usefulness of SRM 2517a would extend well beyond that period. Second, and more importantly, many respondents could not quantify the loss in sales, and therefore profits, that would occur without traceability to NIST of their wavelength calibrations. And third, the benefit estimates reflect only the benefits to the purchasers of the NIST SRM 2517a artifacts; they do not capture the additional benefits to users further down the supply chain.[13] Given these sources of downward bias, we believe that, on balance, the benefit estimates used to compute the evaluation metrics to characterize the outcomes of SRM 2517a are conservative.

Use of SRM 2517a results in:

- *Production related engineering and experimentation cost savings:* Users of SRM 2517a regularly conduct what we call production related engineering experimentation.[14] These activities are an important aspect of production. The new more accurate measurement technology associated with SRM 2517a lowered the cost of these activities and hence represents a cost-savings benefit. Also experimentation costs for industry have been lowered because of industry's interaction with the NIST scientists that developed the artifact.[15]

- *Calibration cost savings:* SRM 2517a reduces the costs of calibrating production equipment and products. It is not uncommon to recalibrate production devices for an optical fiber network on a daily basis, or even more frequently. SRM 2517a reduces the cost of each calibration; it permits equipment to be calibrated on the production floor. The alternative would be to purchase tunable lasers, which not only are more costly but also must be set for one frequency at a time, whereas the SRMs provide a fingerprint covering a whole range of the spectrum of wavelengths. In addition, tunable lasers entail additional operating time using well-trained technicians involved in production.[16]

- *Increased production yields:* Production yields have increased because SRM 2517a improved process control and thereby reduced the costs of product failure. Manufacturers of optical fiber network components manufacture to the customer's specifications and needs. SRM 2517a, as well as other SRMs in the 25xx series, provide useful reference points across a stable wavelength range for the tuning of the components for optical communications systems. As a costly and less accurate alternative, the points of reference could be simulated with expensive cascades of optical filters strung together.[17]

- *Negotiations cost savings:* Negotiation with customers over disputes about the performance attributes of products are reduced because of SRM 2517a and the traceability to the NIST standard that it provides. In the absence of wavelength stability, manufacturers and customers would both have grounds to disagree about performance characteristics. Without SRM 2517a and the traceability that it provides, costly negotiations and testing would occur.[18]

- *Reduced marketing costs:* Marketing costs are reduced because of the traceability of an important new standard to NIST that SRM 2517a allows, and sales are greater than for SRM 2517 because of the confidence inspired by the new standard traceable to NIST.[19]

Quantitative estimates of each of the above categories of benefits were obtained from the five manufacturers with whom we spoke. According to Dr. Gilbert, these five companies collectively have purchased about 30% of the SRM 2517a cells sold to date. The benefit data in Table I captures industry-wide benefits. Each datum in Table I is the product of the sum of the dollar values for each respondent multiplied by 3.33 (3.33 = 1/0.30), and all dollar values are converted to year 2000 dollars.

To be conservative, the estimated benefits from SRM 2517a are truncated after ten years. Respondents indicated that the SRM 2517a provided knowledge that would be commercially useful for the foreseeable future. Some respondents emphasized that, as a standard, the knowledge embodied in SRM 2517a would last and be useful virtually forever. However, industry may require even more development of the standards for measuring the wavelength of light as time passes, and the respondents as a group believed that a commercial lifetime of ten years would be a conservative estimate for the period of industrial use of SRM 2517a.

The observed variance through time in the benefits (in year 2000 dollars) reflects three key things. First, there are different periods of primary incidence for the various cost savings. For example, production-related engineering cost savings occur primarily in the early years of the time series and in some cases even before the introduction of SRM 2517a.[20] In contrast, the costs of reduced yields (benefit of increased yields) are avoided throughout the time series after SRM 2517a was introduced and the technology transferred to industry. Second, the introduction of SRM 2517a occurred in late 2000 and partial-year benefits are reported; benefits increase in subsequent years since the SRM is used throughout each year. Third, the variance over time reflects the collapse of optical fiber communications industry sales from record highs in 2000–2001 to low levels in 2002. Projections by industry then reflect an expected recovery of industry sales to the levels experienced in 1999—levels that in 1999 were between one-third and one-half of their subsequent peaks in 2000–2001 before the bubble burst—by 2004–2005. Thereafter, the projections reflect

TABLE I
Industry benefits truncated at 10 years (year 2000 dollars)

Year	Production cost savings ($1000s)	Calibration cost savings ($1000s)	Increased production yield ($1000s)	Decreased negotiation costs ($1000s)	Decreased marketing costs ($1000s)
1999	$3,193.9				
2000	$3,266.5	$401.0	$2,613.3	$245.0	$473.7
2001	$1,388.3	$1,832.6	$10,531.7	$1,094.3	$1,894.7
2002	$1,682.3	$353.5	$2,106.3	$218.9	$383.0
2003	$1,388.3	$441.8	$2,632.9	$273.6	$478.8
2004	$1,388.3	$589.7	$3,514.2	$365.2	$639.0
2005	$1,388.3	$735.8	$4,384.6	$455.6	$797.3
2006		$846.8	$5,046.5	$524.4	$917.7
2007		$973.8	$5,803.2	$603.0	$1,055.2
2008		$1,119.9	$6,673.7	$693.4	$1,213.5
2009		$1,287.8	$7,674.7	$797.5	$1,395.6

Note: Production related engineering and experimentation cost savings decrease in 2001 because, although some experimental production uses of the measurement technology were reported after the introduction of the SRM, the most intense realization of such experimental benefits came from the application of the new measurement technology—gained in industry's interaction with NIST through publications, presentations, and ongoing interaction with the researchers—to production problems encountered by industry as it coped with the need for the actual improved SRM and substituted experimentation for it. Publications about the SRM 2517a technology started appearing in 1999. The other categories of industry benefits increase after the introduction of the SRM 2517a because those benefits reflect the actual use of the SRMs once they were available for use.

TABLE II
Estimated costs associated with SRM 2517a
(year 2000 dollars)

Year	ATP Funds ($1000s)	Industry pull cost ($1000s)
1998	$72.6	
1999	$76.7	
2000		$16.3
2001		$73.5

TABLE III
Estimated total costs and estimated total industry benefits associated with SRM 2517a (year 2000 dollars)

Year	Total costs ($1000s)	Total industry benefits ($1000s)
1998	$72.6	
1999	$76.7	$3,193.9
2000	$16.3	$6,999.5
2001	$73.5	$16,741.6
2002		$4,744.0
2003		$5,215.4
2004		$6,496.4
2005		$7,761.6
2006		$7,335.4
2007		$8,435.2
2008		$9,700.5
2009		$11,155.6

what knowledgeable industry observers expect to be a 15% rate of growth.

The costs associated with the SRM 2517a project are in Table II. The actual costs of the ATP intramural project are shown along with estimates of the pull costs for industry. Respondents were asked to estimate any initial costs, over and above any fees paid to NIST for SRM 2517a to be able to use (i.e., pull in) the artifact in production. These pull costs are one-time costs.

Table III aggregates the cost and benefit estimates from Tables I and II.

Results of the economic analysis

Table IV summarizes the four evaluation metrics calculated for this case study.[21] Clearly, based on

one or all of the metrics in Table IV, the ATP intramural funded SRM 2517a project was successful from society's economic perspective. The internal rate of return is 4,400%, the benefit-to-cost ratio is 267 to 1, and the net present value in 2002 in year 2000 dollars is 76 million.

The metrics in Table IV reflect the social return on investments, and these are the returns

TABLE IV
Evaluation metrics for the SRM 2517a case study

Metric	Estimate
Real internal rate of return	4,400%
Benefit-to-Cost ratio	267 to 1
Net present value using 1998 as base year in year 2000 dollars	$58.1 million
Net present value using 2002 as base year in year 2000 dollars	$76.2 million

TABLE V
Revised evaluation metrics for the SRM 2517a case study using total benefits (net gains in the total of producer surplus and consumer surplus) (year 2000 dollars)

Metric	Estimate
Real internal rate of return	5,500%
Benefit-to-Cost ratio	331 to 1
Net present value using 1998 as the base year in year 2000 dollars	$72.0 million
Net present value using 2002 as the base year in year 2000 dollars	$94.4 million

that economists call producer surplus. Producer surplus is the profit resulting because of the use of the infratechnology embodied in SRM 2517a. Although the estimate will be a rough one, we are also able to provide a first-order approximation of the consumer surplus gains as well. Figure 1 represents the situation for the typical company selling a differentiated product that uses SRM 2517a in the production process.[22] The availability of the new standard reference material lowers the unit costs as shown in the figure from "unit cost 2517" to "unit cost 2517a." Consequently, the company chooses a lower price and sells more of its product or service.[23] The company's profit maximizing price falls from P_1 to P_2, and the optimal output increases from Q_1 to Q_2. The new surplus—resulting because of the new lower unit costs of production enabled by SRM 2517a—is the sum of the areas A, B, C, and D. Area A represents the new producer surplus on sales of the original amount of output. Area B plus area C represents the new producer

surplus from the sale of additional output. Finally, area D represents the net gain in consumer surplus (new consumer surplus that does not simply offset a loss in previously existing producer surplus).

Details about price, output and unit cost are considered highly confidential and the industry respondents were typically unwilling to provide such information. However, one of the respondents was willing to provide detailed information, for its own production, about P1, P2, Q1, Q2, and unit cost both before SRM 2517a was introduced and then after it replaced SRM 2517. For that company, the ratio of net new consumer surplus to new producer surplus, $D/(A + B + C)$, equals 0.238. That company conjectures that its experience with the cost lowering effect of replacing SRM 2517 with SRM 2517a would be similar to the experiences of others in the industry. Therefore, as a first-order approximation of consumer surplus gains because of the process innovations from applying SRM 2517a, we multiply the new producer profits—the industry benefits column of Table III—by 0.238. Table V recalculates the metrics for the SRM 2517a project by using the total of the net gains in producer and consumer surplus (the industrial benefits from Table III multiplied by 1.238) as the social return on the investment.

5. Concluding observations

Public agencies have taken their own idiosyncratic approaches to respond to the Government Performance and Results Act of 1993 (GPRA), and researchers have offered a variety of evaluation methods in the pages of this jour-

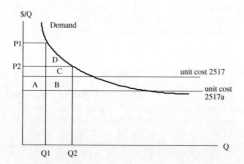

Figure 1. Demand, unit cost and net gain in producer and consumer surplus from the use of SRM 2517a.

nal and others. Whatever the merits of the numerous alternatives to the approach based on the Griliches/Mansfield estimation of the social rate of return for the public investments, the Griliches/Mansfield method is the preeminent way to evaluate public investments' social value from an economic perspective.[24] The Griliches/Mansfield methodology is so important that it could usefully have a category of its own among the subset of categories in the *Journal of Economic Literature* category for technological change (O300—Technological Change; Research and Development: General). We hope that our case study has illustrated the usefulness of their methodology for evaluating public investments.

Appendix: Quantifying Social Rate of Return Metrics

Using the time series for costs and benefits, measured in constant dollars, the internal rate of return, the benefit-to-cost ratio, and the net present value for the project were calculated in this case study using the year when each project began as the base year. In addition to those three customary metrics, net present value referenced to year 2002 was also computed since it is the year in which the calculations were originally performed.

The metrics are calculated from the time series of costs and benefits in year 2000 dollars. Costs and benefits were converted to constant dollars to allow all dollar figures to be directly comparable. All dollar figures have been converted to year 2000 dollars using the chain-type price index for gross domestic product provided in the *Economic Report of the President*.[25] Year 2000 was chosen because, at the time that the case study was conducted, that was the most recent year for which complete annual data were available.

Internal rate of return[26]

The internal rate of return (IRR) is the value of the discount rate, i, that equates the net present value (NPV) of the stream of net benefits associated with a research project to zero.[27] The time series runs from the beginning of the research project, $t = 0$, to a terminal point, $t = n$.

Mathematically,

$$\text{NPV} = [(B_0 - C_0)/(1 + i)^0] + \cdots + [(B_n - C_n)/(1 + i)^n] = 0 \quad (1)$$

where $(B_t - C_t)$ represents the net benefits associated with the project in year t, and n represents the number of time periods—years in the case study evaluated in this paper—being considered in the evaluation.

For unique solutions for i, from equation (1), the IRR can be compared to a value, r, that represents the opportunity cost of funds invested by the technology-based public institution. Thus, if the opportunity cost of funds is less than the internal rate of return, the project was worthwhile from an *ex post* social perspective.

Benefit-to-cost ratio

The ratio of benefits-to-costs (B/C) is the ratio of the present value of all measured benefits to the present value of all measured costs. Both benefits and costs are referenced to the initial time period, $t = 0$, when the project began as:

$$B/C = \left[\sum_{t=0}^{t=n} B_t/(1 + r)^t\right] \bigg/ \left[\sum_{t=0}^{t=n} C_t/(1 + r)^t\right] \quad (2)$$

A benefit-to-cost ratio of 1 is said to indicate a project that breaks-even. Any project with $B/C > 1$ is a relatively successful project as defined in terms of benefits exceeding costs.

Fundamental to implementing the ratio of benefits-to-costs is a value for the discount rate, r. While the discount rate representing the opportunity cost for public funds could differ across a portfolio of public investments, the calculated metrics in this paper follow the guidelines set forth by the Office of Management and Budget (1992), which states that: "Constant-dollar benefit-cost analyses of proposed investments and regulations should report net present value and other outcomes determined using a real discount rate of 7%."

Net present value

The information developed to determine the benefit-to-cost ratio can be used to determine net present value (NPV) as:

$$NPV_{initial\ year} = B - C \qquad (3)$$

where, as in the calculation of B/C, B refers to the present value of all measured benefits and C refers to the present value of all measured costs and where present value refers to the initial year or time period in which the project began, $t = 0$ in terms of the B/C formula in equation (2). Note that NPV allows, in principle, one means of ranking several projects *ex post*, providing investment sizes are similar.

To compare the net present values across different case studies with different starting dates, the net present value for each can be brought forward to the same year—here year 2002. The $NPV_{initial\ year}$ is brought forward under the assumption that the NPV for the project was invested at the 7% real rate of return that is recommended by the Office of Management and Budget as the opportunity cost of government funds. NPV_{2002} is then a project's NPV multiplied by 1.07 raised to the power of 2002 minus the year that the project was initiated as:

$$NPV_{2002} = NPV\ (1.07)^{2002-initial\ year} \qquad (4)$$

Acknowledgment

This paper is based on research conducted under the sponsorship of the National Institute of Standards and Technology's Advanced Technology Program. We are grateful for comments and suggestions from Stephanie Shipp and Jeanne Powell on earlier versions.

Notes

1. The Government Performance and Results Act of 1993 (GPRA) required that public institutions' research programs identify outputs and quantify the economic benefits of the outcomes associated with such outputs. Some public agencies have skirted the issue by arguing that the research they do or that they fund is peer reviewed, and thus it is sound; and if the research is sound, it must be socially valuable. Many embrace the importance of having research peer reviewed both at the pre-funding stage as well as upon completion. However, the peer review process certainly does not address in any precise or reliable way whether or not the research is socially valuable from an economic standpoint. It is not so much that a formal analysis of social economic rates of return is officially out of bounds for the peer review process; rather, such an analysis is simply not a part of the peer review process as it currently exists. Other public agencies are attempting to be more exact in their approach to meeting the GPRA requirement to quantify outcomes' benefits. However, the hurdle that is difficult to clear for most public agencies is how to quantify benefits in a methodologically sound and defensible way.

2. The origin of this assumption can be traced at least to Bush (1945), although Link and Scott (1998, 2001) have placed this assumption in a specific policy context.

3. For background information about ATP see, for example, Link and Scott (1998, 2001).

4. Because of fundamental molecular absorptions when light is projected through the absorption cell filled with acetylene gas, the power transmitted through the cell is distinct at specified wavelengths, allowing accurate references to those wavelengths. Those references can then be used to calibrate instruments for industry.

5. Gilbert, Sarah L., and Swann, William C., Acetylene $^{12}C_2H_2$ Absorption Reference for 1510 nm to 1540 nm Wavelength Calibration—SRM 2517a, NIST Special Publication 260–133, 2001 Edition, Standard Reference Materials, Issued February 2001 (Washington, D.C., U.S. Government Printing Office, 2001), p. 2.

6. The rough breakdown of all of the SRM 2517a sales by industry category is 45% to manufacturers of test equipment, 30% to manufacturers of components, 10% to companies providing network systems, and 15% to other users—mostly research laboratories—of the SRM. According to Dr. Gilbert, a company will typically purchase one SRM 2517a.

7. Link and Scott have developed, through ongoing evaluations of federal research programs, an alternative approach to the *economic* evaluation of publicly-funded research. This approach differs from traditional evaluation methods that have been used in addition to peer review. The alternative approach is needed to provide additional insights because the traditional evaluation methods are limited in an evaluation world that is performance accountable. The genesis of this approach is in Link (1996a), and recent applications are in Link (1996b) and Link and Scott (1998, 2001). Link and Scott, and others, have used this approach in a number of the evaluation studies sponsored by the Program Office at NIST, as well as in several ATP-sponsored projects. More specifically, and in general terms, Link and Scott argue that asking what is the social rate of return to an innovation and asking how that compares to the innovator's private rate of return may not always be the most appropriate question to ask. The fact that the social rate of return is greater than the private rate of return does indeed provide evidence that there are benefits spilling over to society. However, the fact that the social rate of return is greater than the private rate of return ignores consideration of the cost effectiveness of the public sector undertaking the research as opposed to the private sec-

tor. In other words, the Griliches/Mansfield traditional evaluation method does not address the efficiency with which social benefits are being achieved. Two alternative evaluation methods could be more appropriate for publicly-funded research. When publicly-funded publicly-performed investments are being evaluated we argue that our Counterfactual Evaluation Method could be appropriate. Holding constant the economic benefits that the Griliches/Mansfield model measures, and making no attempt to measure that stream, the counterfactual evaluation question is: What would the private sector have had to invest to achieve those same benefits in the absence of the public sector's investments? See as an example of the Counterfactual Evaluation Method Link and Scott (1998). Alternatively, when publicly-funded privately-performed investments are being evaluated, we argue that our Spillover Evaluation Method could be appropriate. The question asked is one that facilitates an economic understanding of whether the public sector should be underwriting a portion of private-sector firms' research, namely: What proportion of the total profit stream generated by the private firm's R&D and innovation does the private firm expect to capture; and hence, what proportion is not appropriated but is instead captured by other firms that imitate the innovation or use knowledge generated by the R&D to produce competing products for the social good? The part of the stream of expected profits captured by the innovator is its private return, while the entire stream is the lower bound on the social rate of return. The extent of the spillover of such knowledge with public good characteristics could determine whether or not the public sector should have funded the research. See as an illustration of the Spillover Evaluation Method, Link and Scott (2001).

8. As relevant, other investment costs will be discussed below. Such investment costs are costs that the private sector will incur to utilize the ATP project's output. These are, stated differently, the costs incurred by the private sector to pull in ATP's output and utilize it efficiently. Hence, these costs are referred to as pull costs.

9. Of course, it is assumed that the benefit information provided by interviewed individuals is accurate and reproducible should subsequent interviews by others take place.

10. The data developed for discussion of the outcomes in this case study are based on discussions with Dr. Gilbert and several industry experts from Wavelength References, Burleigh Instruments, Corning, Agilent, and Chorum Technologies.

11. The information about the industry-wide coverage of our sample of respondents in industry was provided by NIST.

12. For a discussion of other optoelectronics SRMs, see:http://patapsco.nist.gov/srmcatalog/tables/view_table.-cfm?table=207-4.htm.

13. As one respondent whose company manufactures commercial gas cells (based on SRM 2517a) for use in instruments stated: "If there were no SRM 2517a, all along the way through the supply chain the additional calibration expenses (suites of equipment and extra labor costs) would be incurred. Roughly half of the optical spectrum analyzers sold to industry incorporate the SRM 2517a technology to calibrate better. There would be extra expense and time at each research site."

14. Our understanding is that these activities fall under the rubric of research and development (R&D), but absent information about how companies classify these activities we refrain from using the policy-sensitive term "R&D."

15. To paraphrase one industry expert: SRM 2517a reduced our investigation costs; we would have invested additional engineering person-years with equipment to maintain production. See also the note to Table 1.

16. One respondent, whose company manufactures locked lasers and gas cells, observed that the alternative to SRM 2517a for calibration is to invest in a suite of equipment and then take the extra time to get the calibration results. A telecommunications company responded that prior to SRM 2517a it relied on its own internal standards based on one frequency and then extrapolated to other frequencies. The company's expert stated that the SRM 2517a standard, with multiple indicators of various frequencies, is a critically important advance for telecommunications.

17. A manufacturer of narrow band optical filters told us: SRM 2517a provides narrow line widths for reference to absolute vacuum wavelengths and this is critical to meeting the performance specification needs of our customers. This artifact gives us an unquestionable reference to absolute wavelengths so that secondary standards can be recalibrated as they drift. Our alternative, over say 30 nm of wavelength range for a particular product, maybe 10 optical filters would be strung together. While the cost of this alternative is not that great, performance tolerances and wavelength stability would be lost. Using the alternative would have resulted in a yield loss of about 30%.

18. One respondent noted that without NIST traceability through SRM 2517a, interactions with the customers over performance characteristics would be like dealing with "a wound that would not heal."

19. Paraphrasing a component manufacturer: There are two parts to the sales/marketing impact of SRM 2517a for our company. First, there is a savings in personnel costs because there is less effort needed to convince customers about the quality and reliability of our products. More importantly, there is a positive effect on our reputation and the customers' confidence in our product line because of having NIST standards integrated in the production process. That positive effect translates into extra sales and extra profits. Paraphrasing a manufacturer of wavelength meters: We use SRM 2517a as we manufacture wavelength meters. SRM 2517a is used to check periodically the calibration of test lasers and equipment used for the qualification of our wavemeters. We can claim traceability to NIST. There are cost savings to us in the sales/marketing category.

20. Industry interacts with NIST and stays abreast of the latest developments through direct communication with NIST scientists, and through scientists' presentations and publications. In this case, some respondents reported that they began benefiting from the new knowledge—gained from interaction with NIST researchers—about wavelength calibration even before SRMs were sold, as industry coped with the need for the actual SRMs but substituted experimental work in their absence.

21. Regarding evaluation metrics, see the appendix to this paper.

22. As is seen in Figure 1, in addition to gaining new profits that we have identified as industrial benefits, industry loses some of its previous profits on the previous amount sold before unit costs fell because the use of SRM 2517a lowers costs and consequently price falls. However, those lost profits (lost producer surplus) are completely offset by a gain of exactly that amount in consumer surplus, leaving just the new profits measured in Table III and represented by A + B + C in Figure 1 as the increase in total surplus because of increased producer surplus. The net gain in consumer surplus (represented by D in Figure 1) is then added to get the change in total economic surplus that is the social return to the use of SRM 2517a—consumers gain more than D, but that additional gain is exactly offset by an equal amount of lost previously existing surplus for producers, leaving D as the net gain in consumer surplus.

23. Note that Figure 1 depicts optimal output in the long run when all costs are variable.

24. As we have noted above, for GPRA purposes, it will sometimes be appropriate to use the development of the Griliches/Mansfield methodology that we have incorporated in our Counterfactual Evaluation Method and our Spillover Evaluation Method.

25. See CEA (2002), Table B-7, "Chain-type price indexes for gross domestic product, 1959–2001." The index number for 2001 was estimated as the average of the three quarterly observations available.

26. The characterization of the three metrics follows Link and Scott (1998).

27. Using the constant dollar figures for costs and benefits, the internal rate of return is a "real" rate of return. In contrast, some economic impact assessments (including many conducted for NIST's Program Office) have presented "nominal" rates of return that were based on time series of current dollars (the dollars of the year in which the benefits were realized or the costs were incurred).

References

Bush, V., 1945, *Science—the Endless Frontier*, Washington, DC: U.S. Government Printing Office.

Council of Economic Advisers (CEA), February 2002, *Economic Report of the President*, Washington, D.C.: United States Government Printing Office.

Griliches, Z., 1958, 'Research Costs and Social Returns: Hybrid Corn and Related Innovations,' *Journal of Political Economy* **66**, 419–431.

Link, A.N., 1996a, 'Economic Impact Assessments: Guidelines for Conducting and Interpreting Assessment Studies,' NIST Planning Report 96-1.

Link, A.N., 1996b, *Evaluating Public Sector Research and Development*, New York: Praeger Publishers.

Link, A.N. and J.T. Scott, 1998, *Public Accountability: Evaluating Technology-Based Institutions*, Norwell, MA: Kluwer Academic Publishers.

Link, A.N. and J.T. Scott. 2001, 'Public/Private Partnerships: Stimulating Competition in a Dynamic Economy,' *International Journal of Industrial Organization* **19**, 763–794.

Mansfield, E., J. Rapoport, A. Romero, S. Wagner, and G. Beardsley, 1977. 'Social and Private Rates of Return from Industrial Innovations,' *Quarterly Journal of Economics* **91**, 221–240.

Office of Management and Budget (OMB), 1992, 'Guidelines and Discount Rates for Benefit-Cost Analysis of Federal Programs,' Circular No. A-94, October 29.

[11]

Econ. Innov. New Techn., 2008, Vol. 17(7&8), October&November, pp. 677–687

INTELLIGENT MACHINE TECHNOLOGY
AND PRODUCTIVITY GROWTH

DAVID P. LEECH[a,b] and JOHN T. SCOTT[c,*]

[a] Business Division, Villa Julie College, Stevenson, MD, USA; [b] TASC, Inc., 1101 Wilson Blvd, Suite 1600, Arlington, VA 22209, USA; [c] Department of Economics, Dartmouth College, Hanover, NH 03755, USA

(Received 1 April 2007; In final form 17 August 2007)

This paper provides preliminary estimates of the productivity impact of intelligent machine technology (IMT) and the rate of return to IMT research and development (R&D) over the next two decades. The paper adapts economists' traditional productivity growth model to enable the use of industrial experts' forecasts of a few key parameters of the model to form the estimates of productivity growth and rate of return. Respondents – from a sample of firms operating in IMT development and applications in the automotive, aerospace, and capital construction industries – anticipate that IMT will generate substantial productivity growth over the next two decades, and the estimated social rates of return to IMT R&D are substantial.

Keywords: Intelligent machine technology; Productivity growth; Research and development

JEL Classification(s): O300; O400

1 INTRODUCTION

Intelligent machine technology (IMT) is the application of computer-based knowledge to enable machines capable of using human-like behavior to perform tasks – that without the technology would be performed by humans – in complex and dynamic industrial environments.[1] IMT is in part enabling technology in that it will allow new machine-intensive and labor-saving production techniques across a wide range of industries.[2] It is in part infrastructure technology in that it will ideally conform to standards ensuring it will provide access across industries to human-performance-like, machine-based, generic technology that is necessary for the development of innovative labor-saving processes.[3] IMT is evolving from current

---

* Corresponding author. Tel.: +1603-646-2941; E-mail: john.t.scott@dartmouth.edu

[1] We use the non-technical, descriptive term 'human-like' behavior; for both technical and philosophical reasons, 'human-level' behavior might be more apt. IMT is computational technology that senses its environment and adjusts its behavior based on modeling of interaction with that environment and evaluation to achieve goals. It can be encapsulated in a computer program, an intelligent sensor, or a robot. Examples of IMT include machine systems such as computer-aided design technologies, computer numerically controlled machine tools, computer controlled inspection systems, enterprise integration information systems, just-in-time production scheduling and inventory control technologies, internet technologies that enable out-sourcing to the most efficient suppliers, and multi-spectral measurement systems for construction site metrology and other applications.

[2] See Link and Siegel (2007, p. 97) for definition and discussion of enabling technologies.

[3] Link and Siegel (2003, p. 63, p. 78) define infrastructure technology and explain its role in innovation.

ISSN 1043-8599 print; ISSN 1476-8364 online © 2008 Taylor & Francis
DOI: 10.1080/10438590701785637

successes in computer-aided industrial operations; in that sense, *new* IMT is incremental innovation. However, the advances anticipated in intelligent machines, as they become capable of assuming industrial tasks currently performed by humans, support the view that the next two decades will see IMT emerging as radical innovation.[4] International competitiveness will require firms to use new IMT.[5] Hence, IMT-induced productivity growth is important to a nation's firms and merits the attention of their government's technology policy.[6]

This paper provides preliminary estimates of the productivity impact of IMT and the rate of return to IMT research and development (R&D) over the next two decades. To develop the estimates, we focus on a sample of firms operating in IMT development and applications in the automotive, aerospace, and capital construction industries. The paper adapts economists' traditional productivity growth model to enable the use of industrial experts' forecasts of a few key parameters of the model to form the estimates of productivity growth and rate of return. IMT-induced productivity growth has been widely anticipated because of the established industrial successes of computer-aided design, analysis, scheduling, inventory control, and numerical control, along with rapid developments in the understanding of how to build intelligent machines. The experts at the National Institute of Standards and Technology (NIST) and in industry with whom we have spoken anticipate that over the next two decades, intelligent machines will be closing the gap between their levels of performance and human levels of performance for specific industrial tasks. Closing the gap is an important policy issue and necessary to ensure continued productivity gains for the twenty-first century industries.[7] It is also exciting from a philosophical as well as technological standpoint as machines progress from winning chess matches to human-like performance of complex tasks in industry.[8] With the exciting prospects in mind, we estimate the range of likely productivity effects by combining the knowledge of the experts with economists' models of productivity.

The approach developed here for the study of IMT-induced productivity growth rates and IMT R&D rates of return is an application based on a very large and well-established literature about productivity growth and rates of return to R&D. For review of that large literature, see Link and Siegel (2003). For a focus on the disaggregated components of productivity, see Tassey (2005). In the present paper, we focus entirely on identifying the effect of one disaggregated component – namely, IMT.

Section 2 explains the measure of IMT-induced productivity growth. Section 3 then describes the sample and provides the productivity growth estimates. Section 4 explains the measure of the rate of return to IMT R&D. Section 5 then provides the rate of return estimates.

---

[4] Link and Siegel (2007, p. 126) provide a window to the literature about radical technologies; IMT is arguably a special case of such dramatic departures in process technology – special because of its pervasiveness, yet radical in the potential for transforming competition in individual industries.

[5] For example, see the description of IMT increasing the productivity of German automobile manufacturer BMW AG in Gumbel (2007).

[6] IMT development entails multidisciplinary research requiring sound technology policy. IMT is an emerging *system* technology, both technically – requiring the integration of technologies governing, as explained by Albus and Meystel (2001, pp. 17–18), sensory processing, world modeling, value judgment, and behavior generation – and institutionally – requiring the collaboration and integration of public, quasi-public, and private sector institutions specializing in basic scientific research, generic technology development, and infratechnology development. See Albus and Meystel (2001, pp. 145–152) regarding complexity of IMT and Tassey (1997) regarding complexity of technology and demands of multidisciplinary research. See Tassey (2005) regarding interaction of institutions in a successful national innovation system.

[7] See US Domestic Policy Council (2006). The goals for the American competitiveness initiative discussed there include capability and capacity in nano-manufacturing, intelligent manufacturing capabilities, and related sensor and detection capabilities.

[8] Computer programs not only play chess, they handle airline reservations, manage financial transactions, control inventories, verify customer identifications, dispense bank drafts, and track package shipments. Respected technologists believe the realization of 'digital people' and 'engineered minds' (autonomous machines) is palpably close (Albus and Meystel, 2001, p. 146).

Section 6 concludes with discussion of the importance of government support for IMT R&D investments.

2   THE MEASURE OF IMT PRODUCTIVITY GROWTH

Our estimation method focuses exclusively on new, IMT-induced growth in output, because we construct the measure of IMT-induced productivity growth as an effect above and beyond the effects for all sources of output growth other than the advance in IMT knowledge. Thus, the growth in output that we identify is that growth that is not explained by the growth in inputs other than IMT knowledge. Stated differently using the conventional categorization of inputs, we focus on only the growth in output that is not explained by growth in labor, in capital goods, in materials, in knowledge capital other than IMT knowledge stock, and in exogenous trends in output growth.[9]

To ensure a consistent focus for our respondents in industry (discussed in Sec. 3), we began with industry-specific credible future scenarios for the likely advances over the next two decades for IMT applications in the automotive, aerospace, and capital construction industries. The future scenarios were developed in consultations with a group of well-respected technology specialists from NIST, industry associations, and academe. The group of specialists also helped us to gain access to knowledgeable individuals within the selected private sector firms surveyed.[10]

To isolate the anticipated IMT-induced growth in output, respondents were asked their expectations about several parameters, which are defined in Table I. Gamma (γ) is defined to be the computational capability multiple – the increase in computational capability per unit of cost – anticipated for the computational tasks used in their industry over each of the next two decades. For example, if computational power per unit of cost for the industry were anticipated to grow by an order of magnitude over the next decade, then $\gamma = 10$.

TABLE I   The IMT productivity parameters.

Parameter	Definition	Empirically based theoretical range (mean)[a]
Gamma (γ)	Computational capability multiple showing the increase in computational capability per unit of cost for the industry's computational tasks	1–35 (7.95)
Alpha (α)	Proportion of an industry's tasks as measured by their costs that can benefit from the application of new IMT	0.0–0.67 (0.325)
Beta (β)	Output quality multiple showing the increase in value of the industry's output attributable to new IMT	1–10 (4.55)

[a]The lower limit is simply the case of no effect – that is, there are no gains in computational capability or in output quality, and hence the multiples γ and β are 1, and none of the industry's tasks can benefit and hence the proportion α is 0. For the upper limit, we can of course only speculate regarding γ and β, and α's admissible upper limit of 1 is not particularly informative. We have responses from industry for each of the next two decades, and also given R&D with typical conditions for appropriating returns versus complete appropriation. To provide a sense of the realistic range for these parameters, reported here, for the upper limits, is the largest value reported by any of the respondents for either of the next two decades given R&D with typical conditions for appropriating return. In parentheses are the average responses for those two decades given the typical conditions. The figures here are based on 18 observations – one in each of the two decades from each of the nine respondents providing the information.

---

[9] Solow's (1957) seminal paper focused on a much more inclusive residual – namely, the residual productivity growth rate after the growth rates in capital and labor were controlled. See Link and Siegel (2003, pp. 27–28) for a discussion of Solow's residual.

[10] A complete list of the technology specialists with whom we consulted and their affiliations as well as the detailed future scenarios are provided in Leech *et al.* (2006).

Alpha (α) is defined to be the proportion of the industry's tasks as measured by their costs that can benefit from the application of new advanced machine intelligence. For example, if one-half of a manufacturing industry's costs are taken by tasks that can benefit from applications of advances in intelligent machines or systems, then $\alpha = 1/2$.

Finally, beta (β) is defined to be the output quality multiple. For example, if the applications of advanced machine intelligence are expected to increase the value of the industry's output by 25%, then $\beta = 1.25$.

Output at time t is Q_t. The cost of the factors of production, the inputs, at time t is F_t. An industry's total factor productivity is the ratio of the value of its output to the cost of its inputs, or $\text{TFP}_t = Q_t/F_t$. At time $t + \delta t$, the cost of the factors of production will be $\alpha(F_t/\gamma) + (1 - \alpha)F_t$. At time $t + \delta t$, the industry's total factor productivity given the effects of new IMT is $\text{TFP}_t = \beta Q_t / F(1 - \alpha + (\alpha/\gamma))$. Then, with a dot over a variable to denote its change per unit of time, the growth rate in total factor productivity induced by the new IMT is:

$$\left.\frac{\dot{\text{TFP}}}{\text{TFP}}\right|_{\text{new IMT}} = \frac{(Q_t/F_t)\,(\beta/(1 - \alpha + (\alpha/\gamma))) - Q_t/F_t}{Q_t/F_t} \tag{1}$$

where $\dot{\text{TFP}}/\text{TFP}|_{\text{new IMT}}$ is the notation to indicate the contribution of new IMT to the growth rate in total factor productivity, Q_t/F_t.[11]

To understand the relations captured by Eq. (1), denote $(\beta/(1 - \alpha + (\alpha/\gamma))) = (1 + r)$. Then,

$$\left.\frac{\dot{\text{TFP}}}{\text{TFP}}\right|_{\text{new IMT}} = \frac{(Q_t/F_t)(1 + r) - (Q_t/F_t)}{Q_t/F_t} = r \tag{2}$$

is the growth rate in productivity attributable to new IMT. Observe that the productivity growth multiple $(1 + r)$ increases as the quality multiple β increases. Also note that the productivity multiple increases as the fraction $1 - \alpha + (\alpha/\gamma)$, the multiplier for the factor cost F, gets smaller. The $(1 - \alpha)$ part of that denominator is the portion of cost that is not affected by IMT, so it gets smaller as α gets bigger. And the (α/γ) part of the denominator gives the portion of cost affected by IMT divided by the IMT capability multiple. The bigger that multiple, the smaller are costs, and the bigger is α, the more important that cost reduction is. So F, the start of period cost, is averaged in with a weight of $(1 - \alpha)$ with the new end-of-period cost, and F/γ, the end-of-period lower cost because of the improved IMT, gets averaged in with a weight of α.

We conclude this section with an intuitive summary statement as follows. Total factor productivity Q/F is the ratio of output's value to inputs' cost, and $\beta/(1 - \alpha + (\alpha/\gamma))$ is the productivity multiple induced by new IMT. Its numerator is the multiplier for the value of output because of the increase in its quality due to IMT improvements. Its denominator is the multiplier for costs (it will be a fraction between 0 and 1) because of the improvement in IMT. If α were 0, then the multiplier would be 1 since costs would not be reduced. If α were 1, then the multiplier would be $1/\gamma$, the reciprocal of the cost improvement multiple (two times

---

[11] We have then a very specialized portion of the residual in the original Solow (1957) formulation. Solow's residual reflected the growth rate in output not explained by the growth rates in labor and capital. That residual was classically attributed to an exogenous rate of output growth and the rate of growth in the stock of knowledge. Here we have focused on the residual attributable solely to new IMT.

the capability implies one-half the cost). Of course, α will in general be a fraction, so the denominator multiple is saying that part $(1 - \alpha)$ of the start of period cost F is unchanged, while the other part (α) gets reduced by the fraction $1/\gamma$.

3 THE ESTIMATES OF IMT PRODUCTIVITY GROWTH

To estimate IMT-induced productivity growth over the next two decades, we surveyed 14 firms.[12] The complete survey instrument is provided in Leech *et al.* (2006). Equation (1) is estimated using the survey responses of the nine companies that provide all of the necessary information. Thus, we rely on expert opinion gleaned from a survey of knowledgeable individuals in industry; that approach results in a small sample, and the limitations of such a sample must be acknowledged at the outset.[13]

We calculate 95% confidence intervals for the means that we present to allow us to capture the uncertainty about the true means for the variables of interest to us. Nonetheless, we emphasize that we would certainly prefer to have a larger sample, and the measures of productivity growth and R&D rate of return that we develop and integrate with survey data can be applied to larger samples if they become available.

Using the conventional categorization of inputs, we focus on only the growth in output that is *not* explained by growth in labor, in capital goods, in materials, in knowledge capital other than IMT knowledge stock, and in exogenous trends in output growth.[14] Table II shows the estimates of the IMT-induced productivity growth rate g per decade, and those rates are converted into compound annual rates of growth shown in Table III.

TABLE II   Anticipated IMT-induced productivity growth rate, g, per decade[a].

Decade	Number of observations	Mean	Standard Error[b]	95% Confidence interval[c]
2006–2015	9	3.69 (369%)	1.13*	1.08–6.31
2015–2025	9	7.38 (738%)	1.95**	2.89–11.87

[a]The period of analysis for this table is 9 years in length for the 2006–2015 scenario, and 10 years in length for the 2015–2025 scenario.
[b]The estimated mean's level of significance for a two-tailed test (based on the t-statistic = the ratio of the coefficient to the standard error) against the null hypothesis of a zero growth rate: * = 0.02, ** = 0.01.
[c]Based on the information provided by the respondents and the model, the anticipated IMT-induced productivity growth rate is within the reported range with probability 0.95. For example, for the first decade the anticipated IMT-induced productivity growth rate is in the range from 108 to 631% with probability 0.95. The reported means provide the point estimates – the expected outcome for the anticipated growth rate.

---

[12] The 14 companies with which we discussed IMT and to which we are grateful for the insights provided by their representatives are Boeing Company, Bechtel Corporation, CH2M Hill, CNH Global, Daimler-Chrysler Company, FANUC Robotics of America, Ford Motor Company, Foster-Miller, Inc., iRobot Corporation, John Deere, Mag IAS, Okuma, Northrop Grumman Corporation, and Toyota Corporation.
[13] We chose experts and firms in industry by using patent data to identify individuals and companies with a considerable stock of applied knowledge about IMT and also by consulting with a group of distinguished technology specialists from NIST, industry associations, and academe.
[14] Even infrastructure technology support from government and cooperative R&D in the industry are held constant at their accustomed levels in recent years. When respondents provided their estimates that have been used with the model to make predictions about IMT-induced productivity gains and about IMT R&D rates of return, the respondents were asked to assume that industry and government activities such as cooperative R&D and government support with infrastructure technology continue in the accustomed way. Estimates about quality multiples and computational capability and so forth are provided for the upcoming two decades and productivity growth rates and rates of return on investment are then derived.

682   D. P. LEECH AND J. T. SCOTT

TABLE III   Annual compound rate of anticipated IMT-induced productivity growth[a].

Decade	Annual rate of productivity growth
2006–2015	0.187 (18.7%)
2015–2025	0.237 (23.7%)

The rates in Table II using the decades as the period of analysis are converted into compound annual rates of growth r. Thus, given that g for the first decade is 3.69 (or 369%), the corresponding value of r is r such that we have $(1+r)^9 = 1 + g$. With $g = 3.69$, r solves as 0.187 or 18.7%. There are 10 years covered for the decade 2015–2025. Thus, with the decade growth rate for the second-decade scenario being 7.38 (738%), we have $(1+r)^{10} = 1 + g$, and the compound annual rate of growth r solves as 0.237 or 23.7%.
[a]For the 9-year span 2006–2015 and the 10-year span 2015–2025.

4   THE MEASURE OF IMT R&D RATE OF RETURN

Equation (1) when combined with IMT R&D intensity allows us to estimate the rates of return to IMT R&D. We have isolated the IMT-induced rate of growth in production. That growth rate is the rate of growth in output that is *not* explained by exogenous growth or by the rate of growth in other inputs – such as labor, physical capital goods, materials, and other types of R&D including government-provided infrastructure R&D. Thus, the IMT-induced rate of growth in production is:

$$\left.\frac{\dot{\text{TFP}}}{\text{TFP}}\right|_{\text{new IMT}} = \frac{\dot{Q}}{Q} - \lambda - \sum_j \eta_j \frac{\dot{X}_j}{X_j} \qquad (3)$$

where Q denotes output, X_j denotes the jth input other than IMT-knowledge stock, η_j denotes the elasticity of output with respect to the jth input, and λ denotes the exogenous rate of growth in output.

The IMT-induced rate of growth in productivity equals the product of the elasticity of output Q with respect to the IMT-knowledge stock R and the rate of growth $\dot{R}/R$ in that IMT-knowledge stock, where $\dot{R} \equiv dR/dt$ and t denotes time. Therefore, the IMT-induced rate of growth in production – the part of the growth rate for output due entirely to IMT-induced growth in output – can be written as the product of the rate of return, dQ/dR, to IMT R&D and the IMT R&D intensity, $\dot{R}/Q$ (the ratio to output of IMT R&D spending during the period) because:

$$\frac{\dot{Q}}{Q} - \lambda - \sum_j \eta_j \frac{\dot{X}_j}{X_j} = \eta_R \frac{\dot{R}}{R} = \frac{dQ}{dR}\frac{R}{Q}\frac{\dot{R}}{R} = \frac{dQ}{dR}\frac{\dot{R}}{Q} \qquad (4)$$

As Link and Siegel (2003, p. 72) observe, the formulation of the rate of return to R&D capital stock given in Eq. (4) ignores depreciation in the R&D capital stock and for that reason using the formulation to estimate the rate of return is expected to give a downward biased result here.[15] Link and Siegel (2003, p. 72) also discuss another source of downward bias when the formulation in Eq. (4) is used with total factor productivity growth rates in the typical econometric study. Namely, as Schankerman (1981) explained, to some extent R&D expenditures are already reflected in the measures of capital and labor for which growth rates, $\sum_j \eta_j (\dot{X}_j/X_j)$, are subtracted from the rate of growth in output to get the residual to be attributed to exogenous growth rate, λ, and the growth rate in R&D capital stock. Thus, the

---

[15] For technical details about why we anticipate a downward bias in the estimated rate of return when, as in the present case, we are estimating a social rate of return, see Scherer (1984, p. 283, endnote 7).

effect attributed to R&D is typically an 'excess rate of return' – a return above and beyond that already captured by the growth in other inputs that to some extent will reflect R&D investments. The 'double-counting' source of downward bias in the estimate of dQ/dR is less likely in our application of the formulation in Eq. (4), because in effect, by asking for estimates of α, β, and γ as described in Sec. 2, we have asked the expert industrial respondents to estimate directly the left-hand side of Eq. (4) – that is, we ask them to estimate directly the productivity effect that is attributable to new IMT.

5   THE ESTIMATES OF IMT R&D RATE OF RETURN

From the method explained in Sec. 2, we have derived each respondent's estimate of $(\dot{Q}/Q) - \lambda - \sum_j \eta_j (\dot{X}_j / X_j)$, the IMT-induced rate of growth in productivity for the industry of an IMT-user respondent and for the industries to which an IMT-developer sells IMT. From the survey responses, we estimate for each respondent the appropriate industry IMT R&D intensity, $\dot{R}/Q$. The respondents have provided multiples to convert company-level data about $\dot{R}$ and Q to industry-level data.

We include in $\dot{R}$ not only the downstream IMT R&D of the using industries, but as well we include the upstream IMT R&D done by IMT developers who sell IMT to the using industries. The sample of IMT developers covers a wide range of IMT, and the respondents provide multiples to convert company-level IMT R&D for the developers into industry totals including all of their competitors. The total industry-wide upstream IMT R&D of the IMT developers is then allocated to the downstream IMT-using industries in the proportions of all IMT patents taken by patents assigned to those downstream industries.[16]

For each respondent, we then have for each decade an estimate of the IMT-induced rate of growth in productivity and an estimate of IMT R&D intensity. Following Eq. (4), dividing the productivity growth rate by the R&D intensity for each of the nine observations provides an observation of the rate of return dQ/dR on IMT R&D. Table IV shows the rates of return with each entire decade as the period of analysis, and Table V shows the compound annual rates of return.

Those annual rates of return are somewhat more than 70%, somewhat higher than most of the estimates, using a variety of models and methods, for the rates of return to firms' overall R&D investments, reviewed by Link and Siegel (2007, Table 4.4, pp. 48–49). In the large literature they review, a majority of the estimated rates of return to firm R&D were in

TABLE IV   Anticipated rate of return, i, to IMT R&D per decade[a].

Decade	Number of observations	Mean	Standard error[b]	95% Confidence interval[c]
2006–2015	9	154.85 (15,485%)	53.95*	30.45–279.25
2015–2025	9	229.25 (22,925%)	54.07**	104.56–353.94

[a]The period of analysis for this table is 9 years in length for the 2006–2015 scenario and 10 years in length for the 2015–2025 scenario.
[b]The estimated mean's level of significance for a two-tailed test (based on the t-statistic = the ratio of the coefficient to the standard error) against the null hypothesis of a zero rate of return to IMT R&D: * = 0.03, ** = 0.01.
[c]Based on the information provided by the respondents and the model, the anticipated rate of return to IMT R&D is within the reported range with probability 0.95. For example, for the first decade the anticipated IMT R&D rate of return is in the range from 3045 to 27,925% with probability 0.95. The reported means provide the point estimates – the expected outcome for the anticipated IMT R&D rate of return.

---

[16] The patent proportions were provided by 1790 Analytics Inc.

TABLE V   Annual compound anticipated rate of return to IMT R&D[a].

Decade	Annual rate of return to IMT R&D
2006–2015	0.752 (75.2%)
2015–2025	0.723 (72.3%)

Table 4's IMT R&D rates of return using the decades as the periods of analysis are converted into compound annual rates of return, s. Thus, given that i for the first decade is 154.85 (or 15,485%), the corresponding value of s is s such that we have $(1 + s)^9 = 1 + i$. With $i = 154.85$, s solves as 0.752 or 75.2%. There are 10 years covered for the decade 2015–2025. Thus, with the decade IMT R&D rate of return for the second-decade scenario being 229.25 (22,925%), we have $(1 + s)^{10} = 1 + i$, and the compound annual rate of growth s solves as 0.723 or 72.3%.
[a]For the 9-year span 2006–2015 and the 10-year span 2015–2025.

the range of roughly 30% to 40%. None of the rates of return they report for total R&D or company-financed R&D are as large as the ones we estimate in Table V. However, we are not only estimating anticipated rates of return, rather than actual rates of return, but also we are examining just IMT R&D; and moreover, we have estimated a social, rather than a private, rate of return to the firm.

The rates of return to IMT R&D are social rates of return because they reflect the benefits and costs to society as a whole rather than solely to the developers and users of IMT that make the IMT R&D investments. On the benefits side, we have social rather than private rates of return because we estimate the gains from increased amounts of output from given resources and from reduction in resources used for given outputs, whether or not the private investors appropriate all of those benefits. We obtain estimates of the rate of growth in output made possible by the new IMT. The sales (the additional output times the price realized from the output) from those output gains will not typically equal the social value of the increased output because of the spillovers to consumer surplus (value to consumers above and beyond what they pay) and those spillovers increase with the competition faced by the firms making the R&D investments. On the costs side, in estimating the rate of return to IMT R&D investment, we have a social, rather than private, rate of return because we have included the costs of R&D investments made upstream (in the IMT-developers' industries) that are embodied in the IMT used in the downstream industries. The method weighs social benefits against social costs, resulting in a social rate of return to IMT R&D investments.

The estimates in Tables IV and V are conservative for a couple of reasons. The fact that we include in R&D intensity the upstream R&D that is useful for the downstream IMT-using industries – as is appropriate in order to have all of the social costs from which social benefits are derived – will make our estimates of the rate of return to IMT R&D smaller than would be the case if – as typically happens – the analysis did not account for R&D embodied in purchased technology.[17]

To be even more conservative in our estimation of the IMT R&D rates of return, we have included in the 'R&D' spending what Scherer (1984, chapter 8) refers to as 'launching costs'. The survey asked the respondents to estimate the amounts that they would spend to advertise the new IMT-based features, teaching customers about the new quality of the newly developed IMT-based products and services, and successfully launching them. Such expenditures to successfully launch new or newly improved goods are an important part of successful R&D because without them the benefits from the R&D would not be realized. Those costs are part of

---

[17] Some studies have accounted for R&D embodied in purchased inputs. A prominent example is Scherer (1984, chapter 3 and chapter 15). For a review and further development of the idea that benefits of R&D done outside the using industry affect R&D rates of return, see Scott (1993, chapter 9).

the social costs of introducing the new and newly improved IMT-based products and services and as such they have been included with the R&D spending to determine the R&D intensity used in calculating the rate of return. The approach of course lowers our estimates of the rate of return on the IMT R&D.

6 CONCLUDING OBSERVATIONS

Our study of IMT has implications for technology policy. IMT-induced productivity growth is expected to be substantial and expected social returns to IMT R&D are high. Moreover, the surveyed firms report that they would invest much more in IMT R&D if they could appropriate all of those social returns. The anticipated R&D investments reported for the scenarios described in Tables II–V assumed that the companies investing in IMT R&D would appropriate returns to the extent that they typically do, with much of the benefit spilling over to other producers and consumers. We asked them how much they would invest if, instead, they could appropriate all of the returns generated by their IMT R&D investments. If IMT developers and users could appropriate all of the returns from their IMT R&D investments, they would invest much more in IMT, with their IMT R&D intensities roughly doubling. Table VI compares the R&D intensities for the two decades under the alternative assumptions of typical conditions for appropriating returns versus complete appropriation of returns. Given the typical finding that incomplete appropriation of returns reduces R&D investment below the socially desirable level, the findings in Table VI support the need for government support of IMT R&D investments to overcome the market failure of underinvestment in socially valuable IMT R&D.

The respondents' opinions reinforce the idea that government-supported IMT R&D investments are an important source of the growth in the IMT-knowledge stock that will underlie the IMT-induced productivity gains. Each respondent was asked about the significance of government-funded R&D for the future developments anticipated by 2025. Significance was assessed on a scale from 1 to 10 with 1 indicating no perceptible influence of government-funded R&D, 5 implying that the government-funded R&D was or was expected to be an *important source* of information, and then the higher numbers indicate increasingly that government-funded R&D significantly affects or is expected to affect the direction and effectiveness of the establishment's R&D. The 14 respondents provided assessments of the importance of government-funded R&D for IMT advances over the upcoming years. The average response was 5.79 with a 95% confidence interval from 4.33 to 7.24. Clearly the

TABLE VI Anticipated IMT R&D intensity per decade for typical versus complete appropriation of returns[a].

Decade/appropriation	Number of observations	Mean	Standard error[b]	95% Confidence interval[c]
2006–2015/typical	9	0.0300	0.00484*	0.0188–0.0412
2006–2015/complete	9	0.0593	0.0116*	0.0324–0.0861
2015–2025/typical	9	0.0332	0.00706**	0.0169–0.0495
2015–2025/complete	9	0.0766	0.0244***	0.0202–0.133

[a]The respondents were asked about their R&D investments given customary or typical conditions for appropriating returns and then alternatively given the counterfactual situation of complete appropriation of returns. As discussed in the text, the R&D here includes 'launching costs' and the upstream R&D embodied in the using industry's IMT.
[b]The estimated mean's level of significance for a two-tailed test (based on the t-statistic = the ratio of the coefficient to the standard error) against the null hypothesis of a zero IMT R&D intensity: * = 0.001, ** = 0.002, *** = 0.02.
[c]Based on the information provided by the respondents and the model, the anticipated IMT R&D intensity is within the reported range with probability 0.95. The reported means provide the point estimates – the expected outcome for the anticipated IMT R&D intensity.

respondents believe that government funding of IMT R&D will be important if the anticipated developments in IMT are to be achieved.

The respondents also report that compliance with industry technical standards is essential to their marketing and sales efforts for new IMT-based products and services. The need for effective standards is undoubtedly an important reason the respondents say government support of IMT investment is needed. Using a scale of 1–10, with 1 denoting that compliance with standards is insignificant and with 10 indicating that compliance with standards is *essential* to the sales and marketing strategy, there were nine respondents. Their mean response was 7.56 with a 95% confidence interval from 6.11 to 9.00. Clearly the respondents believe compliance with industry technical standards is important for the success of the next generations of IMT-based products. Such standards have been important to date. There were 13 respondents providing an evaluation of the importance of standards for IMT-based goods and services to date. Their average assessment was 7.54 with a 95% confidence interval from 6.90 to 8.17.

Although there is considerable uncertainty about the future advances in IMT, we conclude with a cautious summary and suggestions for future research.[18] In sum, our respondents anticipate IMT will generate substantial productivity growth over the next two decades. They report that their IMT R&D intensity would roughly double if they could appropriate all of the returns from the R&D, implying that the value created by their IMT R&D spills over to other firms to a substantial extent. They also report that government-funded IMT R&D has been and will continue to be important for the achievement of IMT advances. The generality of our findings is limited by our small sample size, and an important task for future research will be to increase the sample size. Developing surveys of academics and researchers in industrial laboratories, as well as surveying more firms with operations based in a variety of countries, will make possible a breakdown of the results by industry and allow estimates with smaller confidence intervals.[19]

Acknowledgements

We thank Albert N. Link and two anonymous referees for numerous helpful comments that have been incorporated into the final version of the paper.

References

Albus, J. and Meystel, A. (2001) *Engineering of Mind: An Introduction to the Science of Intelligent Systems*. New York: John Wiley & Sons.

Gumbel, P. (2007) BMW Drives Germany. *Time*, **170**(3), *ProQuest* document ID 1300201821. Available online at: http://proquest.umi.com/pqdweb?did=1300201821&sid=1&Fmt=3&clientId=4347&RQT=309&VName=PQD.

Leech, D., Burke, J., Russell, M., Waychoff, C. and Scott J.T. (consultant) (2006) *Future Economic Impacts of Investments in Intelligent Machine Technology, 2006–2025, Final Report to the National Institute of Standards and Technology*. Arlington, VA: Northrop Grumman.

Link, A.N. and Siegel, D.S. (2003) *Technological Change and Economic Performance*. London and New York: Routledge – Taylor & Francis Group.

Link, A.N. and Siegel, D.S. (2007) *Innovation, Entrepreneurship, and Technological Change*. Oxford: Oxford University Press.

Schankerman, M.A. (1981) The Effects of Double-counting and Expensing on the Measured Returns to R&D. *Review of Economics and Statistics*, **63**(3), 454–458.

Scherer, F.M. (1984) *Innovation and Growth: Schumpeterian Perspectives*. Cambridge, Massachusetts and London: MIT Press.

---

[18] We gain insight about the uncertainty of future advances in IMT from the range of the respondents' responses about γ, α, and β and hence the range for predicted IMT-induced productivity growth.

[19] Although a number of the corporations surveyed are multinational, the survey is focused on the US; future surveys should broaden the sample.

Scott, J.T. (1993) *Purposive Diversification and Economic Performance*. Cambridge and New York: Cambridge University Press.
Solow, R.M. (1957) Technical Change and the Aggregate Production Function. *Review of Economics and Statistics*, **39**(3), 312–320.
Tassey, G. (1997) *The Economics of R&D Policy*. Westport, Connecticut: Quorum Books.
Tassey, G. (2005) The Disaggregated Technology Production Function: A New Model of University and Corporate Research. *Research Policy*, **34**(3), 287–303.
US Domestic Policy Council (2006) *American Competitiveness Initiative: Leading the World in Innovation*. Washington, DC: Office of Science and Technology Policy.

Research Evaluation **21** (2012) pp. 105–112
Advance Access published on 24 March 2012

doi:10.1093/reseval/rvs005

Public gains from entrepreneurial research: Inferences about the economic value of public support of the Small Business Innovation Research program

Stuart D. Allen, Stephen K. Layson and Albert N. Link*

*Department of Economics, University of North Carolina at Greensboro,
Greensboro, NC 27402, USA*
*Corresponding author. Email: anlink@uncg.edu.

This article presents a systematic analysis of the net economic benefits associated with the Small Business Innovation Research (SBIR) program. We offer a derivation of producer and consumer surplus to estimate economic benefits. Fundamental to the implementation of these models is a specific value of the elasticity of demand, but in its absence we estimate what its value would be when the benefit-to-cost ratio associated with public support of the SBIR program equals unity. We infer from these calculations, and from general knowledge about the ability of SBIR-funded firms to exploit their monopoly position, that the SBIR program likely generates positive net economic benefits to society.

*Keywords: entrepreneurship; innovation; technology; SBIR program; benefit-to-cost ratio;
program evaluation; producer surplus; consumer surplus.
JEL Codes: O31; O38; O22; H43.*

1. Introduction

The Small Business Reauthorization Act of 2000 mandated that the National Research Council (NRC) within the National Academies conduct 'an evaluation of the economic benefits achieved by the SBIR [Small Business Innovation Research] program' and make recommendations to the Congress for 'improvements to the program'. The NRC steering committee, charged with the design of the study, took several approaches to the evaluation. These approaches included multiple award-recipient firm surveys, Principle Investigator and firm interviews, and over 100 case studies.[1] Based on descriptive information from the surveys and insight from the case studies, the NRC made important recommendations to the Congress regarding, in particular, increases in the size of each award.[2]

Although the NRC and others used its survey data to provide well detailed descriptions of the program in their reports and testimony to the Congress, their analyses were narrow and did not include any evaluation metrics to quantify the broader-based net economic benefits from such use of public resources.[3] Rather, the NRC and others relied primarily on case studies and descriptive statistics from the survey data to illustrate the importance of the program to the award-recipient businesses and then only suggestively to the society as a whole.

This article presents the results of a systematic analysis of the net economic benefits associated with the SBIR program using the data collected by the NRC for the Department of Defense (DoD), the National Institutes of Health (NIH), the National Aeronautics and Space Administration (NASA), the Department of Energy (DOE), and the National Science Foundation (NSF).[4]

The remainder of this article is outlined as follows. In Section 2 we provide institutional background on the

SBIR program. In Section 3 we describe the NRC's data collection effort and the resulting database that is used herein. In Section 4 we offer a derivation of producer and consumer surplus to estimate economic benefits; estimation of producer and consumer surplus from these models is based on an elasticity of demand value for the technology-based products resulting from the SBIR-funded research. Absent specific information about the elasticity of demand, we calculate in Section 5 what its value would be when the benefit-to-cost ratio associated with public support of the SBIR program equals unity. And, we infer from these calculations, and from general knowledge about the ability of SBIR-funded firms to exploit their monopoly position, that the SBIR program generates net positive economic benefits to society. Section 6 concludes the article with a summary statement.

2. Background on the SBIR program

The SBIR program is a public/private partnership that provides grants to fund private-sector R&D projects. It aims to help fulfill the government's mission to enhance private-sector R&D and to complement the results of federal research.[5]

A prototype of the SBIR program began at NSF in 1977 (Tibbetts 1999), and because of the success of that program, the Congress passed the Small Business Innovation Development Act of 1982 (Public Law 97-219; hereafter, the 1982 Act). It required at that time all government departments and agencies with external research programs of >$100 million to establish their own SBIR program and to set aside funds equal to 0.20% of their external research budget. In 1983, that set aside totaled to $45 million.

Specifically, the 1982 Act stated that the objectives of the program are to: stimulate technological innovation, use small business to meet federal research and development needs, foster and encourage participation by minority and disadvantaged persons in technological innovation, and increase private sector commercialization of innovations derived from federal research and development.[6]

As part of the 1982 Act, awards were structured and defined by three phases (National Research Council 2004). Phase I awards were small, generally <$50,000 for a 6-month award period, and they were to assist businesses assess the feasibility of an idea's scientific and commercial potential in response to the funding agency's objectives. Phase II awards, capped at $500,000, and generally lasting 2 years, were to support the business develop further its proposed research that was to lead to a commercializable product, process, or service. Post-Phase II research occurs in what is called Phase III. No SBIR funds are awarded during Phase III; it defines the period during which third-party financing (e.g. from venture

capitalists) is obtained to move the Phase II developed technology into the marketplace.

As stated in the 1982 Act, to be eligible for an SBIR award, the small business must be: independently owned and operated; other than the dominant firm in the field in which they are proposing to carry out SBIR projects; organized and operated for profit; the employer of ≤500 employees, including employees of subsidiaries and affiliates; the primary source of employment for the project's principal investigator at the time of award and during the period when the research is conducted; and at least 51% owned by US citizens or lawfully admitted permanent resident aliens.

In 1986, the 1982 Act was extended through 1992 (Public Law 99-443). In 1992 the SBIR program was reauthorized until 2000 through the Small Business Research and Development Enactment Act (Public Law 102-564). Under the 1982 Act, the set aside had increased to 1.25%; the 1992 reauthorization raised that amount over time to 2.50% and re-emphasized the commercialization intent of SBIR-funded technologies. The reauthorization also increased Phase I awards to $100,000 and Phase II awards to $750,000, although it has not been uncommon for awards to exceed the $750,000 threshold. The 1992 reauthorization broadened the 1982 objectives to focus on women: 'to provide for enhanced outreach efforts to increase the participation of . . . small businesses that are 51 percent owned and controlled by women'.

The Small Business Reauthorization Act of 2000 (Public Law 106-554) extended the SBIR program until 30 September 2008 and kept the 2.50% set aside. It retained the 2.50% set aside but did not increase the amounts of Phase I and Phase II awards.

The Congress did not reauthorize the SBIR program by the legislated date of 30 September 2008, even given the NRC's report to Congress on the program's accomplishments and its recommendation to do so. Rather, the Congress has continually extended the program through a series of short-term reauthorizations. On 31 December 2011 the program was reauthorized until 30 September 2017 under the National Defense Reauthorization Act of 2012 (Public Law 112-81).

Currently 11 agencies participate in the SBIR program: DoD, NIH, NASA, DOE, NSF, the Environmental Protection Agency (EPA), and the Departments of Agriculture (USDA), Commerce (DoC), Education (ED), Transportation (DoT), and most recently, Homeland Security (DHS). In 2005 (the year of the NRC survey from which the data analyzed herein come), DoD maintained the largest program, awarding about 51% of total dollars and funding of about 57% of the total awards in that year. Five agencies—DoD, NIH, NASA, DOE, and NSF—account for nearly 97% of the program's expenditures, with NIH being the second most important, accounting for 30% of total dollars and 19% of awards in 2005 (Table 1).

Table 1. SBIR awards and dollars for FY2005 by agency

Agency	Phase I awards	Phase I dollars	Phase II awards	Phase II dollars	Total awards	Total dollars
DoD	2,344	$213,482,152	998	$729,285,508	3,342	$942,767,660
HHS[a]	732	$149,584,038	369	$412,504.975	1,101	$562,089,013
DOE	259	$25,757,637	101	$77,852,565	360	$103,610,202
NASA	290	$20,183,648	139	$83,014,853	429	$103,198,501
NSF	152	$15,054,750	132	$64,101,179	284	$79,155,929
USDA	91	$7,195,211	40	$11,738,536	131	$18,933,747
DHS	62	$6,158,240	13	$10,241,202	75	$16,399,442
ED	22	$1,646,603	14	$6,749,980	36	$8,396,583
DoC	34	$2,373,433	19	$5,469,846	53	$7,843,279
EPA	38	$2,652,216	14	$3,540,251	52	$6,192,467
DoT	7	$679,154	3	$1,765,468	10	$2,444,622
Total	4,031	$444,767,082	1,842	$1,406,264,363	5,873	$1,851,031,445

[a]NIH is under the Department of Health and Human Services (HHS).
Source: US Small Business Administration (2006).

Table 2. Population of SBIR Phase II projects 1992–2001 by agency

Agency	Completed Phase II projects	Percentage
DoD	5,650	50.38
NIH	2,497	22.27
NASA	1,488	13.27
NSF	771	6.88
DOE	808	7.21
Total	11,214	100.00

Table 3. Descriptive statistics on the National Research Council survey of Phase II awards by agency

Agency	Phase II sample size	Respondents	Response rate (%)	Random sample
DoD	3,055	920	30	891
NIH	1,678	496	30	495
NASA	779	181	23	177
NSF	457	162	35	161
DOE	439	157	36	154
Total	6,408	1,916		1,878

Not only is their variability in funding levels across agencies, as shown in Table 1, but also there are cross-agency differences in programmatic goals. The primary goal of DoD's SBIR program is to provide technologies that can be used as part of our nation's defense system, which is the mission of DoD. In contrast, NIH's primary mission for its SBIR program is the development of fundamental knowledge and its application for improving health. Pioneering the future of space exploration, scientific discovery, and aeronautical research is the mission of NASA and its SBIR program. The DOE's SBIR program supports technical knowledge related to the agency's program areas. Finally, NSF's SBIR program promotes science and the commercialization of science.[7]

3. The NRC database

The NRC conducted an extensive and balanced survey in 2005 based on a population of 11,214 projects completed from Phase II awards made between 1992 and 2001 by five agencies: DoD, NIH, NASA, DOE, and NSF. It was assumed as part of the NRC's sampling methodology

that Phase II awards made in 2001 would be completed by 2005.

The five agencies surveyed accounted for nearly 97% of the program's expenditures in 2005, as shown in Table 1. Table 2 shows the distribution of the population of 11,214 projects by the funding agency, and the percentage of each agency's Phase II projects that was surveyed. The total number of projects surveyed from the 11,214 population of projects was 6,408. The number and percentage of respondents from these 6,408 surveyed projects is shown in Table 3. The total number of responding projects was 1,916, and the average response rate across all five agencies was about 30%.[8]

Also shown in Table 3 is the total number of projects in the final random sample of completed Phase II projects by the agency. The NRC surveyed a number of non-randomly selected projects because they were projects that had realized significant commercialization and the NRC wanted to be able to describe to the Congress such success stories. The non-randomly selected projects are not considered herein.

Responses to project survey questions are used in the evaluation analysis below.[9] The first survey question

Table 4. Descriptive statistics on Phase II project costs and revenues ($1000) by agency for projects reporting data

Agency	Random sample	Projects reporting data	Phase II award amount		Phase II award amount ($2005)[a]		Sales through 2005		Licensing or outright sale of the business through 2005	
			Mean (SD)	Range	Mean (SD)	Range	Mean (SD)	Range	Mean (SD)	Range
DoD	891	383	744.20 (324.41)	(99.30–3750.0)	873.27 (378.91)	(112.02–4599.20)	2594.65 (12003.17)	(0–208848)	299.99 (1935.67)	(0–21600.0)
NIH	495	223	645.97 (215.02)	(14.83–1571.2)	758.11 (247.93)	(19.38–1810.79)	1666.40 (7610.13)	(0–100000.0)	1674.11 (9682.13)	(0–100000.0)
NASA	177	76	582.11 (48.27)	(439.3–731.57)	689.60 (49.07)	(574.0–855.53)	1342.96 (2709.75)	(0–15055.0)	9.84 (54.52)	(0–365.87)
NSF	161	74	377.20 (77.83)	(249.85–500.0)	436.51 (72.94)	(312.81–551.57)	871.83 (1156.47)	(0–6267.0)	3103.96 (23313.66)	(0–200000.0)
DOE	154	79	684.77 (103.2)	(387.29–900.0)	811.75 (112.87)	(441.26–992.83)	940.94 (1928.01)	(0–13541.63)	230.46 (1210.1)	(0–8800.0)

[a]Award amount adjusted by the GDP Implicit Price Deflator (2005 = 100).
Source: NRC surveys, by agency.

asked for the amount of Phase II funding awarded to support the project. The second survey question asked for total sales and licensing revenues to date (i.e. in 2005) from the Phase II technology. Table 4 provides descriptive statistics on these variables.[10] Also shown in the table are the award amounts in the current and $2005.

The amount of the Phase II award measures the public sector's investment into the private sector's generation of new technology, and thus it is the project cost in the benefit–cost analysis of the program. In the following section we present a framework for translating sales and licensing revenues into the value of producer and consumer surplus, the economics-based concepts related to the social benefits associated with Phase II funding considered herein.

4. Derivation of producer and consumer surplus

Griliches (1958) and Mansfield et al. (1977) are heralded as pioneering the so-called traditional approach to the evaluation of publicly funded research.[11] In their model, costs are measured in terms of public allocations in support of private research and benefits are measured in terms of the economic surplus that results through time. For existing businesses that receive publicly funded research support and that face a downward sloping demand curve, the resulting innovation lowers the marginal and average cost of producing a good sold in a competitive market generating an increase in consumer surplus.[12]

In contrast to the traditional model used by Griliches (1958) and Mansfield et al. (1977) which assumes that the firms receiving public funding sell their products in competitive markets, we assume that the firms receiving SBIR awards have temporary monopoly power. Figure 1 shows a monopolist, with constant marginal and average cost c and facing demand D, that sells its monopoly product or service in amount x^* at price p^*. In Fig. 1 the area defined by the triangle ABP* represents consumer surplus. Producer surplus is represented by the rectangle P*BEF.

The entrepreneurial businesses that receive Phase II SBIR awards are being funded to research a new technology and eventually either bring it to market or license it to others. Our model of producer and consumer surplus accounts for these two possibilities.

A business that brings a new technology to market enjoys monopoly power for some period of time. Assume constant long-run marginal and average cost equal to c. Profit, π, or producer surplus, PS, is:

$$PS = (p - c)x = \frac{(p - c)px}{p} \tag{1}$$

where p represents price and x represents output quantity.

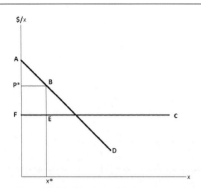

Figure 1. Graphical description of consumer surplus and producer surplus.

The profit-maximizing monopolist will price its output where the profit margin $\frac{(p*-c)}{p*} = \frac{1}{\varepsilon}$, for ε being the price elasticity of demand.[13] Thus Equation (1) simplifies to:

$$PS = \frac{1}{\varepsilon}p^*x^* \qquad (2)$$

where * denotes the profit maximizing price and output quantity.

Thus profit or producer surplus is total sales divided by the price elasticity of demand.[14] To illustrate Equation (2), if the price elasticity of demand is 2 then producer surplus is 50% of sales.[15]

To determine consumer surplus, CS, for the monopolist that brings a new technology to market, assume that demand is linear and is given by $p = a - bx$. In this case, CS is:

$$CS = \frac{1}{2}(a - p)x \qquad (3)$$

For profit maximization, set marginal revenue (MR) equal to marginal cost (c):

$$MR = a - 2bx = c \qquad (4)$$

Solving Equation (4) for profit maximizing price and output quantity yields $x^* = \frac{a-c}{2b}$ and $p^* = \frac{a+c}{2}$. Substituting these results into Equation (3) yields $CS = \frac{1}{2}\pi$. Given Equation (2), it follows that:

$$CS = \frac{1}{2\varepsilon}p^*x^* \qquad (5)$$

To illustrate Equation (5), if the price elasticity of demand is 2, then CS is 25% of sales.[16,17]

For the case of a business that licenses its technology to others or is sold outright, producer surplus equals licensing sales or the selling price of the business [see Equation (1)

for $c = 0$] and consumer surplus equals zero because no product is being marketed.

5. Calculated value of the elasticity of demand when benefit-to-cost ratio equals unity

The calculation of economic benefits in terms of producer and consumer surplus requires a complete sales and licensing history of each business beginning at the time that it received the Phase II award. That information is not known; all that is known from the NRC database is the sales and licensing history of each business from the time that it received its research award to 2005 (the year of the NRC survey).

Using sales and licensing revenue as of 2005 to approximate producer and consumer surplus clearly understates the economic value of benefits. Some businesses will have generated $0 in sales and licensing revenues from the funded project by 2005, but might begin to generate sales and licensing revenues in the future. Similarly, those businesses that have generated such revenue might continue to do so beyond 2005. And, no information is available on the producer or consumer surplus generated by those companies that purchase a funded-business's technology or that license it.[18]

The social costs associated with producer and consumer surplus from the funded Phase II research projects have at least three components, two of which represent public support to those businesses that received Phase II awards and the third represents the business's own resources devoted to the Phase II project. The first component is the amount of the Phase II award. The second component is the amount of the Phase I award that each business that received Phase II funding was previously awarded. The third component is the amount of own R&D that the business devoted, as complementary resources, to the funded Phase II project.

The amount of the Phase II award is reported in the NRC database; each award amount was referenced to 2005 using the GDP Implicit Price Deflator (2005 = 100).[19] The NRC database does not contain information about the amount of the Phase I award that each business received; however, each business did receive a Phase I award.[20] The maximum amount for a Phase I award, over the time period covered by the NRC data, is $100,000.[21] Finally, no information is available on the amount of own R&D that the business allocated to the Phase II research project or to marketing, successfully or unsuccessfully, the resulting technology. However, the five-agency case studies conducted by the NRC to complement the construction of its database (National Research Council 2008), as well as earlier case studies associated with DoD's SBIR program, suggest that this amount is

Table 5. Calculated values of the elasticity of demand when the benefit-to-cost ratios for Phase II SBIR awards equals unity by agency

Agency	n	Calculated elasticity
DoD	891	3.151
NIH	495	>50
NASA	177	1.290
NSF	161	>50
DOE	154	1.518

minimal, and more likely zero (Link 2000; Link and Scott 2000; Scott 2000).

We iterate over alternative values of the elasticity of demand to determine that value for which the benefit-to-cost ratio equals unity. Benefits are measured in terms of producer and consumer surplus as defined by Equations (2) and (5), respectively.[22] Recall, too, that producer surplus equals licensing sales or the selling price of the business for such businesses, and consumer surplus equals zero for such businesses because no product is being marketed. Costs are measured as the sum of the Phase I and Phase II award to each project regardless if the project has any measurable producer or consumer surplus. Phase I awards are valued at $100,000 for each project, and Phase II awards are valued as the amount of the award ($2005).

To illustrate, as shown in Table 4, 383 of 891 DoD-funded projects reported sales and licensing information on the NRC survey. It is assumed that the other 508 projects had zero sales or licensing revenues, but all 891 projects were considered in the calculation below. In other words, as shown in Table 5, for an elasticity of demand value of 3.151, the benefit-to-cost ratio averaged over 891 projects equals unity. That calculation is based on 891 projects, 508 of which have a benefit-to-cost ratio of zero and 383 of which have a benefit-to-cost ratio equal to $((PS + CS)/(\$100,000 + \$Phase\ II\ award))$.

Regarding the values reported in Table 5,[23] if the actual elasticity of demand for the new technology-based products sold and licensed by DoD-funded businesses is less elastic than 3.151, then the calculated benefit-to-cost ratio will be greater than unity. Unfortunately, we have no independent estimates of the elasticity of demand for new technology-based products sold by a monopolist. Certainly, the businesses selling or licensing such products will enjoy monopoly power for some period of time, and then it will dwindle as others slowly enter the market.[24] But, the time frame for the data analyzed in this study is relatively short (1992–2001), thus it might not be unreasonable to conclude that the actual elasticity of demand for DoD-funded projects' products is closer to 1.00 than to 3.151.

For NASA and DOE, a similar story holds. If the actual elasticity of demand for the new technology-based products sold and licensed by the respective funded businesses is less elastic than 1.290 and 1.518, respectively, then the calculated benefit-to-cost ratios will exceed unity.

NIH and NSF are interesting cases. As shown in Table 4, licensing revenues from NIH-funded projects are, on average, equal to sales revenues; and, licensing revenues from NSF-funded projects are, on average, ~3.5 times as great as sales revenue. Thus, the calculation of producer and consumer surplus for these projects are less sensitive—far less sensitive in the case of NSF project— to alternative values of the elasticity of demand. It is not unreasonable to conclude, based on elasticity of demand values that exceed 50, that the benefit-to-cost ratio for both NIH- and NSF-funded projects exceeds unity.

6. Concluding statement

The National Research Council (2008) points out:

> Comparisons between SBIR programs...must be regarded with considerable caution....[D]iffering agency missions have shaped the agency SBIR programs, focusing them on different objectives and on different mechanisms and approaches. Agencies whose mission is to develop technologies for internal agency use via procurement—notably the Department of Defense (DoD) and the National Aeronautics and Space Administration (NASA)—have a quite different orientation from agencies that do not procure technology and are instead focused on developing technologies for use outside the agency.

Thus, caution should be exercised if making a judgment about the net economic value of one agency's SBIR program with another.

Although one cannot say with certainty that on average the net economic value of the SBIR program is positive, the evidence presented here is suggestive of that fact.

To generalize about the method adopted in this study of the SBIR program in the five largest participating agencies, it is directly applicable to an evaluation of other publicly funded programs. While in the case of SBIR an evaluation was mandated by the Congress, there is a broader mandate in place. The 103rd Congress stated in the Government Performance and Results Act (GPRA) of 1993 (Public Law 103-62) that federal agencies should be accountable for program results. More recently, it was stated in a memorandum from the then Director of the Office of Management and Budget (OMB) Peter Orszag that 'rigorous independent program evaluation can be a key resource in determining whether government program are achieving their intended outcomes'. Some agencies, such as DOE and the National Institute of Standards and Technology (NIST) have taken bold steps in that direction. Perhaps the readily implemented method in this article will become a methodological foundation for other agencies to do the same.[25]

Notes

1. See National Research Council (2008) for an overview of these studies, and see the accompanying agency reports for additional details.
2. See Bearse and Link (2010) for an initial analysis of the economic implications associated with increasing the amount of each award.
3. See the testimonies of Audretsch (2011), Link (2011), Siegel (2011), and Wessner (2011).
4. We thank Dr Charles Wessner of the NRC for making these data available to us for this study.
5. For a discussion and a model of the economic role of the SBIR program, see Link and Link (2009) and Link and Scott (2009, 2010, 2012a).
6. For an analysis of the probability that a SBIR project's technology is commercialized, see Link and Ruhm (2009) and Link and Scott (2009, 2010).
7. A more detailed description of SBIR program goals is in National Research Council (2008) and Link and Scott (2012a).
8. Others, for example, Link and Ruhm (2009) and Link and Scott (2009, 2010, 2012a), have estimated sophisticated econometric models to test for selection bias and they have accepted the null hypothesis of no bias. This conclusion was also reached independently using descriptive analysis by the NRC (National Research Council 2008).
9. The NRC database contains project information. In only a few instances in the data considered did a given business receive two SBIR project awards and those projects were in distinctively different technology areas. Thus, below we refer to the project data describing business behavior because our model of economic surpluses relates to business behavior.
10. Typical descriptive statistics are shown in Table 4. For additional descriptive statistics, see National Research Council (2008) and Link and Scott (2012a).
11. The Griliches/Mansfield approach follows from Schultz's (1953) agriculture illustration. For a review of applications of the use of producer and consumer surplus to evaluation see, for example, Bengston (1985), Georghiou and Roessner (2000), Feller and Nelson (1999), Banzhaf (2009), and David et al. (2009). See Link and Scott (2005) for an application of estimating the producer and consumer surplus from survey data. See also the papers in Link and Scott (2011b).
12. See Link and Scott (2011a) for a critique of the Griliches/Mansfield approach.
13. See Tirole (1988).
14. A unitary price elasticity of demand is not reasonable in this case; it assumes that marginal cost equals 0.
15. These results hold without any assumption about the shape of the demand curve. Unfortunately, we do not have exact measures from the NRC database or from the case studies conducted by the NRC on the price elasticity of demand. And, there are no comparable studies from which an approximation can be gleaned.
16. If demand is convex, consumer surplus will be $>25\%$ of sales; if demand is concave, consumer surplus will $<25\%$ of sales.
17. We do not consider the case that this measure of consumer surplus is not a measure of new consumer surplus because it is a cannibalization of previous existing surplus (Scherer 1979). Our reasoning is that the funded projects are often the small, entrepreneurial company's first effort in researching the subsequently commercialized technology.
18. In addition, the technologies emanating from the funded projects might be complementary to other products produced by the business or by those companies that purchase/license the technology. To the extent that this is the case, the SBIR-funded research will have leveraged gains in producer and consumer surplus from existing products about which we have no information.
19. It may be reasonable to expect that respondents to the NRC survey reported cumulative sales in nominal rather than in $2005. If so, this referencing of costs to 2005 understates the true benefit-to-cost ratios calculated below.
20. Of those businesses that successfully complete a Phase I project, a percentage, which varied by year and by agency, is invited to apply for a Phase II award.
21. It is not uncommon in the policy evaluation literature to treat such pre-award costs as sunk costs. See, for example, Gallaher et al. (2012) and Link and Scott (2011a, 2012b).
22. To the extent that a respondent had projects with positive sales but did not choose to report it on the NRC survey, our final ratios are biased downward.
23. As noted above, Link and Scott (2009, 2010, 2012a) have shown that, in general, selection bias is not present when analyzing the probability that a funded project commercializes its technology. Because commercialization is related to sales and licensing revenues, we view these calculations as being unbiased.
24. Anecdotally, Reynolds International Pen Corporation sold its first ballpoint pens in 1945 for between $12.00 and $20.00; its per-pen production cost was 80 cents. By 1948, its market share fell to close to zero as competitors entered the market (Whiteside 1951).
25. See Ruegg and Jordan (2011) and Link and Scott (2012b).

References

Audretsch, D. B. (2011) 'Testimony Before the House of Representatives Committee on Small Business', <http://smbiz.house.gov/UploadedFiles/David_Audretsch_SBIR_Testimony.pdf> accessed 14 March 2012.

Banzhaf, H. S. (2009) 'Objective or Multi-Objective? Two Historically Competing Visions for Benefit-Cost Analysis', *Land Economics*, 85: 3–23.

Bearse, P. M. and Link, A. N. (2010) 'Economic Implications of Raising the Threshold Funding Limits on SBIR Awards', *Science and Public Policy*, 37: 731–5.

Bengston, D. N. (1985) 'Economic Evaluation of Agricultural Research: An Assessment', *Evaluation Review*, 9: 243–62.

David, P. A., Mowery, D. and Steinmueller, W. E. (2009) 'Analysing the Economic Payoffs from Basic Research', *Economics of Innovation and New Technology*, 2: 73–90.

Feller, I. and Nelson, J. P. (1999) 'The Microeconomics of Manufacturing Modernization Programs', *Research Policy*, 28: 807–18.

Gallaher, M. P., Link, A. N. and O'Connor, A. (2012) *Public Investments in Energy Technology*. London: Edward Elgar.

Georghiou, L. and Roessner, D. (2000) 'Evaluating Technology Programs: Tools and Methods', *Research Policy*, 29: 657–78.

Griliches, Z. (1958) 'Research Costs and Social Returns: Hybrid Corn and Related Innovations', *Journal of Political Economy*, 66: 419–31.

Link, A. N. (2000) 'An Assessment of the Small Business Innovation Research Fast Track Program in Southeastern States'. In: Wessner, C. (ed.) *The Small Business Innovation Research Program: An Assessment of Fast Track*, pp. 184–210. Washington, DC: National Academy of Sciences.

——. (2011) 'Testimony Before the House of Representatives Committee on Small Business', <http://smbiz.house.gov/UploadedFiles/Al_Link_SBIR_Testimony_for_4.7.11.pdf> accessed 12 March 2012.

Link, A. N. and Link, J. R. (2009) *Government as Entrepreneur*. New York: Oxford University Press.

Link, A. N. and Ruhm, C. J. (2009) 'Bringing Science to Market: Commercializing from NIH SBIR Awards', *Economics of Innovation and New Technology*, 18: 381–402.

Link, A. N. and Scott, J. T. (2000) 'Estimates of the Social Returns to SBIR-Sponsored Projects'. In: Wessner, C. (ed.) *The Small Business Innovation Research Program: An Assessment of Fast Track*, pp. 275–90. Washington, DC: National Academy of Sciences.

——. (2005) 'Evaluating Public Sector R&D Programs: The Advanced Technology Program's Investment in Wavelength References for Optical Fiber Communications', *Journal of Technology Transfer*, 30: 241–51.

——. (2009) 'Private Investor Participation and Commercialization Rates for Government-sponsored Research and Development: Would a Prediction Market Improve the Performance of the SBIR Programme?', *Economica*, 76: 264–81.

——. (2010) 'Government as Entrepreneur: Evaluating the Commercialization Success of SBIR Projects', *Research Policy*, 39: 589–601.

——. (2011a) *Public Goods, Public Gains: Calculating the Social Benefits of Public R&D*. London: Oxford University Press.

——. (2011b) *The Economics of Evaluation in Public Programs*. London: Edward Elgar.

——. (2012a) *Employment Growth from Public Support of Innovation in Small Firms*. Kalamazoo, MI: W.E. Upjohn Institute for Employment Research.

——. (2012b) *The Theory and Practice of Public-Sector R&D Economic Impact Analysis*. Gaithersburg, MD: the National Institute of Standards and Technology.

Mansfield, E. et al. (1977) 'Social and Private Rates of Return from Industrial Innovations', *Quarterly Journal of Economics*, 91: 221–40.

National Research Council. Wessner, C., ed., (2004) *SBIR: Program Diversity and Assessment Challenges*. Washington, DC: National Academy Press.

——. Wessner, C., ed., (2008) *An Assessment of the SBIR Program*. Washington, DC: National Academies Press.

Ruegg, R. and Jordan, G. B. (2011) 'Guide for Conducting Benefit-Cost Evaluation of Realized Impacts of Public R&D Programs'. U.S. Department of Energy report.

Scherer, F. M. (1979) 'The Welfare Economics of Product Variety: An Application to the Ready-to- Eat Cereals Industry', *Journal of Industrial Economics*, 28: 113–34.

Schultz, T. W. (1953) *The Economic Organization of Agriculture*. New York: McGraw-Hill.

Scott, J. T. (2000) 'An Assessment of the Small Business Innovation Research Program in New England: Fast Track Compared with Non-Fast Track Projects'. In: Wessner, C. (ed.) *The Small Business Innovation Research Program: An Assessment of Fast Track*, pp. 104–40. Washington, DC: National Academy of Sciences.

Siegel, D. S. (2011) 'Testimony before the House of Representatives Committee on Science and Technology', <http://science.house.gov/sites/republicans.science.house.gov/files/documents/hearings/Siegel%20Final%20SBIR%20testimony.pdf> accessed 14 March 2012.

Tibbetts, R. (1999) 'The Small Business Innovation Research Program and NSF SBIR Commercialization Results' Mimeograph.

Tirole, J. (1988) *The Theory of Industrial Organization*. Cambridge: MIT Press.

U.S. Small Business Administration. (2006), <http://tech-net.sba.gov/>.

Wessner, C. W. (2011) 'Testimony Before the Senate Committee on Small Business and Entrepreneurship', <http://www7.nationalacademies.org/ocga/testimonySmall_Business_Innovation_Research_Program.asp> accessed 14 March 2012.

Whiteside, T. (1951) 'Where Are They Now?' *New Yorker*, 17 Feb. 1951: 39–58.

[13]

ELSEVIER

Research Policy 31 (2002) 145–158

www.elsevier.com/locate/econbase

Public/private technology partnerships: evaluating SBIR-supported research [☆]

David B. Audretsch [a], Albert N. Link [b,*], John T. Scott [c]

[a] *Institute for Development Strategies, Indiana University, SPEA, Suite 201, Bloomington, IN 47405, USA*
[b] *Department of Economics, University of North Carolina at Greensboro, Greensboro, NC 27412, USA*
[c] *Department of Economics, Dartmouth College, Hanover, NH 03755, USA*

Received 21 October 2000; received in revised form 1 December 2000; accepted 12 December 2000

Abstract

This paper evaluates public support of private-sector research and development (R&D) through the Department of Defense's (DoD's), Small Business Innovation Research (SBIR) Program. Based on alternative evaluation methods applicable to survey data and case studies, we conclude that there is ample evidence that the DoD's SBIR Program is stimulating R&D as well as efforts to commercialize that would not otherwise have taken place. Further, the evidence shows the SBIR R&D does lead to commercialization, and the net social benefits associated with the program's sponsored research are substantial. © 2002 Elsevier Science B.V. All rights reserved.

Keywords: Small business; Innovation; Public/private partnership; R&D; Program evaluation

1. Introduction

As greater attention is paid to public support of private-sector research and development (R&D) by participants in the innovation process, it becomes imperative for policy makers to offer an economic rationale for their support of public/private technology partnerships as well as to formulate and demonstrate means for evaluating such relationships. While scholars and policy makers have long debated the economic role of government in the innovation process and the importance of market failure as an element of that rationale, Baron (1998) has offered a focused rationale for the Small Business Innovation Research (SBIR) Program: "[T]he rational for SBIR is the same as the general argument for government R&D—positive externalities (meaning) social benefits exceeding private ones."

When market failure is the broad justification for public support of R&D performed in the private sector, the situation is not only one where social benefits exceed private benefits. As a consequence of the divergence of social benefits and costs there must be, absent support from the government, underinvestment in R&D from society's perspective. The fact that social benefits exceed private benefits is not sufficient to establish underinvestment. [1] Furthermore,

---

[☆] An earlier version of this paper was presented at the January 2000 American Economic Association meetings in the session "Government as Venture Capitalist: Evaluating the SBIR Program." We appreciate the comments and suggestions from participants at that session as well as those from two anonymous referees.
* Corresponding author.
E-mail addresses: daudrets@indiana.edu (D.B. Audretsch), al_link@uncg.edu (A.N. Link), john.t.scott@dartmouth.edu (J.T. Scott).

[1] See Baldwin and Scott (1987).

if government wants to justify public support with an argument based on market failure, policy makers must establish that government failure would not prevent improving R&D performance with a proposed policy. [2]

The government has at its disposal mechanisms to address market failure and hence, to overcome private-sector underinvestment in R&D. [3] These mechanisms include creating and maintaining an economic environment conducive for innovation. Examples of such mechanisms include the patent system and the passage of the National Cooperative Research Act of 1984 to encourage research joint ventures; tax incentives to stimulate innovative investments through, for example, the 1981 R&E tax credit and its periodic renewals; and direct public/private technology partnerships to subsidize R&D, with the SBIR Program being one of several such programs. [4]

In addition to its important role in surmounting market failure, government should also be held accountable for its legislated policies. As Link and Scott (1998) point out, the concept of public accountability in the US traces at least to the early 1920s. But, the passage of the Government Performance and Results Act (GPRA) of 1993 emphasized the social importance of performance accountability, especially in the areas of science and technology, and has brought accountability back to center stage.

Our focus in this paper is on the SBIR Program. We do not debate the appropriateness of the government's support of that program but take that as a historical given and turn directly to evaluating the program's results. [5] In Section 2, we briefly describe the SBIR Program, with particular emphasis on the Department of Defense's (DoD's) SBIR Program. In Section 3, we outline our evaluation methodology and present our findings with an emphasis on the social returns associated with SBIR-funded research. Concluding remarks are presented in Section 4.

2. An overview of the SBIR Program

The SBIR Program began at the National Science Foundation in 1977. [6] At that time, the goal of the program was to encourage small businesses— considered by many to be engines of innovation in the US economy—to participate in NSF-sponsored research, especially research that had commercial potential. Because of the early success of the program at NSF, Congress passed the Small Business Innovation Development Act of 1982. The 1982 Act required all government departments and agencies with external research programs of greater than US$ 100 billion to establish their own SBIR Program and to set aside funds equal to 0.2% of their external research budget. [7]

The 1982 Act states the following objectives of the program:

1. To stimulate technological innovation.
2. To use small business to meet Federal research and development needs.
3. To foster and encourage participation by minority and disadvantaged persons in technological innovation.
4. To increase private sector commercialization of innovations derived from federal research and development.

In 1987, the funding percentage increased to 1.25%. The Act was later reauthorized by the Small Business Innovation Research Program Reauthorization Act of 1992, and the funding percentage increased to 1.5%. Since 1997, agencies have set aside 2.5% of their external research budgets for SBIR.

---

[2] While closure on the economic rationale for government policies supporting innovation may be at hand, Klette et al. (2000) explain that documenting both market failure and successful government programs to overcome it is quite difficult (and when government programs are not successful in overcoming market failure there is government failure). Kealey (1997) even challenges the conventional wisdom that government support for science is useful.

[3] Martin and Scott (2000) associate various policy mechanisms with sector-specific market failures that the mechanisms address.

[4] See Link (1999) for a review of public/private partnerships in the United States.

[5] See Lerner (1999) for a discussion of the appropriateness of the government as a venture capitalist through SBIR Programs. See also Lerner and Kegler (2000) for a review of the literature related to SBIR Programs.

[6] Tibbetts (1999) provides a history of the development of this program.

[7] As a set aside program, the SBIR Program redirects existing research funds rather than appropriating new research funds.

D.B. Audretsch et al./Research Policy 31 (2002) 145–158   147

Justification for the reauthorization, as stated in the 1992 Act, was that the program:

> ... has effectively stimulated the commercialization of technology development through federal research and development, benefiting both the public and private sectors of the Nation.

Clearly, given the complete list of stated objectives of the program dating from the 1982 Act, its rationale would be broader than the objective of correcting the market failure of underinvestment in R&D. In addition to addressing underinvestment in R&D, the SBIR Program has as well the goal of promoting diversity per se in the population of firms doing R&D.[8] Here, we focus on the market failure, underinvestment justification for the SBIR Program.

The DoD is the largest federal agency participating in the SBIR Program. Administratively located in the Office of Small and Disadvantaged Business Utilization within the Office of the Secretary of Defense, the SBIR Program funds projects of interest to the Army, Navy, Air Force, Defense Advanced Research Project Agency (DARPA), the Ballistic Missile Defense Office, the Defense Special Weapons Agency, the US Special Operations Command, as well as general DoD research and development.[9]

The DoD's SBIR Program solicits proposals from eligible small businesses twice a year, and the awards are of three types.[10] Phase I awards are relatively small, generally less than US$ 100,000. The purpose of these awards is to help firms assess the feasibility of the research they propose to undertake for the agency in response to the agency's objectives. Phase II awards are larger, averaging about US$ 750,000. These awards are for the firm to undertake and complete its proposed research, ideally leading to a commercializable product or process. So-called Phase III awards do not come from DoD, but rather from the

Table 1
DoD SBIR budgets and awards, by fiscal year[a]

Fiscal year	Budget (US$ (M))	Phase I awards	Phase II awards
1983	16.70	281	0
1984	42.79	368	115
1985	79.00	513	282
1986	153.00	1031	254
1987	202.00	1264	401
1988	221.80	1056	334
1989	234.40	1021	362
1990	239.26	1140	415
1991	233.53	963	318
1992	241.84	1063	434
1993	384.82	1285	535
1994	276.19	1371	417
1995	445.25	1263	575
1996	453.46	1372	613
1997	543.02	1526	639
1998	553.44	1286	674
1999	541.31	1393	569

[a] Source: http://www.sbirsttr.com/sbirmisc/annrpt.html.

private sector to the researching company to pursue commercialization. Table 1 provides a funding history of DoD's SBIR Program.

3. A methodology for evaluating the SBIR Program

Our methodology for evaluating DoD's SBIR Program, which can be applied to other programs, includes three elements:

1. A broad-based statistical analysis of SBIR recipients.
2. A case-based investigation of recipients regarding the impacts associated with SBIR awards.
3. A case-based investigation of the social rate of return from SBIR-funded research.

Data limitations associated with the SBIR Program, as well as with most public/private partnerships, and the multi-faceted nature of program evaluation per se, led us to adopt a broad-based evaluation methodology. Although survey-based information on SBIR recipients is used to conduct what some may view as a traditional evaluation exercise (Section 3.1), we are reluctant to draw program evaluation conclusions

---

[8] Scott (2000b) shows that the private sector is much less likely to provide funding to DoD SBIR-funded projects that are in certain technology areas, in certain geographic regions, or minority-owned. Such projects may well address underinvestment, but they could also promote diversity as an independent goal in itself.

[9] For an overview of the program, see http://www.acq.osd.mil/sadbu/sbir/overview.html.

[10] An eligible independently owned (at least 51% owned by US citizens) and operated company must be for-profit with 500 or fewer employees.

from only that analysis since the respondent sample is limited in size and since there is a limited literature to which these econometric findings could be compared. [11] We have relied on case studies (Sections 3.2 and 3.3) to complement our statistical analysis and to facilitate asking broader evaluation questions. Of course, case studies are not without their limitations including representativeness issues and possible interview biases. However, as a whole, our approaches are complementary and our findings are robust, both of which are important elements of a systematic evaluation effort. We conclude that DoD's SBIR Program is encouraging commercialization from research that would not have been undertaken without SBIR support; and, moreover, it is overcoming reasons for market failure that cause the private sector to underinvest in R&D.

3.1. Innovation and commercialization efforts of SBIR awardees

As noted above, two of the legislated goals of the SBIR Program are "to stimulate technological innovation" and "to increase private sector commercialization of innovations derived from federal research and development." As a first step toward an evaluation of the DoD's SBIR Program, we sought to understand the extent to which innovation and commercialization have been achieved among SBIR awardees. This background analysis in and of itself does not constitute an evaluation of the SBIR Program, but rather it provides some initial insight into the magnitude of the commercialization that occurs, and the characteristics of companies that are commercializing SBIR-funded products.

We rely on data collected by the National Academy of Sciences (NAS) for a representative sample of DoD SBIR awardees. [12] The Academy's mail survey went to a sample of 379 SBIR companies that received a Phase II award, since 1992. A total of 232 surveys were returned partially or totally completed. The 112 completed surveys with all of the information needed for our analysis are analyzed here.

Since, the purpose of this background analysis was to gain a better understanding of the commercial-

ization activity that has occurred, we considered a model to explain cross-company differences in actual sales realized to date (the survey was administered in early 1999) from the technology developed during the DoD-funded Phase II project (ActSales). [13] Thus, our model is

$$\text{ActSales}_i = f(\boldsymbol{X}_i) \tag{1}$$

where the subscript i indexes each awardee company and the vector $\boldsymbol{X}_i$ contains company-specific characteristics as described in Table 2. The dependent variable in Eq. (1), ActSales, is the actual sales realized to date from the technology developed during the Phase II project, measured in dollars. Although the mean of ActSales is US$ 175,021, that reflects the fact that 78 of the 112 projects reported no sales. For the 34 projects reporting sales, the mean of ActSales is US$ 576,539.

One clear implication of these survey data is that SBIR awardees do commercialize products and services based on their SBIR-sponsored research. That general finding does show the two stated purposes of the SBIR Program noted above—stimulation of socially desirable R&D and innovation that would not occur without the SBIR Program and commercialization of the R&D results—are met. We turn now with an econometric model to details of the commercialization.

Least-squares analysis is not appropriate for estimating Eq. (1) since the dependent variable is truncated at zero. [14] Least-squared results do not explicitly use the information about threshold effects on sales, and thus, such estimation would predict negative sales for some observations. We use the tobit model to estimate Eq. (1); the tobit model can be interpreted as predicting a measure of the value of sales from the SBIR project. If the predicted value is positive, then the company commercializes a product or service and then has sales; otherwise, sales

---

[11] See Lerner and Kegler (2000) for a review of this literature.
[12] These data are described in Cahill (2000).

[13] See Audretsch et al. (2000a) for a preliminary analysis of *expected* sales.
[14] However, in the present case, the results reported regarding the signs and significance of the explanatory variables and the general conclusions about commercialization do obtain in the corresponding least-squares regressions. The least-squares results were presented in the earlier version of this paper that was presented at the American Economic Association's meetings, and they are available on request from the authors.

D.B. Audretsch et al. / Research Policy 31 (2002) 145–158

149

Table 2
Characteristic variables in Eq. (1) ($n = 112$)

Variables	Definition	Mean	Range	S.D.
AgeBus	Age of the company measured in years	11.13 years	1–36	7.417
ExpFounder	Equals to one, if the most recent employment of the company founder(s) was in another private company as opposed to a university or government agency, and zero otherwise	0.786	0/1	0.412
Revenues	Company revenues were reported in ranges: less than US$ 100,000; US$ 100,000–499,999; US$ 500,000–999,999; US$ 1,000,000–4,999,999; US$ 5,000,000–19,999,999; and over US$ 20,000,000. The midpoint of each range was used with US$ 50,000 defining the midpoint of the lower bound and US$ 25,000,000 defining the midpoint of the upper bound	US$ 5,547,321	US$ 50,000–25,000,000	7162364
PhaseII	Number of previous Phase II awards	6.01 awards	0–81	12.384
Complete	Equals to one, if the current Phase II award is completed, and zero otherwise	0.366	0/1	0.484
Market	Equals to one, if the company has underway or has completed a marketing plan, and zero otherwise	0.589	0/1	0.494
Active	Number of years since the awarding of the most recent Phase II award	2.82 years	1–6	1.195
Electronics	Equals to one, if the relevant technology area of the award is electronics, and zero otherwise	0.500	0/1	0.502
Computer	Equals to one, if the relevant technology area of the award is computer, information processing, and analysis, and zero otherwise	0.214	0/1	0.412
Materials	Equals to one, if the relevant technology area of the award is materials, and zero otherwise	0.071	0/1	0.259
Mechanical	Equals to one, if the relevant technology area of the award is mechanical performance of vehicles, weapons, and facilities, and zero otherwise	0.045	0/1	0.207
Energy	Equals to one, if the relevant technology area of the award is energy conservation and use, and zero otherwise	0.098	0/1	0.299
Environment	Equals to one, if the relevant technology area of the award is environment and natural resources, and zero otherwise	0.045	0/1	0.207
LifeScience	Equals to one, if the relevant technology area of the award is life sciences, and zero otherwise	0.027	0/1	0.162
FastTrack	Equals to one, if the Phase II award was a Fast Track award, meaning that outside private-sector funding was committed to the project before the SBIR award was made, and zero otherwise	0.161	0/1	0.369
ProbResponse	Probability of response to the original NAS survey (the Probit model predicting probability of response used variables that were available for 109 of the 112 observations)	0.659	0.271–0.998	0.175

D.B. Audretsch et al. / Research Policy 31 (2002) 145–158

Table 3
Estimated tobit results from Eq. (1) (asymptotic *t*-statistics in parentheses)

Variable	Estimated coefficient	Estimated coefficient
Intercept	−2310466 (−3.161)***	−1406461 (−1.292)
AgeBus	−13045.5 (−0.457)	−11542.7 (−0.419)
ExpFounder	−43146.1 (−0.127)	11598.1 (0.034)
Revenues	0.0532968 (2.250)**	0.0432694 (1.760)*
Phase II	−7401.9 (−0.521)	−6718.9 (−0.476)
Complete	707243.6 (2.117)**	536615.9 (1.583)
Market	1147888 (3.082)***	1171060 (3.213)***
Active	62991.5 (0.414)	29066.1 (0.178)
Computer	654036.6 (1.801)*	597507.1 (1.660)*
Materials	849108.7 (1.773)*	899354.4 (1.884)*
Energy	379947.9 (0.769)	254938.4 (0.519)
Environment	919731.2 (1.710)*	821494.6 (1.555)
LifeScience	124461.1 (0.165)	20594.2 (0.028)
FastTrack	−82285.4 (−0.213)	2868.0 (0.007)
ProbResponse	–	−1078063 (−1.134)
Log likelihood	−540.98	−539.41
χ^2	41.95 (13)***	43.15 (14)***
n d.f.	112	109

* Significant at the 0.10 level.
** Significant at the 0.05 level.
*** Significant at the 0.01 level.

are zero. The results for the tobit estimations are in Table 3.[15]

The tobit results in column (2) of Table 3 lead us to conclude that companies are indeed commercializing products from their SBIR projects. Those that have done so to date are the larger companies in the computer technology area, materials technology area, and environmental technology area that have both completed their Phase II research as well as have formulated a marketing plan.[16] The specifica-

tion reported in column (3) includes an additional explanatory variable, ProbResponse. If the probability of responding to the NAS survey is associated with actual sales (ActSales), and if that response effect in the error term is correlated with the variables included in *X*, the estimates in column (2) of Table 3 could be biased, hence, the inclusion of the variable ProbResponse.[17]

Using the tobit models in Table 3, we estimated for each project the expected value of sales conditional on the tobit index function being greater than zero (and hence, conditional on the realized sales being greater than zero). Formally, we estimate the conditional mean of the tobit index function in the positive part of its distribution for each observation. The average of these conditional means is US\$ 603,231

---

[15] The intercept reflects an effect for electronics and mechanical technologies. There are just five firms in the mechanical technology area, and a dummy variable for that technology area is a perfect predictor for the occurrence of US\$ 0 of sales. However, our a priori knowledge of projects in that area tells us that the probability of sales is not zero; rather, with just five observations, it was happenstance that none of those projects had actual sales. We have included these five cases, along with the 56 firms in the electronics technology area, 44 of which have US\$ 0 in actual sales, in the intercept term. In alternative tobit estimations (available upon request from Link or Scott), we deleted these mechanical technology cases from the sample, and the qualitative findings (signs and significance and approximate magnitudes) are unchanged.

[16] As shown in Audretsch et al. (2000a), Fast Track projects have higher *expected* sales, other things held equal in an OLS estimation, but those projects did not begin until 1996, and therefore, by 1999

they had realized less actual sales than the older projects, although the effect is not significant.

[17] There are just 109 observations available for the specification including ProbResponse, because three of the 112 observations did not have all of the variables used in the probit model of response. We also calculated a response hazard rate but its inclusion in Eq. (1) in place of ProbResponse gives results similar to those reported in column (3) of Table 3 (results are not reported here but are available upon request from Link or Scott).

D.B. Audretsch et al./Research Policy 31 (2002) 145–158   151

for the specification without the control for response bias and US$ 598,698 for the specification with the control. [18] Estimating the expected sales for each observation given X_i (that is, the probability weighted sum of the outcome of US$ 0 of sales as well as the positive outcomes), we find on average for all of the observations the expected sales are US$ 217,267 for the specification without control for response bias and US$ 223,244 for the specification with the control. [19]

These findings, along with case-based information that in the absence of SBIR support the SBIR firms would not have pursued Phase II research or would have pursued it on a very limited scale, lend support for our preliminary conclusion that the program is meeting two of its stated goals. [20] We reach these conclusions based on our interpretation of the statistically significant tobit coefficients and models.

However, because two program goals are being met, in total or in part, is in our opinion insufficient information upon which to base even a preliminary economic evaluation of the overall program. What must be shown is that companies would not have undertaken the research on their own because of insufficient private returns *and* that SBIR funding overcomes market failures benefiting society with a large social return. In the following two sections, we, therefore, add two more elements of evaluation. We use case studies to show that the SBIR Program encourages new entrepreneurs, actually changing the career paths of some researchers and bringing their talents and ideas into the commercial world. Then, additional case studies are used to demonstrate the large social return from the projects that are made possible by the SBIR Program.

3.2. Entrepreneurial behavior and the SBIR Program

To develop information about the extent to which the SBIR Program changes the behavior of knowledge workers and thereby helps to create a science-based entrepreneurial economy, Audretsch et al. (2000b) use case studies along with responses to a survey of a broader sample of firms with SBIR projects. Although the authors emphasize that their results are exploratory and based on a small sample, their results do show that the SBIR Program has influenced the career paths of scientists and engineers by facilitating the startup of new firms. Additionally, the experience of those knowledge workers in commercializing products and services with a small business has had a spillover effect by influencing the career trajectories of their colleagues.

Audretsch et al. report that both their survey and their case studies provide consistent evidence that:

1. A significant number of the firms would not have been started in the absence of the SBIR Program.
2. A significant number of the scientists and engineers would not have become involved in the commercialization process in the absence of the SBIR Program.
3. A significant number of other firms are started because of the demonstration effect by the efforts of scientists to commercialize knowledge.
4. As a result of the demonstration effect of SBIR funded commercialization, a number of other scientists alter their careers to include commercialization efforts.

Especially for scientists and engineers without previous experience with knowledge-based small firms, the SBIR Program appears to encourage the development of knowledge about commercialization possibilities and facilitate commercialization from research-based knowledge.

3.3. Estimating social returns from SBIR-supported projects

3.3.1. Conceptual framework for analysis
It is well known that risk and the closely related difficulties of appropriating return to investments in technology—R&D specifically—will lead

---

[18] There is little qualitative difference between the results when a response hazard rate is substituted for the probability of response in the specification. Using the response hazard rate, the average of the conditional means is US$ 602,483.

[19] For the specification that replaces the probability of response with the hazard rate, the average value of expected sales is US$ 223,450.

[20] See Link (2000), and Scott (2000a) for case-based information that these companies report that in the absence of SBIR support they either would not have pursued Phase II research, or would have done so on a very limited scale.

152   *D.B. Audretsch et al. / Research Policy 31 (2002) 145–158*

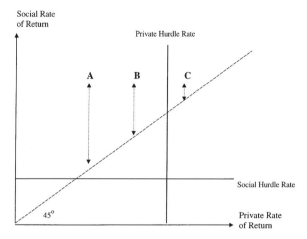

Fig. 1. Gap between social and private rates of return to R&D projects.

to a divergence between private and social benefits. The social rate of return will be greater than the private rate of return as illustrated in Fig. 1.[21] The purpose of this simple heuristic device is to characterize private sector projects with returns not only less than the expected social returns but also less than the private hurdle rate for projects normally undertaken by the firm. In those cases, the divergence of private from social returns can imply the market failure of private underinvestment in socially desirable R&D.

The social rate of return is measured on the vertical axis of Fig. 1 along with society's hurdle rate on investments in R&D. The private rate of return is measured on the horizontal axis along with the private hurdle rate on investments in R&D. A 45° line (dashed line) is imposed on the figure to emphasize that for the projects depicted the social rate of return from an R&D investment exceeds the private rate of return from that same investment. The three illustrative projects discussed below are labeled as project A, B, and C.

For project C, the private rate of return exceeds the private hurdle rate, and the social rate of return exceeds the social hurdle rate. The gap (short vertical double arrow line) between the social and private rates of return reflects the spillover benefits to society from the private investment. However, the inability of the private sector to appropriate all benefits from its investment is not so great as to prevent the project from being adequately funded by the private firm. Hence, it is not a candidate for public support.

Consider projects A and B. The gap between social and private returns is larger than in the case of project C; neither project will be adequately funded by the private firm. To address this market failure the government has two alternative policy mechanisms. It can use a tax policy to address the private underinvestment in R&D or it can rely on public/private partnerships as a direct funding mechanism.

If the private return to project B is less than the private hurdle rate because of the risk and uncertainty associated with R&D in general, then tax policy may be the appropriate policy mechanism to overcome this underinvestment. Risk is inherent in a technology-based market, and there will be certain projects for which the rewards from successful innovation are too low for private investments to be justified. Tax policy, such as the R&E tax credit, may in these

---

[21] A more complete explanation for this figure and for the theoretical model underlying the derivation of social and private returns is in Link and Scott (2001). See also Jaffe (1998) for an application of a similar figure to the Advanced Technology Program.

D.B. Audretsch et al./Research Policy 31 (2002) 145–158   153

situations reduce the private marginal cost of R&D sufficiently to provide an incentive for the project to be undertaken privately. For projects like project B, a tax credit may be sufficient to increase the expected return so that the firm views the post-tax credit private return to be sufficient for the project to be funded.

However, for projects like project A, a tax credit may be insufficient to increase the expected return enough to induce the private firm to undertake the project. Such projects could include for example projects expected to yield an innovative product that would be part of a larger system of products. Even if technically successful there might be substantial risk that the product would not interoperate or be compatible with other emerging products, and direct funding rather than a tax credit may be the appropriate policy mechanism to stimulate socially desirable investments in systems.

A priori, it is difficult to generalize about the way that any one firm's under-funded projects will be distributed in the area to the left of the firm's private hurdle rate. However, some generalizations can be made about the portfolio of private sector firms' projects in general. For those R&D projects, like project B, for which the firm will appropriate some returns but for which the overall expected return is slightly too low, a tax credit may be sufficient to increase the expected return to the point that the expected return exceeds the private hurdle rate. Such projects may be of a product or process development nature and are likely to be a part of the firm's ongoing R&D portfolio of projects. For those R&D projects, like project A, for which the firm has little ability to appropriate returns even if the marginal cost of the project is reduced through an R&E tax credit, the firm may not respond to such a tax policy but may respond to a direct funding policy mechanism. Such projects may be of a generic or fundamental technology nature, that is technology from which subsequent market applications are derived and that enable downstream applied R&D to be undertaken successfully. Thus, the economic rationale for public/private partnerships is that such partnerships represent one direct-funding R&D policy appropriate to overcome market failure and that they are more likely to be necessary, compared to fiscal tax incentives, when the R&D is generic or fundamental in nature.

Drawing upon the foregoing arguments, we maintain that a candidate project for SBIR awards is one like project A in Fig. 1. That is, given that the proposed research aligns with the technology mission of DoD, SBIR should fund such projects for which there is a significant potential social benefit but also that are characterized by substantial downside risk such that the firm's expected private return is well below its private hurdle rate.

Case-study information reported by Link (2000) and Scott (2000a) confirms for a small sample of SBIR-supported projects that not only are the firms' private returns less than their private hurdle rates but also that outside investors are unwilling to sponsor fully the research because of both technical and market risk. Hence, at the outset of an SBIR project, not only is a firm's private hurdle rate not expected to be met, neither is the required return for a third party. In conjunction with the evidence presented below that the projects have high social returns, the findings support the belief that the SBIR Program corrects the market failure of underinvestment in socially-valuable research in emerging technologies.

3.3.2. Preliminary estimates of social returns

Link and Scott (2000) interviewed SBIR award recipients for 44 projects in 43 companies for this part of the evaluation study. Each was interviewed toward the end of its Phase II award period. Information collected made possible the calculation of a lower-bound of the prospective expected social rate of return associated with each project and a comparison of that expected social rate of return to both the expected private rate of return to the firm had it pursued the project in the absence of SBIR support and the private rate of return expected by the firm with its SBIR support. The analysis clearly indicates that SBIR is funding projects like project A in Fig. 1, and given such funding the projects have become similar to project C.

The sample of projects studied may not be statistically representative of all projects funded by SBIR. To make such a claim, all would have to be interviewed to obtain information similar to the information collected. This was not done because of resource constraints and the availability of SBIR staff to identify specific individuals to be interviewed and to make initial contacts. Thus, the sample of 44 projects is simply one sample, and the findings are not necessarily

Table 4
Variables for the prospective expected social rate of return calculations

Variable	Definition	Source
d	Duration of the SBIR project	DoD files, verified and updated as necessary during interviews
C	Total cost of the SBIR project	DoD files, verified and updated as necessary during interviews
A	SBIR funding	DoD files, verified and updated as necessary during interviews
r	Private hurdle rate	Interview
z	Duration of the extra period of development beyond Phase II	Interview
F	Additional cost for the extra period of development[a]	Interview
T	Life of the commercialized technology	Interview
v	Proportion of value appropriated	Interview
L	Lower bound for expected annual private return to the SBIR firm	Derived
U	Upper bound for expected annual private return to the SBIR firm	Derived

[a] The additional costs considered were research and development costs and not the costs associated with searching for or negotiating with venture capitalists. See Gans and Stern (2000).

Table 5
Descriptive statistics on variables used in the social rate of return model ($n = 44$)

Variable	Mean	Range	S.D.
d	2.68 years	2–3.5	0.36
C	US$ 1,027,199	US$ 448,000–3,450,000	461901
A	US$ 782,000	US$ 448,000–1,099,966	127371
r	0.33	0.2–0.5[a]	0.08
z	1.30 years	−0.375–5.0[b]	1.07
F	US$ 1,377,341	US$ 0–15,000,000	2972266
T	10.56 years	1–30[c]	7.23
v	0.16	0.0045–0.60	0.16
L	US$ 902,738	US$ 34,842.6–5,300,500	1228850
U	US$ 1,893,001	US$ 258,830–8,666,330	1733581

[a] Eight of the respondents were uncomfortable estimating the private hurdle rate that outside financiers would apply to their projects at their outset. For those, the average value of r for the respondents in their region was used in the calculations.

[b] One observation for z has a negative value because commercial returns started before the end of Phase II.

[c] One respondent reported that T would be several decades, and another reported that T would be forever. In both cases, T was conservatively entered as the value 30 years. However, because the relevant discount rates are so high, the difference between 30 years and "forever" is not significant. In the integrals in the mathematical model, the term with T entered negatively as an exponent would become zero, but with a large value of T the term is very small in any case.

representative of all SBIR projects. However, because the findings are strong, and because the anecdotal information obtained from SBIR staff indicates the sample was a reasonable cross-section of funded companies, we are comfortable generalizing to some degree about the findings. In any event, the methodology of Link and Scott (2001) is sufficiently general to be applied to other samples. [22]

---

[22] A complete description of the sample of companies is available upon request.

Table 4 lists the variables required for the implementation of the model. As noted in the table, data on selected variables were independently available from DoD project files, but all such information was also verified during the interview process and corrected when discrepancies were found. Descriptive statistics for these variables are in Table 5.

Phases I and II values for project duration, total cost, and SBIR funding, were combined into one value to cover both Phases I and II of the project. That is, each project is viewed from the time that Phase I began, and

D.B. Audretsch et al./Research Policy 31 (2002) 145–158   155

expectations from that point forward are estimated. It is at that point in time that the market failure issues discussed above are especially relevant. Respondents reported the additional period of time beyond the expected completion of Phase II until the research would be commercialized and the additional cost required during that period.

The variable v, the proportion of value appropriated, deserves some explanation. Firms cannot reasonably expect to appropriate all of the value created by their research and subsequent innovations. First, the innovations will generate consumer surplus that no firm will appropriate, but that society will value. Link and Scott ignore consumer surplus in the calculations of the prospective expected social returns thus motivating the claim that the estimates are lower-bound estimates. Second, some of the profits generated by the innovations will be captured by other firms. Larger firms, for example, will observe the innovation and will successfully introduce imitations. Each respondent as part of the interview process was asked to estimate the proportion of the returns to producers (themselves and other firms) generated by their anticipated innovation that they expect to capture. Then, in an extended conversation, other possible applications of the technology developed during the SBIR project were explored. Each respondent was asked to estimate the multiplier to get from the profit stream generated by the immediate applications of the SBIR project to the stream of profits generated in the broader applications markets—beyond the applications to be made by the SBIR firm—that would reasonably be anticipated. We calculated v as the product of two proportions. The first is the proportion anticipated by the SBIR firm of the profits from the development and commercialization of the specific applications it planned for the technology being developed. The second is the proportion of profits from all possible applications—including those beyond the applications that the SBIR firm anticipated making itself—taken by the respondent's planned applications of the generic technology being researched and developed in the SBIR project. Thus, v is the total proportion of the value of the technology appropriable by the researching firm. For example, if an SBIR firm anticipated appropriating 50% of the profits generated by its planned types of applications of its SBIR technology, and if the profits from the types of applications

planned by the SBIR firm were expected to be 50% of the profits from all applications of the technology, then the SBIR firm would expect to earn 50% of a profit stream that itself was 50% of the total profit stream attributable to the SBIR generated technology. The firm, therefore, would anticipate appropriating 25% of the profits generated by its SBIR project.

Link and Scott then find the lower bound for the annual private return to an SBIR-sponsored project by solving their investment model for the amount that the private firm must earn to meet its private hurdle rate, or its required rate of return, on the portion of the total investment that the firm must finance. [23] The firm would not invest in the SBIR project on its own unless it expected at least that lower bound for the annual private return on its investment.

To determine the upper bound for the annual private return, the investment model is solved for the expected annual return that if exceeded would imply that the expected rate of return earned by the private firm would be greater than its hurdle rate in the absence of SBIR support, and therefore, SBIR support would not be required for the project.

Sequentially, Link and Scott estimate the average expected annual private return to the firm as the average of the upper and lower bounds, U and L. Knowing the average expected annual private return is $((L + U)/2)$ and knowing the portion of producer surplus that is appropriable, v, then total producer surplus equals $((L + U)/2v)$. This value for total producer surplus is a lower bound for the expected annual social return. Again, it is a lower bound because consumer surplus has not been measured.

The expected private rate of return without SBIR support is the solution for the internal rate of return—the rate of return that just equates the present value of the expected annual private return to the firm to the present value of research and post-research commercialization costs to the firm in the absence of SBIR funding.

Finally, the lower bound on the social rate of return is found by solving the investment model for the

---

[23] The theoretical mathematical model is available from either Link or Scott. A complete and detailed description of the model, along with an illustrative implementation of it based on project data from the Advanced Technology Program is in Link and Scott (2001).

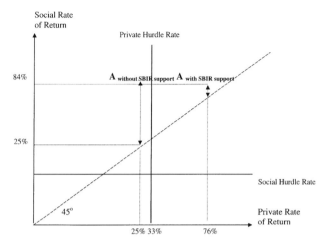

Fig. 2. Gap between social and private rates of return to the average SBIR project, $n = 44$.

internal rate of return with the average expected annual private return $((L + U)/2)$, replaced with the lower bound for the average expected annual social return $((L + U)/2v)$.

The investment model was estimated for each of the 44 SBIR-sponsored projects. Mean values of the two resulting important rates of return, averaged across the 44 projects, are shown in Table 6. There are two important points to be seen in Table 6. First, the average of the expected private rate of return in the absence of SBIR support is 25%, clearly less than the average self-reported private hurdle rate of 33% (see Table 5). Thus, in the absence of SBIR support the sample of firms would not have undertaken the research, and in fact each of the sampled firms stated that explicitly during the interviews. Further, the expected social rate of return (lower bound) associated with SBIR fund-

Table 6
Rates of return for the average SBIR project ($n = 44$)

Variable	Definition
$i_{\text{private}} = 0.25$	Expected private rate of return without SBIR funding
$i_{\text{social}} = 0.84$	Lower bound for expected social rate of return

ing of these projects is at least 84%, and hence, the projects are expected to be socially valuable.

We cannot conclude that a social rate of return of at least 84% is "good" or "bad," or "better" or "worse" than expected. However, we can compare the estimate of the lower bound of the social rate of return to the opportunity cost of public funds promulgated by the US Office of Management and Budget (OMB). Following the guidelines set forth by OMB (1992) mandating a real discount rate of 7% for constant-dollar benefit-to-cost analyses of proposed investments and regulations, clearly a nominal social rate of return of 84% is above that rate and thus, reflects projects that are socially worthwhile in terms of the OMB standard. [24]

The expected private rate of return with SBIR support for each of the 44 projects can be calculated as the solution for the internal rate of return in the investment model given the actual time series of private investments and private returns. The estimated private rate of return with SBIR support averages 76% for the 44 cases, this value is noticeably above the average private hurdle rate of 33%. However, there is

---

[24] Link and Scott (1998) discuss the use of this guideline for NIST economic impact assessments.

D.B. Audretsch et al. / Research Policy 31 (2002) 145–158   157

no way for the SBIR Program to have calculated the optimal level of funding for these 44 projects, or for any projects, unless, as part of the Phase I application all relevant data, including hurdle rates, could have been assessed. In the absence of such information, which in practice would be difficult to obtain because of, if nothing else, self-serving reporting by proposers, the funding implemented by the SBIR Program may be as close to optimal as possible. [25]

Fig. 2 summarizes the estimated values for the average SBIR-sponsored project. Based on the sample of 44 projects, the average gap between the lower-bound social rate of return and the estimated private rate of return without SBIR funding support is 59%.

Two points need to be emphasized, along with our previous comments about the statistical representativeness of the sample of 44 companies. First, the social rates of return estimated for the SBIR projects are very conservative, lower-bound estimates because they do not include consumer surplus in the benefit stream. Second, some might be skeptical about the SBIR awardees' earnest belief that without SBIR funding the projects would not have been undertaken or at least would not have been undertaken to the same extent or with the same speed. With the SBIR Program in place, certainly the pursuit of SBIR funding would perhaps be a path of least resistance. However, if the research would have occurred without the public funding, the estimated upper bound and (hence the average of the upper and lower bounds for the expected private returns) would be too low, and the actual lower bounds for the social rates of return would be even higher than estimated. Further, the gap would remain, although that would not in itself necessarily justify the public funding of the projects.

4. Concluding remarks

Based on our three-part evaluation analysis, and the caveats associated with each, there is ample evidence to support the conclusion that the net economic

benefits associated with DoD's SBIR Program are positive. More specifically, our broad-based statistical analysis of SBIR recipients demonstrates that two of the program's objectives—stimulating technological innovation and increasing private sector commercialization of innovations derived from federal research and development—are being met. In addition, the case-based analyses demonstrate that the SBIR Program redirects the efforts of award recipients toward commercial activity that would not otherwise have taken place, and that commercial activity and its attendant spillover effects generate substantial positive net social benefits.

Although our conclusions are robust, it is important to emphasize that our analysis is specific to DoD's SBIR Program. Until studies of other agencies' SBIR programs take place, one should be extremely cautious about generalizing from our DoD SBIR findings to the entire SBIR Program. [26]

References

Audretsch, D.B., Link, A.N., Scott, J.T., 2000a. Statistical analysis of the national academy of sciences survey of small business innovation research awardees: analyzing the influence of the fast track program. In: Wessner, C.W. (Ed.), The Small Business Innovation Research Program. National Academy Press, Washington, DC, pp. 291–306.

Audretsch, D.B., Weigand, J., Weigand, C., 2000b. Does the small business innovation research program foster entrepreneurial behavior? Evidence from Indiana. In: Wessner, C.W. (Ed.), The Small Business Innovation Research Program. National Academy Press, Washington, DC, pp. 160–193.

Baldwin, W.L., Scott, J.T., 1987. Market Structure and Technological Change. Harwood, London.

Baron, J., 1998. DoD SBIR/STTR Program Manager, Comments at the Methodology Workshop on the Assessment of Current SBIR Program Initiatives, Washington, DC, October.

Cahill, P., 2000. Fast track, is it speeding commercialization of the department of defense small business innovation research projects. In: Wessner, C.W. (Ed.), The Small Business Innovation Research Program. National Academy Press, Washington, DC, pp. 43–103.

Gans, J.S., Stern S., 2000. When does funding research by smaller firms bear fruit? Evidence from the SBIR program. NBER Working Paper No. 7877, September.

[25] Scott (1998) has proposed using a bidding mechanism that, if applied, would result in the SBIR funding being just sufficient to ensure that the private participants earn just a normal rate of return. The proposal is a novel one, however, it is yet untried. Successful implementation would require additional development in order to reduce it to practice.

[26] As these studies take place, by agency, consideration should be given to having matched samples of firms, that is firms with and without SBIR support, to obtain comparative evaluation estimates of the marginal impact of the program. See Wallsten (2000).

Jaffe, A.B., 1998. The importance of spillovers in the policy mission of the advanced technology program. Journal of Technology Transfer 23, 11–19.

Kealey, T., 1997. The Economic Laws of Scientific Research. MacMillan, London.

Klette, T.J., Møen, J., Griliches, Z., 2000. Do subsidies to commercial R&D reduce market failures? Microeconometric evaluation studies. Research Policy 29, 471–495.

Lerner, J., 1999. The government as venture capitalist: the long-run impact of the SBIR program. Journal of Business 72, 285–318.

Lerner, J., Kegler, C., 2000. Evaluating the small business innovation research program: a literature review. In: Wessner, C.W. (Ed.), The Small Business Innovation Research Program. National Academy Press, Washington, DC, pp. 307–324.

Link, A.N., 1999. Public/private partnerships in the United States. Industry and innovation 6, 191–217.

Link, A.N., 2000. An assessment of the small business innovation research fast track program in southeastern states. In: Wessner, C.W. (Ed.), The Small Business Innovation Research Program. National Academy Press, Washington, DC, pp. 194–210.

Link, A.N., Scott, J.T., 1998. Public Accountability: Evaluating Technology-Based Institutions. Kluwer Academic Publishers, Norwell, MA.

Link, A.N., Scott, J.T., 2000. Estimates of the social returns to small business innovation research projects. In: Wessner, C.W. (Ed.), The Small Business Innovation Research Program. National Academy Press, Washington, DC, pp. 275–290.

Link, A.N., Scott, J.T., 2001. Public/private partnerships: stimulating competition in a dynamic market. International Journal of Industrial Organization 19, 763–794.

Martin, S., Scott, J.T., 2000. The nature of innovation market failure and the design of public support for private innovation. Research Policy 29, 437–447.

Office of Management and Budget, 1992. Economic Analysis of Federal Regulations Under Executive Order 12866, mimeographed.

Scott, J.T., 1998. Financing and leveraging public/private partnerships: the hurdle-lowering auction. STI Review 23, 67–84.

Scott, J.T., 2000a. An assessment of the small business innovation research program in New England: fast-track compared with non-fast track projects. In: Wessner, C.W. (Ed.), The Small Business Innovation Research Program. National Academy Press, Washington, DC, pp. 104–140.

Scott, J.T., 2000b. The directions for technological change: alternative economic majorities and opportunity costs. Review of Industrial Organization 17, 1–17.

Tibbetts, R., 1999. The Small Business Innovation Research Program and NSF SBIR Commercialization Results, mimeograph.

Wallsten, S., 2000. The effects of government-industry R&D programs on private R&D: the case of the small business innovation research program. Rand Journal of Economics 31, 82–100.

Index